Ethical Relativism and Universalism

Ethical Relativism and Universalism

SARAL JHINGRAN

MOTILAL BANARSIDASS PUBLISHERS
PRIVATE LIMITED • DELHI

First Indian Edition: 2001

ISBN: 81-208-1820-2

Also available at:
MOTILAL BANARSIDASS
41 U.A. Bungalow Road, Jawahar Nagar, Delhi 110 007
236, 9th Main III Block, Jayanagar, Bangalore 560 011
8 Mahalaxmi Chamber, Warden Road, Mumbai 400 026
120 Royapettah High Road, Mylapore, Chennai 600 004
Sanas Plaza, 1302 Baji Rao Road, Pune 411 002
8 Camac Street, Kolkata 700 017
Ashok Rajpath, Patna 800 004
Chowk, Varanasi 221 001

Printed in India
BY JAINENDRA PRAKASH JAIN AT SHRI JAINENDRA PRESS,
A-45 NARAINA, PHASE-I, NEW DELHI 110 028
AND PUBLISHED BY NARENDRA PRAKASH JAIN FOR
MOTILAL BANARSIDASS PUBLISHERS PRIVATE LIMITED,
BUNGALOW ROAD, DELHI 110 007

To

Ishan and Pallavi
With lots of love

Foreword

The controversy over relativism and universalism is very old and has been articulated in different forms - sociological, ontological and linguistic. These forms are not necessarily exclusive. Universalism has its own different types - strict or absolute and context-sensitive. One comes across variety in relativism as well. For example, we often hear of global relativism and local relativism. Some modern and postmodern versions of relativism claim to be beyond both local relativism and global relativism. The vast and growing literature on the subject and its related themes is available not only in the West but also in India.

Dr. Saral Jhingran, who is intimately familiar with the Indian traditions of philosophy, has made a thorough study of the fundamental problems of moral philosophy. Her approach is critical and analytical. She seems to be sympathetic even towards the views criticized by herself. The expository and critical parts of Dr. Jhingran's work are followed up by her own constructive views on the subject. From sociology of knowledge, various versions of postmodernism and realism to existentialism and universalism are among the wide-ranging themes of her study. She has been able to do justice to Indian thought also which for understandable reasons could not be discussed at length within the scope of this book.

Dr. Saral Jhingran's scholarship and style of presentation have made the book highly readable and instructive. I hope this book will be received well by the scholars, students and also general readers.

D.P. Chattopadhyaya

Centre for Studies in Civilizations
Delhi and Calcutta
October 2, 2000

Preface

Quite a few years ago I became interested in what I then called religious experience of humankind (*The Roots of World Religions*, 1982). Having been earlier trained in Vedanta, my instinctive search was for basic similarities in the three major world religions that I had chosen for my study. I found amazing similarities in the experiences of the mystics and those for whom religion was a matter of inner faith, piety, or experience. At the same time, I was overwhelmed - first, by the evidence for diversity of, or even contradictions between, the beliefs, creeds and values of different religions; and second, by the vociferous declarations of their immense diversity and uniqueness by Western philosophers, such as R.C. Zaehner, and men of religion, such as Karl Barth. I also heard a sane voice of Ninian Smart out of the cacophony of declarations of diversity. Ninian Smart is a staunch advocate of the above thesis, but also believes in the possibility and desirability of interreligious dialogue. But does not dialogue mean mutual understanding, and does not mutual understanding imply common grounds and shared moments?

I have always had an instinctive faith in, or assurance of, the basic affinity of humankind which underlies all cultural and religious differences. This faith has had a strong battering from the protagonists of cultural diversity and relativism, but has still persisted. Gradually I became more and more interested in the phenomenon of cultural diversity and whatever it implies, especially in the field of morals which have been my major concern. At first, I concentrated on the writings of socio-anthropologists, because they were the persons who talked of cultural diversity the most. At that stage I naively thought that it should not be difficult to question the thesis of ethical relativism, as it could be easily pointed out that even if the empirical fact of cultural diversity and the thesis of relativity were accepted in toto, this would not prove ethical relativism.

But so far I had not reckoned with postmodern thought for the simple reason that I was not conversant with it. Postmodernism has been largely confined to the Continent and has been generally ignored in the English speaking world; and Indians, including me, are much more at home with the writings of English speaking scholars. As a result, while postmodernism has become increasingly fashionable and popular among certain philosophico-literary circles in India, it has mostly remained a strange philosophical movement for the rest of Indian intellectuals.

Then my friend, Prof. V.K. Bharadwaja almost forced me to read postmodern philosophers before attempting to write anything on ethical relativism. Needless to say that it was tough going for me at first. I realized that given the postmodern premises, the kind of ethical universalism that I wish to propose in this work becomes automatically questionable. Postmodern thought takes cultural-ethical relativism further back to metaepistemological and metaontological levels, thus making any anti-relativist thesis false by definition. Various postmodernist contentions aim at proving the problematic character of knowledge and the illegitimacy of epistemology. They also reject any cross-cultural or universal criteria of judgment and comparative evaluation. In sum, they reject *ex hypothesi* the possibility of even a minimum universal morality.

Although the challenge of postmodernism to any kind of ethical relativism seems formidable, it can be successfully met in critical moral discourse. The more I read postmodern scholars, the more I became conscious of the internal inconsistencies of their standpoint. This is not to undermine the role of postmodernism as a corrective to various semi-dogmatic assertions of the Enlightenment inspired Western thought, or the reasonableness of some of its theses, such as the unjustifiability of judgment from an external point of view. I only want to say that it would be highly naive and inconsistent to take it as the final word against any moderately universalist position in ethics.

Diversity is all around us, not only at the intercultural level but also at the intracultural ones. But what does this empirical fact of cultural diversity prove - that it is the 'universal truth' about human condition? Or, that the mere empirical fact of cultural diversity can prove ethical relativism in some basic, universal, and almost absolute sense? The fact is that relativism of any kind becomes inconsistent when it tries to present itself as a universally applicable thesis.

I accept most of the arguments put forward by cultural-ethical relativists, such as the fact of widespread moral disagreements; the relevance of the cultural-institutional context in deciding the rightness or wrongness of a particular course of action; sociological determination of our beliefs, norms and valuational preferences; and the fallibility of our moral assertions. But I insist that none of these arguments prove ethical relativism, or the doctrine that whatever is believed or practised *is* right, true, valid or good within its own cultural-conceptual framework.

On the positive side, I argue in this work that we are not prisoners of our conceptual frameworks, and can transcend the limitations of our inherited beliefs, concepts and norms. We can understand others, communicate with them, as well as claim cross-cultural validity for some basic universal principles or criteria. This means that moral discourse is 'essentially' universal, that is, whenever I offer a moral judgment, or support a moral principle, I expect that the same judgment or moral principle would be applicable to all relevantly similar cases. And, in most cases relevant similarities need not be those of contingent cultural conditions.

I have also argued for the cognitivity and objectivity of most moral assertions. That is, when we offer a moral judgment, we at the same time assert that we 'know' that it is so. By the objectivity of the moral judgment I mean both its independence from its subject, as also some form of causal relationship between the judgment and its object. I have further argued for the rationality of meaningful moral discourse; that is, a moral judgment or a moral principle is by definition one which is justifiable on rational grounds.

I have however *presumed* that at least some universal moral principles, such as the sanctity of life and the dignity of the person, are 'true' irrespective of any empirical considerations, or the number of persons who agree or disagree with them. These universal moral principles are neither the product of any specific culture or its conceptual framework, nor that of dialogue and agreement among various 'experts', but are in some sense *a priori*, that is, assumed in most ethical discourse.

The first two Chapters of the present work are purely descriptive and present various formulations of the relativist point of view. The next two Chapters attempt a critique of various relativist theses. The fifth Chapter discusses the realist and universalist approaches to various ethical issues. In the last three Chapters, I have presented my own views, arguing for a universal rational moral point of view, and the need for open-ended cross-cultural rational moral dialogue.

I could not have undertaken the ambitious task of examining what is perhaps the most crucial problem of contemporary ethical discourse, i.e. the 'relative' merits of the relativist and universalist approaches to ethics, but for the constant help and guidance of Prof. Bharadwaja. He read two or three drafts of the work and gave me his valuable comments and suggestions at every stage of the development of this work, for which I am very grateful to him.

My son Anant has helped me with the correcting and editing of the final draft of the work, including preparing the bibliography. I appreciate his love and concern for me. I also appreciate the support and love I got from my husband, son Dhir, and daughters-in-law Smita and Renu, during the many years it took to bring this book to fruition.

Saral Jhingran

New Delhi
August 2000

Contents

CHAPTER 1

Cultural and Ethical Relativism

I. Cultural Relativism

I.1 Relativism in thought and morals is a common enough doctrine known to both ancient Greeks and Indians[1]. Pre-Socratic sophists were famous for their radical relativistic stance which comprehended both knowledge and practice. Protagoras' oft-quoted saying that "man is the measure of all things" seems to present relativism in a nutshell. He declared that things are for every individual what they appear to him/her. Whatever appears as true, right, or desirable to a person is so for him/her. Human knowledge is not universally valid or true, but is just an opinion which grows out of momentary perception. It is valid only for that person who has it. True and false, right and wrong, good and evil are all matters of opinion. Individual person is the measure of all things.

Similarly, post-Vedic Indians were well aware of the cultural diversity among people of different ages and regions. The Dharmasãstras and Epics (the *Rãmãyana* and the *Mahābhārata*) frequently point out how the ways and customs of people of North and South India differ from each other. This diversity is not evaluated from an ethnocentric point of view; instead, it is made a basis for quite a radical form of relativism and a doctrine of tolerance. According to this view, customs (*ãcãra*) are an important source of norms of conduct of various communities. Tradition or customary pattern of conduct (*ãcãra*) is generally defined as that which has been handed down by earlier generations, which is practised by the good men (*śiṣṭas*) of society, and which is not opposed to religious texts (Vedas and Smṛtis).[2] The emphasis in Smṛtis and other religio-moral literature is throughout on traditional norms and ways; and it is clearly stated that those norms of conduct which are in vogue in a given community are authentic and valid for the members of that community alone. It is added that the following and practice of the same norms and customs by the members of another community would constitute sin.[3]

Moreover, Indian (Hindu) thinkers were also well aware of the power of time, and the changes it brings in the values, perceptions and ways of the people; and acknowledged that even the norms, prohibitions and injunctions of the religious texts which have become abhorrent to the subsequent generations can be abandoned by them.[4]

The *Mahābhārata* asserts that the injunctions and prohibitions of Vedas (signifying universal norms) cannot be applicable to all people alike. It points out that with changing times, circumstances in people's lives also change, so that whatever was normally right in the earlier times may not be so in later times. It further contends that since different sages affirm different things, we cannot accept one of them only as authoritative. It even says that there is no ethical norm or custom which is conducive to the good of all equally.[5]

In the West, Plato seems to have demolished relativism with his theory of transcendental, universal, archetypal ideas. In middle ages, of course, there was no scope for relativism due to the unquestionable authority of the Church which claimed to be in possession of final knowledge in all spheres of life.

Though the thinkers and pioneers of Renaissance, Reformation and Enlightenment successfully challenged the authority of the Roman Church, they, like the medieval thinkers, believed in universal knowledge and values. Not only the knowledge achieved through science but even fundamentals of religions (expressed in the form of deism) and basic principles of morality were asserted as universal, i.e. worthy of universal belief and compliance.

A relativistic approach to culture and morality was revived there when the Westerners moved into Asia and Africa in search of markets, or with imperialist ambitions. They were accompanied by Christian missionaries. At first both groups, the men who sought power over Asian and African countries, and the missionaries who wanted to convert their populace to Christianity, took it for granted that there was nothing worth preserving in the thought and culture of the people who were subjected to their imperialist and christianizing zeal. Gradually however, this Euro-centric approach began to be questioned.

Westerners who were naturally ethnocentric became more so when they confronted weaker Asian and African countries, and assumed the superiority of their newly acquired science, technology and liberal views. At the same time, they also became conscious of the immense diversity in the ways, beliefs and practices of people belonging to distant cultures.

After a while anthropologists came to the scene, who, for reasons best known to them, concentrated on far-off cultures which had little contact with the outside world. The anthropological data on the ways and beliefs of these preliterate people were put forward as weird, entirely alien, and hence as an uncontroversial proof of the cultural diversity and relativity of mores and ways of separate cultures. Thus was born cultural relativism which simply affirms the indubitable fact of diversity in the beliefs, norms, values, goals and ways of people of different regions and ages, or different cultures. This diversity with which humankind was familiar all through its history is made striking by the anthropologists' insistence on choosing extreme examples to prove their point.

Sociological or cultural relativism may be merely a descriptive thesis which need not lead to ethical relativism. That is, one can accept the fact of cultural diversity in every field of knowledge and practice, and yet opt for a universalist or even absolutist view of knowledge and morals. Ethical relativism, on the other hand, does not merely claim that different people believe in different acts to be right and wrong, or that there is an immense, irreconcilable diversity of ways among people of different places and times; they also assert that the beliefs, norms, or practices of different people are right, valid, and authoritative for them separately.

Cultural relativism starts with the empirical fact of cultural diversity in moral beliefs, customs, norms and values. It points out that whatever is thought and practised as right in one society may be often thought and prohibited as wrong in another society. Or, things which may be a moral issue for a community may be either a non-moral issue, or no issue at all for another community. Or, some thing may be regarded as a morally good practice in one community at one time but may become morally reprehensible to the same community at a different time. Or, some practice which is regarded as a moral issue in one community at a certain time may become a non-moral issue in the same community at a later time.[6] It is called the diversity thesis.

Of course, the fact of cultural diversity has been known to humankind since ancient times; and it has been rightly pointed out by some scholars that all the painstakingly gathered anthropological data aiming to prove cultural diversity do not add anything new to the already existing knowledge.[7]

I.2 Apart from cultural diversity, relativists also emphasize a culture being an integrated whole whose various aspects or dimensions are integrally related to each other and to the ethos or *Weltanschauung* of the culture as a whole.

These relativists find support in the theories of early anthropologists and sociologists who always conceived culture as a unit or homogeneous whole and emphasized the autonomous and integrated nature of various cultures. This view asserts that neither the moral norms, nor even concepts and perceptual patterns of a people can be studied in isolation, but require the context of an entire culture. Since the culture of a given society or group is an integrated whole, its various aspects are so intimately related and interdependent that any one aspect of that culture can neither be explained, nor even understood, without reference to the context of entire culture. T.F. Hoult has used the phrase "socio-cultural compatibility" to express this relation between various aspects of a culture. The culture of every society is an intricate pattern of interaction between and interdependence of various aspects of personal and social life. Different aspects or dimensions of a culture, such as religion, philosophy, morality, art, science, technology, socio-political structure, economic order etc, are interdependent; so that each aspect influences and is being influenced by other aspects.

Anthropologists, A.L. Kroeber and Clyde Klukohn understand the integral nature of a culture with reference to the concept of pattern. Each culture embodies traditional patterns of behaviour which express the basic ideas and values of that culture and provide the very foundations of the superstructure of culture.

Another anthropologist, Radcliff Brown understands culture in terms of social structure. It is assumed that "each structural system is a functional unity in which all the component parts contribute in a harmonious way to its existence and continuity." It is further contended that all kinds of social phenomena - from morals and religion to law - must be studied "not in abstraction or isolation, but in their direct or indirect relations to social structure."[8]

The above views of cultural pattern and social structure are holistic, that is, they view culture as an integrated whole. As a result, moral values, norms and standards of a people are taken to be an integral part of, dependant upon, or relative to, their respective cultures. In the words of John Ladd:

> Cultural relativism maintains that there is an irreducible diversity among cultures because each culture is a unique whole with parts so intertwined that none of them can be understood or evaluated without reference to the other parts and to the cultural whole, the so called pattern of culture.[9]

Ladd quotes Edward Sapir: "The worlds in which different societies live are distinct worlds, not the same world with distinctt labels attached."[10] What Sapir means is that not only ethical norms but also world-views, conceptual frameworks and perceptual patterns, as well as attitudes and emotional responses of persons, are different from society to society. This is so because all these cognitive and emotional patterns are integrally bound together, and are determined by the culture, or the way of life of that society. It is argued that,

> Ethics as part of culture cannot be understood or evaluated apart from the distinct world or society to which it belongs. Hence, cultural relativism implies ethical relativism.[11]

In another context I have also understood and described Hindu morality as integrally related to various other aspects of Hindu culture, and even coined a new phrase 'religio-culture' to express the holistic nature of Hinduism. I argue there:

> Hinduism is an integrated whole in which religion, philosophy, morality and social culture are so intimately related that neither morality, nor any other aspect of Hinduism, can be studied in isolation without reference to its other aspects.[12]

Therefore, "a proper understanding of both Hindu religion and philosophy becomes a prerequisite for any worthwhile attempt at understanding and evaluating Hindu morality."[13]

I.3 Cultural relativists further advocate what is generally called dependency thesis. Anthropologists, sociologists and psychologists join hands in pointing out that the values and norms of an individual are directly derived from her society or culture. A child learns her moral code from her society, through her parents, teachers and peers. The theory of innate ideas is now totally rejected; and it is now an accepted fact that no beliefs, attitudes and moral values are inborn. All our beliefs, attitudes and patterns of behaviour are learnt from our social environment. Even our deepest convictions about moral rightness or wrongness of certain kinds of acts, practices or patterns of behaviour are but introjected or interiorized views of our culture. Our very conscience is formed by internalizing of sanctions used by our society to support its moral norms.

The dependency thesis thus asserts that the only source of a person's beliefs, norms and attitudes is her culture. Most sociologists go on to say that even the ultimate moral principles on the basis of which our moral norms are generally justified are culture-relative. It follows that the moral norms, values etc. of an individual or group are nothing but the products of a particular culture, and cannot have any transcultural or universal validity.

I.4 Relativism is also sought to be argued on the basis of the philosophy of empiricism, as propounded by David Hume, William James and John Dewey. According to it, all our concepts and ideas have their source in experience, and not in reason or any other mysterious entity like God or a transcendental self.

As it is not reason but experience which is the source and justification of all our ideas, and experience is notoriously variable, depending upon so many contingent factors, no beliefs or norms, whether everyday ones or moral, can claim universality or finality. Cultural-ethical relativists use a combination of empiricism and naturalism to prove their thesis. According to empiricist philosophers, such as Hume, James and Dewey, as well as various anthropologists and psychologists, experience is the only source of all our knowledge, perceptual and ideational. Moral ideas are synthetic, and no synthetic ideas can be *a priori* as Kant argues; or self-evident as W.D. Ross, G.E. Moore and other intutionists claim. Instead, concepts are derived from experience, and necessarily refer to experience. M.J.Herskovits, an anthropologist, explains relativism as the "theory that judgments are based on experience, and experience is interpreted by each individual in terms of his own enculturation."[14]

David Hume has given us the most famous passage regarding the impossibility of deriving 'ought' from 'is'. Yet his moral philosophy is best understood as some form of empiricist-naturalism. Hume's basic thesis is that all knowledge consists of perceptions (impressions) and ideas based on them; and there cannot be any innate ideas or *a priori* knowledge in any field of life. He categorically denies that reason plays any part in our moral assertions. The rules of morality, therefore, are not conclusions of our reason. Rather, morals are a matter of feelings or passions; and these latter cannot be "pronounced as either true or false, or be either contrary or conformable to reason."[15] He frankly reduces moral terms, like good, right, wrong etc, to the sentiment of approbation or disapprobation "which arises in you towards this action."[16]

Hume tried to mitigate the relativist implications of his thesis by emphasizing that our feelings of pleasure and displeasure, or approval and disapproval, towards some act or character trait are a matter of (universal) human constitution. Yet, even though the feelings of approbation and disapprobation, as well as compassion, are universal in humankind, they are mostly directed to different acts and persons in different cultures, i.e. are culturally conditioned. Hume's empiricism therefore comes precariously close to relativism.

From the empiricist - naturalist point of view, our moral assertions are related to, or based upon, our experiences, responses, or experiential needs. R.B. Perry's definition of value in terms of interest is a classical example of naturalistic - relativist point of view, and leads to relativism in ethics. Though Perry does not consider himself a relativist, interests and desires are notoriously variable, and if ethical value is realized through the fulfillment of desires or interests, then naturally morality would be contingent and relative.

Empiricism in ethics also means that ethical concepts and judgments can be understood and evaluated by empirical methods. Moore rightly defines naturalism in ethics as the view that "Ethics is an empirical or positive science: its conclusions could be all established by means of empirical observation and induction."[17] Empiricism is closely related to naturalism which seeks to define ethical terms in empirical terms. All kinds of moral sentiment theories and approbation theories would come under this head.

I.5 Sociological relativism is the name of the theory that is developed by sociologists and some other thinkers using anthropological data, as also some basic sociological concepts. The name sociological relativism covers a wide spectrum of views, from the common anthropologists' cultural relativism to the radical conceptual relativism of 'postmodernists'. According to Paul W. Taylor:

> We mean by sociological relativism, then, the view that all of the following empirical claims are true. There is extreme variation among the moral norms of different societies. The moral attitudes and beliefs of every individual are originally derived from his society's moral code. The belief that there is but one true morality is, for most people, a reflection of their ethnocentricism.[18]

The observations and assertions of sociologists under the head of sociology of knowledge have been an important source of cultural relativism. Both the term and the approach it signifies are a twentieth century phenomenon. Its essential claim is that social circumstances and culture of a given society condition or shape the understanding and person of the subject, and also to some extent determine the objects which come to be known through socially determined categories. It was Karl Mannheim who first developed this idea that all knowledge is conditioned or determined by sociological circumstances. He defines the sociology of knowledge as a theory of the social or "existential determination of knowledge (or thought)." The emergence and crystallization of thought are influenced decisively by extra-theoretical factors which he calls existential factors. The existential determination of thought is found in the genesis of ideas, as well as in the concrete content of knowledge, in our experience, and in the perspective of the subject.[19]

Sociological factors or processes condition or determine the formulation of problems or issues, the selection of relevant data from experience, and all efforts at the resolution of problems. Thus, both the attitudinal responses and theoretical concepts are derived from the conceptual framework of a given society. The historical or sociological conditions in which a given knowledge or idea is developed determine both its form and content. To quote him:

> The world is known through many different orientations because there are many simultaneous and mutually contradictory trends of thought (by no means of equal value) struggling against one another with their different interpretations of "common" experience. The clue to this conflict, therefore, is not to be found in the "object in itself"..... but in the very different expectations, purposes, impulses arising out of experience.[20]

These different orientations to knowledge are called 'perspectives' by Mannheim. A perspective, according to him, "signifies the manner in which one views an object, what one perceives in it, and how one construes it in his thinking." These perspectives differ qualitatively among themselves, as a result of which two persons may agree on their factual, or scientific, or methodological beliefs, and yet come out with very different judgments regarding the same issue.[21] He goes on to argue that, "the same word, or the same concept in most cases, means very different things when used by differently situated persons."[22]

Mannheim gives the example of the concept of freedom which was understood so differently by conservative feudal lords of middle ages and nineteenth century liberals. Actually, he does not support relativism either in science or in morals. His thesis is purely sociological; and he is more concerned about sociological or intracultural factors that determine the form or content of the knowledge of a group in particular sociological situations.

Later protagonists of the sociology of knowledge have developed these ideas in a manner which emphasizes the social determination of knowledge and strengthens both relativism and skepticism. Emile Durkheim particularly emphasizes social determination of human thought. He affirms the social genesis of the categories of thought, and argues that concepts are embedded in the language of the society around us, which means that our concepts are a product of the society. The acceptance or rejection of concepts is not determined merely by their objective validity but also by their consistency with other prevailing beliefs in that society.[23] Yet Durkheim is not fully a cognitive relativist; social determination of categories does not make them wholly arbitrary. And in some sense "conceptual thought is coeval with humanity itself."[24]

There is considerable diversity of opinion concerning the social factors which should be regarded as determinative of human knowledge. While some, like Marx, regard only certain factors, such as means of production, as determinative of human knowledge and behaviour, others regard the social structure as a whole as determinative of our knowledge and praxis. There is debate also regarding the extent of the influence of social factors on human mind. The main question, however, is regarding their epistemological significance. If society partially or totally determines knowing and thinking, how does this affect their validity ?

Scholars, like Mannheim and Durkheim, emphatically acknowledge the role of social factors in determining not only knowledge but also its truth or validity. And if different societies are constituted differently, then truth would depend on conventional or contingent factors. And there would be no universal truth.

On the other hand, Max Weber and M. Scheler conceive social influence on mental activity as giving direction only. Our knowledge is conditioned by the system of values and goals of our society, but the latter do not determine its truth or validity. Generally, it is accepted by the sociologists of knowledge that the content and validity of knowledge are not affected by sociological factors; only the choice of problems and data, as also the different emphases on various aspects of the subject matter, are thus influenced.[25] They also exempt scientific knowledge fully from the limiting influence of sociological factors.

They argue that morality, religion, art and the entire way of thinking of people are determined by the historical circumstances, the stage of scientific and technical knowledge, the mutual relationships between different institutions of the society etc. Since all these sociological factors are fully interdependent and historically conditioned, it is but natural that they are different in different societies and times, depending upon historical and sociological circumstances, the level of knowledge etc. The morality of a people would be conditioned by all the above historico-sociological factors, and hence different in different societies.

II. Approval Theories

In the first half of twentieth century, various theories regarding the subjective or sociological origins of human ethical concepts were developed. These theories are different from those of the earlier thinkers like Shaftsbury and Hume, in that most later thinkers consciously recognize the relativist implications of their thought.

Approval theories can be classed under both normative theories and metaethical theories. In both forms, they have relativistic implications. Approval theories are behind all sociological theories that understand morality in terms of the moral codes of different societies. Right or good is what is approved by a society; and different societies may well approve or disapprove different acts and traits according to different historico-cultural circumstances. These theories imply a relativist approach to morality by directly or indirectly undermining reason and reducing the meaning of ethical terms to our feelings of approval and disapproval which, in turn, are arguably culturally conditioned.

Approval theories resemble cognitive - naturalist view which equates ethical terms to empirical ones, and ethical discourse to empirical discourse in science. This view also asserts that ethical issues can be settled by the empirical method of science, that is, by gathering data about what is believed and approved in a given society, thus, methodologically reducing ethics to empirical science. Like traditional science, their methodology is universalist and monist, that is, we can answer all ethical questions, and at least seek to resolve all ethical disputes, through an appeal to empirical data.

They reject the idea of any basic or foundational ethical principles. The approval or disapproval of certain acts, character traits, or behaviour patterns by a certain society is both constitutive, and the source of knowledge, of the norms and standards of rightness and goodness prevailing in that society. And inasmuch as the sentiments or attitudes of approval and disapproval are not guided by rational considerations, they come close to the emotive responses of logical positivists, or attitudes of Charles L. Stevenson. Thus by the simple definition of right, good and their opposites in terms of what is approved or disapproved by a particular society, the way is cleared for a full-fledged relativistic normative theory.

Edward Westermarck, an anthropologist, was one of the most influential of those thinkers who used the term 'ethical relativism' perhaps for the first time in Western thought in his work *Ethical Relativity.* Westermark emphasizes the diversity in the moral judgments of different groups and individuals. He attributes these differences mostly to the fact that moral ideas are rooted in emotional responses. For him, the approval or disapproval that determines the meaning of ethical terms is generally that of the individual or appraiser of moral acts. Significantly, the moral terms discussed most by Westermark have emotional overtones, such as reprehensible, praise-worthy and duty. To say that an act is reprehensible, according to him, is to say that "I have a tendency to feel moral disapproval towards the agents of all acts like this one."[26] To quote him in some detail,

> I maintain.... that the qualities assigned to the subjects of moral judgments really are generalizations derived from approval or disapproval felt with regard to certain modes of conduct. (When we call certain acts good, or bad we do so).... because they have evoked moral approval or disapproval in ourselves or in other persons from whom

> we have learned the use of those words.... A judgment which contains such a concept may be said to be true if the person who pronounces it actually has a tendency to feel the emotion in question with reference to the subject of judgment.[27]

Though he assert that these emotions should be impartial and disinterested, the idea of impartial and disinterested emotions is rather self-contradictory. Westermark, therefore, remains a typical naturalist-relativist who rejects the idea that there can be any valid moral judgments independently of how we feel about the issues involved. Ethical terms are reduced to naturalistic terms (approval or disapproval) which can be known through empirical methods. Since our approvals and disapprovals are both necessarily conditioned by our socio-cultural circumstances, and are naturally variable, this view is relativistic at both normative and metaethical levels. Such a view reduces moral judgments to mere assertions of one's feelings; and thereby it negates the possibility of moral disagreements, and the truth or falsity of a given moral judgment.

Durkheim can be taken as a representative of social approbation theories. Moral terms and norms express the approval or disapproval of a particular society. The "prevailing sentiments" in a society provide the only standard for all our moral pronouncements. He emphasizes that any moral discussion should be undertaken only on the basis of what he calls moral facts. Ethics, according to him, should be treated as a science with moral phenomena or facts as its subject matter. Such a science would concern itself with the rules and precepts which actually prevail in a society rather than with those which someone thinks ought to prevail.[28] Durkheim, like Westermarck, makes moral terms and judgments relative by definition. We can include his views under the head of approval theories, as also under sociological relativism.

Thus, cultural relativists start with the empirical observation that there are different beliefs, norms and patterns of behaviour in different cultures and times; and that people judge various acts and persons according to the norms and standards of their respective societies or cultures. They further seem to contend that one and the same act can be judged as right or wrong by two groups of people according to their different cultural norms; and there is no way that they can be comparatively evaluated.

All such views seem to reject the very possibility of moral disagreements, which fact is crucial to almost the entire moral discourse. No meaningful disagreement is possible if the two parties are merely talking about their respective emotional attitudes of approval or disapproval without finding any common ground for agreeing or even disagreeing about.

III. Ethical Relativism

III.1 Most cultural relativists simply argue that not only the same act can be judged as right and wrong in different societies, but both these opposing judgments would also be true or valid for their respective societies. That is, what is right in one society may be wrong in another, or vice versa. In other words, what is considered right or wrong in a given society is true, valid, or justified for that society. It is added that we have no right to judge or evaluate the customs, norms and patterns of behaviour of other societies by the standards which can only come from our own culture. The crucial link between a simple statement of cultural diversity or cultural relativism and ethical relativism consists in this assertion that what is believed, affirmed, or sanctioned in a given society *is* true or morally justified for that society.

Taylor understands ethical relativism as the doctrine that two groups of people may hold contradictory ethical beliefs without either of them being mistaken. That is, the same act may be right in one society and wrong in another, according to the norms of the two societies. Moral norms are valid only within the society that has adopted them; they are not valid outside that society. Thus ethical relativism is developed in conscious contradiction to ethical absolutism which affirms that right and wrong, good and bad are concepts which are true, irrespective of the society or culture in which these norms are to be applied.

Now, when it is said that what is wrong in one society may be right in another, it may mean that different things are thought or believed to be right or wrong in different societies, and are sanctioned by one society's norms and prohibited by other society's norms. So far it is just cultural relativism.

But the expression "what is wrong in one society may be right in another" may mean something more radical. It may be taken not as a mere factual assertion but as a normative claim.It may mean that the ethical judgments are relative to the society and its moral norms which are the bases or standards of those moral judgments. It may also mean that those norms and judgments are valid only within that society which has adopted them as parts of its way of life. Such norms are not to be considered valid outside that society. And the latter is a very different assertion than a mere recognition of cultural diversity.[29]

When an ethical relativist asserts that different moral norms are true, valid, or justified only for their respective societies, she is going beyond sociological relativism, and is making a normative claim. She is denying universal validity to all moral norms. She is saying that a moral standard or rule is applicable only to those who are members of that society which has adopted them. She, therefore, thinks it illegitimate to judge the conduct of the members of a given society by the norms and criteria of her own society. Any such exercise, we are told, would be misplaced, as moral norms and standards are by nature relative to their respective cultures, and can have no absolute or universal validity.[30]

According to Ladd, ethical relativism has two possible versions- a negative one and an affirmative one. The negative version is that there are no universally valid moral principles (or moral codes); the positive version is that every moral principle (or moral code) is equally valid.[31]

III.2 This view found particular favour among anthropologists of late nineteenth-early twentieth centuries. They, as we have seen, at first concentrated on far-off isolated cultures and were generally struck by dissimilarities between the cultures or the ways of life of preliterate people and their own modern Western culture and way of life. They were further inspired by a liberal ideology which valued tolerance above all and intensely disapproved of the missionaries' and colonialists' attempts at 'improving' the morals and ways of these societies, which invariably resulted in destabilizing them. These anthropologists insisted on first, the basic differences between the cultures of different societies; second, the need for tolerance; and third, the supposed fact that the value of tolerance directly follows from the thesis of cultural relativism.

The advocacy of tolerance of other cultures or ways of life was done by the anthropologists and sociologists in conscious contradistinction to the Enlightenment *Weltanschauung*. which mainly consisted in the search for universally valid or certain knowledge through scientific approach. The Enlightenment thought gradually gravitated towards positivist view of knowledge and praxis. Positivism deprecated whatever could not be sustained (verified) through scientific method, e.g. religion, morality and arts. The excessive emphasis on scientific method and the understanding of scientific knowledge as infallible further resulted in an utter contempt for all those areas of human interest, belief and praxis, or ways of life that were apparently not so based on the foundations of science. This approach also meant an attitude of immense superiority on the part of the white race, and a sense of "white man's burden" to reform the other backward cultures by making them reject their age-old traditions and ways of life.

The supporters of sociological relativism argue that outsiders have no right to interfere in the beliefs and ways of various heterogeneous people because first, each culture is a well-integrated way of life and cannot be understood, far less evaluated, from an outside point of view; and second, there is no universal (cross-cultural) criterion by reference to which various cultures can be comparatively evaluated. As we have seen, these sociologists generally exempt scientific knowledge from their relativism. Their relativism is moderate or half-hearted compared to the later postmodernist relativism. Also, their chief motive in asserting cultural - ethical relativism seems to be a liberal spirit which emphasizes the basic equality of all human beings (a typical tenet of nineteenth century liberalism), the right of all humans to live the way they choose, and a condemnation of all chauvinistic or Euro-centric claims to superiority.[32] Cultural or sociological relativism, as it has been presented by early anthropologists, sometimes seems to be more of a normative theory than a theory meant to explain sociological phenomena.

Ruth Benedict was one of the most vociferous anthropologists who passionately advocated cultural relativism, as they thought that this is the only humane, liberal, or tolerant approach to cultural diversity. In her own words,

> The recognition of cultural relativity carries with it its own values.....(In recognizing it) we shall arrive then at a more realistic social faith, accepting as grounds of hope and as new bases for tolerance the coexisting and equally valid patterns of life which mankind has created for itself from the raw materials of existence.[33]

These anthropologists sincerely believed in the value of tolerance, and an integral relation between tolerance and cultural relativism. It was taken for granted and never questioned that tolerance of other ways of life naturally follows from the thesis of cultural-ethical relativism. In fact, all their arguments seem to have but one aim, to emphasize the value of tolerance instead of the earlier Western assertion of the indisputable superiority of modern Western culture. According to Herskovits,

> The very core of cultural relativism is the social discipline that comes of respect for differences. Emphasis on the worth of many ways of life, not one, is an affirmation of the values in each culture. Such emphasis seeks to understand and harmonize goals, not to judge and destroy those that do not dovetail with our own.[34]

Anthropologists started by first reducing morality to a collection of folkways, mores, customs and tribal taboos etc. of peoples of particular places and times.[35] They further argued that a culture's mores and norms carry their own authority and stand in no need for rational justification. According to William Graham Sumner, whose work *Folkways* was a pioneer work in anthropology advocating the thesis of ethical relativism, strongly argues for the justifiability or validity of all mores *per se* :

> Everything in the mores of a time and place must be regarded as justified with regard to that time and place...... For the men of the time, there are no "bad" mores. What is traditional or current is the standard of what ought to be.[36]

He adds that "we do not study them in order to approve some of them and condemn others." If at all any comparison is to be made, it should be among the mores of the same society to see which of the mores serve the purpose of that society better. The beliefs of the people who persecuted witches "were as justified as those of modern times who believe in the dogma" that all men are equal. Thus, all mores are equally worthy of attention just because they have existed.[37]

Since all mores, norms, beliefs and ways are not only relative to the society or culture in which they are in vogue, they are also valid and authentic for that particular society alone; and since *exhypothesi* there can never be a cross-cultural standard or moral principle with reference to which various divergent and even mutually opposed norms can be comparatively evaluated, no claim to superiority on the part of any moral code or system of moral norms can be entertained. Since no system of moral norms can be affirmed as higher or lower, superior or inferior, it follows that all moral systems are equally right or valid for their respective societies. It also follows that all norms should be tolerated and accepted as equally worthy.

III.3 Ethical relativism is further justified by these anthropologists and sociologists by adopting a sort of definist position in which what 'is' is taken as the sole criterion of what 'ought to be'. Sumner naively offers the empirical fact that the common man, especially in traditional societies, hardly ever questions the authority of the tradition as a proof that traditional mores are the only source, authority and justification of any practice and value. These scholars are using the natural psychological authority of mores as a proof of their validity within a particular community in which they are in vogue. Since tradition is the only source, basis and justification of the rightness or wrongness of certain acts and character traits, they are right or wrong when they conform to or deviate from those mores:

> For the people of a time and place, their own mores are always good, or rather that for them there can be no question of the goodness or badness of their mores. The reason is because the standards of good and right are in mores.[38]

Ethical relativism is thus reached by the protagonists of sociological relativism by the simple device of declaring that whatever is believed in a particular society is the sole criterion or standard of whatever *is* right or good in that society.[39] Since tradition is the sole source of authority and justification of the rightness or wrongness of certain acts, and since traditions (mores) differ so much, it follows that there can be no universal criterion of judgment with reference to which different mores and customs (moral codes) can be comparatively evaluated. And since no justification of the mores and norms is needed other than the fact of their existence, or being in vogue, it follows that at every time and place whatever is believed and practised *is* true and right simply by virtue of its being so believed and practised. And this is ethical relativism.

This view denies the distinction, accepted both by philosophers and commonsense, between thinking and believing on one hand and truth or validity on the other. It is simply assumed that what is thought or believed in a society *is* valid for that society. For ethical relativists, the question of truth and falsity of an ethical assertion does not arise and they mostly talk only of the validity of moral norms within particular societies. Even their use of the term 'valid' is not in accord with the lexical meaning of the term. It seems that ethical relativism is based principally on the equation between belief or assertion and truth or validity. In other words, it simply says that 'what is' *is* 'what ought to be'. Whatever is usually believed in or approved of in a society is what ought to be so practised.

Ethical relativism generally consists of five interrelated theses : First, there is immense diversity in the customs and norms of morality of different cultures. Second, society or culture is the source of all one's morals. Third, the justification of moral assertions is relative to the conceptual framework, or way of life of a culture. That is, whatever is believed and practised in a given society *is* right or valid for that society. Fourth, there are no universally valid norms or standards which can be applicable to all societies, or which can be used for comparative evaluation of these diverse norms and standards. Fifth, it follows, according to this view, that moral norms or values of these societies are all equally valid or justified. It means that if an action is judged right in one culture C_1 and wrong in another culture C_2, then both these judgments are correct or justified. A member of C_1 would be right if he judges action A as right; and a member of C_2 would be right if he judges the same action A as wrong. More important, a member of C_1 would be wrong if he judges that action wrong when his society pronounces it right. And the same would be true of the second society whose members would be wrong if they pronounce action A as right, since their society considers it wrong.

Further, any ethical judgment, norm, or character trait is right or good if it harmonizes with the beliefs, norms and the whole way of life of a society. A trait or value is neither good, nor bad in itself; it is good or bad only with reference to the culture in which it is to function. That is, the cultural setting, conceptual and normative frameworks, or the way of life of a people are the source and sole basis of justification of any morality. Hence a given moral code can neither be questioned, nor comparatively evaluated with reference to other such codes. Each code is true, valid and justified for the society in which it is in vogue, and deserves as much respect as any other moral code.

Philippa Foot gives a slightly different analysis of the basic tenets of relativism. According to her, relativism in ethics consists of three assertions: First, there are wide variations in moral judgments between different cultures and generations. Second, no one set of these opinions appears to have any more claim to truth than any other. And third, the concepts of 'objectivity' and 'truth' apply to moral judgments only within a community of shared reactions, although these judgments do not report these reactions.[40]

Moral judgments are not reports of these reactions, i.e. moral approbation or disapprobation of a group, or a person. Instead, moral judgments are applications of interpersonal objective standards to individual cases; only these standards belong to separate communities or groups. Such judgments are to be evaluated according to the standards of the society or group to which the person making the moral judgment belongs. That is, they can be justified only on internalist grounds, and there is no question of comparative evaluation.

This has an interesting implication. If an action A is declared right in a culture C_1 and wrong in another culture C_2, so the argument goes, there is no contradiction involved. The two judgments pronouncing the same act A as right and wrong respectively are not contradictory, since the act A is being judged according to two entirely different standards, and contradiction ensues only when two opposite judgments are pronounced on the basis of one and the same standard. Foot gives a slightly different version of the same argument. According to her, relativism does not involve any contradiction since one and the same person does not pronounce the same act A as both right and wrong, because no one can use two standards simultaneously.[41]

We may remember here that Foot is not a relativist herself. She even tries to argue for some universal element in morality on the basis of our common human needs.[42] But her outright rejection of Hare's distinction between description and evaluation, her emphasis on thick concepts, such as rudeness, and her implicit acceptance of internalism in judgment lead her to a relativist stance in morality.[43]

Here we may refer to an intresting distinction between justification and explanation of a moral practice, made by Ladd. According, to him, an explanation is one which we, as anthropologists or scientists give for an apparently curious or alien phenomenon in a preliterate culture; while a justification is one which is offered by a member of that culture who believes in and practises that custom. Ladd opines that justification occurs in the informant's discourse; and, in contrast to explanation which is introduced illegitimately into the descriptive ethics, the informant's justification is an intrinsic component of his ethical system.[44]

III.4 A related view contends that the apparent differences in morality are not actually differences in moral values but in conceptual meanings. That is, the system of factual and ontological beliefs, or the conceptual framework, as also the institutional structure, of a given society determine the meaning or understanding of an act which, in turn, determines its evaluation in that society or culture. These different evaluations, it is argued, do not reflect differences in basic values but in their conceptual meanings.

A favourite example in all such arguments is the practice of killing or letting one's aged parent die among Eskimos and South Pacific islanders. It is argued, that even though the outward act is similar, the meaning of killing is different for them than it is for us. The Eskimos' life conditions are so very hard and different from those of developed societies, and when it is a case of survival of either one's children or one's aged parent, killing of one's parent supposedly takes on a different meaning, and so on. Similarly, in the case of South Pacific islander, it is argued, his ontological beliefs determine the meaning of the act of killing. We are told that the islanders believe that a person gets the body in the other world exactly similar to the one at the time of his death. So, for the South Pacific Islander, it is a matter of filial duty to kill his father at the age of 60 when his body is still in a relatively good condition.

It is being argued here that the value of filial duty is the same among the Eskimos or the South Pacific Islanders on one hand, and Romans or modern Westerners on the other. Only the meaning of the apparently similar act of killing one's father is different in these cases. For Eskimos, the killing of father means the survival of one's children; for the islanders, it means that the father would get a healthy body in the other world; while for the Romans it meant murder done from avarice.[45] Karl Dunker, an anthropologist, first developed this thesis according to which "ethical valuation is not concerned with acts as abstract events in space-time. The ethical essence of an act depends upon its concrete pattern of situational meanings."[46]

Solomon Asch, another anthropologist, correctly points out the objective character of duty or obligation. He is also right when he contends that duty or,

> requiredness is not a property that belongs to an action irrespective of its setting and relations. Every judgment of the value of an act takes into account the particular circumstances under which it occurs. There follows the important consequence that the same act may be evaluated as right because it is fitting under one set of conditions, and as wrong because it violates the requiredness of another set of conditions.[47]

Asch himself is not a relativist, but his understanding of different life situations and their moral implications for basically similar acts is quite relativistic. Thus, he seeks to excuse the Eskimos for killing or letting the aged parents die on the basis of different life situations. In this context, he brings to our notice the fact that "Eskimos do not have homes for the aged, or retirement pensions."[48] The entire argument is curious, to say the least, and its relativist thrust is only too evident.

IV. Institutionalism and Ethical Relationism

IV.1 Another very important argument in this context is one which understands morality in the institutional context. It is argued that a morality cannot be developed or understood in a vacuum. It arises, is practised, and can be evaluated, only in the context of the institutions of a given society. This argument rightly emphasizes the integral relation between social structure and morality.

When the social context of morality or its social function is emphasized, the conception of morality in terms of separate moralities naturally ensues. Scholars, such as Stephen. E. Toulmin, John R. Searle, P.F. Strawson, and John Rawls, constantly refer to institutional facts or institutions which should be taken into consideration while judging an act. Though their purposes and emphases are different, they all underline the descriptive element in moral judgments, the necessary relation between description (or descriptive criterion) and evaluation, and the importance of institutional facts. These institutional facts provide bridges between 'is' and 'ought'. All our duties and obligations arise out of institutions which we have either voluntarily accepted, or which are an integral part of our society's moral code. They correctly distinguish between the justification of an individual act which falls within the ambit of an institution, and that of the institution itself. While the former can be justified with reference to a particular institution, the latter cannot be justified, or rather does not need a justification.

Toulmin considers the nature of morality and moral reasoning, and contends that : First, morality can be practised and justified only in a social context; and ethics has a definite function in a social life, that of regulating the behaviour of the members of a particular society with a view to harmonizing their desires and actions.[49] Second, the question as to which traits of character and/or actions are conductive to social harmony is to be decided almost exclusively with reference to the moral code of that community. In other words, any society's moral code is the final criterion for, and the ultimate justification of, human conduct and moral judgments. In most cases no other justification is required. He contends that all questions regarding what a person ought to do can be answered simply by referring to the moral code of that society and ascertaining whether or not the act or practice being discussed is in conformity with it.[50] A moral code gives the framework within which all relevant moral questions can be asked and answered. And it does not make sense to question the framework itself because it is the ultimate point of reference and justification. In his own words,

> so long as one confines oneself to a particular moral code, no more general 'reason' can be given for an action than one which relates it to a practice (or principle) within that code... within the framework of a particular moral code one can ask of most individual actions - 'Is this really right?' but the standards of rightness cannot be questioned.[51]

Toulmin acknowledges the possibility of questioning the moral code or rather the way of life of a society; but this questioning can be undertaken only by the members of that society, and that too with the definite purpose of improving it so as to make it more suitable to changed circumstances and sensibilities. He definitely refuses the possibility of comparatively evaluating the different moral codes, or even some aspect thereof, and avers that, "If corresponding standards in two moral codes are found to be different, the question 'Which of these is really right?' cannot arise." This means that most moral questions can be answered only within the framework of an institutional setting. Thus, we cannot even put the question whether monogamy is better than polygamy, as they are, according to him, two separate institutions, and not two forms of one institution, i.e. marriage. Since they are different institutions, belonging to different ways of life, having different meanings and implications, they cannot be compared or evaluated on a comparative scale. We can only judge or evaluate different acts falling under an institution but not two separate institutions.[52]

Toulmin is right when he asserts that to question the rightness of a particular action is one thing, to question the justice of a practice as practice is quite another. We can justify a given action with reference to a social practice, but the question of justice, or justifiability, of the practice is entirely different.[53] Critical examination of social practices or institutions is undertaken at the critical level of morality. But even at this higher or more developed level, the critique of the various aspects of the moral code can be undertaken only from within, and not from an external point of view.

Similarly, John Hartland-Swann argues for an integral relationship between a society's institutional structure and its moral norms and practices. The latter cannot be evaluated in isolation from the former, as institutions, practices and norms of a given society hold together forming one integrated way of life.[54] He emphasizes the basically social character or social orientation of morality, and thus seems to reject the claim to autonomy on the part of ethics. Since the ways of life of different communities naturally differ, and since any given act or practice can be judged only by an internalist criterion, that is, with reference to the entire set of rules, institutions etc. of that community, it means that we cannot evaluate any behaviour pattern or institution from the moral point of view which claims to have more or less universal validity.

Secondly, according to Hartland-Swann, morality consists of socially important customs, or those rules and norms which are found to be useful for the conservation and harmony of social order. Morality is developed by a given society for a specific purpose. It is, therefore, always someone's or some society's morality, and consists in "keeping or violating of customs considered socially important...." In other words, we have no morality or a universal set of norms and principles which is fully rationally justified and universally applicable. We cannot say that this or that act is morally right or wrong, but only that this or that act is enjoined or prohibited by a community's moral code. It follows, according to him, that,

> there is nothing which is 'intrinsically', or 'unconditionally', or 'absolutely' moral or immoral, what is moral, or immoral depends on the degree of social importance attached to its performance, or avoidance, by some particular community at some particular time and in some particular place.[55]

Strawson has argued that an affective moral code necessarily refers, or responds, to the needs of the specific institutional structure of a given society. He defines morality as that system of "rules or principles governing human behaviour which apply universally within a community or class."[56] And, moral obligation is always that of an individual in a particular society :

> The fundamental idea is that of a socially sanctioned demand made on an individual in virtue merely of his membership of the society in question, or in virtue of a particular position which he occupies within it, or a particular relation in which he stands to other members of it.[57]

Duties and obligations go with offices, positions and relationships to others, or the various roles an individual is expected to play in her community. These roles and their corresponding socially sanctioned demands depend upon the institutional structure of a given society. For example, the roles of father and mother are so different in a traditional Indian family (where father is the provider and mother looks after the entire extended family) from those in a modern Western one (in which not only the demands of the extended family are totally absent but also the roles of father and mother *vis-a-vis* the children are no more well defined). Thus, both the socially sanctioned demands and the duties related to them change from society to society according to their respective institutional structures. And "there is no reason why a system of moral demands characteristic of one community should, or even could, be found in every other."[58]

Moral behaviour, according to him, is not one which is demanded of man as man. He points to the diversity of moral demands which are relative both to the social structure and the place or role of the individual in it. In the beginning itself of his article, he contends that, "The region of the ethical..... is a region of diverse, certainly incompatible and possibly practically conflicting ideal images or pictures of a human life, or of human life."[59]

In his famous article, "How to Derive 'Ought' from 'Is'?" Searle has made an important distinction between regulative and constitutive rules. Regulative rules regulate activities whose existence is independent of rules. They are both contingent and easily changeable. On the other hand, "constitutive rules constitute (and also regulate) forms of activity whose existence is logically dependent on the rules."[60] These constitutive rules together form the institutions of a society. All moral judgments and decisions are based on 'institutional facts'; that is, once we accept them most moral obligations, commitments, rights and responsibilities would follow. If we accept that all, or most, of our moral obligations are derived from the institutions of the community we happen to belong to, and also the empirical fact that these institutions differ from society to society, ethical relationism seems to follow.

Whether we say that our duties are determined by the moral code of our particular society, or say that they are derived from the institutions or institutional roles within our society, relativism follows. Of course, there is truth in the above assertion. Neither are our moral duties and obligation recognized, nor are moral judgments pronounced in a vacuum. They always presuppose a social organization, its institutional structure, and institutional roles, i.e. the system of 'socially sanctioned demands' (Strawson's phrase), or what these scholars call 'institutional facts'.

Rawls makes a similar distinction, but calls the regulative rules 'the summary concept' of rules, and the constitutive or institutional rules 'the practice concept' of rules. The practice concept of rules alone is morally relevant; and it allows the important distinction between the justification of a particular act falling under a particular practice, and the justification of that practice itself.[61] But Rawls is no relativist.

While Searle does not discuss the problem of justification of institutions and Strawson and Rawls accept, but do not elaborate upon, the need for such a justification in view of the requirements of justice it is Toulmin alone who takes up the matter. And as we have seen above, he understands the justification of institutions or practices in quite a relativistic manner.

Thus, institutionalism, as understood by the above philosophers, leads to ethical relativism, even though of a milder kind. It expresses a basic truth about ethics, that it is mostly concerned about concrete moral maxims, and even more concrete practical situations, and abstract, formal moral principles do not go far in helping us in solving our day-to-day moral problems.

Richard. B. Brandt, a utilitarian and a universalist by implication, accepts the possibility of universal moral principles, but adds that such principles would have to be very abstract. The moment we try to put some content into them, they become culture-specific. He cites the example of Ten Commandments, most of which seem quite simple and universal to us. But, he points out that, "every one of these acts (such as restraint from adultery) presupposes a specific local, institutional or cultural structure of private property, monogamous marriage, courts of law......."[62]

Though most of the above scholars are not relativist in their basic stance, they acknowledge that ethics or morality largely consists, not in the formulation of abstract ethical principles but, in providing such regulatory maxims or rules as can help us choose the right course of action in day-to-day life. And since such choices and decisions are made only in concrete life situations, they have to be relative to particular, and very different, ways of life. It is further accepted that even moral rules and principles are relative to a particular way of life or culture. Any proposed universal moral principle would have to be abstract, and as such would not be able to guide our moral decisions or serve as criteria for our moral judgments.

IV.2 Nineteenth century idealist philosophers, such as Hegel, Fichte and Bradley, emphasized the importance of state or society as the larger whole in and through which alone the individual self can realize itself. Of course, Marx is the most important example of the thinkers who saw the individual not as a person but as a unit of a community or class.

In the first half of the last century, existentialist thought was very influential. According to it, 'existence' is 'being in the world', and the being of the 'other' is essential for the very being of the self. Even though the idealists (Hegelians) and the existentialists advocate very different world-views and philosophical approaches, for both, community is the source of all human ideas and values, as well as the necessary context in which alone the human self can act or be moral.[63]

A very important support for ethical relativism comes from the contemporary emphasis on the values of plurality, particularity and ethnicity. The term ethnicity has its roots in the concept of race. Since biology does not provide any basis for racial differences, contemporary sociologists base their concept of ethnic differences on political and cultural factors. The terms ethnicity and ethnic identity are now increasingly being used to fight the idea of mainstream, often called assimilationism.

Though the motivation for the ethnic movements are largely political, their emphasis on differences, pluralism and particularity, as against any universalist theory, have strong relativist overtones. These ethnic movements are not only opposed to universalism but also to individualism. This approach emphasizes group-based particularities shaped by historical and cultural factors, specific to "particular groups situated in particular ways in a particular social order."[64]

Ethnicity, that is, socio-cultural and political diversity is regarded as constitutive of identity of both groups and persons. Various ethnic groups, some natural, some created for political reasons, are said to be constitutive of the personal identities, so that any view that tries to conceive man as man falsifies the lived facts and experiences. It is further argued that in all socio-political matters these constitutive differences must be taken into account.

The conception of separate ethnic identities has been largely developed in conscious contradistinction to Enlightenment universalism and nineteenth century liberalism. It is also against Enlightenment rationalism. Rationalist tradition from Descartes to Kant and Hegel emphasized reason as the essence of human beings, and the universality of reason. This undermined, or seemed to do so, the specific contribution of various historical or socio-cultural factors. The emphasis on the universality of reason and essential similarity of human race (the theory of basic racial differences among human beings has long been discarded) is seen by postmodernists as a rejection of particularity and uniqueness of different peoples and cultures.

Postmodern philosophers, as we shall see in the next Chapter, challenge the view that conceives some human characteristics as inherent in, or as the universal essence of, humanity, and regards the racial or ethnic differences as merely accidental. In its place, Lucius Outlaw advocates due recognition to "the play of differences" and a critical appreciation or respect for "group-based particularities."[65]

IV.3 Gilbert Harman, one of the most vocal advocates of relativism, holds that the main issue between relativism and absolutism is the age-old dispute between naturalism and autonomous ethics. According to him, naturalism which he endorses involves moral relativism, and the latter :

> denies that there are universal basic moral demands and says different people are subject to different basic moral demands, depending on the social customs, practices, conventions, values and principles that they accept.[67]

To quote another relativist, Richard A Schweder :

> The aim of relativist teachings is to give permission to diversity and difference by justifying the permission it grants

> on the grounds of coequality or noncomparability of divergent forms.[68]

While some ethical relativists, like Ruth Benedict, contend that all ways of life are of equal worth, most others are reluctant to accept this logical conclusion of their relativism. They admit, though often half-heartedly, that we can relatively evaluate ways of life or conceptual frameworks, but add that such evaluations are only tentative. And in the end we are left with several conceptual frameworks and ways of life which are equally deserving. All our moral norms, principles and standards not only remain relative to the way of life, or conceptual framework of a given culture, they are justified or valid within that culture only. What is believed or practised in a given society is right for it, so that different, even opposing, moral judgments can be true. In other words, moral terms, norms, and criteria are true and valid only within a particular culture or way of life, and there can be no universal moral principles which would hold in every culture and time.

Thus, ethical relativism consists of three basic assertions : First, the morality of a person or group is strictly relative to the form of life of that group or community, which includes not only religion, world-view and system of values but also many other interrelated socio-cultural factors. Second, there is multiplicity of such forms of life. And third, there is no way we can judge which morality and form of life are better than others. David B. Wong puts it succinctly:

> When we find diversity on the most fundamental levels, we despair of finding any genuinely neutral and independent standard of justification that will allow us to say which of the many conflicting systems is the best.[69]

CHAPTER 2

Positivism, Postmodernism and Ethical Relativism

I. Metaethical Theories

We have briefly discussed in the previous Chapter some common formulations of ethical relativism, the most common or popular form being the one which is generally based on the empirical fact of cultural diversity, coupled with certain anthropological-sociological theses. The latter are : each culture is an integrated whole; these separate and diverse cultures are the only source of all the beliefs, norms and values of human beings; the norms and practices of each culture are valid only within that cultural whole; and there is absence of any cross-cultural criteria for their comparative evaluation. This kind of ethical relativism also presupposes an empirical-naturalist position, according to which normative conclusions follow from certain empirical assertions.

Another form of ethical relativism consists of approbation theories. Their basic contention that whatever is believed, practised, or approved of in a given society is right or valid for that society expresses a definist-naturalist position in metaethics. The approbation theories, therefore, can be classified under both normative and metaethical theories.

The third formulation of ethical relativism is one which understands morality as a response to the needs and demands of the institutions of a given society, so that 'right' and 'good' are whatever fits in harmoniously with the institutional structure, beliefs and practices of that society. All these views seem to reduce the 'right', 'good', or 'ought' to whatever 'is'. However, these views are not difficult to challenge.

Those forms of ethical relativism which seek to found themselves on some form of metaethical relativism stand on a firmer ground and are more difficult to challenge than those which mostly talk of cultural diversity and other related beliefs. An ethical relativism forms a cohesive system wherein metaethical and normative relativism form two sides of the same coin. We cannot refute ethical relativism without first challenging metaethical relativism, whereas we can refute normative relativism without challenging the sociological (empirical) thesis of cultural relativism. And challenging metaethical or cognitive relativism is a more difficult task than just challenging diversity-based ethical relativism. It has become especially so in view of the postmodern trends against rationalism and generally against all claims to knowledge.

Traditionally, ethics has been understood largely as what we call normative theory. But most ethical theories presuppose or include some conceptions about the nature of ethics, ethical judgments, meaning of ethical terms and so on. This aspect of an ethical theory may be labelled as metaethics. Take for example, the theories of G.E. Moore and R.M. Hare. These are normative theories, but they also include their metaethical views regarding the meaning of ethical terms, the nature of ethical judgments and the method of their justification.

A majority of ethical thinkers, such as Hare, John Ladd and William Frankena, however, believe that our choice of metaethical theory has nothing to do with our preference for some normative theory. In other words, metaethical theories are normatively neutral.[1] They either describe how we think, or prescribe how we should think in moral matters. But they do not give us the normative conclusions or norms of praxis.

On the other hand, there is much to be said for the view that our choice of metaethical theory influences our normative views. A cognitive non-naturalist metaethics generally leads to absolutist ethics; while a naturalist theory, whether cognitive or non-cognitive, generally results in a relativist ethics. Also, non-cognitivist metaethics has a greater tendency towards normative relativism, as compared to some form of cognitivism. Take the example of logical posisivists' clear-cut non-cognitivst metaethical theory which results in an extreme normative theory, rejecting all ethical assertions as meaningless.

There are three general problems in metaethics: those dealing with the meaning of moral terms and judgments; those dealing with the nature of moral judgments; and those concerned with the justification or defence of moral judgments.

The questions regarding the meaning of moral terms and the nature of moral judgments are interrelated, and are not generally dealt with separately by moral philosophers. Thus, while Moore discusses the *sui generis* nature of the 'good', he also argues for the autonomy of ethics and a basic difference between naturalistic description or analysis and normative assertion. Hare concentrates on the problems concerning the nature and conditions of moral discourse (judgments) which are generally labelled as metaethical; and his metaethics has a substantial normative content. While laying down the necessary conditions (prescriptivity and universality) for moral assertions, he is in fact giving us a normative standard for them.

It means that even though the relation between metaethical theories and normative theories may by equivocal, generally we can assume that the former do affect the latter. At the same time, our metaethical theories are not free of normative elements. If our contention is right, it will help us in identifying those metaethical theories which lead to ethical relativism.

Then there is the third metaethical problem concerning the justification of moral judgments. The question of justification of moral judgments has gradually taken centre-stage for ethical discourse. The earlier query whether moral judgments can be pronounced as true or false is now changed into the question whether moral assertions can be justified. If the answer is in the affirmative, then the question follows as to how this can be done, that is, with reference to which standard or principle this justification can be attempted, and also whether this standard or principle can itself be justified. In other words, can there be an ultimate ground for the justification of ethical judgments ?

The answer to the last question regarding the justification depends on one's approach to the first two questions concerning the meaning of ethical terms and the nature and function of ethical assertions. For example, logical positivists, starting with the verificationist theory of meaning, have no problem in denying any universal validity to, and rational justification for, moral assertions. Postmodernists, as we shall see, start with the view that all beliefs, practices and norms have both meaning and validity within a given conceptual framework. It follows, so it is argued, that they cannot have any universal validity or ultimate justification.

II. Positivism and Ethics

II.1 Logical positivists or the philosophers of Vienna Circle, reject all ethical, religious and aesthetic assertions as mere expressions of the speaker's feelings or attitudes. As such, they are both relative to the feelings and socio-cultural conditioning of the speaker; and have no claim to validity or truth. This conclusion is supposed to follow from what positivists regard as axiomatic, i.e. no statement can be true (or false) which is not either analytically true, such as mathematics, or empirically verifiable (or falsifiable). Ethical assertions which impute some positive or negative value to an act or character trait are not only not factual statements but are also not statements about the speaker's feelings; and so cannot be verified. Their sole function is to express some feelings and/or invoke similar feelings in others.

We would take up in brief the views of A.J. Ayer as representing the emotivist theory of meaning in ethics. According to him, when I call an action wrong, "I am simply evincing my moral disapproval of it.... I am merely expressing certain moral sentiments." And,

> In every case in which one would commonly be said to be making an ethical judgement, the function of the relevant ethical word is purely "emotive". It is used to express feelings about certain objects.[2]

Since a wide variety of words may express feelings in very different contexts, the ethical relevance of feeling-expressing words lies in the fact that they at the same time seek to invoke similar feelings in others. Secondly, they must not be used in any descriptive or assertive sense. In using ethical terms I am not making any assertion about any facts, including my feelings. It follows, according to Ayer, that,

> If a sentence makes no statement at all, there is obviously no sense in asking whether what it says is true or false...... moral judgements do not say anything. They are pure expressions of feelings and as such do not come under the category of truth and falsehood. They are unverifiable for the same reason as a cry of pain or a word of command is unverifiable - because they do not express genuine propositions.[3]

Ayer concludes that ethical propositions have no validity, and do not come under the purview of truth or falsehood. Further, he denies the possibility of genuine disagreement in ethical matters. Ethical dispute may be about some matters of fact which can be easily resolved; or it may be about the feelings we have towards the object of judgment. Dispute about feelings cannot be settled by argumentation, or appeal to facts. If the two partners of a moral dispute have undergone different processes of moral 'conditioning', then even if they agree with all the facts of the case, they would continue to disagree about the moral value of the action under discussion. In that case, none of the partners can convince the other about the superiority of his own moral judgment through any argumentation. No genuine disagreement is possible if both the disputants are talking about their respective emotional attitudes of moral approval or disapproval. Moral assertions are simply expressions of the subject's feelings, and they, in turn, are a matter of social conditioning.[4]

The task of moral philosophy is, therefore, not to justify certain moral principles, or comparatively evaluate different principles, but simply to describe various people's feelings towards certain acts and traits, and their sociological causes. In fact, these are the tasks of phychology and sociology.[5]

II.2 Charles L. Stevenson is the most influential writer after Ayer who advocates an emotivist theory of meaning with certain modifications. According to his view, moral terms are not meant to give information. Their major function is to create an influence on the hearer. He goes on to distinguish between the 'descriptive' and 'dynamic' uses of language. Ethical discourse mainly involves the dynamic use of language, which is closely related to the emotive meanings of ethical terms.[6] For example, the word 'good' has a laudatory emotive meaning which is also dynamic, that is, influences the attitudes of others.

The relationship between our beliefs and attitudes is not logical but empirical and contingent. Stevenson further analyzes ethical assertions as consisting of two parts : an expression of one's own attitude towards a given moral subject, and an exhortation to the hearer to adopt an attitude similar to that of the speaker. Stevenson's theory of meaning contains several interrelated ideas - distinction between the descriptive and emotive meanings of ethical words; the primacy of emotive meaning; and the causal theory of meaning, that is, the view that ethical words are primarily used to arouse similar emotions in others. According to him, while disagreement in beliefs is concerned with how matters are truthfully to be described and explained, the disagreement of attitudes, "is concerned with how they are to be favored or disfavored and hence with how they are to be shaped by human efforts."[7] Thus, all ethical assertions consist of a cognitive part containing factual beliefs which are capable of being objectively true or false; and a non-cognitive part consisting of our emotional or attitudinal response which is not capable of being objectively true or false.

Stevenson claims that his version of emotive theory of meaning is free of the relativism that haunts both naturalist theories and earlier emotive theories. He argues that while naturalist theories make ethical propositions relative to some natural factors; and emotivist theories deny both the validity of moral judgments and the possibility of moral disagreement, his theory grants them both.

Stevenson seeks to recognize the role of reasoning in moral discourse. But even for him, moral argumentation is mostly persuasive, and persuasion is neither valid nor invalid, neither true nor false. We can give factual arguments in favour of our own views, and these evidences and arguments would be governed by rules of reasoning, and would be true or false. But whether they can persuade the hearer or not will depend upon the latter's prior attitude, or her own willingness to be persuaded.

Stevenson's causal theory of meaning of moral terms, his assertion of attitudes and emotions as the primary element in our moral assertions, and his candid acceptance that differences in attitudes cannot be resolved through reasoning - all these factors seem to lead to the conclusion that he has failed to establish reason's role, or the possibility of rational agreement in moral discourse. If moral judgments are based on, or are expressions of, our emotional attitudes which depend upon social conditioning, such a theory has to be relativistic.

Logical positivists are not relativists in the common sense of the term, since, excepting Stevenson, they have all sought to brush aside ethical discourse as merely emotive, and meaningless. Of course, their emphasis on emotions and attitudes as the determining factor in our ethical assertions has strong relativistic implications.

Existentialist school of thought developed during the same period as logical positivism, i.e. first half of twentieth century. While logical positivism can be regarded as a natural extension of the Enlightenment-inspired rationalism and empiricism, existentialism expresses a revolt against them. Though both philosophies, or rather philosophical movements, were born in the Continent, logical positivism gained greater acceptance in the English speaking world, while existentialism has been more influential in the Continent . Existentialist philosophy has been resurrected and reinterpreted by philosophers, mostly belonging to the Continent, who are generally known as postmodernists.

III. Postmodern Cognitive Relativism

III.1 The so-called postmodern thought has been the greatest challenge to any universalist claims on the part of ethics, and for that matter of all knowledge. I use the word so-called in the sense that it seems presumptuous to me to declare the 'modern' period as finished and done with.

Before we turn to the 'postmodern', we must first understand what the word 'modern' itself signifies. In briefest outline, modern period in Western history starts with eighteenth century Enlightenment, Bacon, Descartes, Locke, Kant and Hegel being its representative philosophers. Both empiricism and rationalism are the products of Enlightenment, and in most cases, especially in science, they have been integrated.

The word 'modern' embodies the spirit of Enlightenment. The *Weltanschauung* of the Enlightenment modernity consists of following theses: First it represents a quest for the indubitable certainty and objectivity of knowledge, arrived at through experience and reasoning. Enlightenment modernity seeks truth which is objective, universal and transcultural. It regards scientific method as the only source and criterion of knowledge and truth. It has often sought to undermine the truth claims of other aspects of human knowledge and experience, e.g. religion, morality and art. The universalist claims of morality and truth claims of religion have been often treated contemptuously by modern thinkers.

Second, modern thought is convinced of the reign of law in nature, and it has been in constant search of such laws and 'truths' which can help humanity control and use nature. Sometimes the same methods of study have been applied to human sciences, and human behaviour is sought to be explained in physicalist behaviourist terms.

Third, the entire modern thought is based on faith in the universality of human reason. Everyone is an heir to this reason. Its functioning and conclusions may be conditioned and modified by societal or cultural values and attitudes, but it remains essentially universal and trans-cultural. That is to say, what is argued and proved by reason is true, irrespective of cultural or traditional attitudes and prejudices.

Fourth, Enlightenment was a revolt against tradition and traditional authority, and that tradition is enshrined in the community or its culture. Therefore, the individual, and not community, is declared as the locus of reason, as well as the subject of dignity and rights. Kant's categorical imperative- "Treat everyone as an end and never as a means" - expresses this aspect of Enlightenment inspired modern thought. Individual is prized for herself, and individual's self-fulfillment or self-perfection is the recognized goal, directly or indirectly, of entire modern ethos.

Fifth, modern thought emphasizes the values of freedom and equality of all human beings, which are taken as naturally implied in their conception as essentially rational beings. There is a natural conflict between freedom and equality, as the exercise of freedom tends to neutralize the affirmation of equality. Modern thought has never been able to overcome this conflict.

Sixth, one slightly independent aspect of modern thought concerns the central place given to epistemology. It might have originated in the unequal emphasis on experience and reason in the empiricist and rationalist sub-traditions of modern period. Empiricist philosophers, such as Locke, Berkeley and Hume, put a question mark on modernist claims to universality and indubitability of all knowledge; while rationalists in general, being committed to mathematical paradigm of knowledge or truth, undermined sense perception. Kant tried to reconcile the two positions by arguing the possibility of *a priori* synthetic propositions. Epistemological question, thus, becomes the basic question for modern thinkers. They do not doubt the possibility of knowledge, but have found it problematic and needing justification.

Modern thought, thus, can be called logocentric, when logocentricism is understood both as referring to the 'word' (language) and reason. The understanding and analysis of ordinary language, as it is used in everyday discourse, has formed a mojor part of later modernist thought.

Seventh, modern thought is also foundationalist in knowledge. For the empiricists, knowledge has its foundations in sense experience or sense data which give us a knowledge of the world outside. This assertion is problematic, and has been the cause of most modern epistemological exercises. The rationalists, on the other hand, have tried to found their knowledge on indubitable rational principles which are the ultimate grounds of all rational thinking and, in their turn, need no rational justification. Both groups of philosophers have taken recourse to the infinite regress argument, saying that we cannot stretch rational justification of knowledge indefinitely, and therefore have to stop at some point, be it sense data, or some rational axiomatic principles, according to one's point of view.

Eighth, both groups of philosophers have generally adopted some form of externalism in judgment. For empiricists, their verifiability criterion appeals to facts, independent of experience or the subject of knowledge, for proving any proposition; while rationalists appeal to some basic universal principles of reason, again independent of the subject, for justifying any proposition or assertion. These rational principles would be different according to the discipline involved but they would be universal nevertheless.

III.2 'Postmodernism' is typically a revolt against each and every dimension of modern thought and approach.[8] Thomas McCarthy gives a concise account of postmodernism as it has been developed in conscious contradiction to Enlightenment or modern *Weltanschauung*

> To the necessity that characterizes reason in the Cartesian-Kantian view, the radical critics typically oppose the contingency and conventionality of the rules, criteria, and products of what counts as rational speech and action at any given time and place; to its universality, they oppose an irreducible plurality of incommensurable lifeworlds and forms of life, the irremediably "local" character of all truth, argument and validity; to the a priori, the empirical; to certainty, fallibility; to unity, heterogeneity; to homogeneity, the fragmentary; to self-evident givenness ("presence"), universal mediation by differential systems of signs (Saussure); to the unconditioned, a rejection of ultimate foundations in any form. Interwoven with this critique of reason is a critique of the sovereign rational subject..... It is no longer possible, the critics argue, to overlook the influence of the unconscious on the conscious, the presence of the irrational,...... the historical and cultural variability of categories of thought and principles of action.[9]

Postmodernism challenges the modernist emphasis on indubitability of some types of knowledge. Such terms and concepts as 'essence', 'universal', and 'necessary' are an anathema to postmodern thinkers. All conclusions of knowledge are inductive and therefore tentative, and can be questioned by subsequent experience, reasoning, or theory.

Postmodernists equally challenge the concept of objectivity and argue that all perception involves subjecivity. Rather, the perceived and experienced world is a construct of the concepts, attitudes, desires and goals of the subject. The point of departure for postmodernism is its opposition to science's claim to provide the correct methodology and final criteria for validating all knowledge. In this context it opposes foundationalist and representationalist views of knowledge which have been more or less taken for granted in modern thought.

The claims of human reason are similarly questioned. There are no necessary universal truths. All truths are relative to various factors, above all, to the conceptual framework of one's culture and society. Along with reason goes the law-governedness of nature. Postmodernism hails freedom, doubt, uncertainty and unpredictability.

The emphasis on freedom should have led to a renewed emphasis on the individual. Instead, the postmodernist writers emphasize the role of community and culture, both in the conceptualization of thought and the development of human personality.

It also rejects the centrality of epistemology in modern thought. It assumes that human thought, experience and praxis are determined by, or are relative to, the community and culture in which one is born and brought up. The conceptual framework of that community in some literal sense 'constructs' the objects of perception. Epistemology's goal of indubitable or certain knowledge is rejected, and along with it epistemology.

Finally, postmodernism advocates internalism in judgment, That is, all our knowledge, judgments and norms are derived from, and are justifiable within, our culture's unique conceptual framework, and cannot be questioned from any position outside that framework. This contention is crucial for the entire postmodernist thought. It is supported by the incommensurability thesis, and a total denial of any cross-cultural criteria of judgment. Postmodernism also supports anti-representationalism in knowledge which implies that the referent of our knowledge can never be positively identified and described. Together, these views lead to a radical form of cognitive and ethical relativism.

Postmodernism is further associated with a glorification of mass culture and common man's point of view. It has become associated with the poststructuralism and deconstructionism of Jacques Derrida, Michael Foucoult and Paul Feyerabend. Though the contexts of the two - postmodernism and poststructuralism - are quite different, they have been generally identified in the popular mind.

III.3 Postmodernist thought, like French poststructuralism, rejects the empiricist idea that language can represent reality, or that the world is accessible to us through language. According to it, language constitutes, rather than represents, the reality. Postmodernism means different things to different people. The common denominator to all its versions is the crisis in representation, a loss of faith in our ability to represent (know) the real. All representations are constructs and are ultimately politically informed.

Richard Rorty argues against the representational view of knowledge and claims of superiority on the part of either science or philosophy in his famous work *Philosophy and the Mirror of Nature*. He rightly traces the representational view of knowledge to British empiricists (Locke and Hume), and emphasizes the constructive part played by the subject in any knowledge. Our knowledge is neither founded on raw, unmediated experience of 'external world', nor on some universal rational principles. It is rather a product of our conceptual framework which we inherit from our community. He calls his view epistemological behaviourism or pragmatism, and describes it as the assertion,

> That nothing counts as justification unless by reference to what we already accept, and that there is no way to get outside our beliefs and our language so as to find some test other than coherence.[10]

It means that there is no way we can decide between various versions of 'objective' reality for the simple reason that the conception of truth as correspondence with the world is suspect. Long intricate philosophical arguments follow which point out how difficult it is to support the contention that scientific theories, as for example those concerning light, represent or mirror something 'out there'.

Interestingly, these philosophers are not only opposed to various metaphysical theories which might want to talk of reality in the abstract, or normative theories which may also want to affirm some universal and inter-subjective (objective) principles as their norms and values, but also to realist or positivist theories of science.

No knowledge, whether empirical or rational, can claim to represent reality, which claim would mean having a privileged relation to reality. What we call epistemic relation is not an outcome of direct relation between the subject and an independent objective reality, but is a product of very intricate relationships between various beliefs, concepts, interests and purposes of human beings in a given community. Traditional thought seeks to understand the world as one, objective and unified, governed by universal laws which, in turn, are knowable by rational-empirical thinking. Feyerabend and others contest the view that all of us live in one world, and our purposes, wishes and perceptions make no difference to the one world. He points out that even physics has failed to give us a unified version of space, time and matter; and concludes that science represents a variety of approaches based on a variety of models, and successful in restricted domains.[11]

Moreover, our practical concerns, and our attempts to mainpulate the natural and social worlds transform them, so that the world that is known to an engineer or a doctor is a different world from the one that is known to a theoretician. It is supposed to follow that there is not one world but many. Not everybody lives in the same world. The world of a forest ranger, and that of a city dweller lost in the woods are different. They are different events or worlds and not simply different appearances of the same world.[12] The perceptions and the resulting worlds of a villager and a city dweller- even if the two happen to be in the same (the word 'same' is a taboo but I know of no other word) surroundings - are different.

The differences between various worlds increase when they belong to different cultures. Different languages posit things having certain properties and standing in certain relations to others. A simple word 'snow' has very different inflectional meanings. Eskimos are said to have a large number of words for snow in its various stages, whereas we generally have two or so. It is even more true of our conceptions of time and space. Evans Prichard studied Nuers and contended that their concept of time differs from ours. According to him, the Nuers do not have a conception of time which is independent of events, is abstract, and in which events take place; instead, they are interested only in events and are not conscious of the passage of time apart from events. That means that not only our concepts and standards of thought and praxis but even our perceptions are a result of enculturation.

III.4 Almost the central thesis of postmodern thought is its emphasis on conceptual schemes, when the latter are conceived as total frameworks of thought and life pattern. As a result, it is argued, any given proposition's meaning can be understood only in the context of its conceptual framework, and it can be justified only from an internalist point of view. It is possible to trace this distinction between content and scheme to Kant's distinction between matter and form of experience. Earlier this distinction was asserted by C.I. Lewis:

> There are, in our cognitive experience, two elements: the immediate data, such as those of sense, which are presented or given to the mind, and a form, construction, or interpretation, which represents the activity of thought.[13]

Nelson Goodman is one of the most vociferous advocates of this distinction. He starts by distinguishing "conventional as the optional or artificial, as contrasted with the mandatory or factual." Even questions regarding such matters of empirical fact as the rotation of the moon should be answered, according to Goodman, by saying: "That depends upon what we take as frame of reference." Even motion is optional, "a matter of convention, of fabrication imposed upon what we find."[14]

He goes on to say that there are always alternative, equally legitimate versions of any empirical phenomenon in terms of other concepts; and the conceptual scheme that we employ in describing a phenomenon is optional. Not only that, it does not mean also that the facts being so described are the same. Rather,

> these objects, observations, measurements, principles are themselves conventional; these facts are creatures of their descriptions..... All convention depends upon fact, yet all fact is convention.[15]

Goodman goes on to argue that there is no way to describe the world as it is independent of our frame of reference. If asked for a clarification or justification of our version of the world, we can only give another version. Thus, the distinction between convention and facts is not absolute; rather it is itself conventional. The two are interdependent. All descriptions are relational (conventional), that is, in every description "some stance or the other is adopted..... A shift in stance affects a resorting." He goes on to proclaim that,

> How can divergent diagrams or versions be of the same facts, the same world ? They must be either of no world or of different worlds. There must be many worlds if any.[16]

Goodman is arguing here that not only facts can be described from many incommensurable points of view, these points of view are equally valid. The choice depends upon our immediate purposes etc., but there is no metaphysical or ontological ground for our choice.

W.E.O. Quine in his influential essay, "Two Dogmas of Empiricism" attacked the two empiricist claims regarding the distinction between analytic and synthetic judgments and verifiability as the criterion of truth. However, he retained the duality of scheme (conceptual framework) and content; that is, experience and our understanding of it include two elements - an invariant content and the variant conceptual forms, or conceptualizations. This distinction supports the commonsense view of the matter, albeit in a radical manner, according to which we live in, or share a common world, and differences in our descriptions of, or theories about, the world are due to our different perspectives. Thomas Kuhn, Imre Lakatos, Feyerabend, Derrida, et al support this view in their different ways. In the words of Richard A Schweder:

> In a Post-Nietzschian world, informed by postpositivist conceptions, objectivity, truth and reality are inextricably associated with, and are not possible without, something prior contributed by the subject.[17]

III.5 Since there is no access to 'the world' as an undescribed or unperceived reality, we cannot compare our description of the world with the world itself. When we try to compare our description with the world, we are actually comparing our description with some other description or conceptualization. Above all, all these versions of the world can be right at the same time, even though they cannot be reconciled to each other, that is, are incommensurable. 'The world' cannot help us pick one right version since we have no access to it; the world, in fact, is an empty idea.

This is the theory of relative truth. We cannot test a version of the world for truth by comparing it to some standard, such as 'the world'. Nor do observational data determine the truth, as they are multifaceted and irregular, and must be arranged into patterns using freely adopted principles or schemes. The use of different principles will result in different patterns, and hence different truths. There can be no single standard for evaluating different versions of the world. Many world versions are available, and which one a person adopts depends upon her purposes etc. There is no valid correspondence between the facts and their descriptions, and hence no privileged description of them. What we consider truth or reality depends upon our framework. To quote Goodman again:

> As meanings vanish in favor of certain relationships among terms, so facts vanish in favor of certain relationships among versions.[18]

The reference theory of meaning is questioned, and more or less rejected. Rorty, Quine and Wilfrid Sellars argue for the inscrutability of reference; that is, a linguistic expression cannot determine the external referent the sentence is about. These writers are challenging the basic commonsense view that science can have definite 'objective reference' to things 'out there' and can tell us things about them which are true since they 'represent' (or correspond to) the external world truly.[19] They question the 'givenness to sense' which is presumed in our commonsense, as well as scientific, view of knowledge. Rorty and others have consistently asserted the 'theory-ladenness of facts' and 'underdetermination' of theories by facts. The two contentions are meant to discredit the representational view of knowledge and any claim on the part of any discipline to 'know' the 'reality'. The conceptions of truth, reference, or givenness to sense etc., we are told, are relative to, or determined by, the conceptual framework of the community or culture we happen to belong to, or are simply a matter of enculturation. In the words of Rorty:

> It seemed possible to say that the question of what was real or true was not to be settled independently of a given conceptual framework, and this, in turn, seemed to suggest that perhaps nothing existed apart from such frameworks.[20]

Both the meaning and justification of all our assertions, whether empirical or theoretical, are relative to our conceptual framework. The truth or falsehood of all such assertions is similarly not to be decided independently of the conceptual scheme or framework in which those assertions are made.

III.6 Conceptual relativism relies heavily on the supposed fact that language shapes our ideas, concepts and even our perceptions. Our thought and experience are determined by our linguistic framework, so much so that we cannot legitimately compare or translate statements made in one language into those in another. The truth of each is to be assessed within the framework provided by that conceptual system. Different languages serve to structure different worlds, and are therefore incommensurable.

Different conceptual schemes may contain and employ different concepts and criteria of truth, and there is no scheme-independent way of determining which is the 'correct' conceptual scheme or criterion. Consequently, when we say that a statement is true, we must indicate which concepts or criteria we are employing. Truth is, thus, relative to the conceptual framework in which a statement is being made.

Above all, these philosophers aim at challenging the very relevance, not to say anything of basicality, of epistemology to any knowledge or praxis. The conceptual tools of epistemology, such as knowledge, representation, correspondence, truth and validity, are all suspect in the eyes of postmodernist scholars.[21]

They start by rejecting the empiricist theory of meaning, that is, the view according to which semantic value or meaning is produced in the relation between the linguistic sign and the object. This view is better known as referential theory of meaning, associated with G. Frege. The aim of Frege's referential theory of meaning, and his distinction between sense and reference, is to emphasize the objective character of propositional knowledge. Whereas realism has an ontological connotation, objectivism has an epistemological one. To know the meaning of a word is to have the knowledge of the object to which it refers.

As against this referential theory of meaning, poststructuralist writers, such as Derrida, advocate what is called metaphorical theory of meaning, which resembles idealist viewpoint. According to it, semantic value or meaning is a product of the relation between different words in a system of language. In order to understand the meaning of a word or a statement we need not go beyond the language and its structure.

Quine argues for the indeterminacy of translation, and inscrutability of reference. He contends that though we can understand the meaning of a particular expression while trying to understand from within the linguistic structure of that particular language, we can never be sure as to what object(s) a word or phrase refers. It also means that we cannot accurately translate a linguistic expression in another language in the absence of a determinate reference point in the 'objective world'.[22]

The concept of meaning has somehow been separated from the context of sense and reference, as conceived by Frege and other realists. Instead, it has been reduced to translatability of one language into another. The idea behind this thesis is to underline the basic differences between the conceptual schemes incorporated in different languages; or what is called incommensurability of different conceptual schemes.[23]

Chinese language has come to acquire special interest in the postmodernist circles. It is so because Chinese supposedly exhibits a unique conceptual scheme, entirely different from that of Western languages. Not only the world-view and general approach of the

Chinese are said to be radically different from those of the Western cultures, their perceptual categories are also said to be different. Long treatises are written how the Chinese divide even the objects of everyday experience into very different categories, and how even the simplest assertions in European languages cannot be literally (accurately) translated into Chinese, because there are no concepts in Chinese parallel to those modern Western men are used to in their normal everyday discourse. For example, A.C. Graham contends that such simple sentences as "the cat sat on the mat" and "the grass is green" cannot be translated into Chinese. In the case of first sentence, it is argued, the conceptions of sitting and mat are very different in Chinese language, as compared to those in English. As to the second sentence, the Chinese language is said to divide the entire vegetation into trees and grass, so that grass includes shrubs etc. And their colour classification is also different, green and blue being included in one category; and so on. He further contends that the contrast in the two languages, Chinese and English, would be still greater if we were to take classical Chinese. Moreover, "Synonymy will of course be even harder to find in the terminology of philosophy and morals."[24]

Graham concedes to commonsense that we can understand another language, but adds that we can do so only by correlating the words within the linguistic scheme. And this would need long acquaintance with various uses of words in different contexts. Even then we cannot translate the two languages into each other. He admits the relativist implications of his view of untranslatability, and goes on to cite examples after examples how no exact equivalents are to be found in Chinese for such simple everyday words as an old man, and so on.

The fact of untranslatability is supposed to prove that the same concepts are not to be found in different languages. It would be even truer for values, norms and perspectival judgments. The idea here is to suggest that language exemplifies the entire ethos of a culture, and the conceptual scheme enshrined in any language is unique. It determines the values, norms and even perceptions of a people.

Different scholars have further argued in detail how the two ways, Chinese and English, of looking at and approaching the world are radically different. While the English concentrate on opposites, the Chinese emphasize complementary concepts. And so on.

III.7 The concept of incommensurability has been constantly asserted and emphasized by postmodernists with different views and sometimes with different purposes. Alsdair MacIntyre contends, like so many others, that,

> each (moral) system has its own standards and measures of interpretation, explanation, and justification internal to itself.... there are indeed no shared standards and measures external to both systems and neutral between them, to which appeal might be made to adjudicate between their rival claims. The two systems of thought and practice (Confucian and Aristotelian) are incommensurable in the sense made familiar to us by Thomas Kuhn.[25]

MacIntyre defines incommensurability as "a relationship between two or more systems of thought and practice, each embodying its own peculiar conceptual scheme, over a certain period of time." He adds that reference to periods of time is meant to bring out the fact that conceptual schemes have a historical existence.[26]

Ethical relativism naturally follows from this radical thesis of incommensurability of languages and their conceptual frameworks. It necessarily means an *a priori* rejection of any thesis of universalism in ethics.

The notion that we could find a common matrix of inquiry, something which overspanned all actual and possible conceptual frameworks, is rejected by postmodernists. Both Thomas Kuhn and Feyerabend emphasize 'the theory ladenness' of facts. It follows, according to Rorty, that,

> if we once admitted that Newton was better than Aristotle not because his words better corresponded to reality but simply because Newton made us better able to cope, there would be nothing to distinguish science from religion or politics.[27]

Kuhn's famous work, *The Structure of Scientific Revolution*, seems to have revolutionized the whole Western thought, or brought it to a point of no return. According to him, each new theory in science is a complex whole, almost unrelated to others. The earlier notion was that different scientific theories understand and explain one common world. Instead, not only their

> explanatory concepts but also their choice of problems and their empirical data are different. These different scientific theories are both incompatible and incommensurable with each other. There is no permanent, neutral, observation language, or common framework of scientific concepts and standards, with reference to which we can evaluate rival and competing theories.

Quine, Kuhn, Feyerabend and Lakatos are generally reacting against the 'Cartesian anxiety', that is, the desire to found our knowledge on some indubitable experience, or rational principle. They seem to be saying that there is no such thing 'out there', at least in the sense that it can be positively determined, or a universal rational principle, with reference to either of which our linguistic assertions can be evaluated.[28]

Kuhn has often talked of loss of data whenever a new scientific theory is adopted, meaning that the new theory does not explain the old data in a better way, as it is usually thought, but selects new data to explain. Kuhn further contends that the proponents of different scientific paradigms can never make each other agree with their respective viewpoints, or even achieve 'complete contact' with each other. In his own words :

> In a sense that I am unable to explicate further, the proponents of competing paradigms practice their trades in different worlds.... before they can hope to communicate fully, one group or the other must experience the conversion that we have been calling a paradigm shift.[29]

Kuhn is denying here any real communication between the supporters of any two scientific theories; which means that they can neither answer each other's questions or problems, nor benefit from each other's insights. The only alternative is a total paradigm shift, or a revolutionary change in one's conceptual framework and even choice of empirical data. Any fruitful communication between the followers of different theories is not possible because they "practice their trades in different worlds", and in some sense "see different things."

Any two scientific views are both mutually incompatible and incommensurable. While incompatibility means being mutually contradictory in the explanation of empirical data, Kuhn's incommensurability thesis denies any common, shared, universal framework in which any two views can be compared and evaluated.[30]

It is further argued that high level theories of science are underdetermined by observational data. And thus was born what Karl Popper has called "the Myth of framework" which supposedly determines not only our understanding and explanation of empirical facts but even our perception thereof.

It may seem here that controversy regarding scientific theories cannot have a direct impact on our ethical problem. However, the postmodernist thinkers always intend their theories to be comprehensive, that is, applicable to different disciplines. Feyerabend thus contends that not only any two scientific theories are mutually incommensurable, various aspects of human life and culture, their values, concerns and concepts, such as science, religion, art and literature, are also incommensurable with each other. Given the general conception of incommensurability, it follows that the concepts, moral norms and values of different cultures are also incommensurable. Here we will not go into the self-contradictions involved in any such assertion but simply describe the relativist views of these scholars.

Richard J. Bernstein gives a concise description of contemporary relativism.

> The relativist not only denies the positive claims of the objectivist but goes further. In its strongest form relativism is the basic conviction.... that in the final analysis all such concepts [as rationality, truth, reality] must be understood as relative to a specific conceptual scheme, theoretical

> framework, paradigm, form of life, society, or culture. Since the relativist believes that there is (or can be) a non-reducible plurality of such conceptual schemes, he or she challenges the claim that these concepts can have a determinate and univocal significance.... Thus, for example, when we turn to something as fundamental as the issue of criteria or standards of rationality, the relativist claims that we can never escape from the predicament of speaking of "our" and "their" standards of rationality - standards that may be "radically incommensurable".[31]

The idea of conceptual scheme and the related thesis of incommensurability, whether applied to science, or to religion and morality, lead irresistibly to an all-encompassing relativism. To quote Bernstein again:

> As I have characterized the relativist, his or her essential claim is that there can be no higher appeal than to a given conceptual scheme, language game, set of social practices, or historical epoch. There is nonreducible plurality of such schemes, paradigms, and practices; there is no substantive, overarching framework in which radically different and alternative schemes are commensurable - no universal standards that somehow stand outside of and above these competing alternatives.[32]

This view resembles Wittgenstein's theory of language games. According to him, as is well known, the main task of philosophy is to understand ordinary language as it is actually used. He asserted that the meaning of words does not consist in 'naming' but in the way they are used in the ordinary language. That is, reference to an object is not integral to linguistic communication. Moreover, to understand a proposition we have to take into consideration the context - the language game - in which that sentence has been uttered. Different language games are said to have different rules of grammar and argumentation, and we have to remain in the confines of the particular game we are playing. Though Wittgenstein did not have intercultural communication in mind, his rejection of reference theory of meaning and his insistence on basic differences in the rules of different kinds of discourse (language games) comes very close to the postmodernist thesis of incommensurability.

III.8 While Enlightenment-liberal tradition made the individual subject and agent the basic unit of society, and the locus of (universal) rationality and dignity, postmodern thought locates the individual in the community, and emphasizes the role of community in knowledge, morality, art, and so on.[33] Rorty, MacIntyre, Michael Sandel and Hans-Georg Gadamer are the chief proponents of this line of thought.

Not only the world we live in but also the subject of experience is constructed by the conceptual framework and culture in which she has been brought up, and above all by the language spoken by her community. The concept of self as an autonomous subject of experience and agent whose identity remains more or less constant throughout her life is rejected. In its place we have the concept of self whose nature or person is largely other-determined and is continuously in a state of flux or process.

Meaning has become social and provisional. There is an emphasis on commonness, opinion and everyday experience, as against theoretical and/or scientific knowledge. In the words of Feyerabend,

> as far as I am concerned truth lies with us, with our "opinions" and "experiences" and we, "the many", not abstract theories, are the measure of things.[34]

Feyerabend is hostile to the role of 'experts'. Every opinion, every version of truth must be amenable to further criticism and revision. Postmodern relativists, however, mean much more than this. They challenge and in fact reject all claims of science as providing knowledge of natural phenomena. To quote Feyerabend,

> But a democracy cannot simply bow to the assertions of scientists and philosophers, it must examine these assertions, especially when they touch on fundamental matters; for example, it must examine this claim of 'objectivity'.[35]

This opposition to all 'modernist' claims to knowledge and search for certainty and objectivity is expressed in a very curious way.

Feyerabend and Rorty discuss the famous controversy between Galileo and the Cardinal Bellarmine regarding the geocentricity of the universe. They give the arguments from both sides in a way which suggests the equal validity of both. If we prefer the scientific version of reality, it is more a matter of choice than of objective truth. According to Feyerabend,

> Galileo did not simply ask for the freedom to publish his results, he wanted to impose them on others.... He simply took it for granted that the special and very restricted methods of astronomers.... were the correct way of getting access to Truth and Reality.[36]

He and Rorty argue in detail how the Churchman was so liberal and open-minded in his controversy with Galileo who was totalitarian and dogmatic in his approach. Rorty, though less radical than Feyerabend, contends that the Enlightenment legacy has been that Galileo was absolutely right, and Ballarmine absolutely wrong. The exponents of the Enlightenment's view of rationality would not even take a suggestion that the Church's view may at least have some claim to validity. For Rorty,

> the crucial consideration is whether we know how to draw a line between science and theology, such that getting the heavens right is a "scientific" value, and preserving the church and the general cultural structure of Europe is an "unscientific value."[37]

Rorty admits that scientific approach, or Galileo's version of the universe was rather true, or at least more desirable. But he hastens to add that "to proclaim our loyalty to these distinctions is not to say that there are "objective" and "rational" standards for adopting them."[38] The choice between the scientific and the Church's points of view is not based on rational, objective considerations, but on our values, and these values are the products of our culture and times. The notions of rationality, disinterestedness etc. are products of educational and institutional patterns of the day. Our choice of data and evidence for any theory are a matter of cultural climate. The change in Western society's understanding of astronomical matters is not a result of rational arguments, but is a product of the times, even as the change in the society's attitude towards slavery, homosexuality etc., is a result of changed ethos of the times. Neither the former, nor the latter, would count as rational.

III.9 Above all, conceptual relativism means a rejection of any possibility of a universal or trans-cultural criterion of truth or comparative evaluation of different perspectives. This is supposedly a stand aimed at countering our natural ethnocentricism. It is contended that the rationality of beliefs and practices of a given society must be measured by the standards of that society itself. According to the Strong Programme, advocated by Barry Barnes and David Bloor, "rules of argument and criteria of truth are internal to a social system." Mary Hesse has argued that truth is internal to given societies, and is determined by "the relevant local consensus." Explanation in terms of sociological factors takes the place of rational justification. Knowledge is simply what is accepted in our culture.[39]

It seems to follow that there is no valid distinction between what is true or reasonable and what is accepted as such in a particular society. According to Barnes and Bloor, "For the relativist, there is no sense attached to the idea that some standards or beliefs are really rational as distinct from merely locally accepted as such."[40] The supporters of what is called the Strong Programme in relativism go much beyond Kuhn's theory of radical shift in paradigms, or incommensurability of various paradigms. According to this view, there cannot be any comparison between different perspectives or forms of life because rationality is local, or internal to a particular culture.

The advocates of Strong Programme are affirming a radical version of cognitive relativism. Its main tenets are : 1. causality, 2. impartiality, 3. symmetry and 4. reflexivity. That is, they understand all beliefs and assertions in terms of the sociological conditions that bring about those beliefs or states of knowledge. They further seek to be impartial towards what are traditionally regarded as true or false beliefs. That is, the same sociological explanation (symmetry) is given to all kinds of beliefs, whether scientific, metaphysical, or ritualistic. Finally, such a view has to be reflexive, that is, in principle its pattern of explanation would have to be applied to itself.[41]

This view is in sharp contrast to the commonsense view that seeks to explain and justify 'true' beliefs on rational grounds, and explain (away) 'false' ones as due to historico-social factors. By insisting on identical explanation -cum- justification in all cases, this view rejects all bases for distinction between 'true' and 'false' beliefs.

Actually, the entire postmodern thought is directed against the positivist claim for scientific method as providing universal and infallible knowledge. This claim was behind the verifiability - falsifiability criterion of logical positivists, Karl H. Popper and Anthony Flew. This further implied the correspondence theory of truth which has now been rejected, not only by postmodernists but also by most other thinkers. Postmodernist writers reject both the verificationist theory of meaning and the correspondence theory of truth. There is no sure method by which we can assess the truth or falisty of our beliefs regarding the world, simply because we cannot go beyond our knowledge to 'the world' which we are supposed to know through our separate versions of the world.

Since every version or knowledge of the world is relative to the conceptual framework or the totality of our beliefs and values in a given culture, at a given point of history, no knowledge or assertion can claim universal, far less absolute, truth.

The above reasoning leads moderate relativists like Bernstein to the thesis that all knowledge is fallible and subject to further corrections. Bernstein avers that it is not relativism. He, however, goes on to assert that the fact that a given belief has been proved incorrect by later scientific research does not mean that the earlier belief was false at the time it was held. Since it was supported by the stage of knowledge or conceptual framework of the time it was true for that society and times.[42] Apparently, the rationality of any belief is a function of the total system of beliefs of a culture; and there can be no questioning of its rationality, except from an internalist point of view. A belief is true, and a practice justified, not because it corresponds to empirical facts, or can be justified by reasons (when reasons and rationality are understood in terms of Enlightenment philosophy), but solely because it is in harmony with the totality of beliefs and values of that culture at a point of time.

Peter Winch in his frequently discussed article, "Understanding a primitive society", takes up the question - "Are there standards of rationality which are valid across cultures?" He takes as the basis of his discussion Evans-Pritchard's study of witchcraft among the Azande, and argues that we have no justification in asserting that the beliefs and practices of pre-scientific cultures, as Azenda witchcraft, are irrational, or even less rational than ours. Pritchard has stated how scientific evidence against the efficacy of witchcraft leaves the Azanda unmoved. Winch argues that Azande system of beliefs and practices does not constitute a theoretical system aiming at scientific understanding of natural phenomena. Rather, they are engaged in a very different type of activity whose rules of rationality differ totally from those of scientific method. Basing his arguments on Pritchard's observations, Winch contends that standards of rationality differ from culture to culture, and those of one culture and activity cannot be used to judge another culture or activity.[43]

On the face of it, conceptual relativism, along with the thesis of incommensurability, seems to imprison each one of us in the enclosure of our conceptual schemes, from which there seems to be no way out. We can neither contact the outside world, nor meaningfully communicate with other persons, inhabiting supposedly different worlds determined by their own conceptual schemes. The most stark expression of relativism comes expectedly from Feyerabend whose lightly made remark "anything goes" has often been used as a slogan representing the spirit of relativism. According to him,

> Reason is no longer an agency that directs other traditions, it is a tradition in its own right with as much (or as little) claim to the centre of the stage as any other tradition. Being a tradition, it is neither good, nor bad, it simply is. The same applies to all traditions - they are neither good, nor bad, they simply are. They become good or bad (rational/ irrational; pious/impious; advanced/ "primitive"; humanitarian/vicious; etc.) only when looked at from the point

> of view of some other tradition. "Objectively" there is not much to choose between anti-semitism and humanitarianism. But racism will appear vicious to a humanitarian, while humanitarianism will appear vapid to a racist. *Relativism* (in the old simple sense of Protagoras) gives an adequate account of the situation which thus emerges.[44]

Feyerabend has frequently argued that good arguments can always be found for opposite sides on any issue.[45] This is meant to suggest that there are no right and wrong sides of any issue; both sides have equal claims to justification and validity. Conceptual relativism, thus, is the most radical form of relativism. All knowledge is perspectival, theory-laden, dependent upon a framework of concepts which somehow determine the way we organize our experiential data. There are no neutral facts independent of our conceptualizations, and there is just no way we can compare and evaluate these different systems of concepts, or conceptual frameworks.

III.10 Various contemporary scholars have tried to reduce the rigour of radical relativism and have proposed a weaker version thereof. Donald Davidson rejects the very distinction between content and scheme which, he hopes, would leave us free to have direct access to empirical facts. He has further argued against the whole idea of incommensurability and untranslatability of languages.[46]

Others, like Charls Swoyer, distinguish between two senses of relative truth - a strong and a weak one. According to the first, a proposition would be true relative to one conceptual framework, and false relative to another. According to the latter (a weak) sense, a proposition can be true in one conceptual framework but inexpressible, and hence neither true nor false, in another. Swoyer supports the latter view, while criticizing the former. But it still makes sense to talk about alternative conceptual frameworks, and about the difficulty in comparative evaluation of different frameworks with a view to determining their 'truth'.[47]

It is further argued in this context that both the relativists and their critics use the term 'truth' in an absolute sense. Various controversies can be avoided if we were to give up this absolute sense of 'truth'. The latter implies first, that a statement is true or false irrespective of the standpoint or perspective of the speaker; and second, that all considerations of truth or falsehood can only be marked on a bipolar scale. The advocates of the so-called moderate or weaker form of relativism argue here that no statement is true or false in itself, but only in the context of a given conceptual framework. They add that the rejection of bipolar view of truth leaves enough scope for meaningful argument and comparative evaluation of different conceptual schemes.[48]

Gerald Doppelt and others have pointed out that even Kuhn did not rule out a common world which is sought to be explained by any two incommensurable theories or paradigms.[49] It is further very earnestly argued that relativism does not mean "any thing goes" as Feyerabend sometimes rhetorically used to say. Schweder interestingly argues that even if "nothing in particular exists independent of our theoretical interpretation of it", that is, the contribution of the subject is inherent in all knowledge; and even if "all theories are inherently underdetermined by facts", 'normal science' has its own value. He goes on to contend that even if there are multiple objective worlds, we must constantly engage ourselves in communicating with each other. He rightly points out that "rationality does not require uniformity or convergence of beliefs."[50]

Bernstein also advocates a milder version of postmodernist relativism. He contends:

> The incommensurability of languages and traditions does not entail a self-defeating or self-referentially inconsistent form of relativism or perspectivism.
>
> The concept of incommensurability is not to be confused with, or reduced to, logical incompatibility or incomparability.....
>
> Incommensurable languages and traditions are not to be thought of as self-contained windowless monads that share nothing in common. ....We must not succumb to "the myth of the framework."[51]

Bernstein, like Schweder, makes a strong plea for "learning to live with (among) rival pluralistic incommensurable traditions." He opines that "an engaged encounter with the other," leads to a better understanding of our own tradition.[52] That may be so. But the writer still cannot understand how the obligatoriness of understanding the 'other' can follow from any theory of incommensurability, howsoever moderately it may be presented. Actually, Bernstein's own definition of relativism, quoted earlier, precludes any such fruitful dialogue.[53]

Similarly, Rorty, while rejecting Enlightenment rationalism, still seeks to leave room for disagreement and meaningful dialogue. He equates relativism with pragmatism. And,

> For pragmatists the desire for objectivity is not the desire to escape the limitations of one's community, but simply the desire for as much intersubjective agreement as possible, the desire to extend the reference of "us" as far as we can.[54]

Objectivity here consists in intersubjectivity, and the latter refers mostly to one's own community. What is shared in one's community is true and valid for that community. Rorty argues that the pragmatist does not have an epistemology, and therefore cannot be accused to have a relativistic epistemological position. He avers that a relativist is not obliged to justify every belief and practice. For him, his own culture and its concepts and values would always remain the point of view from which he views other cultures. Thus, a certain amount of ethnocentricity is supposedly natural or inevitable.[55]

MacIntyre believes that the incommensurability of various cultural systems does not mean their total incomprehensibility. Nor does it mean, as Davidson argues, that we can understand others by reducing their beliefs and conceptions to ours. But here he makes another point. He avers that in order to understand other cultures, either our own language should be neutral between competing systems of beliefs, which, of course, is not possible, or we would have to learn to occupy alternate viewpoints in order to understand different systems of belief and practice.[56] But all these hermeneutic attempts do not detract from the fact that,

> there is after all no mode of thought, enquiry, or practice which is not from some particular point of view, and whose

judgments do not therefore take place on the basis of what Edmund Burke called prejudices, prejudgments.[57]

III.11 Gadamer thinks that the understanding necessarily involves interpretation, and interpretation always has scope for freedom. Moreover, our interpretation would naturally be governed by our prejudices. Gadamer emphasizes the positive role of 'prejudgments' and 'prejudices' in understanding. Prejudices which arc constitutive of our being and historicity may be negative and blind; but they also open us up to experience. We always understand from our own situation and horizon. That is why we often understand 'the same thing' differently. All dialogue and agreement can be only among those who belong to the same tradition. Community plays a very decisive role in Continental thought. Not only the norms and standards of an individual's thought and practice, but her very self is said to be determined by the community. Gadamer is a strong protagonist of authority and tradition and their determinative influence on our thought, praxis and personhood.[58]

Jürgen Habermas, like Gadamer, acceptes that we cannot escape from our own horizon in seeking to understand what appears alien to us, and that it is almost impossible to try to assume the point of view or position of a disinterested observer or theoretician while studying other forms of life. That is to say, there is no escape from ethnocentricity. (Of course, he finds this escape in communicative action, but that is another theme.)

In order to make any sense of the idea of incommensurability and their relativistic stance on one hand and their insistence on dialogue and agreement on the other, these thinkers accept the possibility of partial understanding of other cultures and conceptual frameworks. This is possible, not because of our common humanity but because we are somehow able to understand the 'other' in our own terms. Rorty, as we have seen, accepts the natural ethnocentricity of our attempts to understand the 'other'. Gadamer and other Continental postsructuralist thinkers emphatically affirm the freedom of interpreation. And Gadamer adds that our interpretation could only be through the prism of our prejudices which constitute our person. MacIntyre is similarly a firm believer in the loyalty or commitment to one's own culture or community. These writers seem at once to accept and reject the possibility of any meaningful communication between any two cultures.

III.12 To recapitulate, conceptual relativism which we may also call cognitive relativism asserts following theses:

(i) Our knowledge - both theoretical and empirical - is necessarily related to, or even determined by, our conceptual framework. Not only our empirical (scientific) beliefs are framed in the concepts available to us in our culture, but also our very perception of the world is determined by the categories or classifications of our culture. This would be even truer for metaphysical, religious and moral beliefs.

(ii) This conceptual framework is enshrined in the language of one's society. The categories, classifications and concepts of each language are correlated and form a more or less integrated system. Linguistic expressions are mostly value-laden. Even our descriptive statements are divergent in different languages, because of the basic differences in the categories and concepts of different languages.

(iii) There is a plurality of these conceptual frameworks and it is near impossible to accurately translate statements from one language to another.

(iv) Various conceptual frameworks present versions of the world, or represent forms of life which are mutually incommensurable and untranslatable.

(v) There can be no common transcultural conceptual framework in and through which members of different cultures can compare each other's beliefs and concepts.

(vi) We cannot transcend our own culturally determined point of view while trying to understand other cultures. We understand other cultures by partially reducing them to our own forms of thought and praxis.

(vii) Nor is there any way we can go beyond our conceptual framework or linguistic systems to 'the world' in order to test the truth of our beliefs. Cognitive relativism emphatically rejects the representational theory of knowledge, and the correspondence theory of truth.

(viii) It further rejects foundationalism in the justification of knowledge, whether the latter appeals to sense experience, or rational principles.
(ix) Thus, we cannot make a comparative judgment of different versions of the world, or forms of life; first, because we cannot test their truth value with reference to that which they are supposed to describe; and second, because there is no intercultural or universal standard or criterion with reference to which they can be evaluated.
(x) It means that the truth or falsity of a given belief, or the justifiability or otherwise of a given practice, can be judged only from an internalist point of view, in the context of an entire system of beliefs and practices, or the conceptual framework of that culture.

Postmodernists accept four theses of cultural relativism as advocated by modern anthropologists and sociologists. They are:
(i) Diversity of various cultures and their conceptual frameworks which, of course, is an uncontroversial empirical fact.
(ii) Dependency, or our culture being the sole source of all our beliefs, norms and values. This thesis is strengthened by the sociology of knowledge which is given a privileged status by postmodernists. It is argued that not only our ethical norms and other values but even our empirical beliefs and scientific theories are conditioned or even determined by sociological factors.
(iii) Integral nature of every cultures which was well recognized in sociologists' cultural relativism, though in a milder form, has been turned almost into a fetish by the postmodernists. Not only the various beliefs, norms and practices of a given culture are integrally related or interdependent, they are also determined by a definite conceptual framework, expressed in a specific language.
(iv) The absence of any cross-cultural standard or critierion with reference to which various cultures can be criticized or comparatively evaluated. Postmodernists express this general proposition in stronger terms, as the impossibility of a common matrix or overarching framework in which the various incommensurable conceptual frameworks can be brought together and compared.

While the various theses of cultural relativists are independently expressed in far stronger terms by postmodernists, their unique contribution to a relativist thesis lies in the twin theses of incommensurability of various conceptual frameworks and ways of life, and mutual untranslatability of various languages. These are expected to underline the total independence of different cultures, their conceptual frameworks, or ways of life. This, in turn, supposedly implies the impossibility (or for moderate relativists extreme difficulty) of mutual understanding of, not to say anything of mutual give and take between, various cultures or ways of life.

The impossibility (or extreme difficulty) of a transcultural framework, or language in which mutual dialogue, comparison and sharing can take place is the other side of the thesis of incommensurability and indeterminacy of translation. Substantial truth belongs only where common standards are presupposed. In the words of Philippa Foot, "all substantial truth is truth relative to one or other of a set of possible standards." And, "Local truth is the only substantive truth that we have."[59]

IV. Ethical Relativism

IV.1 According to this later version of relativism, the beliefs and practices of people are relative to, or determined by, the entire system of beliefs, concepts and values of a given culture, and they cannot be questioned, judged, or evaluated except from an internalist point of view. This is cognitive or metaethical relativism, which cuts at the very roots of any kind of ethical universalism. Ethical relativism follows. Not only the ethical beliefs and patterns of behaviour are relative to the totality of beliefs etc., or the conceptual framework of that culture, they cannot be understood and evaluated from any outside point of view.

All the above theses are generally presented in an extreme uncompromising way, at least by a majority of postmodernists. When combined together, they present an almost rigid theory which excludes *a priori* any possibility of universal norms or standards, either in knowledge or in praxis. That cuts at the roots of any possibility of even a minimal universal ethics. Once postmodernist conceptual relativism is accepted, no further argument is needed in support of the thesis of ethical relativism. If *ex hypothesi*, all our beliefs, norms and even perceptions are relative to our conceptual scheme; if these conceptual schemes are not only plural but also mutually incommensurable; if all beliefs and practices can be understood and justified only from an internalist point of view; and if there is no possibility of any cross-cultural framework, or neutral language, then total ethical relativism is the only alternative theory left to us.

IV.2 Ethical relativism is further inherent in postomodernist thought because of its communitarian bias. Wheather it is Rorty, MacIntyre, or Gadamer, the emphasis is on communitarianism, both in theory and praxis. The Enlightenment-liberal tradition took the individual as the locus of reason, the subject of duties and rights, and as a moral agent. This reason was not only conceived as universal, the individual's being rational and/or autonomous were also seen as due to her essential humanity. Entire humanity was supposed to share the norms and rules of rational thinking, and according to Kant, even the categories of perception. Thus, Enlightenment thought was both individualistic and universalistic. It is because individual was the primary unit, the subject of experience and thought, and a moral agent, that she could be related to the whole of humanity. Enlightenment-liberal thought affirmed a total continuity between the individual and the humanity as a whole, and therefore it could pass easily from one to the other. The principle of universalization, first affirmed by Henry Sidgwick, and later on by R.M. Hare, Marcus G. Singer and others, was generally taken for granted as an axiomatic truth. Universal morality, at least a minimal one, was affirmed as a natural presumption in this context of essential affinity of the whole of humanity.

Postmodernists, on the other hand, regard community as the prime or basic unit of socio-moral thought. According to MacIntyre, individual is what she is due to the determining factors of community, its institutions, and the roles the moral agent is expected to play in her society.[60] Our moral concepts, standards or criteria, the demands of society, and even our individual needs, differ from society to society, so that even an apparently universal principle, such as justice, is conceptualized very differently in different societies:

> it is not simply that A and B advance principles which produce incompatible practical conclusions. The type of concept in terms of which each frames his claim is so different from that of the other that the question of how or whether the dispute between them may be rationally settled begins to pose difficulties.[61]

MacIntyre is not even a relativist, but being a strong protagonist of communitarian approach to morality he says much the same thing. According to him, "when two such distinct linguistic communities confront one another,.... each will represent the beliefs of the other within its own discourse in abstraction from the relevant tradition and so in a way that ensures misunderstanding."[62] And,

> it is not only a choice between two mutually incompatible sets of beliefs, but one between sets of beliefs so structured that each has internal to it its own standards of truth and justification.[63]

These scholars despair of any possibility of arriving at some genuine understanding of the 'other', because, "there is no access to any subject matter which is not conceptulized in terms that already presuppose the truth of one set of claims rather than the other." MacIntyre concludes that to use the terms 'is true', or 'is justified' means nothing more than to claim that, it "seems true to this particular community" or "seems justified to this particular community."[64]

Both community and tradition (including their conceptual framework) have become central to contemporary, largely Continental, thought. It is asserted that any moral judgment can hope to apply only within the particular community; and that the truth or falsity of that moral judgment can be judged only with reference to the norms and standards of that community, i.e. internally.

Generalization principle, though retained, can be applied only within the community. The argument here is that the thesis, that the same judgment must apply to all cases which are similar to the first in all relevant aspects, does not understand how relevant aspects are impossible to match in any two incommensurable lifeworlds/forms of life/cultures. In contrast, the relativists argue that apparently similar acts have different meanings, and naturally different evaluations in different cultures with their diverse beliefs, values and conceptual frameworks. It means that we can never find an act similar to the one on which we have just pronounced a moral judgment in other cultures or lifeworlds, so that the same judgment cannot be applied in the two cases - howsoever similar they may appear. This gets rid of the generalization principle, and any hope of ever being able to justify a universalist approach in morality.

IV.3 Gilbert Harman's much discussed article "Moral Relativism Defended" is worth discussing here once again. He starts off by stipulating a definition of morality which "arises when a group of people reach an implicit agreement or come to a tacit understanding about their relations with one another."[65] Moral judgments make sense only with reference to some one agreement or the other. He calls genuine moral judgments "inner judgments" which are concerned with voluntary actions and tell that someone ought or ought not to have done that act; or it was right or wrong of him to have done so. We make inner judgments about someone, he goes on, only if we suppose that he is capable of being motivated by the relevant moral considerations. Furthermore, inner moral judgments can be applied only when the actor and appraiser share common moral principles and attitudes (motives). Second kind of judgments are those in which we pronounce a person as evil, but do not say that he/she 'ought' not to have acted in the manner he/she did.

This strange argument would become eaiser to handle with the help of his own examples. Accordingly, our moral judgments would not apply to beings from outer space; nor will they apply to cannibals. We may say resentful things against them, but we can't say that they 'ought' not to have eaten their victims. The same applies to the imaginary case of a contended employee of Murder, Incorporated, Ltd. We cannot say that he ought not to have murdered another person; though we may still say that this action was wrong. The same is true for Hitler's genocide of Jews. We may bemoan the fact of so much loss of life, but we cannot say that Hitler 'ought' not to have undertaken the extermination of Jews.

It is so because inner judgments imply first, that the agent has reason to do something; and second, that the speaker in some sense endorses those reasons and supposes that the audience also endorses them. Harman adds that rationality alone cannot provide reasons for actions, but certain desires, goals, or intentions are also necessary. Unless, the speaker and his audience share the motivational attitudes of the agent, no inner judgment can be passed. These motivational attitudes are derived from agreements in a given community. His main thesis is that an act cannot be judged right or wrong independently without reference to the context of entire conceptual framework and motivational attitudes of the agent and her group or community. For some reason he does not use the usual terminology of postmodern relativism, consisting of conceptual framewrok, lifeworld etc. He rather prefers to emphasize the agreement among a group of people to the effect that they would all act on a given set of norms. He derives from above the conclusion that if a society A practises slavery, and there are no dissenting voices against the practice within it, then we cannot pass strictures against its members' practice of slavery, though we can still denounce the institution of slavery. On the other hand, if there are dissenting voices against slavery in another society, that is, some people are conscious of the evils of slavery, then we can pass an 'inner judgment' that they ought not to have practised slavery.

First, he insists that we cannot pass judgment on the actions of persons with whom we do not share their motivational attitudes. Secondly, each group can have its own code of morality, even the group called Murder Incorporated, the only condition being that all the members of that group agree to abide by these norms. Thirdly, Harman himself acknowledges that there is no criterion which can prescribe the minimum size of the group that can have a morality of its own. He admits that there can be a single member group, that member deciding his own form of life.[66]

Most of these arguments are not only controversial, they actually seek to dissolve all moral issues in a conglomerate of vague agreements, and still vaguer motivational attitudes. The long and short of this approach seems to be that not only there can be no universal morality, there can also be no morality which would be accessible to rational argument or dialogue. He clearly affirms that we cannot convince the cannibals or Hitlers of the world that their actions are wrong. More importantly, he seems to say that as far as the agents of these heinous acts are concerned, their actions are morally right. Here Harman is not simply saying that we cannot praise or blame these agents whose mental horizons are limited to their group's morality; he is making them beyond the reach of any moral judgment. But it is not simply cannibals or members of outer space who are thus beyond the reach of our moral judgment; any group of persons, or rather any one, who does not have sufficient reason or motivation to follow our moral norms and principles is hereby exempted from our moral judgment.

This leads us to an extreme kind of ethical relativism which totally rejects the possibility of any cross-cultural norm or criterion for moral judgments. (Harman's concession for the possibility of comparative evalution is not convincing in the face of his type of ethical relativism.) According to this view, any action is justified solely on the basis of the norms and principles a group of persons accepts, when neither the size of the group, nor the rationality or ethicality of the norms is decided by any rational or universal criteria.

Let us leave Harman's extreme ethical relativism. Even otherwise, postmodernist stance necessarily leads to some form or the other of extreme relativism. If each community has its own well-integrated culture or way of life with a unique conceptual framework and a unique language which determine not only its norms and values but also its empirical knowledge, beliefs and perceptions, and if these various ways of life and their conceptual frameworks are per definition incommensurable, and if it is impossible to develop any cross-cultural conceptual or linguistic framework in which to communicate with the 'other', it follows necessarily that there cannot be any universal morality whose concepts, values and standards can be shared cross-culturally. Postmodernist emphasis on communitarianism is obviously a protest against the Enlightenment universalism, and their emphasis on pluralism, incommensurability and so on makes any kind of universalism *ex hypothesi* impossible.

CHAPTER 3

Cultural-Ethical Relativism: A Critique

I. The Limited Validity of Cultural Relativism

I.1 We have seen in the first Chapter how most 'modern' ethical relativists first describe and emphasize the now too well - recognized fact of cultural diversity in the beliefs, norms and patterns of behaviour adopted by, and approved of, in different societies; and how they thereafter simply switch over to ethical relativism, without making any attempt to connect their naturalist empirical description to their normative conclusion.

To recall the earlier discussion, cultural relativism consists of four main theses : (i) diversity thesis; (ii) dependency thesis; (iii) culture being an integrated whole of interdependent parts; and (iv) internalism in judgment.

In other words, since the moral code of the individual agent is derived from her culture; and since it is integrally related to other aspects of culture, it supposedly follows that individual's moral code is relative to the culture or way of life of that society in which the individual happens to be living. Since obviously, there is a large number of these moral codes, and since the criteria of moral judgment and evaluation are derived from their respective cultures, it is not possible to make comparative evaluation of different ways of life or moral codes. It is supposed to follow that all moral codes and ways of life are equally valid and worthy of our respect.

My main contention in this Chapter is that the kind of relativism that is expressed in the last paragraph does not follow from the empirical thesis of cultural relativism.

As to the first three theses of cultural relativism, we can accept them as true at the empirical or sociological level. But there are two riders - first, that even cultural relativism is not to be accepted unconditionally; and second, that ethical relativism does not follow from the fact of cultural relativism.

The fact of cultural diversity was very well known to ancient Greeks and Indians; and modern anthropologist' laboriously collected data on this diversity does not add anything new. The fact that people differ in their moral codes does not mean that all these diverse moral codes are normatively right or valid. In fact, cultural diversity is a purely descriptive thesis which is both indubitable, and yet quite irrelevant. What does cultural diversity prove? Only this much, that peoples of different parts of the world hold apparently divergent beliefs and norms of moral behaviour. But ethical or normative relativism can never be derived from this descriptive thesis. What *is* can never be the major premise in any argument that seeks to assert what *ought* to be.

Significantly, the thesis of cultural diversity is very general and nebulous. It cannot provide us with any criterion as to which segment of world population should be accepted as a self-sufficient unit with a unique culture of its own. Nor can it help us in identifying the norms, standards or ideals which are constitutive of a society's moral code, as any society at a given point of time has innumerable socially sanctioned customs and mores, and not all of them can be constitutive of the moral code. We have to, first of all, define what is moral, and only then try to assert the diversity of moral norms and values. It is a commonplace that almost half of a society's code of conduct concerns amoral issues, like rules governing social ettiquette, role models, or other interpersonal relationships. Once the field of morals is identified, perhaps we would find that the differences in people's moral norms and values are not so drastic as they appear at first glance.

I.2 Secondly, cultural relativism points out that an individual learns all her beliefs, norms, goals and values from her society, so that each one of us naturally practises the moral code of one's own society. It follows that each person's morality is relative to her culture.

Having origins in one's culture is supposed to mean that both the explanation and rational justification of the beliefs and practices of a people are to be found in their culture or way of life. It also supposedly implies that there can be no cross-cultural criteria which can be applied to such beliefs and practices which have their source in different cultures.

The fact, however, is that since time immemorial, human beings have shared ideas. Ideas travel faster than human beings, so that it is difficult to say decisively that the source of all our beliefs and values is our society. Religion and ideology travel equally far and wide. Ideologies, such as Marxism, and religions, such as Islam, have always rejected the relevance of social or national boundaries. Western ideals of Enlightenment and liberalism have penetrated to the far corners of earth and influenced those cultures. Now-a-days not only we learn our ideas from our parents and peers but also from books, and above all, from electronic media, and now internet. Even before the revolution in mass communication, one's limited society was not the only source of one's beliefs and norms. Those who come into direct contact with other cultures, or those who are fond of reading the literature of other cultures are open to so many liberating influences. It was the ban on foreign travel that led to the extreme backwardness of Hindu society in medieval India; and it was the spurt in foreign travels under the pressure of industrialization that led to European Enlightenment.

Human spirit is constantly trying to expand its mental horizons, and transcend the limits of its spatio-temporal environment. While the masses mostly accept the morality of their society uncritically, those who have had the opportunity of direct communication with other cultures, or have reached the critical level of morality, welcome such beliefs and norms of other cultures which appeal to them. The dissenting voice in a society, acknowledged even by the arch-relativist, Gilbert Harman, could not have been possible if human thought and practice orginated in their totality in one's society and culture.

This means that the third thesis of cultural relativism, regarding human beliefs and norms having their source exclusively in one's society, and hence being totally relative to the culture to which the agent happens to belong, is also only partially true.

More importantly, even if it were fully true, it would not have made ethical relativism more probable. There is no logical necessity why anything which has its origin in the agent's society should be true and right by virtue of the fact of its origins in the agent's society. This fact gives the practice or norm an added psychological authority only, and not any moral authority, or claim to validity.

I.3 Thirdly, cultural relativism rightly asserts the integral nature of any given culture, so that no belief, norm, pattern of behaviour, or value can be evaluated without taking into consideration all other beliefs, norms and values of that culture which together constitute its way of life. It is a true sociological assertion, and I myself have affirmed it in the context of Hindu ethics, saying that Hindu way of life is a whole in which morality cannot be studied separately from other aspects of culture.[1] Elsewhere also I have acknowledged that culture is an integrated way of life:

> The culture of every society is an intricate, complex pattern of interaction between a number of elements. Each of these elements is but one part of a larger whole, each influencing and being influenced by other factors.[2]

But none of the above contentions can be seen as an argument in favour of ethical relativism. All that is being asserted is that morality as it is practised in day-to-day life is relative to the culture of that society in which the particular moral code is in vogue.

The relativists, however, suggest as if each culture incorporates a homogeneous or monolithic way of life which inspires or determines all its aspects, from religion and morality to politics and arts.[3] Such a homogeneous way of life is a myth or at best a working hypothesis. Each culture is a complex, multi-dimensional whole whose various dimensions or aspects are often mutually incompatible.

Life is complex, and all attempts at reducing its complexities to well-defined descriptions or slogans - including the latest ones-cannot do justice to its profundity and complexity. Hindu 'religio-culture' provides a unique example of a culture in which its various aspects are at once mutually interdependent and in a state of dynamic tension.[4]

Let me give a specific example from Hindu-India's history. Medieval Hindu society was generally dominated by caste distinctions, ritualistic concepts of impurity, and a polytheistic, ritualistic and externalistic religion. The same middle ages saw the emergence and spread of the Bhakti movement throughout the length and breadth of India. The Bhakti tradition was theistic, spiritualist and extremely egalitarian,as against the polytheistic, ritualistic (externalist) religion and caste hierarchy-based social order of Brahmanism. It was the direct antithesis of the Brahmanic way of life in every aspect; and yet, not only both traditions thrived in one and the same society and culture, most Hindus somehow managed to cling to both ways of life simultaneously. Meanwhile, both traditions interacted and influenced each other; but they could never be synthesized into a homogeneous way of life.

It is not that Hinduism or Hindu culture and way of life are peculiar. In the case of any given culture, unless it is totally cut off from the rest of the world, its beliefs, norms and values are in a constant state of flux, due to historical conditions, or the inner dynamics of and tensions between its own traditions, or above all due to the impact of other cultures with which it is constantly engaged in active interaction. How are we to decide which way of life, or which dimension of culture, or which stage of its history, represents the way of life of that culture as a whole?

First, the concept of culture, as having a readily identifiable homogeneous or monolithic way of life which determines all other aspects of that culture, does injustice to the highly complex, multifaceted *Weltanschauung* of every culture. Second, it undermines the flexibility and inner dynamics of every culture which makes it change and adapt itself to changing historical circumstances, levels of scientific knowledge, technology etc. Third, and perhaps most important, no culture can thrive in a vacuum; it is in constant interaction with other cultures, and cannot remain uninfluenced by that interaction. No culture is like the windowless monad of Leibnitz, and no amount of talk of incommensurability can alter the fact of constant interaction between different cultures.

If the above contentions are true, that is, no culture is monolithic, static, and devoid of any contact with other cultures, then no culture can have a homogeneous, determinate, closed way of life. If so, the moral code of no culture can be conceived as a once for all closed affair. Like other aspects of a culture, the moral code of a society is in constant interaction with other moral codes, and is influenced by them.

Human ethnocentricity often works against this interaction, and helps to strengthen the case for relativism. Every society or culture is convinced that its own beliefs, values, customs, or way of life are the best, and that particular culture has nothing to learn from others. Each of the prophetic religions claims final or ultimate truth for its own faith, values and way of life.

But inspite of all their ethnocentric claims, each culture, when confronted with other cultures, takes note of their ways, norms, and values; in the process becomes a little more self-conscious; and consciously or subconsciously borrows from those other cultures. Impact of Greek thought brought the Renaissance in Europe; and impact of Western Enlightenment and liberalism effected an even more far-reaching transformation in Indian society.

An active interaction with other cultures results in inner tensions and conflicts which may or may not be resolved. But the impact of such an interaction leaves an indelible mark on every culture, thus forcing it to change or modify itself in the light of new ideas, and new impetuses. Of course, the second culture and morality would not remain untouched by this mutual confrontation.

One more thing. Changes in a society and its culture or way of life are inevitable, but they are gradual. While new ideas are incorporated, old ones continue due to inertia, or because of the authority of the tradition. The gradualness of most changes in any society ensures continuity. It also means that there is no particular period of society for which we can say that this represents the way of life of that society. We cannot neatly compartmentalize different periods of a society's history, each having its own way of life or *Weltanschauung*, because the life's flow cannot be arbitrarily cut and divided into separate periods. We can neither say that the way of life and moral code of each period of history of a society are distinct units; nor can we calim that the society or culture as a whole has a constant, easily identifiable way of life.

Different cultures (excepting a few favourite examples of anthropologists) are in constant interaction with other cultures, influencing and modifying each other. There are no rigidly defined and closed systems of thought and moralities which are confronted with each other, but which cannot mutually communicate due to their supposed incommensurability. Interaction between cultures goes back to three millenniums or so. Though these contacts were largely for trade, cultural and religious exchanges also regularly took place. This fact is proved by the large-scale spread of Buddhism before the Christian era. In modern times when communications have increased hundredfold due to revolutionary advances in technology, and when we are talking global in every context, even the talk of self-contained cultures having incommensurable ways of life feels odd.

Even if we leave out the contemporary world which is both transformed and shocked by information explosion, the facts of internal diversity of each culture; constant changes in every culture; and constant interaction between different cultures belie the favourite relativist thesis of each culture having an identifiable, determinate way of life which provides not only the norms of conduct but also the criteria of all judgment, and so on. It is not to deny that each culture does have its own way of life, or unique pattern in which all its dimensions are organized; but only to say that the extreme way in which this sociological thesis is presented is not true to the facts of life.

Neither the uniqueness of each culture, nor their plurality and mutual differences need be undermined. But to talk of plurality and differences is one thing, and to talk of each culture being a self-sufficient, or even self-enclosed whole, and different cultures being so different and incommensurable that no communication is supposedly possible between them, is quite another. The latter stance has sometimes been suggested by modern sociologists and anthropologists, but is developed fully only in postmodern thought.[5] Such a view of culture and human nature cannot do justice to the natural affinity between human beings, so well recognized in 'modern' Western and Indian thought.

I.4 Fourthly, it is argued that every act, behaviour pattern, or practice can be evaluated only in the context of the whole of culture and way of life of that society. This view is generally known as internalism in judgment which rejects the possibility of cross-cultural comparison and evaluation.

Since *ex hypothesi* each culture is a homogeneous unit no part or aspect thereof can be studied or evaluated independently of the context of all other beliefs, norms and institutions of that culture or way of life. If an act or practice is in harmony with other beliefs, norms and institutions of a given society, it is right for that society. As we know, Toulmin has refused even to consider polygamy and monogamy as two forms of the same institution, and regards them as two separate institutions which are to be evaluated in the contexts of two very different ways of life.

However, when the modern anthropologists and sociologists assert the integral nature of each culture and some form of internalism in judgment, they do not intend this to mean the total incommensurability of various cultures or ways of life. They simply want to express a positive celebration of plurality and diversity, as also the value of universal tolerance. This was the need of the times, as the aggressive rationalism of Enlightenment way of thinking, the Eurocentricity of modern Western thought, and reformist zeal of nineteenth century liberals - all tended to suggest a denouncement of the religions, cultures and moralities of Asian and African peoples. The sociologists' emphasis on the value of plurality or diversity, and the illegitimacy of judging other cultures from an ethnocentric point of view, were very much needed as a corrective to the aggressive Eurocentricity and universalism of Western thought. At the same time, this thesis of advocating internalism in judgment is more of a normative thesis, or a part of ethical relativism than that of cultural relativism. We would, therefore, come to it during our discussion of ethical relativism (Section III.3. infra).

I.5 Modern ethical relativism bases itself on, and seems to derive its normative conclusions from, a naturalist-empiricist understanding of the issues involved.[6] According to it, experience is the only source of our knowledge, whether empirical or theoretical and there are no *a priori* criteria or standards of our choices and judgments. Whatever inspires in us feelings of pleasure (approval) is good or right; and its opposite is bad or wrong (Hume). Or, whatever satisfies our interests or desires is good or right (Perry).

Here the empiricist approach comes very close to naturalism, and is open to the same criticism as the latter. Inspite of the philosophical controversy initiated by Moore's criticism of naturalism, I believe that the former still holds. (We would come to it later in section III.2 infra). Empiricism's distinct thesis, however, is that experience is the source of both our normative assertions and their justification or verification. Ethical assertions can be verified or falsified by a simple reference to facts, just like normal empirical assertions.

Naive empiricism is now arguably not defensible even in the field of empirical knowledge; it is far less so in other spheres of knowledge and judgment, such as ethics, aesthetics and religion. First, experience is not the only source of our beliefs and values. Especially, ethical discourse implies certain basic normative principles which are neither derived from experience, nor from reason, but which are nevertheless rationally (and intuitively) justifiable. Secondly, experience, or referring back to 'facts' is now no more acceptable as the only correct method of justification or validation of any propositions; it is even less so in the case of ethical assertions. Nor can we accept the naive version of correspondence theory of truth. It means that there need not be objective facts corresponding to our ethical terms as 'good' or 'bad' which alone are expected to validate our ethical assertions; and the latter would still remain eligible to be judged as true or false.

I.6 Further support for ethical relativism comes from the school of thought known as sociology of knowledge. The latter was developed at first strictly as a sociological exercise. Karl Mannheim, as we have seen in the first Chapter, argued that sociological factors or processes condition our understanding of, and reasoning about, any problem. The world is known through many different orientations or perspectives, and the latter include not only various sociological factors but also our expectations, purposes, impulses etc. These perspectives are qualitatively different, so that any two persons may agree on their facts and yet come up with opposing judgments.[7]

Now, any non-relativist, such as myself, would agree with the above view. We do perceive and evaluate things and issues from different perspectives, and the latter consist of our ideologies, or our conceptions of what is right, wrong, good and bad, and our interests, goals etc. Moral arguments or debates and disagreements about real life issues are common in all developed societies. These debates, such as on abortion and euthanasia, in contemporary Western societies, express quite divergent perspectives. Significantly, these opposite perspectives are to be found in the same society; and their diversity cannot provide any support either for cultural relativism, or for the thesis of determinative influence of culture on human beliefs and values. Ethical disagreements only imply that we understand and evaluate socio-moral issues from different perspectives.

In fact, Mannheim himself was largely concerned about intracultural conflicts rather than intercultural ones, which means that he acknowledged that every culture contains various perspectives. His writings in a way support my contention of internal diversity of every culture. Moreover, his perspectives are not totally determined by the society or culture but are also conditioned by individual's goals, desires etc. Does it not mean that society alone is not the source of our perspectives and that individual's personality also plays an important role?

Equally important is the distinction made by most sociologists of knowledge between knowledge and its validity. While the content of knowledge is sociologically determined, its validity is an independent question. Mannheim advocates the thesis that human beliefs are conditioned or even determined by the social structure and the totality of the beliefs, norms etc. which are prevalent therein. But he cautions,

> Relating individual ideas to the total structure of a given historico-social subject should not be confused with a philosophical relativism which denies the validity of any standards and of the existence of order in the world.[8]

He goes on to explain that the relational point of view of the sociology of knowledge tells us about the origins and content of knowledge but,

> the mere factual demonstration and identification of the social position of the asserter as yet tells us nothing about the truth-value of his assertion. It implies only the suspicion that this assertion might represent merely a partial view.[9]

Max Weber and Max Scheler have opted for a still milder version of the sociology of knowledge. According to Scheler:

> the sociological character of all knowledge, of all the forms of thinking, perception, cognition, is indubitable : not, of course, the content of all knowledge and still less its objective validity, but the selection of its objects according to the *ruling social-interest perspective*; (original italics)[10]

Scheler and other sociologists distinguish between several kinds of knowledge from myth (as the lowest) to the positive knowledge of mathematics, natural sciences and technical knowledge (as the highest).[11] We may not agree with this hierarchy, but it shows that many sociologists, if not all, conceive knowledge in terms of the subject matter and level of rationality, and not merely as a product of some rigid and circumscribed conceptual framework of some particular society.

Of course, Durkheim and others have emphasized the social determination of human thought much more. But even his thesis of social genesis of categories of thought and various concepts does not prove that the truth of any belief, or the validity of any thought or praxis, depends exclusively on that particular society's structure or the totality of its prevailing beliefs. All these may determine our affirmation or rejection of certain beliefs or practices, but they cannot validate or justify those beliefs and practices.

In fact, the early sociologists of knowledge were interested in identifying various sociological factors that condition or determine our beliefs and values. They did not always venture into the field of epistomology, and when they did so their pronouncements were moderate. Also, they mostly exempted scientific knowledge from sociological determination. Even when some affirmed such a determination, they never suggested that the truth or validity of mathematics, or scientific and technological knowledge, is a function of sociological determination. Many sociologists, such as Scheler and Hans Speier, clearly rejected such an idea:

> From the fact that ideas are constantly being functionalized for the satisfaction of needs it cannot be inferred that they are indeed functions of those needs. It is impossible to impute them to a given social situation because the ethos of a society never coincides with the ethos of theoretical reasoning; that is, the social order is never wholly reasonable. So far as it is not, ideas must be "ideological," must transcend the contingencies of the social reality in which they occur,[12]

Given the above version of the sociology of knowledge, anybody and everybody would agree with it. It is only too true that most of our thought, beliefs, values and practices are determined by the society around us and its prevalent beliefs and values. But: First, these beliefs and practices etc. are themselves divergent and do not form a harmonious whole, so that their determination of our thought and praxis is always nebulous and often tenuous. Secondly, the conditioning influence of sociological factors is not total or suffocating, and any person, especially at the critical level of morality, is always open to new ideas and values, and is capable of criticizing those of her own society.[13] Sociology of knowledge thus can give some conditional support to cultural relativism but none to ethical relativism.

II. Approbation Theories

II.1 Approbation theories provide the best example of naturalist-relativist theories, as they reduce normative terms (good, right, etc.) to psychological or sociological facts (of approval or disapproval of the individual or society) which can be easily measured and verified through scientific methods (Durkheim).

Hume was one of the earliest proponents of moral approbation theory. He reduced the rightness or wrongness of an action to the feelings of pleasure (approval) or displeasure (disapproval) which "arises in you (the appraiser) towards this action." He did not face the fact that his own criticism of naturalism in ethics could be directed against him. He seems to offer a clear-cut naturalistic theory of moral judgments when he reduces the goodness and badness of any act to the feelings of approval or disapproval in the heart of the appraiser. Hume however avoids relativism by emphasizing that the sentiments of approval and disapproval, as well as that of sympathy, are present in a very similar manner in the entire humankind.

Though I have a natural sympathy with any view regarding the basic affinity of the intuitive perceptions and emotional responses of humankind, any such assertion has to be viewed cautiously. The influence of the culture and conceptual framework of the society over human responses must be acknowledged.

Edward Westermarck and Durkheim have advocated appraiser approbation theory in tis individual and social forms respectively. But such a theory is no lenger taken seriously. Relativists, of course, have rejected the possibility of any cross cultural appraisals. Moral approvals and disapprovals, they opine, are totally culturally conditioned, and they cannot be natural or universally shared. If so, the appraiser's sentiments do not count unless the appraiser and the agent belong absolutely to the same lifeworld. If they do so belong, then relativism remains the only alternative. Though relativism is established, it is at the cost of turning moral discourse into an empirical one which is confined to a group only, and which has no normative content. On the other hand, from a universalist point of view, (universal) moral principles and judgments cannot be founded on such a variable thing as human sentiments of approval or disapproval.

Approval theories are open to the general criticism labelled against naturalist theories by Moore, especially to 'his open question'. That is, we can always ask of particular character traits or acts that are approved or disapproved, whether they are actually moral or immoral, and whether the approval and disapproval are actually valid or justified from a moral point of view. We shall return to Moore's criticism in our next section.

II.2 Approbation theories can be included in both cultural-ethical relativism, and metaethical relativism. As metaethical theories, that is, theories that seek to understand and explain ethical terms and judgments, they deserve greater attention. By reducing ethical properties and assertions to 'whatever is approved or disapproved by x they make ethical matters relative by definition. And then by combining this metaethical understanding of ethical discourse with the anthropological fact of cultural diversity they seem to arrive at a surer form of ethical relativism. Ethical relativism which simply bases itself on cultural diversity finds itself confronted by the age-old problem of whether or not a normative conclusion can be derived from a merely descriptive one. But approbation theories start with the definist position, according to which whatever is approved or practised in a particular society *is* right for that society. Once this is conceded, 'ought' naturally follows from 'is', or rather, the two become identical. Durkheim even asserts that ethics is a science whose task is to collect the data regarding what people approve or disapprove.

Thus, approbation theories make relativism true by definition. If whatever is approved by an individual or society is *ex hypothesi* right for that person or society, it means the rightness or wrongness of an action is not based on the nature of that action, nor on the application of any universal principle or norm to that act or practice, but solely on personal or societal fiat. Add to it the fact of cultural diversity, and we have a perfect case for ethical relativism.

First, all these theories are naturalist in their approach, and are open to Moore's criticism of such theories (even if we do not call it a naturalistic fallacy). They are further open to Moore's open question : "whether what is approved of as right, or is regarded as good, is really right or good?"

Secondly, approbation theories seem to imply that a person or society can never be wrong in her/its judgment, since good, right, and wrong are not something objectively true but are themselves constituted by the approval or disapproval of the individual or society. The contemporary relativists will, of course, happily agree with the above contention.

But any such assertion goes against all our moral instincts and commonsense notions of morality. We all talk as if a person or society can be mistaken in her or its moral judgments. The distinction between (objective) right or wrong which is firmly affirmed by the commonsense seems to have been denied by such theories. Since whatever is approved is right, neither the objective content of what is approved, nor apparently basic moral principles, such as justice, seem to matter.

Thirdly, the assertion that whatever is approved in a given society is right implies that my feeling approval of a practice is quite compatible with others feeling disapproval of it. It is also supposed to mean that one and the same act or practice can both be right and wrong - for different societies.

Fourthly, the talk of approval and disapproval concentrates on emotions. And though these theories do not reject the cognitive element in morality, their general conception of moral judgment is such that it undermines morality's cognitive and rational character. In everyday morality it is presumed that we approve or disapprove of those acts which we cognize to be good or bad in an objective sense; it also means that the characteristics of goodness or badness are presupposed by our approval or disapproval, not constituted by them.

Finally, the theories, according to which that 'morality' alone is right or valid for a particular society which suits or responds well to the demands of the institutional structure of that particular society, implicity identify 'is' with 'ought'. The moral code (Toulmin), institutional structure (Brandt, Strawson et al) as they exist are accepted as beyond any need for moral or rational justification.

I however think that : First, social institutions and practices should be as much a matter of rational critical evaluation, as the specific actions and norms. Secondly, even if there are separate moralities to suit separate societal institutions, it is no argument against the possibility of a universal morality which either forms the core of these separate moralities, or provides the rational standards for critical and normative evaluation of these moralities.

III. 'Is' and 'Ought' Controversy

III.1 Having accepted cultural relativism and its constitutive theses, ethical relativists add a few contentions of their own:

(i) Relativists seem to take up a naturalist-definist position, according to which right and wrong are simply what are so believed in a particular society. Given this definition, any act which is in accordance with the norms of a given society becomes automatically right, or vice versa. Beyond pointing to one's moral code, no other reason is required in order to justify one's conduct.

(ii) Anthropologists, such as William Graham Sumner and Ruth Benedict, argue here that culture's mores and norms carry their own authority. According to Sumner, everything in the mores of a time and place must be regarded as justified with regard to that time and place. The natural psychological authority of the customs and mores of one's culture is taken by anthropologists as proofs of their validity.

(iii) Not only the same act is judged right and wrong in different societies, but also both these judgments would be true or valid for their respective societies. It means that what is believed, affirmed and approved in a society is true, valid or justified for that society.

(iv) It also seems to mean that the same act may be right in one society and wrong in another. That is, the same act when done by the members of one society which regards it as right would be right, and would be wrong when done by the members of another society which regards it wrong.

(v) All our beliefs and norms not only have their origin in our respective cultures, their explantion and justification are also to be sought in their origins. A person holds a belief A - because ...... (explanation); his belief A is justified or valid because....... (justification in terms of the same sociological factors). In other words, a person's believing in something is relative to her culture. And the validity of that belief or norm is also relative to that culture or the sociological factors which created her beliefs and norms in the first place. According to this view, the simplest and surest way of justifying an act or judgment is to refer it to the moral code of the agent's society. A moral code is the ultimate framework with reference to which all moral questions are decided, while the moral code itself generally needs no justification.

(iv) Others have pointed to the institutional pattern which not only provides context or framework for all moral judgments but also constitutes the moral norms and standards for that society. As Rawls has put it, institutional rules are constitutive rules, and a given practice cannot be understood, far less evaluated, without reference to the institution which gives it legitimacy.[14] A certain moral norm, or the entire moral code would be right or valid for a society if it is in harmony with the society's institutional framework and its demands. Another very different moral code would be valid for another society which has a very different set of beliefs, practices and institutions.

(vii) Since moral codes, being the ultimate framework of moral judgments, cannot be rationally justified, it follows that any evaluation of an act, pattern of behaviour, or character trait can be undertaken only from an internalist point of view. All justification and criticism can be only from within, that is, the criterion for evaluation can come only from within the particular culture whose members' actions and conduct are being evaluated. This is the internalist view of justification which gives a strong support to ethical relativism.

(viii) Internalism in justification implies that there cannot be any cross-cultural criteria which can be applied to all cultures or which can help us comparatively evaluate them. It is wrong to judge a society's customs and ways from an externalist point of view, that is, with reference to a standard which is external to it. Every culture is conceived as if it were a closed unit with no communication with other cultures. There are no intercultural bridges of our common humanity.

(ix) In the absence of any cross-cultural criteria, and in view of the fact that we can judge a moral code only from an internalist point of view, it seems to follow that any particular norm or code would be as valid as another. According to Philippa Foot, the concepts of truth and validity are relevant only within a community.[15]

According to some anthropologist-relativists, such as Ruth Benedict and M. Herskovits, all ways of life are equally justified and are worthy of equal respect.[16] It seems to follow that there is nothing to choose between them.

III.2 The basic question that confronts us is whether or not ethical relativism follows from cultural relativism, or from any of the anthropological-sociological-psychological arguments that are offered by ethical relativists.

The first and most important contention of ethical relativists is that what is believed, affirmed and sanctioned in a given society is right, valid, or justified for that society. This brings us to the age-old problem whether 'ought' can be derived from 'is'. Till a few decades back, this question was taken very seriously, but contemporary moral philosophers tend to brush it aside as non-significant.

In spite of the unwelcome repetitiveness of this venture, let me discuss here in the briefest outline the issues involved. When the relativists say that what is believed or practised in a society *is* right for that society, they are definitely taking up a naturalist position. They are defining moral right or 'ought' in terms of what is believed and affirmed in a society; in other words, they are reducing the ethical to the nonethical, the normative to the descriptive.

Hume's one passage has been quoted innumerable times in the context of 'is'- 'ought' controversy. The passage, as is well known, comments upon ethicists' smooth transition from 'is' to 'ought' According to him,

> In every system of morality which I have hitherto met with, I have always remarked that the author proceeds for some time in the ordinary way of reasoning... when of a sudden I am surprised to find that instead of the usual copulations of propositions *is* and *is not*, I meet with no proposition that is not connected with an *ought* or an *ought not*. This change is imperceptible, but is, however, of the last consequence. For as this *ought* or *ought not* expresses some new relation or affirmation, it is necessary that it should

> be observed and explained; and at the same time that a reason should be given for what seems altogether inconceivable, how this new relation can be a deduction from others which are entirely different from it.[17]

Critics have contended that this criticism is equally applicable to Hume's own system, which seems to identify what is right or wrong with what is approved or disapproved by the appraiser. That may or may not be so. But his contention seems to be reasonable enough that the concept of 'ought' expresses an entirely new relation which simply cannot follow from any statement regarding what 'is'.

It was G.E. Moore who presented a full-fledged argument against naturalism, or the tendency to reduce ethical characteristics to non-ethical ones, and called it the naturalistic fallacy.

Moore's definition of naturalism is generally accepted even though his criticism thereof is not. He defines naturalism as, "ethical theories which declare that no intrinsic value is to be found except in the possession of some one natural property other than pleasure;" This is what, according to him, is to commit naturalistic fallacy.[18] When we say that a thing's being good, or an act's being right is because we prefer it, or approve of it, we should remember that,

> the goodness of the thing - that *of* which you think - is, for that very reason, obviously *not* the same thing as your preference of it. Whether you have a certain thought or not is one question; and whether what you think is true is quite a different one, upon which the answer to the first has not the least bearing. The fact that you prefer a thing (or approve of it) does not tend to shew that the thing is good, even if it does shew that you think it so.[19]

He goes on to argue that we can always distinguish between what we think true, and what *is* true. And,

> what I think true may nevertheless be false. When, therefore, I assert that it is true I mean to assert something different from the fact that I think so. What I think, namely that something is true, is always quite distinct from the fact that I think it.[20]

To be true is not the same thing as being cognized. When we say "that we *know* a thing, we mean to assert not only that our mind is cognitive, but also that which it cognises is true."[21] Similarly, when we think a thing good, we generally have a special attitude of will or feeling towards it, "but the two things are not, in the strict sense, identical."[22]

Naturalist (e.g. advocates of approbation theories) reduce the normative concepts of 'goodness' or 'rightness' and their opposites to some such natural quality as conduciveness to happiness, or being the object of some one's, or some group's approval or disapproval. They thereby falsify the normative character of ethics. Approving and 'goodness' or 'rightness' are two distinct things, so that the same naturalistic mistake is made when it is affirmed that whatever is approved *is* 'good' or 'right'; and whatever is disapproved *is* 'bad' or 'wrong' Commonsense usage suggests that our approval and disapproval *presuppose* a character trait's or an act's being good or right and evil or wrong respectively. That is, our approval or disapproval refers to character traits or acts whose goodness (rightness) or otherwise is not the product of our approval or disapproval, but is rather the cause or basis thereof. If so, then the whole thesis which is central to all formulations of cultural-ethical relativism, that is, whatever is approved in a society *is* right for its members, and whatever is disapproved *is* wrong, seems to falter.

William K. Frankena has argued against the very conception of naturalistic fallacy.[23] His main argument is that when someone equates ethical characteristics with non-ethical ones, no logical fallacy or error is being committed. He is right; but he has still not proved that 'ought' can be simply reduced to, or derived from, 'is'.

Frankena has analyzed the position of the critics of 'naturalistic fallacy' as consisting of three assertions:

1. Ethical propositions are not deducible from nonethical ones.
2. Ethical characters are not definable in nonethical terms
3. Ethical characteristics are different in kind from nonethical ones.

The three contentions hang together. However, Moore only uses the second and third contentions in his argument against 'naturalistic fallacy', his main contention being that ethical characteristics are different in kind from nonethical ones, and hence not definable in terms of the latter. Frankena also seems to concentrate on the last two contentions in his argument against the thesis of naturalistic fallacy.

But as far as I can understand, Frankena's argument does not influence the first contention that ehtical propositions are duducidble from a set of mere nonethical assertions. It was R.M. Hare who developed and elaborated upon this idea, and it is this contention in which I am particularly interested here.

Hare, as is well known, equates ethical with the prescriptive, and contrasts them with the indicative or descriptive statements. The chief function of ethical assertions is to command or prescribe a course of action; and those naturalistic theories which seek to derive evaluative assertions from statements of fact "leave out the prescriptive or commendatory element in value judgments,"[24] Hare endorses Moore's argument and says:

> Value terms have a special function in language, that of commending; and so they plainly cannot be defined in terms of other words which themselves do not perform this function.[25]

A moral judgment has two main constitutive parts or premisses- a descriptive one and an evaluative one. While the descriptive premise classifies the act as belonging to a certain class of acts; the major premise consists of a universal moral principle which declares that all such acts are right or wrong. Hare's main contention here is that evaluation, being a very different linguistic activity, cannot be derived from mere descriptive statements whose function is entirely different:

> No imperative [i.e. ethical] conclusion can be validly drawn from a set of premisses which does not contain at least one imperative.[26]

Hare's view has been criticized on two main counts : First, it seems to leave no point of contact between normative principles and empirical reality, so that the description of the situation can make no contribution to the evaluative or presecriptive judgment. And second, Hare conceives moral reasoning in syllogistic terms wherein the conclusion can contain nothing which is not already contained in the premisses. This concept of reasoning has been criticized persistently, one of the main arguments being that linear deduction is not the only form of valid reasoning. It has been argued by his critics that it is not necessary that the premisses of the argument must contain an evaluative principle, as Hare himself acknowledges in a later work.

Two attempts by J.R. Searle and Philippa Foot towards proving that the 'ought' of ethical judgments can be derived from the 'is' of descriptive assertions are worth mentioning. Searle[27] at first uses the simple device of expanding the statement: "Jones ought to pay the money," i.e. keep his promise, into a series of linguistic assertions, which give the impression as if ethical conclusion naturally follows from the fact of Jones having uttered certain words indicative of promise which, in turn, is supposed to be a descriptive statement. Searle asserts that merely uttering the word "I promise" entails the obligation to keep the promise; or in other words, the obligation inheres in the utterance itself. He further takes recourse to the distinction between brute facts and institutional facts, which distinction has also been advocated by Foot and Rawls. Searle argues that once we accept certain institutions, the obligations and commitments naturally follow, as they are institutional facts.

The whole argument begs the question of Jones' obligation to keep the promise. Simply breaking up some statement containing 'ought' does not prove that the 'ought' is derivable from the 'is', or from any set of empirical statements. The moral obligation to keep the promise may be explainable by taking recourse to 'institutional facts'; or it can be more simply and directly explained by an appeal to a universal moral principle that one ought to keep one's promises. I agree with Hare that promise keeping is a moral principle which is presupposed even by the institution of promise keeping. The utterance of the words "I promise" would entail the obligation to keep the promise only when the moral obligation to that effect, or the prescriptive principle is already acknowledged.[28]

Admittedly, not all duties or obligations are directly derived from abstract universal principles, most of them being derived from institutional rules which largely constitute the actual moral code of the society. As pointed out by Searle and Rawls, institutional rules are constitutive of moral practices. According to this thesis, supported separately by Searle, Rawls, Foot and Toulmin, an institution provides the framework within which relevant acts are understood, evaluated and justified. Within the institutional framework whatever is *is* right, and the source of 'ought'. We would come back to this thesis in a later section.

I strongly suspect that the entire argument is precariously based on a confusion between sociological and psychological observations on one hand and normative assertions on the other. That a large portion of my obligations is derived from the society I happen to live in is a sociological fact; while the sense of obligatoriness attached to social norms is a psychological fact. But that both these obligations and the institutions on which they are based are right, or what ought to be the case, is a normative assertion.

The so-called institutional facts can be understood equally in terms of sociological factors or facts. A particular conception of duty or even a particular institution is a sociological fact, a product of so many historico-sociological factors, and compatible with other practices and institutions of that society. None of these sociological facts, however, proves that the moral 'ought' is derivable from the 'is' of the institutions, or their constitutive rules. A society's institutions do provide a framework or pattern of life for its members ; their rules become constitutive rules of the customs, practices and patterns of behaviour of that society. These institutions further aim at regulating and even controlling the conduct of its members, who accept these institutions and their rules because of the social sanctions, and also because of the psychological authority these social institutions possess for its members. But these sociological facts cannot prove that these institutional facts, rules, or the institutions themselves are right or just. Like Searle Philippa Foot in her much discussed "Moral Arguments"[29] does not prove anything more. The context of her argument is different from that of Searle. She does not take the view that 'ought' cannot be derived from 'is' seriously, and brushes it aside by simply asserting that premisses together can easily lead to a conclusion which is not contained in any of them. Foot's main concern, however, is the view supposedly held by Stevenson and Hare that there is no logical connection between statements of facts and those of value. She argues in response that factual premisses constitute evidence for evaluative conclusions.

Probably she is right in both her contentions. But all she has to say in support of her second and main thesis is that descriptive criteria are involved in the use of such evaluative terms as 'rude', so that given a certain description of someone's behaviour we must conclude that she is rude. She grandly concludes that here is "an example of non-evaluative premise from which an evaluative conclusion can be deduced."

She is right that evaluation follows, or is even implicit in, the description in the case of such thick and relatively less important concepts as 'rude'. In spite of her argument that 'rude' is a different concept from those of conventional behaviour or ettiquette, the fact is that rudeness or its opposite is more a matter of ettiquette rather than that of morality. Moreover, such an analysis will not hold good for more abstract and general principles, and it is the latter that constitute the core of morality. Any argument which is exclusively based on thick concepts hardly proves anything about morality as such.

Foot may also be right when she contends that a set of premisses together may include more than what is contained in the premisses themselves. This may also mean that an evaluative conclusion may be derived from descriptive premisses. And yet, Foot herself has to labour hard in order to justify the leap from mere description to normative judgment by appealing to a vaguely presented thesis of our 'common humanity'.

III.3 I cannot hope to make any substantial contribution to the long drawn controversy regarding the relation between 'is' and 'ought'. However, my contention that 'ought' cannot be derived from 'is', is not a general one which is being questioned by Frankena and Foot but, is made with reference to a specific context. That is, I only want to contend that the rightness (ought) of a moral code cannot be simply asserted or derived from the descriptive sociological fact that this code is in vogue in some society.

I agree with Foot that the empirical facts or descriptive statements can be evidence for evaluative judgments, such as given a description of an act of willful cruelty, we can say without hesitation that it is wrong. At the same time, this has nothing to do with the question whether what is believed or practised in a society is a sufficient basis for the normative judgment that it is the right thing to believe and do.

It seems to me that there is some confusion at the basis of the 'is', 'ought' controversy. The controversy has two versions; or it is discussed in two different contexts. According to the first or main version, enunciated by Hare, evaluative judgments cannot be derived from descriptive ones, as the two have very different kinds of function. The second, or anthropologist - relativist version, simply says that whatever is *is* right, that is, whatever is believed or practised in a society *is* right for that society, or is what *ought to be* the norm for that society. Any argument against the first or Hare's version of the thesis that 'ought' cannot be derived from 'is' cannot affect the simple contention being argued here that what is right or just *is* not the same as what is believed or practised in a society. The rightness of an act, or the 'ought' of duty may well be a function of the situation and its description, but it is not the same as to say whatever is *is* right.

Moore and Hare are both right when they insist that evaluation and description are very different kinds of activity. When an anthropologist is describing the customs, mores and practices of some alien culture, she is engaged in a legitimate activity of description. Of course, description is always value-laden, but the two - description and evaluation - remain distinct. That is why, when another anthropologist, such as Ruth Benedict, pleads for "equal validity of all patterns of life", she is engaged in a very different kind of activity.[30] The second is a normative claim and needs some rational justification other than the mere fact that it is so.

Similarly, when W.G. Sumner describes how the customs, mores and norms have a strong psychological authority for the members of the community in which they are in vogue, how they are never questioned by the people because of their socio-psychological authority, he is combining an anthropological description of observed facts with a psychological explanation, all of which may well be true.[31] Sumner is right when he asserts that morality of a group mainly consists of traditional norms, and that it is "historical, institutional and empirical." But he says much more than this:

> The standards of good and right are in the mores...... Everything in the mores of a time and place must be regarded as justified with regard to the time and place.[32]

What does the 'are' here mean? That it is a sociological fact that customs and mores are understood and followed in everyday life as the standards of what is right or wrong? Or, does he mean that the customs and mores *are* the standards of what is true or right from a normative or ethical point of view ? If the latter, then Sumner is wrong. We may derive our standards of right and wrong from various sources, but then there would always be the requirement of rational justification for them. The procedure of rational justification may be still vague or even controversial; but it would still remain a legitimate question whether the standard or criterion being appealed to in a judgment is a right or justified one.

Moore's 'open question' argument cannot be brushed aside easily. Moore simply says that for any kind of naturalist definist position we can always ask - "Is ..... really good?" We can also question; "Is everything that is believed in, and practised by, a society really good?" Just the fact that certain practices and norms are in vogue in some society does not mean that they *are* morally right or just. The normative 'ought' is not derivable from the empirical 'is'. Regarding every norm, practice, or institution, we can always ask whether this norm or practice is really right, just or good ? As far as I can understand, any naturalist-definist position that equates what is believed, practised, or approved in a society with what is right or good, or what ought to be so believed and practised, takes an unwarranted leap from 'is' to 'ought', i.e. from description to evaluation. Even if it is not a fallacy in Moore' sense, as argued by Frankena, the equation of 'is' with 'ought' remains unjustified.

III.4 Mere believing or practising cannot make an assertion true, or a practice right. If a certain people believe in the earth being flat, or the universe being created a few thousand years ago, the fact of believing does not make these assertions true. In spite of all the postmodernist arguments to the contrary, commonsense dictates that belief does not guarantee truth. If it could, the earth could be both flat and round; and so on.

Richard T. Garner and Bernard Rosen have argued in detail that in both science and ethics, believing something to be the case does not guarantee either its truth, or its validity, or rightness[33] Referring to the anthropologists' practice of justifying the apparently immoral acts of alien cultures on the basis of their beliefs, the two authors argue that there are some acts, such as killing another human being, which would always be wrong; so that,

> the mere fact that these two people live in different cultures does not seem to be relevant, as the ethical relativist seems to be maintaining, to the rightness or wrongness of their actions.[34]

Referring to the ethical relativists' thesis that whatever is believed or practised in a society *is* true or right for them, the authors contend that "The expression, "it is true for them" in this context seems to mean neither more nor less than "they believe it is true."[35] They add that the simple fact of some one's having a belief does not prove anything:

> We are considering the truth or justifiability of the belief, *not* the fact that people have it. It is a mistake to suppose that all beliefs are true, or that a proposition becomes true simply because someone believes it.[36]

It seems that ethical relativism can be proved only if we first start with the assumption that it is true! The ethical relativists' contention, that different people believe the same act to be right or wrong, therefore it is right or wrong for them, presupposes ethical relativism. That is, unless you presume that what is believed and practised *is* right, you cannot take the leap from cultural to ethical relativism. But this presumption is yet to be proved.[37] In short, the mere fact of some people believing certain acts or practices to be right or wrong, that is, cultural relativism cannot be a proof of ethical relativism.

Paul W. Taylor has similarly argued that some people's believing something to be right or wrong does not make it so:

> Whether a given moral opinion is true or false depends not on who believes it or how many believe it, but on whether reasons can be given to justify it.[38]

He contends that a moral belief is justified not on the basis of agreement or disagreement among various people but on that of its rationality. He adds that just as moral disagreement cannot prove ethical relativism, the possibility of agreement of entire humanity as regards certain ethical beliefs would not prove ethical absolutism.[39]

Marcus Singer suggests that this kind of relativism arises out of a question-begging assumption that if a certain practice prevails in a certain place, then it is right in that place; that if a rule is not reconginzed or observed by a group, then it does not apply to them. That way anyone can claim exemption from a rule by refusing to recognize that rule against any immoral practice. "It is one thing", say Singer, "to record a practice. It is another to determine its moral standing."[40]

According to him, the variety of moral practices and rules is no greater than the variety of beliefs and procedures for arriving at some conclusion in empirical and/or logical discourse. If the diversity of beliefs in such discourses has never been expected to lead to logical relativism, argues Singer, then the diversity of moral beliefs and norms does not establish that ethics is relative:

> The fact that a group of people believe something does not make it true, the fact that a group of people practice something does not make it right.[41]

Rules and practices may be diverse and relative for several

reasons. But those reasons do not determine the validity of moral principles. Ethical relativists have somehow confused socio-psychological explanation of a belief or practice with its rational justification. They argue that the cause of a subject A believing something to be right or wrong is the fact that the society around her believes so, or approves of the act. Therefore the belief is relative to the society. From this they somehow conclude that the truth of A's belief is relative to the society's believing it or approving of it. Here the psychological causes of believing are equated without much ado with the reasons or grounds of its justification, or truth. The source of a belief can be an important factor in its sociological and psychological explanation, but it cannot be the reason or ground of its justifications, or truth. To quote Taylor again,

> No contradiction is involved in asserting that all moral beliefs come from the social environment, and denying normative ethical relativism. For the fact that a belief is learned from one's society does not mean it is neither true nor false, or that, if it is true, its truth is "relative" to the society in which it was learned. All of our beliefs, empirical ones no less than moral ones, are learned from our society...... So the fact that our moral beliefs come from our society and are learned in our homes and schools has no bearing on whether they have any universal validity. The origin or causes of a belief is one kind of inquiry, the reasons that justify it or the methods of verifying it is another.[42]

Relativists further contend that there is more than one valid or justifiable answer to any ethical question. Richard Brandt comments on this :

> It does not follow directly from the fact that the Romans approved of infanticide and we do not, that infanticide was really right for them and really wrong for us or that it is neither right nor wrong for everybody.
>
> The second point is that it is one thing to have a scientific theory, in the sense of a *causal understanding* of an individual's

> or group's belief that some conduct is right or wrong; it is quite another thing to have a normative ethical theory which shows that some conduct is really right or wrong.[43]

Brandt rightly contends that knowing why someone believes and behaves in a certain manner is not even relevant to any judgment regarding the rightness or wrongness of any belief or practice, even as knowing why someone or some group rejects the theory of evolution is irrelevant for deciding the satisfactoriness or otherwise of the theory.[44]

The advocates of ethical relativism confuse two types of moral judgments: First, in which we apportion praise or blame to the agent, and while doing so take into consideration various sociological and psychological factors. And second, in which we evaluate the act itself, and while doing so take into consideration both the demands of the situation (sociological factor), and some universal moral principle as a criterion of right and wrong. Thus, while we may not condemn the South Pacific Islander for committing patricide (because we think that he can only act in the light of the beliefs of his society), we can definitely pronounce that act as wrong.m

III.5 The thesis of ethical relativism has two parts : First emphasizes the integral nature of culture and the relativity of moral norms to that culture, as also an internalist theory of moral judgment. And the second rejects the possibility of any intercultural criteria of moral evaluations and judgments. It asserts that inasmuch as the moral norms, standards, or criteria of right and wrong are relative, or internal, to a culture or way of life of a society, there can be no intercultural or universal criteria which can be appealed to while judging an alien culture, or trying to comparatively evaluate any two moral codes.

The emphasis in cultural relativsm on the integral nature of a culture leads to internalism in moral judgment which, in turn, provides the strongest basis for ethical relativism. The thesis of internalism in judgment, as advocated by sociologists and relativists, goes beyond cultural relativism, in that it not only asserts relativity of moral norms and values to their respective cultures, but also their unconditional validity for them. And that is what ethical relativism is all about. If all acts or practices can be judged only with reference to the moral code of the society to which the agent belongs, it means no moral standard or criterion can ever be appealed to in our moral judgments, other than the one that is internal to that culture. The rejection of cross-cultural criteria presupposes the internalist view of moral judgment. It is only when we assume that no one can ever be judged except on the basis of the standards of her own culture, that we are led to reject any cross-cultural criteria. I have argued earlier for internal pluralism of various cultures which means that each culture, not being a monolithic whole, contains a large number of criteria of judgment; and the latter may be mutually divergent. These different criteria may belong to different sub-cultures constituting that society, or different dimensions of that culture. The culture and its criteria also undergo constant change. As a result, it is difficult to pinpoint which criterion, or moral code, or way of life at which point of its history should be taken as representative of the culture as a whole, with reference to which all actions and practices of that society are to be judged.

Ethical relativists might say here that each sub-culture of a society should be taken as an independent unit within which all actions and practices should be judged internally. But it would be a very unrealistic position to take. Each community, or each sub-culture, within a society is in constant active interaction with other communities and sub-cultures. In fact, the division of a pluralist society, like India's, into various sub-cultures is more of a theoretical exercise; in actual life, all ways of life and sub-cultures overlap, and their boundaries are so fuzzy that it is very difficult to identify them in day-to-day life.

No culture is a monolithic whole. And the argument, that whatever is in harmony with other beliefs and practices and total way of life of that culture is right for that society has problems. Total harmony is not to be found in real life. A given act, value, or practice may be in harmony with certain aspects of that culture, but it may well be out of tune with others. A closed culture, with a definite unique way of life and determinate standards of judgment, is an anthropological myth.

On one hand, we have internal differences within each culture; on the other, the boundaries of most cultures are fuzzy. All cultures, except a few preliterate ones, are constantly interacting, and borrowing from each other. Some cultures are much more divergent than others, as the traditional Chinese and modern Western one, while some others are very similar, e.g. the cultures of neighbouring European countries, or Arab countries. The constant references to radical differences between the conceptual frameworks of the Chinese and European cultures, with a deliberate neglect of the similarities between neighbouring cultures, gives a lopsided view of the whole affair.

Various cultures are in constant interaction with each other. Sometimes, the influence of other cultures brings out revolutionary changes in any given culture, For example, Indians' introduction with modern Western liberal ideas triggered off a late renaissance in India. Not only the learned Rammohan Roy, but even partially educated Jyotiba Phule and so many other social reformers took inspiration from Western liberal thought, and undertook serious criticism of Indian customs, norms and even values from a more or less Western rationalist and liberal point of view. If there could not be any just criticism except from an internalist point of view, then the above criticisms would not have been possible and the religio-social transformation that Hindu society witnessed would never have been effected. (Of course, these criticisms were welcomed because they came from Indians, thus suggesting that a foreign criterion can be used in judging only when it has been first somewhat internalized.)

Such criticisms and evaluations, as well as mutual comparisons, are done commonly; and there is no reason why such attempts should be discredited, provided they are honest and impartial. Take for example, Toulmin's contention that we cannot ask whether polygamy is better than monogamy, because they are two different institutions which can be judged only from their respective internal points of view. I think that not only they are not two different institutions but only two forms of the institution of marriage, they can also be comparatively evaluated from several perspectives, e.g.

humanitarian, feminist etc. These humanitarian and feminist points of view do not belong to this or that culture but to humanity in general.

To exempt any institution or practice from criticism, whether it is female infanticide among the Rajputs of India, or it is instant divorce among the Muslims, or it is the neglect of old persons by their progeny in Western cultures, from a humanitarian point of view would be to deny our own humanity. It does not mean that I am taking humanism as the sole criterion for intercultural comparisons and evaluations. There can be many others, such as rationality of a practice, its universalizability, its contribution to human welfare, or to the fulfillment of the human person, and above all, justice.

Without undermining the uniqueness of different cultures, I have argued above that any given culture is not a closed affair and has both internal differences and constant communication with other cultures. If my argument is even possible, there is no reason why we cannot accept the possibility of intercultural criteria of moral judgment. Obviously, it must not come from the appraiser's culture alone. In a way, anthropologists and other cultural-ethical relativists have done a great service to humanity by rejecting cross-cultural criticism which provided a misguided rationale for the white man's burden, resulting into the oppression and subjugation of so many weaker Asian and African cultures. That means the cross-cultural criteria required for a just evaluation of other cultures has to be carefully developed through a process of reasoning and mutual dialogue. We would come to this point in our last chapter.

Let me repeat here that a given morality (I am not talking here of the mores and folkways of preliterate cultures) definitely has its roots in some culture; but it equally definitely has some elements which it shares with the moralities of other cultures, and for which it can claim universality. Every culture is both multi-faceted and in constant communication with others. People may be ethnocentric, but they often learn from each other. They share as a matter of course their knowledge - both theoretical and technical - with others, as also ideas, values and common concerns (e.g. world peace, preservation of global environment etc.). Mutual disagreements may come to the fore during these constant contacts, but such disagreements are largely based on conflict of interests. Alongside these disagreements, agreements and sharing of ideas, values and criteria also emerge during mutual communications. Above discussion at least shows that there is no basis for any assertion regarding the impossibility of any cross-cultural criteria.

IV. Some Further Arguments Concerning Ethical Relativism

IV.1 Some other anthropologists, such as Karl Dunker, have advanced the thesis that various cultures share basic human values, but the historical situations in different cultures are so very different that these common values acquire different 'situational meanings'. Moral quality of an act depends on the situational meaning of an act for the people concerned.

"I think" says Dunker, ".....that the mere fact of "killing" is too abstract a topic to allow for any serious ethical consideration."[45] It is so because "ethical valuation is not concerned with acts as abstract events in space-time. The ethical essence of an act depends upon its concrete pattern of situational meanings." (original italics)[46] He goes on to argue how killing of an aged parent can have so many meanings, like sparing him a lingering death, or even a dull existence. However, such rationalizations may be a part of modern anthropologists' conceptual framework, but they just cannot represent the tribesmen's 'situational meanings'. He further explains the killing of aged people as something which might be done for the interests of the survival of the group:

> He is of no further use, and life may be hard and food scarce to the point of starvation. Surely then it is more reasonable to cast off that part of the ballast than to kill young and healthy members.[47]

Though these anthropologists talk of situational meanings, they seem to be mostly talking of the demands and constraints of the situation. Thus, Soloman E. Asch contends that the act of killing will not have the same meaning under all conditions. He picks up the favourite example of anthropologists - the killing or letting die of aged parents by Eskimos, and argues :

> When an Eskimo family permits an old person to expose himself to death this must be viewed in relation to their situation, their problems, and the alternatives open to them. The act does not have the same meaning for them that it would have for us today; Eskimos do not have homes for the aged or retirement pensions. If we take the given circumstances into account the possibility is present for understanding diverse actions in terms of the same operations of valuing.[48]

Actually Asch, no relativist himself, has weakened the case against relativism in a confused attempt to explain it. Here he seems to be justifying the killing of aged parents in situations where there are no old age homes or retirement pensions. I do not appreciate the role of situational meanings in the above contention. What Dunker and Asch are arguing is that the circumstances of Eskimos are so hard that they choose to kill their aged parents in order to save food etc. for other healthier members of the group. It is at worst the rule of the jungle, and at best a very unpleasant apology for the practice of Eskimos. Simplest and truest explanation would have been that given the extremely harsh living conditions, Eskimos are forced to kill their parents, and we may not blame them because their very survival depends upon their callously following the law of the jungle which can never be an acceptable practice from an ethical point of view.

Instead, these anthropologists undertake long winding apologies for the Eskimos. All this appeal to situational meanings is irrelevant from the ethical point of view. When Asch talks of the absence of old age homes and pensions for the aged as justifying factors for the Eskimos' practice, he brings Eskimos at par with most societies which do not have old age homes. But that does not give them the right either to kill off their aged, or to claim that the killing of the aged has a different situational meaning for all of them.

Dunker even suggests that the old people might be killed as a sacrifice to gods. I wish that Dunker could have first enquired whether this is the case. Of course, even if it were the case, it would not make killing of the aged less heinous. Similarly, Asch suggests that infanticide may be due to the belief that infants are not fully human yet. Again, it would be better to enquire from the people who practise infanticide whether they think so.

Romans who exposed their infants to the elements did so because they valued strength and power more than human life. Indian Rajputs who kill their infant daughters even now do so because they value their (false) pride more which is supposed to suffer in being the father of a daughter. Infanticide is perpetrated not because it has a different situational meaning but because the perpetrators have a hierarchy of values in which pride and strength come much higher than life itself. We cannot possibly have any excuse for such a lopsided hierarchy of values.

Above all, what exactly is meant by situational meanings? How can we ever distinguish between the meaning of a norm or value and the norm or value itself? Our values are what we conceive them to be, or what we understand by them (i.e. their meaning for us). The example of far-off preliterate cultures are given by anthropologists to prove the differences in situational meanings. But do they understand those cultures sufficiently in order to make any positive assertion about them? At best such attempts are good arguments for the policy of tolerance, since it may be rightly claimed that the ontological and other beliefs and customs of these people determine the particular practice being discussed, and perhaps they could not help themselves. But any talk of situational meaning cannot prove that they have the same values as modern Europeans.

Am I arguing against my own thesis by insisting that differences in cultures are those of values and not merely those of situational meanings? I do not think so. It has been my consistent position that acknowledgment of cultural differences does not mean arguing for ethical relativism.

IV.2 A more substantial argument for cultural-ethical relativism is the one which is based on differences in the institutional patterns, and their determining role in their respective moral codes. We have discussed previously (Chapter 1, Section III,) the views of such philosophers, as Stephen Toulmin, Richard B. Brandt, R.B.Perry, Kurt Baier and P.F. Strawson who have emphasized the determinative role of the institutional structure of a society on its morality. None of these philosophers is a relativist; they are simply emphasizing the social function of morality.

Every society has some structure or institutional pattern in which its various institutions, like marriage, ownership of land, means of production, the structure of the state, etc. are organized. Its moral code is developed according to the demands of the institutions and their norms. At the same time, the institutions themselves are influenced by the values of that society. Thus, the moral code and the institutional pattern are fully interdependent.

According to Perry, "Morality is man's endeavor to harmonize conflicting interests."[49] It is a sociological fact that the conflicts of interests which morality seeks to resolve mostly depend upon the institutional structure. The nature and extent of the conflicts of interest in a feudal society would be different from those in a capitalist-liberal society, or a communist one. Naturally, the ways and means of resolving those conflicts through moral norms and rules and regulations would be equally different. While ready obedience to one's superiors would be a virtue in feudal and communist societies, it would be a misfit in a capitalist social structure. And while aggressive self-assertion and exuberant self-confidence would be appreciated in a capitalist society, they may be sanctioned in a community-based morality.

Strawson affirms the universal applicability of the rules and principles of morality; but hastens to add that this universality refers to a community or class only. He conceives morality as a system of "socially sanctioned demands." Morality is not something abstract and general but is a system of specific moral demands which pertains to specific positions and situations which are, in turn, conditioned by (relative to) the institutional structure.[50]

Baier, a staunch universalist, acknowledges that there are many separate moralities which are evolved in the process of the development of society's institutions and rules. These institutions create specific injunctions and prohibitions in order to preserve socio-moral equilibrium.[51]

What these authors are saying is simply that morality being a practical discipline cannot be discussed in an abstract theoretical context. Instead, it is conceived, evolved and practised in the context of day-to-day living, and that context is the lived context of a specific society with specific institutions, and their norms. Thus, Brandt contends that even the supposedly universal moral principles, such as the Ten Commandments, are relative to, or presuppose, a specific institutional structure; and therefore, cannot apply cross-culturally.[52]

The above thesis has merit. However, if we accept it, then we would also have to accept that morality as a practical discipline cannot be abstract, universal or absolute. If morality is developed in response to concrete situations in a concrete institutional context, Kant's categorical imperative cannot be taken as the paradigm of morality.

Now, this is not a final blow to our position, as it is only half the truth. It is true that morality is developed in response to concrete situations; but if it were only that, it would be reduced to practice rules, or rules of thumb, a matter of mere expediency (e.g. whatever leads to social stability, given the actual institutional structure, is morally right). But this is not what we mean by morality. Morality is much more than this, and transcends considerations of expediency. It may well aim at harmonizing conflicting interests, or at helping men to meet socially sanctioned demands, or may be developed in the context of concrete historical institutions. But a morality or moral code would not be one if it tried to achieve these goals with a view to expediency alone, without reference to some basic moral principles.

These moral principles are presupposed by every moral code, even though their understanding and interpretation may differ somewhat. That is to say, all developed moral codes necessarily consist of two elements - universal moral principles and specific moral norms and rules. It is the latter which are conditioned by, or are relative to, a society's institutional structure. I am not arguing here for a universal moral core in all moral codes, though I myself am sympathetic to any such contention. This is too important and complex a subject to be dealt with in the short space left in this Chapter.

Most of the protagonists of institutionalism in ethics, such as Toulmin and Rawls, have affirmed the distinction between the justification of an act and that of the institution under which it falls. While an act can simply be justified by pointing out that it is according to the rules that constitute the given practice or institution, the institution itself cannot either be questioned, or if questioned, it would require a very different kind of reasoning to justify it.[53]

I feel that the real issue is that of the possibility of a critical evaluation of the present institutions with a view to modifying, or even rejecting them. Even if individual acts, as also particular moral rules or norms, are to be judged with reference to the institutions and moral code as a whole, it does not mean that those institutions and specific moral codes themselves cannot be rationally questioned and examined from a humanitarian or moral point of view. The question, whether a given particular institution, such as slavery, caste hierarchy, low status of women, in any society is itself a moral or just one, is a legitimate question. This would be a natural extension of Moore's 'open question' argument. Not only a particular institution, but the entire institutional pattern of a society and its moral code can, thus, be questioned. (See Section 2. and III.5 supra.)

IV.3 Rationality, as I shall argue in a later Chapter, is an important condition for, or characteristic of, all worthwhile moral judgments. Hare calls moral judgments a rational activity which consists in the search for universal, rational moral principles and the testing of the actual norms and practices against these principles.[54] And Baier argues that the best course of action from the moral point of view is one which is "supported by best reasons". Rationality or a critical approach to the conventional rules of conduct is regarded by Baier as the chief criterion of morality.[55]

Baier questions the practice of anthropologists and sociologists of listing various divergent beliefs and practices of different groups of people. Such enumerations can at best establish that these types of conduct are believed to be right or wrong in particular societies. They cannot even prove that those practices are right or wrong even in those particular societies. They can far less prove that they are right from the point of view of morality as such. He contends that the injunctions and prohibitions of every moral code could always be put to moral scrutiny; and the question asked whether what the moral code prohibits or enjoins is really morally wrong or right. In other words, morality proper, as against customs or mores, is a rational discipline. Moral precepts are those which can be subjected to rational scrutiny. The latter helps us to distinguish between "those moral rules which are *genuinely moral* and those which merely happen to be *part of the morality of the group*." (original italics.)[56]

Now, if the so-called moral code of a people contains norms and rules of conduct which have nothing to do with morality proper, then they should not be treated as being true or valid for the people among whom they are in vogue, etc. They can have no moral authority and are open to rational criticism just as any other belief or custom. It is not to say that moral rules and norms proper that are left after sifting of customary rules and semi-ritualistic patterns of social behaviour are not open to critical scrutiny. Moral norms, rules, and even socio-moral institutions of a given society should be equally open to critical appraisal. That is, not only the non-moral customs etc. but also the moral institutions, norms and standards cannot be immune from critical scrutiny. To quote Baier,

> embodiment in the morality of the group is no final guarantee of the morality or immorality of the type of conduct in question. The morality or immorality of the group may be wrong. The moral convictions of the group may be mistaken.
>
> .... it is the very meaning of 'a morality' that it should contain a body of moral convictions which can be true or false, that is, a body of rules or precepts for which there are certain tests,[57]

There is no denying the fact of distinct and possibly quite contradictory moralities. It is also possibly true that it is these separate 'moralities' which serve the function of guiding and regulating interpersonal behaviour in differently structured societies. As Baier rightly points out, the answer to the day-to-day questions regarding one's obligations in concrete life situations cannot be given in generalities but requires critical examination of specific moralities; and this can be done only by "means of standards and against principles which are not tied to any group." Not only this, such a critical testing "involves the asking and answering of questions which would be the same in any culture context whatsoever."[58]

IV.4 Lastly, the cultural-ethical relativists have failed to provide the most crucial criterion for their relativism, that is, the criterion to determine the social unit to whose way of life morality is relative. Though sociologists and anthropologists have always tried to tackle these issues, ethical relativists have not bothered to answer the question regarding the nature and extension of that segment of population which is supposed to have a separate, unique culture of its own, and an equally indigenous moral code.

Since anthropologists have been concentrating on far-off, secluded, preliterate cultures, it is easier for them to identify the group which is supposed to have an autonomous culture. But in the rest of the world where even the boundaries of nation-states are fuzzy, and keep changing; where every society contains within it several ethnic and other groups which claim to be different from the mainstream, due to either religion, or language, or some other basis; and where people keep moving from one place to another, how do we define the society or community with a determinable culture, or way of life ? In view of the pluralist construction of many nation-states, they cannot be the archetypal society with an autonomous way of life. At the same time, the sub-groups within the nation-states also cannot be declared to be such a society, since in spite of all the contemporary emphasis on pluralism, ethnicity and incommensurability, these sub-groups are not so clearly defined and definitely do not have an independent way of life which can be distinctly identified. The various sub-groups in India and other pluralistic societies constantly overlap, and the individuals belonging to them have multiple identities. We would return to this problem of defining the 'community' to which individual moral agents supposedly belong exclusively, in our 7th Chapter.

Equally important, radical relativists are not interested in large cultures, or communities. They are more interested in smaller groups, because only by allowing the smallest possible group the right to have a separate moral code could relativists put their radical thesis in a glaring focus. However, as W.T. Stace has put, the relativist herself has difficulty in saying who are the 'people' who have an autonomous way of life and their own moral standards:

> when once the whole of humanity is abandoned as the area covered by a single moral standard, what smaller areas are to be adopted as the *loci* of different standards ? Where are we to draw the lines of demarcation ? .... Does the *locus* of a particular moral standard reside in race, a nation, a tribe, a family, or an individual ? ..... Each such group, we shall be told, has its own moral code which is, for it, right. But what *is* a "group"? Can anyone define it or give its boundaries ?[59]

Stace gives the same argument which I have tried to present in this Chapter, that is, to divide humankind into smaller and smaller groups distorts the facts of life, where the boundaries between different groups are fuzzy, so that to identify a given group as the locus of a way of life, culture and moral code is either impossible, or arbitrary. It is not to deny the differences between various cultures and ethnic groups, but only to point out that these differences cannot negate innumerable points of mutual communication and overlapping. Above all, these differences of culture or moral code cannot be, at least in most cases, cited as an excuse for exemption from humanity's moral judgment. (I am aware that 'humanity's moral judgment' is still a questionable contention, and would try to argue my point in the 7th Chapter again.)

IV.5 Ethical relativism, like any other ideology, is a product of its times. It was born as a revolt against the Enlightenment legacy. The latter, as represented by Kant and Hegel, was rationalist, universalist, absolutist, and on some interpretation intolerant. In other words, both postmodernism and ethical relativism seek to reject the universalist claims of reason and celebrate the empirical, the conventional, the plural and heterogeneous.

But the Kantian thesis of universal reason was not totally false; at most its emphasis was one-sided. Could it not be that the similar (over)emphasis on pluralism, ethnic conflicts, diversity and incommensurability of cultures is equally one-sided ? Perhaps absolutism in metaphysics and ethics is false and misleading, as everything that is, is contingent, historically conditioned, and so on. Also, in the phenomenal world - and we know of no other - there is nothing that is necessary and absolute. Perhaps all that cultural relativism says is true, that is, that there is an immense diversity of beliefs, norms and everything else; that all these diverse beliefs etc. originate in, and are integral to, a culture. But does it prove that there is nothing but plurality, diversity and heterogeneity ? Are our cultures and moral codes really so incommensurable that human beings are left with nothing to share ? Is every culture or society (remember we yet do not know the extension of these concepts) a windowless monad of Leibnitz, from within which we cannot even peep through to have a glimpse of other cultures ? If yes, then nothing more is left to say, and we are left imprisoned in a radical skepticism.

If the answer is no, then perhaps both sides of the debate - the universalist and the relativist and pluralist - are right but to a limited extent. Also, both sides can be complementary so that they can together understand and develop a more balanced and comprehensive view of the matter.

Pluralism and incommensurability are two concepts which have dominated the entire contemporary socio-cultural or socio-moral discourse, and we would return to them in our next Chapter again.

IV.6 It is often claimed that the greatest virtue of ethical relativism is its providing a basis for a policy of tolerance. As we know, early anthropologists, such as Benedict and Herskovits, pleaded passionately not only for tolerance, but also for equal validity, of different cultures, ways or 'patterns' of life. They also further believed that the cultural-ethical relativism, being expounded by them, provided the best basis or reason for the ideal of universal tolerance.

But does relativism actually provide a basis for tolerance ? Brandt rightly argues that if relativism were accepted, the value of intolerance would be as much justified as the value of tolerance. At most the relativist may say that she prefers tolerance to intolerance, but can't praise tolerance as a value superior to intolerance. A relativist may advocate tolerance as a matter of personal preference, or as a relative normative judgment, but she can never assert that relativism as a metaethical theory entails tolerance.[60]

Geoffery Harrison, himself a relativist, points out that the value of tolerance is a normative value and can be justified internally on the basis of some particular moral system. But relativism is a morally neutral metaethical theory and cannot provide a basis for tolerance. Harrison argues that in order to derive the value of tolerance from the relativist thesis we need a normative premise to the effect that no one has a right to interfere with another's moral code.[61]

However, I would accept here that relativism does encourage tolerance, even if it cannot prove the worth of tolerance. A universalist approach tends to project some particular moral code as the universal and true one, and breed self-righteousness and intolerance for others' values and ways. But relativism's talk of the equal validity of all norms and values tends to encourage an attitude of tolerance and even benevolence for others. If your ways are right or valid for you, and mine are right for me, there is no reason why I should interfere in your ways.

The problem here is regarding the limits of tolerance. If norms are a matter of social convention, and values that of personal preference, and if each of them is valid, true, or justified *for* the person or group which holds them, then we may not interfere with or try to change the norms and values of others, even as we do not bother to influence and change the personal tastes of others, or amoral conventions of other societies. But what happens when those personal values and social conventions seem to us to be really immoral, or they result in avoidable suffering to others? What happens when a society with feudal underpinnings tends to oppress its weaker sections and the womenfolk ? What happens when a given society insists on its right to prompt its widows to burn themselves (as in medieval India)? What happens when a community practices female infanticide from a false sense of honour (as among Indian Rajputs)? What happens when another (Muslim) society thinks that divorcing a hapless woman with a horde of children at the spurt of moment is a male's prerogative, and that male has no responsibility either towards his ex-wife or towards his own children ?

Above all, what happens if a Hitler indulges in a genocide, or a group of people from an association Murder Incorporated Ltd. start murdering others? Gilbert Harman seems to think that if the perpetrators of these crimes have different norms and concerns which give them sufficient reason to indulge in their genocide and other such crimes, then there is nothing we can do about it, except wishing that things were otherwise.[62] At this point ethical relativism seems to stand on its head. Any group, or even any individual may declare itself or herself as an autonomous unit with its/her own moral code, and do whatever it/she wants. And the people around them could do nothing in the name of relativism. This is sheer nihilism, and denial of all morality and humanity. We cannot accept any such position in the name of relativism.[63]

IV.7 Lastly, relativism has never come out with a satisfactory answer to the single question - how does it propose to justify itself? The whole conception of ethical relativism is paradoxical. Any theory, in order to be accepted, needs to have some justification of itself. But when we ask whether the theory of relativity itself is relative or absolute as regards its truth value, relativism fails to give a satisfactory answer. If the theory is absolute, that is, true in all circumstances and applicable to all cultures, this would amount to rejection of relativism. But if relativism boldly accepts that it is itself a relative theory, that is, it is a product of its times and is relative to certain aspects of modern Western culture, then we are led to the conclusion that relativism is highly negligible. Let me quote Ernst Grünwald, one of the early protagonists of the sociology of knowledge:

> it (relationism) claims absolute validity for this same proposition, that all thought is only relatively valid..... In each proposition it advances, relationism is thus obliged to

> contradict its own thesis. One could say: if sociologism is true, then sociologism is wrong; if its thesis is correct, that all thought wrongly claims absolute validity, then sociologism cannot correctly raise its claim to truth either.[64]

Hans Speier accepts social determination of ideas but clearly distinguishes it from the rational justifiability or otherwise of those ideas. Speier acknowledges the dependence of the development of particular ideologies and fields of knowledge on the specific needs of a given society, but these needs etc. are irrelevant as far as the validity or justifiability of some knowledge is concerned.[65]

It is not to deny or even undermine the role of various sociological factors in the development of human knowledge and ideas; but the role of these factors mostly relates to the selection of problems or issues to be faced, and different emphases on the goals to be persued. Even so, first, the answers given to these issues by particular societies need not be above critical scrutiny and cross-cultural comparisons. Of course, while appraising any given answer we would have to consider whether it fulfills the particular needs and expectations of that society; but we can and must always ask whether the answers, ideologies and other cognitive or normative assertions of a particular society are rationally justified. Secondly, not all the problems and issues tackled by human mind in different societies are socially determined, that is, they are pursued independently of sociological conditions. As Speier says, "Philosphers have access to the thinking of all times."[66] The same would be true for moral philosophers.

Sometimes it is affirmed that relativism is a metaethical theory which is applicable to all ethical theories but which itself needs no justification. I do not agree that metaethical theories are beyond rational questioning and justification. It seems that ethical relativism has an irresistible tendency to merge into an irrational subjectivism, or skepticism. In the end, ethical relativism seems to be saying only that whatever is *is* right. John Ladd brings out the inherent irrationality and one-sidedness of cultural-ethical relativism, though in a slightely exaggerated manner:

> It we try to formulate the doctrine of ethical relativism in more abstract terms, we find two possible versions, a negative one and an affirmative one. The negative version is that there are no universally valid moral principles (or moral codes); the positive version is that every moral principle (or moral code) is equally valid.
>
> The net effect of ethical relativism when it is construed negatively is that nothing is right or wrong in itself rightness and wrongness are due only to what people think; ethics is only "opinion".... If pursued consistently, this position finally becomes ethical skepticism or nihilism; nothing is right or wrong; everything is permitted. In other words, negative relativism leads to absolute ethical neutralism, the denial of the distinction between right and wrong.....
>
> The affirmative version operates in exactly the opposite way but with the same ultimate effect. For in affirming the equal validity of every moral principle (or moral code) that is accepted by any society, it entails that the same action can be both right and wrong and neutral as well. If *any* principle is acceptable, everything is permitted.[67]

Ladd goes on to argue that anthropologists who talk of every action being right or wrong in the context of its own culture, and all ways of life being equally valid, do not mean the above extreme and rather absurd thesis. They are instead arguing for the limited validity of ethical norms; that is, these norms are binding only on those within a particular group. Such thinkers are identifying morality with customs ; and in the final analysis such identification cannot be maintained because customs relate to issues which are not so vital or basic as those which concern morality.[68]

But Ladd's contention, that ethical relativism deals only with limited validity and therefore its relativism is not as radical as it appears at first, seems unwarranted. Limited validity means : First, no ethical norm, standard or principle is valid or rationally justified in the sense that it can claim universal applicability. And second, everything that is practised and believed in a particular society is valid or right for that society. The thesis of limited validity, proposed by Ladd and other ethicists, therefore, does not seem to be very different from ethical relativism we have been discussing so far.

I agree with Stace when he says that "If taken seriously and pressed to its logical conclusion, ethical relativity can only end in destroying the conception of morality altogether."[69] However, we need not resort to rhetorical language in order to bring home the fact that ethical relativism is not able to do justice either to the concept (meaning) of morality, or to our moral experience. The very meaning of morality implies not only a distinction between right and wrong acts but also between 'right' and 'wrong' guiding principles of human conduct, and a hierarchy of vlues or goals. If whatever is *is* right, every custom or rule becomes correct, right, or valid as any other; and there would be no incentive left for acting in accordance with the 'right' or 'true' moral principle. If whatever is *is* right, there can be no morality, at least in the Kantian sense of the term.

CHAPTER 4

Relativism: Positivist and Postmodern: A Critique

I. Recapitulation

I.1 In Chapters 1 and 2, I have attempted a descriptive presentation of two major types of ethical relativism : first, the early and more common one that seeks to automatically derive ethical relativism from the anthropological- sociological facts regarding the diversity in cultures, moral codes and institutional structures of different societies; and second, the more recent version thereof which starts with some form of relativistic metaethics or cognitive relativism, from which ethical relativism seems to follow.

I have then attempted a comprehensive critique of the first type of relativism in the 3rd Chapter. There I have argued against the relativist thesis which affirms that each culture has an identifiable, determinate way of life which provides not only all norms of conduct but also the criteria of all judgment. I have contended that a homogeneous closed culture or way of life is a myth, and every culture is multi-faceted, and consists of diverse traditions and sub-cultures which are not separate but constantly overlap. Moreover, a culture or a society is constantly changing due to various internal and external factors. As a result, it becomes impossible to identify one world-view or way of life which can represent the whole of that culture in all its dimensions and historical stages. Nor is it possible to identify separate autonomous sub-cultures as locuses of separate independent lifeworlds or forms of life within a larger society.

I have also argued that individuals may well derive most of their norms from their society, but they are also influenced by the values and ways of other cultures. And at the level of critical morality people do question the norms and values of their culture and seek to transcend its limits.

I have further contended that the relativist thesis that reduces truth and right to whatever is believed and practised in a society seems to be precariously based on a confusion between anthropological-sociological facts on the one hand and normative conclusions on the other. I have supported the Moore - Hare thesis that mere factual assertions alone cannot provide sufficient ground for normative conclusions. Even if we were to reject the traditional gap between 'is' and 'ought', the positions of Moore and Hare still seem to be sensible. Regarding any moral belief and practice we can still apply Moore's 'open question' argument, and ask whether the given belief is really true, and the given practice really right, or just. Or, we can ask with Hare for moral bridge premisses, saying that reduction of the normative to the merely descriptive is not convincing at all. Or, we can say with W.T. Stace and Paul W. Taylor that the question is not of who and how many believe in a certain premise, but whether the norm or principle is right or just.

The same arguments would apply (as we have seen in our 3rd Chapter, Section II) to approbation theories. First, whatever is approved or disapproved in a society need not be identified with what is morally good, bad, right, or wrong, though they may well be reliable indicators of 'true' moral norms or standards. Secondly, approval or disapproval are emotional or attitudinal responses, and as such cannot be the cause or basis of our moral judgments. Rather, we approve or disapprove of whatever we 'cognize' as good or bad, right, or wrong, that is, the cognitive response is mostly prior to, or at least simultaneous with, our moral pronouncements.

I agree with the relativist thesis that an effective moral code is one which is developed in response to the demands of the existing institutions, but reject the view that the institutions of the society, being integrally related with the way of life of the people, are beyond any critical, moral appraisal. We can always critically examine separate moral codes and institutions of the society, and decide whether or not they are just or justifiable from a moral -humanitarian point of view. The moral point of view itself is rationally justifiable and in some way presupposed in all ethical discourse.

Regarding the relativist thesis rejecting any cross-cultural criterion of judgment, and advocating internalism in judgment, I have contended that the entire thesis relies too much on the myth of a culture's being an organic, homogeneous whole. Cultures and individuals do interact with other cultures and persons at various levels, thus making cross-cultural criteria possible, at least tentatively. That means that a mere appeal to some empirical-sociological facts, such as cultural diversity, or some sociological explanatory theses regarding every culture being an integrated whole, and the culture or way of life of every society being the main or basic source of beliefs, norms and values of its people, may justify some kind of sociological-psychological relativism, but these arguments alone cannot justify ethical relativism.

I.2 There is the second kind of relativism which I have labelled metaethical relativism, by which I mean any theory which seeks to understand and explain ethical judgments in such a way that makes ethical relativism true by definition. It starts with the *necessary* relativity of all ethical discourse to the culture, way of life, conceptual scheme, and so on. This kind of relativism is more difficult to challenge as it takes the issue of relativism further back, and seems to make relativism a premise rather than a conclusion of any ethical, i.e. normative, argument.

In this category we can include approbation theories, logical positivism, and cognitive relativism of contemporary writers or postmodernists. We can also divide relativist metaethical theories into cognitivist-naturalist relativism, under which head will come all approbation theories, as well as the entire postmodernist relativism, and noncognitive relativism of the positivists.

Approval theories are an important example of metaethical relativism which makes ethical relativism true by definition. But their cultural-intellectual milieu is nearer to the common form of 'modern' cultural - ethical relativism. While approval theories say that whatever is approved in a society *is* right for its members, cultural-ethical relativists say that whatever is believed and practised in a society *is* right for it. Though the intellectual thrust and conceptual framework of approval theories as well as modern ethical relativist theories are quite different from those of postmodern relativism, they at the same time form a continuum. Both kinds of theories share some conception of each culture being a separate organic whole with its own moral code, conceptual framework and institutional structure. Both theories seem to reject any cross-cultural criteria of moral judgments: earlier ones do so implicitly and to a moderate extent, while later ones do so explicitly and in an extreme sense.

Above all, both types of theories are more or less cognitivist-naturalist, and argue for a milder or stronger form of cognitive relativism. As against this approach, the noncognitivism of logical positivists (including C.L. Stevenson) follows a very different approach to, and understanding of, moral discourse. If so, a discussion of postmodern relativism should follow that of approbation theories. But we have to consider the noncognitivism of logical postivists first before we attempt a critique of postmodernist cognitive relativism for two reasons - first, because positivism is prior to postmodernism historically; and second, because the latter logically presupposes the former. Postmodernism was developed as a reaction to the scientism of positivism.

II. Non-cognitivist Theories:

Positivists start with their verification theory of meaning, and go on to contend that moral assertions do not tell us anything about either objective facts, or even about our feelings, and are merely expressions of our feelings. Hence they are incapable of being true or false; they are simply meaningless. While A.J. Ayer and M. Schlick boldly declare all moral assertions as meaningless, Charles Stevenson has tried to find a role for reason in moral discourse. But in the end for Stevenson, as for others, moral agreement or disagreement mainly consists in trying to influence or even change others' attitudes. Moral disputes can be resolved not by an appeal to moral facts, or to moral principles, but by an appeal to others' feelings/emotions/attitudes. Above all, their thesis of factual verification as the only criterion of meaningfulness and truth makes all discourse, other than the empirical one (or perhaps not even that), meaningless per definition.

Verification thesis has been criticized on many counts. We shall here refer here only to those points which are relevant to our problem. First, it has been argued that verification principle is very vague. Positivists' heavy reliance on verification principle which, in turn, is exclusively understood in terms of sensory experience, leads to many related questions. How can a statement reporting a sense experience be ever verified ? No verification of a given statement can ever be final. We can go on giving other statements reporting perhaps wider and more reliable observations. But further observations may falsify our most trusted assertions, or prove an earlier assertion as true which was so far regarded as false. Even Carnap abandoned the use of the term 'verification' later on.

Secondly, the foundationalism implicit in positivism is open to criticism. It is asserted in response to positivist foundationalism that we can never have direct access to reality. All we can do is to offer other statements based on possibly more reliable observations. But there can never be a final verification of any given statement.

Verification is conceived mainly in terms of protocol sentences which are supposedly reports of atomic sense data. These sense data could not be but subjective experiences, in which case this would lead to skepticism. This skepticism is only matched by the declaration of other disciplines, such as ethics whose assertions cannot be reduced to protocol statements, as nonsense (skepticism), or a matter of mutually divergent emotions or attitudes (relativism).

The very idea of breaking up all propositional knowledge into protocol sentences, and the reductionism involved in this kind of foundationalist epistemology have been severely criticized. Now no one advocates the kind of naturalist foundationalism that was advocated in the positivist philosophy. W.V.O. Quine has criticized the assumption that isolated statements can be confirmed or infirmed. Rather, our beliefs face "the tribunal of experience" collectively, and not one by one. Once the verificationism and empiricist foundationalism are questioned, the positivist condemnation of moral assertions as meaningless falls to the ground; and morality emerges unscathed.

I do not agree with the total rejection of foundationalism. I feel that the problem is not with the general idea of foundationalism, but with the positivists' version thereof; and their narrow and culturally-determined version of verification in terms of sense experience, or what is generally called scientism.

Thirdly, it is commonplace now to assert that the principle of verifiability itself becomes meaningless, if its own criterion of meaning is applied to it. The verification principle is neither an empirical generalization, nor a tautology - the only two kinds of statements that are accepted as true in this theory. Since the verifiability principle can neither be verified, nor falsified, the principle can never claim any truth or authenticity for itself, and becomes meaningless.

Fourthly, we ordinarily enquire into the meaning of words and sentences, and not of statements or propositions (I am using the terms 'statements' and 'propositions' as synonymous in order to avoid any confusion). Propositions are what sentences assert or mean and not something which has meaning. On the other hand, it is propositions which are verified or falsified, and described as true or false. How then, can verifiability be identified with meaning?

Fifthly, and importantly, what does verification actually mean ? There can be many ways of verifying a proposition, in accordance with the discipline or context of that proposition, or its content. Propositions in positive sciences would be verified in a different way than those in human sciences. Even with positive sciences the method and theory of verification would be different according to the subject matter involved (e.g. physics has a very different methodology than biology).

It means that if we want to verify, justify, or test the truth claim of any assertion in morality, we would need an entirely different set of rules of argumentation, criteria of relevance of evidence and so on. Just because empiricist method of verification does not apply here, there is no reason why we should despair of discussing the truth claim of ethical assertions.

Sixthly, the reduction of meaning to empirical verification implies that even many scientific theories should be declared as meaningless since they could not be verified in the specified way. Though the positivists accepted logic and mathematics as true, arguably they could not have done so, as logical and mathematical propositions are either merely analytical and hence vacuous; or synthetic, in which case they cannot be empirically verified. It would be reasonable to think that a theory that declares three-fourths of our knowledge (including science, mathematics and logic) as meaningless is wrong.

Reducing *all* our knowledge to some hypothetical principle of verifiability which centres around sensory experience is unjustified, to say the least. If so, there can be assertions which can be verified/tested/justified on other grounds. Such assertions will have their own method of justification of truth claims, their own rules of meaning and reasoning, and need not be subjected to some narrow verification principle. All assertions in religion, ethics and aesthetics, most in human sciences, as well as some in science and logic, would not be amenable to verification principle; but need not be declared invalid or meaningless on that basis. Every discipline must be understood in its own terms. And this is not to support ethical relativism.

Finally, we can simply point out that positivist philosophy and metaethics go against every single assertion of commonsense and moral discourse. They are:

(i) Commonsense affirms that moral judgments are not simply expressions of emotions. In fact, emotions or feelings may or may not accompany moral judgments.
(ii) Moral judgments claim to be cognitive, that is, they imply knowledge of 'moral facts'. We talk of knowing that an act A *is* right or wrong, a character trait C *is* good or bad.
(iii) Commonsense affirms, and those engaged in moral discourse endorse, that moral statements are true or false. When we declare an act as right or wrong, we never mean that we are merely evincing our feelings. We presume that we have given a normative assessment of 'moral facts' and that assessment is true (or false).
(iv) Commonsense implicitly accepts that either the acts, traits, or practices which are being judged have some 'moral property', additional to, or consequential upon, its natural properties; or at least, all moral discourse implies shared, causally fixed referents of moral terms.

(v) Truth and falsity of moral judgments can be ascertained by ordinary canons of reasoning plus some moral principles which might be agreed upon at a cross-cultural level. (This is too important an assertion and we would take it up again in the final Chapter.)

I am aware that each of the above contentions is challenged by the postmodernist - relativists whose views and theses have been discussed in the 2nd Chapter. It means that I must first confront postmodern relativism and try to answer their various arguments against any universalist approach to either knowledge or praxis, before I attempt to develop my own universalist understanding of the moral point of view. I will now try to critically examine various theses of this later and more substantial kind of relativism.

III. Postmodern Cognitive Relativism:

III.1 Since postmodernism is a child of revolt against all that represents the modern *Weltanschauung*, it is confident of itself, and does not often try to defend its stand. To recapitulate, postmodernists start by challenging the modern emphasis on epistemology and indubitability of at least some aspects of knowledge, i.e. empirical experience and rigorous rational thinking. They equally challenge the idea of objective knowledge, and argue that all perception and knowledge involve a very important element of subjective construction. The claims of reason are similarly questioned. All propositional truths are relative to various sociological factors, and above all, to the conceptual framework of one's community and culture.

Postmodernism represents a radical brand of cognitive relativism. All judgment, knowledge, and even perception are relative to the conceptual framework of the society/culture/life-world/language to which a person happens to belong. When combined with the incommensurability thesis - which asserts that these various frameworks, to which human thought and action are relative, are mutually incommensurable and untranslatable - the postmodernist cognitive relativism becomes a radical and somewhat vulgar relativism.

The opposition of postmodernism to epistemology is mainly directed against its claim to provide some foundations to knowledge in order to help men arrive at certain indubitable knowledge of the world and some basic rational principles. Modern epistemology directly or indirectly presupposes - or used to presuppose - foundationalism and representationalism.

Richard Rorty has been in the forefront of attack on epistemology. He advocates the substitution of hermeneutics for epistemology. Hermeneutics is understood as a holistic approach to knowledge, and is implicitly based on a distrust of the whole epistemological enterprise. Rorty, Quine and Wilfrid Sellars do not aim at presenting a new account of knowledge, but at pointing to the futility of any such account.[1]

Rorty is piqued at the naive positivist view that knowledge represents the world out there, and small protocol sentences report atomic sense data. This kind of naive representationalism should not have been put forward in the first instance, as Kant had long back proved that we cannot have an access to the knowledge-independent world. It follows that we can never be sure that our knowledge represents or corresponds to some world outside our knowledge.[2]

With the representational view of knowledge goes the idea of necessary objective reference in all knowledge. Foundationalism, representationalism and the theory of objective reference are not integrally related, but they mostly go together. Universalism or the concept of universal reason and its necessary principles is another idea which is closely related to foundationalism. Kant did not believe that knowledge represents the objective reality (the thing-in-itself); but he emphatically asserted the foundational and universal character of knowledge. This could be possible because the perceptual framework supplied by the reason or understanding was conceived as universal or common to the entire humankind.

Postmodernism is opposed to each single tenet of the above thesis. It is opposed to foundationalism, representationalism and objective reference; and of course, to all ideas of universalism. It favours pluralism, not only a pluralism of lifeworlds, but sometimes a pluralism of physical worlds also. In short, it advocates that different cultures are different lifeworlds, each having its own language and conceptual scheme. The latter creates its own world in which the objects are perceived and organized differently from those of other cultures. Various lifewrolds or conceptual schemes have almost nothing in common - they are incommensurable.[3]

The entire postmodernist attack on modern thought and epistemology seems to revolve round the idea of incommensurability. This thesis is supposedly integrally related to two other theses of duality of scheme and content and an irreducible plurality of these schemes or conceptual frameworks. Above all, as Thomas Kuhn says, there is no "permanent natural observation language, or common conceptual framework of scientific standards by which we can evaluate rival and competing theories."[4] Each theory can be understood and evaluated from within its own conceptual scheme.

The same thesis is easily extended to morality and other dimensions of human life. When science which is the popular paradigm of certain shared knowledge is declared as consisting of incommensurable schemes, ethical, aesthetic and religious phenomena are far more easily seen as diverse and even incommensurable.

Each culture is declared as a unique whole or lifeworld with a unique language and conceptual scheme which cannot be translated into other languages with different conceptual schemes. Moreover, somehow meaning has been reduced to translatability, so that a language and its conceptual framework are understood in terms of their translatability (or lack of it) in another language. Since it is taken for granted that a language and its conceptual framework cannot be translated into another-what is known as indeterminacy of translation - it follows that various languages and their conceptual frameworks are incommensurable.[5]

III.2 First of all, even though it is repetitive or commonplace, we have to point out that relativism, or what Hilary Putnam calls anarchism, is self-refuting. If all languages and conceptual schemes are both mutually untranslatable and incommensurable, then the thesis of incommensurability can be true only for the culture and conceptual scheme in which was born, that is, modern Western culture. It can be neither translated, nor explained, into other languages, or conceptual frameworks; far less can it be acceptable to them. Referring to Nelson Goodman's extreme view of multiple external worlds corresponding to the multiplicity of versions of the world, Putnam dramatically points out that anyone can tell Goodman: "Not all versions are true for you, Professor Goodman, but so what?"[6] Relativism may appear true to the contemporary postmodernist European thinkers, but that does not entail that it should be true for all other cultures and times.

It is a simple matter of logic that if relativism is true, that is, if every belief and theory is relative to the culture and conceptual framework of its genesis, then relativism is but a local viewpoint which cannot have any validity outside the local culture of its genesis. In other words, if relativism is true then it is worthless. That is, if relativism is true, then all theories are true only within their respective lifeworlds, cultures, or conceptual frameworks, and cannot have any cross-cultural validity. If relativism holds, then it can be true only for contemporary Western (largely Continental) culture, and not for others. However relativists, like logical positivists, are not always willing to acknowledge the self-refuting character of their thesis; and go on arguing for the relativity of all beliefs, norms and values to their respective cultures; not *for* them alone but, as some kind of metaphysical and metaethical truth. Relativism's claim for truth gets converted into some kind of metaphysical or transcendental theory which is presupposed by all knowledge, explanation and justification. But this is simply self-contradictory.

Of course, some extreme relativists as Barry Barnes and David Bloor accept the self-reflexivity of relativist thesis.[7] But then they are reduced to making an almost worthless assertion that they and some other persons in their culture believe in relativism. Postmodern radical relativists are fond of a certain extreme version of the sociology of knowledge. According to it, every belief, whether veridical or false, owes its genesis to sociological causes; that is, both true and false beliefs are caused by the same sociological factors (the thesis of 'symmetry' or equivalence). If we grant this, then the thesis of incommensurability becomes a mere product of sociological factors and is to be explained in their terms. Since veridical beliefs are supposedly not any different from irrational ones, there is no reason for us to assume that relativity thesis also is anything but a contingent product of local and historical causes. Relativism and its thesis of incommensurability are the children of their times.

Various relativist theses are a reaction to the universalism and scientism of modern *Weltanschauung*. The arguments put forward by Rorty and Paul Feyerabend in support of the thesis, that Cardinal Bellarmine was as much justified in his views regarding the geocentricity of the world, as Galileo was in his view regarding the heliocentricity of the solar system, challenge science and its claim to know the physical world.[8] Both philosophers seek to discredit Galileo by contending that he tried to make others believe in his theory and presumed that the Church theory was totally wrong; both argue that Cardinal Bellarmine was much more tolerant and rational in his approach to the controversy, and conclude that Galileo's stand verged on fanaticism. Both claim that every view is contingent, tentative and fallible. While Rorty accepts some sort of superiority of the scientific approach, Feyerabend denies even that. It seems that the philosophical contribution of postmodern thought is confined to its somewhat rhetorical challenge to the scientism of modern thought; while its own positive these are equally questionable.

III.3 In morality the postmodern relativist position seems to be a metaethical one, rather than a normative one, or a merely descriptive one. The problem is not with the relativity of beliefs and morals which may be accepted as descriptively true but which should - if at all - have come at the end of some argument. The problem is with the whole thesis of relativity and incommensurability itself which comes first, that is, as the basis of ethical relativism. It presumes that the relativity of all ethical (and other) judgments to their cultures or conceptual frameworks is a 'truth' which applies to, or is presupposed by, all thought, so that from this relativity we can smoothly argue for ethical relativism. The incommensurability thesis is taken as an explanatory thesis of the entire spectrum of world cultures. But how can it be ? If relativism is true, then it can have no cross-cultural validity. That is, it cannot be true for cultures other than the contemporary Western ones. Others, including the writer, can turn to the relativist and tell her, "You may be right, and relativism may be true *for* you, but it is not true *for* me, and *for* most of the world." The relativists, if they want to be self-consistent, cannot claim wider (cross-cultural) validity for their thesis, more than they are ready to allow to other viewpoints. If relativism is 'true', then it can have no other status than that of a relative viewpoint which we are under no obligation to accept.

Hilary Putnam has criticized relativism on similar grounds. His argument is a little long but cannot be appreciated unless given in full. Putnam compares relativism to solipsism. There are two types of solipsism, according to him: One which self-consistently declares that the subject's ego or self and its creations are the only reality. But there is another and milder kind of solipsism which concedes that there are other selves also, and they create their own worlds. Putnam argues that the second kind of solipsism is inconsistent and involves self-contradiction, in that the relation of symmetry cannot exist between myself and other selves. It is so because for me everything else, including other selves, is but the creation of my self or ego, and other selves cannot be given equal status self-consistently.

Putnam goes on to argue that the relativist is in the same predicament. If he says that the norms of his own culture alone are true for him, he is at least being self-consistent. But if he says that norms of other cultures are true *for others*, he lends himself into self-contradictions. For example, if someone, say a German, Karl, says 'Schnee ist weiss', the relativist has to affirm that Karl says this as determined by the norms of his culture. But the assertion, that "Schnee ist weiss' is true by the norms of German culture', is true by the norms of the relativist's culture. Putnam elaborates upon this argument, and contends that no meaningful discourse is possible if every time we say something we have to specify the cultural norms with reference to which the given assertion is true. Also, all such assertions could be accepted only if they are expressible in the speaker's language and cultural conceptual framework.

Relativism becomes nonsensical in the end, says Putnam, when it tries to say that an assertion is true only as determined by the norms of the language in which the assertion is made; but the entire foregoing assertion can have meaning *for me* (the speaker) as being true only according to the norms and standards of my own language.[9] Putnam concludes that like the solipsist, the relativist also cannot consistently recognize other cultures, their norms and standards as long as he sticks to his thesis that truth *for him* is determined by the norms of his culture.[10]

III.4 Moreover, mutual translation being impossible, there is no way one can ever know whether a given assertion is true or false by the standards of another culture. Surely, the relativist is not intending to deny all distinctions between true and false assertions even within a given conceptual framework. Even when she says that every proposition is true *for* the language and culture in which it is asserted, and one and the same proposition may be both true and false in two different cultures or languages, she has to answer two questions: First, if the two languages are mutually untranslatable, then how can we ever determine whether any two statements are expressing self-same or even similar assertion which can then be declared as true in one culture and false in another ? Second, even if the first extreme thesis were true, that is, a given assertion may be both true and false in two conceptual frameworks, there is the problem of distinguishing between true and false assertions within one and the same linguistic framework. Surely not *all* assertions of any given culture can be true. No rational dialogue and praxis can occur even within one culture without any such distinction. In fact, relativism does seek to eliminate all distinctions between true and false propositins in any language. When it asserts that the sociological causes of all possible assertions in any field of knowledge are the same, and the explanation and justification of all propositions in any linguistic framework are identical, it denies any distinction between true and false beliefs. According to this view, as pointed out above, a scientific assertion about a given natural phenomena and a dogmatic, superstitious belief about the same have the same sociological causes, that is, it is not that the scientific belief has to be explained and justified with reference to scientific or rational laws and dogmatic beliefs are to be understood with reference to sociological conditions, as commonsense understands. Rather, every belief is to be understood with reference to the self-same sociological factors. If so, the distinction between true or false beliefs in every field of life, from science to morals, seems to evaporate.

Here relativism seems to be asserting two quite different propositions: first, that one and the same belief can be both true and false in two linguistic frameworks; and second, that in the final analysis there is no hard and fast distinction between true and false beliefs. Add to this, its primary thesis that the beliefs, ideas, concepts and terms of one language and culture cannot be translated into another so that we have no way to know whether one and the same proposition is both true and false in two different languages; and we have a thesis which is so self-contradictory that it is impossible to express it in a rational form.

IV. Indeterminacy of Translation, Inscrutability of Reference, Conceptual Schemes, and Incommensurability:

Postmodern cognitive relativism mainly consists of the above four theses. It is generally assumed that they are integrally related, that is, are supportive of each other. However when considered more closely, we find that there is considerable tension between them which makes them untenable. These various contentions are further against commonsense and reason (as it is generally understood). We would take up these theses separately and in conjunction with each other.

IV.1 The two theses regarding the indeterminacy of translation and incommensurability of viewpoints are presented as integrally related. Together they constitute the main thesis of postmodern relativism. Let us take up the impossibility of translation from one language to another. Elaborate arguments are given how each language has its own conceptual framework; how the latter determines not only what and how we shall conceptualize but also what we shall perceive. That is, the people speaking a particular language are supposed not only to have unique concepts which differ widely from those of the other cultures or conceptual frameworks; these concepts also organize their perceptions in a way which is very different from the way people speaking another languages, say Chinese, organize their experiences.[11]

W.V.O. Quine calls this thesis the indeterminacy of translation and inscrutability of reference. According to this thesis, the concepts and percepts enshrined in a language are so unique that we cannot find any equivalent concept or expression in one language for another language's concepts and percepts. At most we can learn another language and understand it from within. And yet, after all the effort in learning a language we can never determine what its words refer to in the outside world.[12]

But in real life it is not so. Translating a word into another language means a prior determination of its reference; that is, when we translate a term in another language we simulteneously equate the reference. As Putnam puts it, it is nonsense to say that a certain word A in another language means wheel in our language; and then to say that it does not refer to wheel in the objective world, i.e. we do not know whether the referent of the term A is the same as that of the word wheel. To say that the term A means wheel is to say that "A refers to wheel." An essential step in every exercise in translation is the determination and equation of objective reference.[13] This point is generally acceeded by most contemporary scholars. For example, Chris Swoyer contends that unless two sentences in two different languages approximately have the same meaning, or the same reference, there is no sense in any comparisons. If the referent is not the same, then the two sentences or terms are referring to two different things ; and hence there is no conflict or incommensurability.[14] That is to say, either there is considerable overlapping of reference and meaning, in which case there is no sense in talking of total untranslatability and incommensurability; or there are two independent objects, in which case the two assertions are entirely different and independent of each other, and there is no incommensurability. In both cases there is no sense in saying that a particular assertion is true in one language and false in another.

W. Newton-Smith argues that the truth of a sentence depends upon both the meaning of the sentence and what the sentence is about. But it is propositions alone that can be true or false, and since propositions are determinate, it cannot be that the same proposition is true in one language and false in the other.[15] He further points out that there is no coherent way of saying that S is true for us, and its translation S_2 is false for others; or S is true for them and its translation S_2 is false for us. Newton Smith, Putnam and others have rightly contended that there is a common observational core to all perceptions and beliefs. This core anchors translation from one language to another. The possibility of translation entails falsity of relativism.[16]

Relativism seems to say that the concept of meaning should be given up. The thesis of indeterminacy of translation means that no sentence of any language has a definite meaning which can be translated in another language in a way so that the meaning and reference of the two sentences can be equated. Chinese language provides a favourite paradigm for the advocates of indeterminacy of translation. It is argued that not only Chinese concepts and categories of thought are very different from those of the writers (modern Western ones), the Chinese perceive and classify even everyday objects differently. For example, the Chinese are said to group together grass and shrubs on one hand and green and blue on the other. (We have referred to this view in detail in the 2nd Chapter, Section III.)[17] Not knowing the Chinese, I cannot answer this argument fully. But it is just unbelievable that the Chinese people cannot distinguish between grass and shrubs, or green and blue. It is also unbelievable that they are incapable of understanding and formulating a simple proposition such as "the cat is on the mat."

We can take it for granted - our entire experience and instincts supporting us - that all humankind perceives the middle range mega objects in the same way. Many of us may not have proper conceptions of micro level objects. Many others might have irrational beliefs about various mega level objects; but all do perceive the world, and generally react to it in a very similar manner. The fact that Eskimos have about 100 words for snow, and modern European languages have just a few does not prove either untranslatability, or incommensurability. It only proves that the natural surroundings of the two people are very different. Those surroundings and the constant struggle faced by the Eskimos make them intensely conscious of the varying moods of nature around them, which are reflected in their language, so that they can cope up with them in a better way. Take another example. Indian languages divide a year's seasons into eight, whereas Western languages divide them at most into four. The reason is not incommensurability of two conceptual frameworks but the simple fact that Indian seasons change continuously throughout the year, which is not the case with Europe.

It is not a fact that translation from one language to another is not possible; such translations are routinely undertaken. Putnam argues here that if one translation is not found satisfactory, we do not conclude that no translation is possible; rather, we try to develop a more suitable scheme of translation. Of course, translation from one language to another is easier if the two languages are neighbouring, share more or less same natural and social environment, and belong to the same family, such as the languages of North India. Translations become more difficult in the case of more remote languages. (The reason why Chinese language is a favourite of the advocates of incommensurability thesis is that it is from a remote region and hence very different from European languages.) When the supporters of incommensurability thesis cite only the example of Chinese and Eskimo languages, and hardly ever refer to the mutual untranslatability of European languages, are they suggesting that the relationship of incommensurability exists only between modern European languages and Chinese and Eskimo languages, and that modern European languages are quite commensurable ? Since apparently they do not mean the above, it is curious and irrational that they totally rely on the examples from Chinese and Eskimo languages.

Translations from one language to another have been undertaken from time immemorial. There are certain concepts which are unique to some cultures and languages and which will be difficult to translate into other languages. Examples are the concepts of *dharma*, *karma*, *moksa* in Indian languages; those of *li* and *ch'i* in the Chinese, and that of *logos* in the Greek and its successor languages. Even these concepts have been translated and understood by others, though they may require some explanatory notes. As compared to these few, there would be innumerable others which have very similar connotations in different languages and can be translated from one to another. Concepts referring to concrete objects and their relationships in the physical world, as well as basic intersubjective relationships and some basic concepts of logic, are found in all developed languages. Sometimes, if the concept is abstract, we may at first fail to catch its full nuance, but given the context we succeed in understanding its full meaning. While it is easier to understand and translate thick concepts with descriptive content, abstract concepts are more elusive, but it is not impossible to understand and translate even them. Sometimes we use the original term even in translation in order to retain the full flavour of the original concept, but we do understand that concept.

Not only can we translate different languages into each other, most of us are bilingual, while some are even multilingual. In a pluralist society, such as India's, a large number of languages are spoken; and a majority of the populace understands and speaks two or more languages. Would we have to say that a bilinguist or a multilinguist cannot understand herself in one language when she is thinking or speaking in another language? Or that she cannot express her ideas which have been first thought in one language into another language ? This single empirical fact of the bilingualism of a large section of humanity should be sufficient to silence all the arguments for untranslatability of different languages, or indeterminacy of translation.

Human beings have an irresistible urge to extend their mental horizons by communicating with larger and more varied groups. No culture can survive, far less thrive, in the absence of communication with other cultures. Cultures and societies need other cultures in order even to recognize their separate identities, just as individuals require other selves in order to know themselves as persons. People of any developing, thriving culture feel the urge to expand their physical and mental horizons through trade and cultural transactions with other societies or cultures. Mutual understanding of each other's language and conceptual framework is the prerequisite for such transactions, specially in the field of culture which includes religion, philosophy, art and science. Cultural sharing and give and take in these areas require that texts or classics of various fields are mutually translated. Trade between far off countries thrived long before the Christian era. Then different religions came on the stage, and there arose the need for translation of their generally abstruse texts. Mutual communication and give and take between different and even far-off cultures were commonplace even when there were no proper means of transport. They continued spontaneously from very ancient times to this date, till we were told by contemporary philosophers that different languages are mutually untranslatable, and various cultures and their conceptual frameworks are mutually incommensurable.

For the advocates of untranslatability and incommensurability, Chinese has always been a paradigm language whose conceptual framework is supposedly entirely different from that of other European languages. But abstract and difficult texts from Pali and Sanskrit were translated into the same Chinese language more than two millenniums ago. History writing being uncommon in India, we owe to two Chinese travellers, Fa-Hien and Hiuen-Tsang, for our knowledge of those periods of Indian history when they visited India.

IV.2 Incommensurability thesis is closely related to the thesis of indeterminacy of translation, as also to what Karl Popper calls "the Myth of Framework". Having discarded the notion of outside world which is independent of our knowledge, and that of truth as correspondence with it, the postmodernists assert that the world as we know it is the product of human construction. But while for Kant the human contribution comes from a universally shared reason or understanding, for the advocates of incommensurability thesis, it comes from some communally shared conceptual framework. And these conceptual frameworks are not only relative, contingent, plural and divergent but also mutually incommensurable. As we have seen in the 2nd Chapter, Rorty, Kuhn, Quine and Sellars are great exponents of the theory of conceptual framework which determines all our thinking, desires and even perceptions. Accordingly, the question of what is real or true is not to be settled independently of a given conceptual framework. And this, in turn, according to Rorty, suggests that perhaps nothing really exists apart from such frameworks. He rejects the idea that we *could* ever find a common matrix of inquiry - something which overspanned all actual and possible conceptual frameworks . He asserts that even giveness to sense is a matter of acculturation."[18]

It was Kuhn who first popularized the ideas of conceptual schemes and their mutual incommensurability. Kuhn asserts that there is no real communication between the supporters of any two scientific theories; nor can they share or benefit from each other's insights. The only possibility is a total paradigm shift, which means a total revolutionary change in one's data and concepts. Kuhn argues that proponents of different scientific theories never achieve complete contact, far less agree, with each other. It is so because the proponents of competing paradigms "practice their trade in different worlds."[19]

These theoretical paradigms or conceptual frameworks literally 'construct' the world we live in, react to, and seek to change. In the words of Richard Bernstein (earlier quoted in Chapter 2), all our intellectual concepts and values are "relative to a specific conceptual scheme, theoretical framework, paradigm, form of life, society, or culture." Moreover, there is a "nonreducible plurality" of such conceptual schemes.[20] And finally, "there is no substantive overarching framework in which radically different and alternative schemes are commensurable..."[21]

Thus there are four basic contentions of incommensurability thesis: First, all our percepts and concepts are determined by, or relative to, our conceptual scheme, language, or the historical milieu in which we happen to be living. Second, there is an irreducible plurality of such conceptual frameworks. Third, these conceptual schemes or lifeworlds are mutually incommensurable. And fourth, there is no neutral language in which the different conceptual schemes can be translated and compared, and no universal standards which are different from the various conceptual schemes and which can be applied to all these various schemes from an outside point of view.

It is contended that our mind provides basic concepts which organize and interpret our experiential or empirical data; and there are alternative sets of conceptual schemes, each of which provides a quite different but equally valid way of interpreting experience.[22] The idea seems to be that one and the same world can be looked upon or interpreted from alternative points of view. The latter are underdetermined by 'facts' or the objects of knowledge. Actually, this is never made clear whether it is one and the same world which is variously interpreted from incommensurable points of view, or even the worlds are different. Goodman has declared that each conceptual framework creates its own world; and "there are many worlds, if any", corresponding to these frameworks. This is an extreme position, usually not endorsed by most relativists. In fact, Goodman is also saying something else, that is, interdependence of facts and versions (conventions). Sometimes it seems that the postmodernist scholars do not want to admit even that it is 'one and the same world' which is being interpreted freely. It is part of the incommensurability thesis that different paradigms or conceptual schemes not only differ in their interpretative concepts but also in the initial data they seek to interpret. Moreover, there is no way we can go beyond the conceptual frameworks to the uninterpreted reality.[23]

We detect an influence of Kant here, but his philosophy seems to have been turned upside down. Whereas Kant sought to establish universality, necessity and certainty of all knowledge; relativists argue for relativity, contingency and uncertainty. If there are innumerable ways to interpret the reality, and if the reality itself is a creation or construct of interpretation, there is nothing left which we can call knowledge, and nothing which we can call the world for sure.

No attempt is made to explain the nature and status of conceptual framework. The very fact that a variety of names are used to convey the idea, e.g. conceptual scheme/framework/ language (linguistic framework) /lifeworld/paradigm/language game/form of life, means that the conception is a very loose one. All that the relativist wants to say is that we do not know the knowledge-independent world; all we know is the world as we experience and know, and that is the one which has already been interpreted by our categories and concepts. This seems to be purely Kantian philosophy, but it is not, as the interpreting conceptual framework is a matter of pure convention and is not *a priori* or transcendantal in the Kantian sense. Above all, these conceptual frameworks are innumerable and do not follow any universal logical rules. They cannot be evaluated or compared.

According to Kuhn, scientific paradigms are incompatible and incommensurable, but comparable. But there is no way in which we can compare rival paradigms in the absence of a common neutral language and logical framework. Since Kuhn's rival scientific paradigms do not even share their data and/or problems, and since there is no way we can say that the latter paradigm explains the same problem in a better way, there is no sense in saying that they are even comparable.

IV.3 At this point the incommensurability thesis gets entangled in the web of its own 'conceptual framework', or theories. First of all, there is no point in talking of incommensurability along with untranslatability. The relativists, such as Kuhn, Feyerabend and Rorty, have talked as if the two are integrally related as two sides of the same medal. On the contrary, the two cannot be maintained together. If a particular language or conceptual scheme cannot be translated at all, there is no way we can say that its contents are incommensurable with those of our own. A comparison of the contents of any two theories, paradigms, or conceptual schemes is impossible because of their mutual untranslatability. Unless we know what the 'other' is asserting we cannot declare its ideas and values as incommensurable with ours. Putnam points out that, "To tell us that Galileo had 'incommensurable' notions *and then go on to describe them at length* is totally incoherent."(original italics) [24] Add to it the fact that we cannot call Galileo's paradigm or conceptual framework incommensurable with some other unless we first understood it, and we cannot understand it unless we first experience a paradigm shift or conversion, so that we have already accepted Galilean conceptual scheme. And if we are already converted to that scheme we could not possibly call it incommensurable.

The same applies to the anthropologists' assertions. First they devoutly affirm the diversity and incommensurability of various cultures, then they go on to describe in detail the beliefs, customs etc. of the culture under study in order to impress upon us how curious or diverse the latter are from those of their culture. The incommensurability thesis asserts the untranslatability and alien nature of other cultures and their linguistic - conceptual frameworks, which in theory cannot be understood in our linguistic framework and compared with ours. The comparison of any two cultures, even with the purpose of declaring their incommensurability, presupposes that the appraiser understands the two cultures and their respective conceptual frameworks; and this is what the thesis of untranslatability denies.

If Kuhn's theory holds, then we cannot understand an alien culture without first getting converted to that culture or form of life. But then our own culture would become alien to us; and we cannot simply pass a judgment of incommensurability without being able to understand the two cultures simultaneously. And if we can understand the other culture (the minimum requirement for the judgment of incommensurability), then its conceptual scheme and its content are neither untranslatable, nor fully incommensurable.

At one place Kuhn suggests that not all scientific theories are equally valid; and we can always choose a 'better' theory. He gives several reasons for such a choice: "accuracy, consistency, scope, simplicity, and fruitfulness."[25] If so, then we can very well compare various theories on the same scale which consists of objective, universal criteria used by all scientists. But then where is incommensurability? Actually, Kuhn's insistence that various scientific theories are incommensurable and yet comparable cannot be sustained.

The thesis of incommensurability is made possible by a prior acceptance of the concept of an all-encompassing conceptual framework. As we have seen, Karl Popper calls it the "Myth of Framework". He contends that this thesis suggests that we are prisoners caught in the framework of our theories; our expectations; our past experiences; our language, so that we cannot communicate with others who are equally encased in 'radically' different frameworks or paradigms.[26]

Bernstein has tried hard to justify or present in a reasonable manner the theses of relativity of our knowledge to our conceptual framework, their immense plurality and mutual incommensurability. He contends that Popper's understanding of incommensurability thesis is not right, rather :

> There is always some overlap between rival paradigms - overlap of observations, concepts, standards, and problems. If there were not such overlap, rational debate and argumentation between proponents of rival paradigms would not be possible.[27]

Bernstein argues that comparison and evaluation are possible in the Kuhnean scheme. He, however, endorses Kuhn's rejection of the objectivist point of view, and the latter's contention that there is some common, universal framework of commensuration, or some neutral language in which all languages and frameworks may be translated and then compared.[28] He is of course right - there is no common framework of neutral language which exists over and above all other languages. By the very nature of things every language and conceptual framework belongs to some one culture or the other, some historical period or the other.

Bernstein further contends that in order to compare and evaluate we do not necessarily need a third neutral framework; and there are multiple ways in which we can compare theories.[29] Again he is right; and this is what I am trying to argue.

However, Bernstein's defence of relativism and incommensurability thesis are not altogether convincing. Even if there are multiple ways of comparison, no comparison could have any worth without some determination and equation of reference and meaning. Relativists are constantly asserting that there are no common reference points in the world which are shared by all perspectives. But comparison of any two assertions or points of view is not possible without first, a definite identification of their subject matter or referent; second, the possibility of mutual understanding or translation; and third, some overlapping of both their subject matters and conceptual frameworks. Comparison also implies the existence of, or the need to develop, a minimal common matrix of terms and concepts in which mutual dialogue can take place.

IV.4 Incommensurability of viewpoints or conceptual schemes is not a totally nonsensical proposition. The demands of rational dialogue often bring us face to face with viewpoints and cognitive-emotional attitudes which are incommensurable, that is, only one of the two can be upheld at a time. For example, scientific approach or conceptual framework is totally incommensurable with the superstitious approach of the masses which was predominant in Western countries during the period before the scientific revolution; and which is still somewhat prevalent in the third world countries. Modern science's understanding and explanation of natural phenomena, especially of diseases and their cures, is totally incommensurable with the superstitious fear of certain diseases, such as smallpox in India. Various abnormal mental phenomena are also explained and treated very differently by medical science and superstitions. We would however be hard pressed if we were called upon to assert that both kinds of explanations are equally 'rational', though their 'rationalities' may be different.

Peter Winch has discussed in detail Azande black magic, and has opined that the 'point' of activity of Azande black magic is quite different from the scientific approach which seeks to explain a given natural phenomenon as death; the implication being that science cannot invalidate the black magic of nonliterate tribes.[30] However, the 'point' of superstitious or magical activities is not very different from the point of scientific activities; both seek to understand and control natural powers to serve human ends. The role of human goals and desires, and the tendency to use nature for those goals are common to both. The basic difference between the two is not in the 'point' of activity but in the rational methodological approach of science, and the irrational manner in which the same goals are sought to be achieved through magic and other superstitious activities. Since the two activities, scientific and superstitious or magical, are quite similar in their goal as well as the subject matter (natural phenomena), they are comparable, and found incommensurable.

In other words, the concept of incommensurability makes sense when applied to any two diverse beliefs, attitudes, points of view, or ways of life; but in order to make sense it can only be partial incommensurability. That is, unless we presume some overlapping of the two beliefs, attitudes, or ways; or unless they have some shared subject matter or reference point, they cannot be compared; nor can they be judged as incommensurable.

Incommensurability of attitudes and points of view can be between those belonging to two separate cultures, or those coexisting in the same culture. For example, contemporary Western culture is swept by a strong feminist movement. But parallel to this is the all-pervading perception of woman as a sex object which is shared by both men and women in those societies. They are two incommensurable attitudes even though they do not come from two totally incommensurable and untranslatable conceptual schemes, cultures, or lifeworlds, but from one and the same culture.

In the terminology of Bernard Williams, the feminist and sexist attitudes to women are in actual confrontation and not in a mere notional one. However, actual confrontation is not a necessary condition for incommensurability. While it is easier to pinpoint any two attitudes or beliefs which are in actual confrontation as (partially) incommensurable, there may be many others which are remote to each other, and are still found incommensurable. The incommensurability and commensurability are complex relationships and cannot be rigidly defined, that is, we cannot say either that incommensurability is possible only in the case of actual confrontation; or that the attitudes and values of any two cultures are necessarily incommensurable.

Thus, while there may be both commensurability and incommensurability between different ideas, attitudes and activities, the relation of incommensurability between any two cultures, lifeworlds, or conceptual schemes conceived as self-contained wholes, is difficult to defend. The thesis of incommensurability of any two cultures, or conceptual frameworks takes it for granted that any one culture is a harmonious whole, with one language, one conceptual scheme, and one way of life. But this is purely a sociological myth. I have argued against this thesis at length in my last Chapter (Section I). It has been my contention there that no culture is a monolithic whole of beliefs, attitudes and values. The plurality of ways of life, goals, beliefs and attitudes found within a culture is an indisputable fact of life. Take any modern society -is it monolithic? Aren't there conflicts and tensions within its various ethnic groups? These tensions highten when the ethnic differences are more prominent, as in Sri Lanka, India's North East, erstwhile USSR and Yugoslavia. They are much less if a given culture has a limited geographic spread and one single language.

Plurality and diversity within any given culture are anyway a must even for its natural growth. It is impossible to pinpoint an identifiable determinate way of life of a given culture which can be declared as incommensurable with those of others. Moreover, each way of life and conceptual framework is constantly changing due to its own inner dynamics, as well as due to the impact of other cultures and ways of life. It is all the while absorbing newer ideas or concepts, and reinterpreting and transforming older ones.[31]

It is not true that an individual's thinking and values are fully determined by her society's traditional values, norms and conceptual framework. History is replete with instances where individuals, or a small group of persons, have revolted against and rejected the norms and values of their society, and in the process have been the heralders of far-reaching social, moral and political revolutions.[32] How could we possibly understand these phenomena unless the conception of incommensurability, as developed by Kuhn and others, is modified or moderated? There is no total incommensurability, far less untranslatability of various languages and conceptual frameworks. Rather, as Bernstein has acknowledged, there is a considerable overlap that makes mutual understanding and give and take possible; which fact makes total incommensurability an untenable proposition.

The various theses and concepts which lead to an extreme kind of relativism have emerged from the fact that anthropologists have totally concentrated on far-off isolated cultures. It is easier to conceive them as exclusive units with well-defined ways of life and concepts (though they are also equally complex and multifaceted). But when we come to more advanced, complex cultures, which are in constant communication with other similar cultures, we find that the conception of culture or lifeworld that suited the simpler, geographically excluded cultures can no more be applied to these later cultures; and there is no simple, monolithic way of life which could represent an entire complex and multifaceted developed culture.

It is not to say that these developed cultures do not have distinctive patterns of their own according to which their various dimensions and stages are more or less organized. It is also not to say that the conceptual schemes and systems of values, or value preferences are not distinctive in each culture. It is only to say that while the patterns of organization or value preferences may be different in different cultures, the raw material, i.e. the feelings, interests, percepts, concepts etc., are more or less common in all human beings. By concentrating on preliterate cultures anthropologists have done humanity a great disservice. Since the preliterate cultures were perceived as so widely different from modern Western cultures it was concluded that all cultures and ways of life are homogeneous wholes; and are mutually incommensurable and untranslatable. The two theses seemed attractive at first because of a faulty initial premise that whatever is true of preliterate cultures would be true of all developed cultures. First, the very universalization of the limited example of a few isolated cultures goes against the thesis of incommensurability and relativism. Secondly, there is a basic difference between geographically secluded cultures and other developed cultures which are in constant communication with each other, so that the evidence of the first cannot prove anything about the second, or developed cultures.

IV.5 The idea of conceptual scheme has created insurmountable problems. We have noted Karl Popper's view that conceptual schemes act like prisons whose walls make all communication with others impossible.

There is a second, equally serious, objection against the conception of conceptual schemes. Conceptual schemes apparently are conventions. If a conceptual scheme is something which is superimposed upon nature or objects of knowledge, we are left with two components in knowledge - conventional and natural or physical; and nothing to connect the two.[33] That is, there is no way we can make out whether our 'scheme' or version of 'facts' correctly or truthfully 'represents' the facts', or which of the various alternative versions of 'the world' is true than others.

Nelson Goodman has dramatically emphasized the duality of scheme and content. First, he declares that any description is necessarily conventional because "There are alternative, equally legitimate versions in terms of other concepts." At the same time, not only descriptions, or the concepts in terms of which we organize our facts are conventional, even the facts which they organize are also so, because "these facts are creatures of their description."[34]

Like Kant, all contemporary philosophers agree that there is no way to reach the reality -as-it-is-independent-of -our-knowledge. Whenever we want to know what the various versions of reality are of, we can only supply another version in response to the query. Goodman concludes:

> How can divergent diagrams or versions be of the same facts, the same world? They must be either of no world, or of different worlds. There must be many worlds, if any.[35]

The problems associated with the thesis of duality of scheme and content has led Donald Davidson to argue against this thesis, and finally to offer a unique conclusion :

> Beliefs are true or false, but they represent nothing. It is good to be rid of representations and with them the correspondence theory of truth, for it is thinking there are representations that engenders thoughts of relativism.[36]

He contends that "empirical knowledge has no epistemological foundation and needs none."[37] He argues that "the idea that there is a basic division between uninterpreted experience and an organizing conceptual scheme is a deep mistake.[38] As a corrective to this mistake, Donald Davidson suggests that the entire concept of conceptual scheme should be abandoned. He adds that it is essential to this dualism that there be something neutral and common that lies outside all schemes. But this common something cannot be the subject matter of contrasting and incommensurable languages and conceptual schemes. In his own words:

> We have found no intelligible basis on which it can be said that schemes are different. It would be equally wrong to announce the glorious news that all mankind - all speakers of language at least - share a common scheme and ontology.
>
> Given the dogma of a dualism of scheme and reality, we get conceptual relativity, and truth relative to a scheme. Without the dogma, this kind of relativity goes by the board.[39]

Davidson suggests that we would establish direct contact with reality once we give up the dualism of scheme and content. To him should go the credit of forcefully bringing out the irrationality inherent in the scheme-content duality. The two basic theses of relativism are : first, all our knowledge being relative to the conceptual scheme, language and culture to which we belong; and second, the plurality and the mutual incommensurability of all such schemes. The two together lead to the affirmation of the total contingency, uncertainty and relativity of all human knowledge and judgments.

The conceptual scheme-based relativism makes all knowledge relative and such that it cannot claim any truth for itself in the absence of any direct contact with reality. But the incommensurability of different conceptual schemes presupppposes a common subject matter which is, at the same time, denied. And in the absence of a common referent, the incommensurability becomes meaningless. In short, relativism not only makes knowledge of any and every kind impossible to achieve, it is itself a self-contradictory thesis.

The problem is much more serious in morality. It is contended that not only the rival conceptual frameworks have divergent beliefs, values, norms and moral criteria, people inhabiting different lifeworlds also perceive the apparently similar practices or acts very differently. Since the latter come to us as alredy interpreted by our respective conceptual frameworks, it would be wrong to say that different cultures pronounce the *same act* as right and wrong; rather, there is *no same act* in two distinct lifeworlds. That is to say the two acts of patricide in the Roman culture and among the Eskimos are two different acts; and while the Romans; condemnation of patricide was right *for them*, Eskimos' silent endorsement of patricide is right *for them* - because, in fact, the two acts are different altogether, or have very different meanings for their respective societies. If so, they cannot be compared. And in the absence of any possibility of some at least overlapping referent (i.e. the act of killing father) we cannot talk of the incommensurability of the two value judgments, perspectives, or ways of life.

V Some Further Comments

V.1 It is contended by the relativists and other postmodernists that while the modern rationalist tradition was foundationalist, absolutist and intolearnt, the postmodern relativist position naturally leads to openness and tolerance. The fact, however, is that in her own way the relativist is also an absolutist and an ethnocentric. Putnam calls the relativist position imperialist. Like any other ethnocentric point of view, the relativist goes on harping on the thesis that the beliefs, norms and standards of her own culture are alone true for her, and she can know, judge and act only according to the norms and criteria of her culture.[40]

It is also to be noted that when a relativist concedes that the norms etc. of other cultures are true or valid for them, she is not necessarily being tolerant; rather she is being arrogantly apathetic towards others. Tolerance, though not a very positive attitude, presupposes a minimum level of knowledge of other cultures, a genuine belief that not only they are right according to their lights, they may also be right as such. Tolerance also presupposes an implicit acceptance that while others may be right, we may be wrong in some areas. But while asserting that everyone is right according to the norms of her society and all are equally right, and we cannot either compare or evaluate the other cultures, the relativist is not being tolerant; rather she is adopting an attitude of apartheid. This approach creates an insurmountable barrier between our culture which is, of course, right for us, and other cultures which are presumably much inferior to our own but which we should let continue in their own ways. This attitude is apparent in the anthropologists' practice of concentrating on far-off preliterate cultures, instead of testing their theories with reference to other developed cultures.

The relativists insist that we cannot understand the 'other culture'; but in the absence of proper knowledge we cannot tolerate the other culture either, we can just let it be. There is a subconscious attitude of superiority when the relativist presents her thesis and argues that it is the best basis for a policy of tolerance. Both Putnam and Newton-Smith have argued that a relativist is not as charitable as she fancies herself to be. By asserting that we cannot translate another language into our own, or understand alien cultures, a relativist is virtually denying rationality and humanity to persons belonging to those cultures. According to Putnam, if we cannot understand 'others', there is no point in saying that 'others' are persons like us.[41]

This attitude is also found when an anthropologist or a relativist philosopher, such as Peter Winch or Charles Taylor, seeks to defend the apparently irrational practices of alien preliterate cultures, as Azande, saying that we must not judge them from our standards of rationality, and that the 'point' of their activities is very different from those of modern Western cultures.[42] Is this emphasis on the very different 'point' of Azande magic meant to imply that those cultures are beyond the purview of 'rationality'? Or, does it imply that Azande magic and modern science have equal validity and worth when judged on the scale of rationality, justifiability etc.? To accept Azande or other preliterate cultures as unique is one thing, to say that they have their own rationality even as we have our own is quite another. The very concept of rationality necessarily includes that of universal applicability. Could it be that by making Azande and others beyond the pale of human rationality, these scholars are unconsciously undermining their very humanity?

Relativism thus often falls into self-contradictions. It seeks to declare those cultures and conceptual frameworks incommensurable which it has also declared as unknowable due to mutual untranslatability of various languages. It declares itself as the philosophy of tolerance, though it does not know what it tolerates. It affirms relativism and negates the possibility of any cross-cultural criteria of mutual comparison and evaluation; and yet assumes that its own viewpoint is valid for all cultures and forms of life. It condemns the earlier ethnocentric approach of Western cultures, and yet assumes the superiority of its own point of view. It declares the equal validity of all lifeworlds and conceptual schemes, and yet by making them totally alien and unknowable it reduces them to apartheid, and to a semi-human status.

V.2 The fact, however, is that not only the objective world but also the ways we perceive it, the categories of perception and conception, and some basic principles of logic or reasoning are more or less shared. We can presume that macro level objects are perceived in a similar manner by all humans. Putnam argues that all human beings perceive and think in a quite similar fashion. Minimum laws of logic and logical words (as, all, not, some etc.) are to be found in every language and culture; without them no language is possible.[43] We can understand each other because we share both - the same world and common ways of perceiving it, as well as a more or less common human nature with similar instincts and interests.

Mutual commensurability of our thought and language is presupposed at every stage of life. Putnam has presented a long persuasive argument for the natural possibility of knowing and understanding others. According to him, "the interpretative success does not require that the translated beliefs come out the same as our own, but it does require that they come out intelligible to us." He adds that. "*Comparison* presupposes that there are some commensurabilities."[44] To quote him again:

> We are committed by our fundamental conceptions to treating not just our present time-slices, but also our past selves, our ancestors and members of other cultures, past and present, as *persons*; and that means, I have argued, attributing to them shared references and shared concepts, however different the *conceptions* that we also attribute. Not only we do share objects and concepts with others to the extent that interpretative exercise succeeds, but also conceptions of the reasonable, of the natural and so on. For the whole justification of an interpretative scheme, remember, is that it renders the behaviour of others at least minimally reasonable by our lights.[45]

V.3 In fact, noncognitivists and relativists face the problem of presenting their thesis in a coherent and plausible form. Vulgar or extreme relativism is self-contradictory and incoherent because it uses a nonrelativist conception of truth to present its thesis that norms and standards of their own cultures are true for the inhabitants of different cultures. If we use the words 'true' and 'valid' in the traditional sense which the relativist seems to be doing, then there can be only one true standard or system of values. Of course, we cannot identify this one true standard and value system with those of any one culture alone. On the other hand, to assert innumerable and mutually incommensurable principles and standards as equally true and valid is a self-contradictory proposition. The additional contention that they are true or valid only for their respective cultures only hightens the confusion and contradiction involved.

It has been suggested as a corrective theory that they should use a relative conception of truth in which nothing is right or wrong, true or false in itself but is so in a particular context or for a particular society. As such, any proposition is neither true (in the absolutist sense) nor false. It also means that all contentions are fallible; what is considered true in a particular culture at a particular time may well be regarded as false in the same culture at another time, or in another culture. It is added that if a particular assertion or perceived truth is found false at a later stage, the latter correction does not falsify what was once perceived as true by that society and times.[45]

The above conception of truth makes relativism somewhat more self-consistent, but also no less extreme. What it in effect says is that nothing is right or wrong but times and society make it so. In other words, whatever is regarded as right or true in a given culture is so. And when later generations proclaim it wrong, it becomes wrong; but at the same time, it does not make the earlier perception wrong.

I do not agree. If the later correction has nothing to say regarding the earlier view, then there is no point in declaring the later view as a correction of the earlier view. Nor is there any point in saying that our viewpoints are fallible; and relativism's contribution lies in making this clear. Fallibility implies the possibility of later corrections, so that the earlier viewpoint is declared as false, wrong, or at least partially so. But this is what is being denied when it is declared that the later view does not affect the truth value of the former view. The relativist is saying that if any given society expresses two different views at different points of time, they are both right for their respective times, and the later view does not correct the earlier view. Even if the earlier view says something drastically different from the later view, the earlier view remains true for its times. This is not fallibilism.

Rejection of bipolar view of truth should mean that different views are not absolutely right or wrong, but are only partially so. The Western mind with its own preoccupations is unable to appreciate the implications of its own views. This conditional or partial sense of truth has long been perfected by the Indian mind, especially in the context of religion and morality. It has been repeatedly affirmed by Indians that no religion is ultimately or finally true, but all are partial glimpses of the one truth. Even if some want to deny the Divine Being, their metaphysical theory, e.g. Buddhism and Jainism, is also partially true, because even the description of the Reality as Divine Being is only partially true, and its rejection would be the other side of the medal. No world-view is wholly true, that is, true in an all-comprehending, absolute sense. And by the same token, no view is absolutely wrong. Jainism perfected this thesis in its elaborate doctrine of *syãdavãda* which is too complex and novel an idea to present here. Instead, let me quote Gandhi who very simply and cogently presented the plurality of perspectives (in the religious sphere) which share some common referent. It means that various perspectives, being by their very nature relative, can never comprehend the whole truth. The latter is simultaneously being perceived, understood and interpreted by innumerable other perspectives. While no perspectival view can claim infallibility, finality, or all-comprehensiveness; no perspective (whether in religion, morality, or in science) is false. All perspectives are partial glimpses of truth, and are always open to future correction and supplementation by other perspectives. This does not mean that people who belong to, or interpret, the 'reality' from any particular perspective have a right to criticize, far less to condemn, the other perspectives (in Gandhi's context - religions). Above all, these perspectives are neither infallible, nor self-contained, nor incommensurable. In his own words:

> After long study and experience, I have come to the conclusion that (1) All religions are true; (2) All religions have some error in them, (3) All religions are almost as dear to me as my own Hinduism...[47]

Gandhi goes on to affirm that the soul of religion is one, while its outer crusts are many. Though I have sympathy with this view, I would disregard it here. Instead I would concentrate on Gandhi's views on tolerance :

> The need of the moment is not one religion, but mutual respect and tolerance of the devotees of different religions. We want to reach not the dead level, but unity in diversity. Any attempt to root out traditions, effects of heredity, climate and other surroundings is not only bound to fail but is a sacrilege.[48]
>
> We belittle our own faults and exaggerate the opponent's that develops an attitude of intolerance. If we would be charitable and tolerant, we would endeavour to see our opponents as they see themselves...
>
> This requires a large heart, otherwise called charity....[49]

And

> I do not like the word tolerance, but could not think of a better one. Tolerance may imply a gratuitous assumptions of the inferiority of other faiths to one's own, whereas *ahiṁsā* (non-violence) teaches us to entertain the same respect for the religious faiths of others as we accord to our own, thus admitting the imperfection of the latter......And if we are imperfect oursleves, religion as conceived by us must also be imperfect.....
>
> Religion of our conception, being thus imperfect, is always subject to a process of evolution and re-interpretation.[50]

It may be objected here that this talk of religion is quite irrelevant in our present discussion. Right; but the gulf between religion and morality on one hand and empirical and scientific knowledge on the other has been considerably reduced by the postmodernists themselves. Since the latter apparently find even the knowledge of the physical world problematic, Gandhi's talk of all our interpretations and conceptualizations of 'reality' being imperfect and "subject to a process of evolution and re-interpretation" should be welcome to the contemporary world.

Another thing: What Gandhi means in the context of religious or metaphysical truth would be equally true in that of morality. Just as no religion can claim finality or absolute truth for its creedal beliefs, no moral principle or norm can claim ultimate validity or unconditional truth for itself. Some moral principles would be more true and more universal than others; some would be more false, local and contextual, and may need some correction from a rational point of view.

A moral norm or principle may be true and universal, but it cannot be absolutely true, as there would always be exceptions to it. Moreover, as Gandhi says, nothing which is the creation of historically conditioned fallible minds can be absolutely true, nor could it be totally false. Whether it is different versions of the Absolute (religions), or it is different versions of the good or right way of life (moralities), none of them is either the final truth about the matter, or a totally false one. Above all, they are not mutually incommensurable; there are marked differences but there are equally marked similarities also. An excessive emphasis on irreducible plurality of lifeworlds and their mutual incommensurability fails to do justice to the underlying humanity of people belonging to different cultures and times.

CHAPTER 5

Anti-Relativist Trends: Realism and Universalism

I. Introductory Remarks

So far I have tried to critically assess the various formulations of ethical relativism. Its first and popular form is one which seeks to take an unwarranted jump from the empirical contingent fact of cultural relativism to the normative principle that whatever is believed, practised and approved of in a society, (or whatever fits in with the institutional structure of that society) is right for that society. I have argued that whatever is believed or approved, as also societal (institutional) demands, and everything else that is contingent, empirical and sociological, are all subject to Moore's open question, that is, 'Is what is being believed and practised, really good or right?' I have also argued that the 'ought' of morality cannot be derived from the 'is' of anthropology and sociology. Further, if a particular system of morality suits a particular sociological or institutional structure, it may be a strong point in favour of that morality, but it does not exempt either that moral system, or that society's institutions, from rational-moral scrutiny.

Positivism simply rejected ethics and many other aspects of human culture as merely emotive, or even nonsensical. Not only universal morality but separate culture - specific moralities are all rejected hereby as mere emotive outbursts. I have observed in response : First, (logical) positivism is self-refuting, as it cannot claim any validity for itself. Second, scientific method and criteria need not be the ultimate court of appeal in every discourse, and each discipline can have its own criteria and rules of argumentation and judgment. And third, morality is not a mere matter of emotional responses but does have a cognitive content. The acknowledgment of the cognitive character of ethics, in turn, may suggest a realist understanding thereof, to which we shall return in our second section.

As to postmodernism : it is a diversified nebulous approach or movement which has successfully challenged the absolutism of Enlightenment and the fanaticism of the positivists. Its five basic theses are : First, the idea of the world being perceived and understood through some conceptual scheme, provided by one's culture and language; and its correlate, the duality of scheme and content; second, the immense plurality and mutual incommensurability of these conceptual schemes or lifeworlds; third, the mutual untranslatability of various languages, and the inscrutability of reference; fourth, internalism in judgment, or the illegitimacy of any judgment from an externalistic point of view; and fifth, the impossibility of any cross-cultural framework of any discourse.

We have found that these tenets are mutually inconsistent. For example, incommensurability of various conceptual frameworks and untranslatability of different languages taken together result in self-contradictions. Similarly, the scheme-content duality leads to various problems and contradictions. If we start with this duality, we can either declare that there is no world beyond our knowledge; or say with Goodman that "there are many worlds, if any."[1]

Thus, the postmodernist cognitive relativism denies the two most basic beliefs and presuppositions of commonsense and reason : the existence of a common world shared by widely different people; and the existence of other selves. The theses of duality of scheme and content and the inscrutability of reference make the common empirical world and its knowledge highly problematic. The two or three related theses, regarding the mutual untranslatability of languages, the determining and limiting character of conceptual frameworks, and the immense plurality and incommensurability of these frameworks, make the existence of other persons and cultures equally problematic. No rational discussion, including that of postmodernist relativism, is possible in the absence of faith in a shared world, other rational selves, and some shared framework of mutual communication.

Relativism is integrally related to postmodernist constructivism or conventionalism. According to it, our language or conceptual framework not only determine our values, goals and norms but also our perceptions. In some sense we, or our conceptual framework literally construct the world, so that there are multiple worlds in correspondence with the innumerable conventional versions of the world that are found in different languages and cultures. Here relativism's metaepistemology (normative theory of knowledge) directly results in, and is integrally related to, a relativist metaphysics. Relativists, at least some extreme ones among them, argue that we do not inhabit a common world which may be interpreted differently, but rather, there is a plurality or multiplicity of worlds, and many of those worlds are legitimate in their respective contexts. There is no way we can reach the world-as-it-is before our conceptualization which is understood as a virtual construction of the objects of perception.[2]

Nor should we ask, says Nelson Goodman, as to which one of these constructed worlds or versions 'copies' the outer world best.[3] Goodman constructs a relativist metaphysics out of this. His primary point is that we have no access to the world as undescribed and unperceived reality, and therefore we cannot compare our descriptions of the world with the world-as-it-it-in-itself. The world cannot help us in picking up the right version thereof. This leads to a notion of relative truth. Each way of worldmaking is a complete system with its own inner concepts and standards. Not only truth but reality also is relative. Many versions of the world are available, and there is no privileged description or version. Which version we choose depends upon our interests and objectives. Nor is there any valid correspondence between our various versions and the world. Opposition here is between what is objectively, i.e. mind-independently, there and what is conventional or made up. Relativism or constructivism is opposed to objectivism, or the idea of the world and its objects being mind-independent.

Postmodern relativism is opposed by contemporary realism at both epistemological and ontological levels. In other words, both the relativist theory of knowledge (consisting of the theses of dualism of scheme and content, extreme plurality of schemes or conceptual frameworks, and their mutual incommensurability), and the relativist metaphysics (which seems to assert multiplicity of worlds corresponding to the innumerable culturally - conditioned versions of the world), are challenged by realism.

II. Realism : Metaphysical and Epistemological

II.1 Realism is opposed to both the postmodernist epistemology (expressed through the latter's rejection of all epistemology), as also its extreme relativist metaphysics.

Michael Devitt, C.A.Hooker and other realists assert that the metaphysical question is more important and should be settled first before the semantic and epistemological ones can be taken up. By this they mean that the realist should start by asserting a realist ontology, and then search which kinds of semantics and epistemology would go well with a realist ontology or metaphysics.[4]

In contrast to the constructivist metaphysical position, realism asserts that the world and its objects are real and independent of our knowledge. Both primary and secondary qualities are powers to make us experience the objects in a certain way. The objects of the world have properties; and these have causal roles, that is, they are the causes of our knowledge and beliefs. The central thesis of realism is that the world exists objectively and independently of the mind, and we can know it due to the causal relation between the world and mind.

Realism, like relativism, also comes in different shades. While scholars, such as Hilary Putnam and Michael Dummet, opt for a milder version of realism which accepts that there can be no direct access to the world-as-it-is-in-itself, and reject the correspondence theory of truth; others take a much bolder stand.

These latter realists start by pointing out a basic confusion in the relativist constructivism. For example, Devitt argues that the conception of objects being independent of the perceiving mind is the most basic one in realism :

> To say that an object has objective existence is not to say that it is unknowable, nor that we cannot have true beliefs about it. It is to say that its existence and nature is in no

> way dependent upon our epistemic capacities. It is not constituted by our knowledge, by the synthesizing power of the mind, nor by our imposition of concepts or theories...
>
> The extent to which and the manner in which we can come to know about an object are, for the realist, epistemic issues which are quite distinct from ontological questions about the object.[5]

We construct our theories of the world, and these theories are, in turn, determined by our experiences and our innate predispositions to respond selectively to our experiences. So we can talk of imposing on, organizing and cutting up, our experience. "But this is not to say", says Devitt, "that we construct the world; it is our experience of the world, not the world itself, that we are imposing on, organizing and cutting up." Devitt adds that "existence-relative-to theory is literally incoherent, and is best taken, like 'imposition on the world', as a metaphor."[6]

Devitt thinks that realism is a basically metaphysical or ontological system, and only secondarily a semantic one. He emphasizes that the ontological issue (of objective reality of the world) should be settled first before we can even take up the semantic and epistemic issues.[7] He further believes that the notion of truth is not primary for realism. And if we got to have a notion of truth, then it can only be that of correspondence. Correspondence truth, in turn, requires reference to the external world, or a referential theory of knowledge.[8] This version of realism is in sharp contrast to the postmodernist theories of duality of scheme and content, indeterminacy of reference, and so on.

Realism starts with the assertion of the objective reality of the world (the furniture of the world); and then goes on to assert that we know the world directly without the mediation of mental objects (e.g. sense data). The most important part of any realist epistemology is its causal theory of reference. This implies correspondence theory of truth which is said to be the only theory that can do justice to a realist ontology. At the same time, Devitt, like other contemparary realists, is fully aware of the problems related with the correspondence theory of truth. That is why, perhaps, he repeatedly asserts that the questions of semantics and epistemology are secondary in a realist scheme of thought.

C.A. Hooker argues in detail how our percepts and basic concepts are theory-neutral or independent. He calls it observational vocabulary or natural language. He points out that a scientist may switch over from one theory to another without any shift in his perceptual experience and commonsense conceptual scheme. The central idea of realism, according to Hooker, is that the knower and the known are related causally. Humans are part of the world and know it through natural interaction. Above all, the realist asserts that there exists a mind-independent reality:

> the independence here must be understood to mean logical independence, not causal independence. The realist can allow very strong causal interactions between mind and reality, for that precisely still involves a reality whose basic character is mind-independent.[9]

Hooker understands realism as a theory which asserts that there are real things and real properties in the world; and even theoretical terms have ultimate (intended) referential status.[10] The basic realist metaphysics, according to him, consists of the following claims:

1. Existence is logically and conceptually independent of epistemic conditions (reality exists independently of knowing).
2. Reality is knowable, and knower and known are related causally and not in any strong constitutive manner.[11]

Hooker claims that if we rid our commonsense knowledge of its explicit and implicit theories, then we are left with a neutral scheme which provides the source of commonsense perceptual experience and which has continued the same for millennia. This elementary conceptual scheme also implies an elementary realist metaphysics. Even when a scientist adopts an entirely different explanatory hypothesis, his perceptual and a large part of his conceptual framework remain unchanged. They consist of certain commonsense concepts and simple general truths, and they belong to what Hooker calls the natural language, or commonsense level of human knowledge.[12]

II.2 This brings us to the second important tenet of realism. It is presented in contrast to the relativist contention of the inscrutaility of reference, argued in the broader context of mutual untranslatability of languages and incommensurability of different conceptual frameworks. As against this, the realist claims that the relativist thesis is made possible due to a confusion regarding the reference of our linguistic terms. They argue that relativists work with a descriptive theory of reference; which leads them to the dualism of scheme and content, and relativism of knowledge and praxis. Instead, the realists argue, we should adopt a causal theory of reference or meaning, which assumes a realist ontology, and leaves relativism of all hues without any justification.

Incommensurability thesis looks feasible when we think that with every theory change, the description of various concepts and their referents also changes, which virtually means a reference change. This reference change would not be acceptable even to the scientists. Instead, the realist argues, if we start with a causal theory of reference, the reference need not change even if its description changes with a change in the particular scientist's theoretical scheme.[13]

Neither incommensurability, nor comparability which is accepted by Thomas Kuhn and others, is possible without a fixing of reference. In every day discourse we presume that our reference is definite and fixed. Referential semantics is almost necessary for a realist world-view. Here even the protagonists of the weaker form of realism, such as Putnam, join hands. According to Putnam, to understand a term is to identify its referent. And when we translate a term we definitely equate the reference. Any comparison between two languages or two theories requires first the equating of two terms and then the identification of their common referent. The common referent in different languages and theories means that it might be interpreted and described differently, but it is not constructed by those different languages.[14]

The realist is also committed to the idea of unity of the world. It may be asked as to how such radically different theories and descriptions of the world can validly describe one and the same world. Hooker here uses the analogy of map and the landscape. We can have a large number of different maps of the same stretch of land; and language is like a complex map.[15]

Devitt contends that scientific theories are convergent. He believes that convergence, along with the correspondence theory of truth, can best explain scientific progress. Convergence thesis is offered as an answer to the radical thesis of incommensurability. It is admitted that neither total convergence of scientific theories, nor a total identification of their subject matter or referent, is possible in practical life. Instead, there is a partial overlapping of reference which makes scientific theories related to each other.[16]

II.3 Analogy of mapping leads to the conception of truth as correspondence. Though it is admitted by almost all realists that realism goes best with correspondence notion of truth, most scholars are half-hearted in supporting it. For example, Devitt has serious reservations about the correspondence notion of truth, though he still does not discard it.

Hooker, on the other hand, boldly accepts the correspondence notion of truth on the lines of Tarski's semantic theory of truth. That is, a given proposition is true if and only if it is the fact of the matter. He believes that a realist epistemology is most in harmony with a realist ontology. He, however, acknowledge that a realist can as well adopt a coherence theory of truth.[17] He adds two semantic realist tenets to the earlier metaphysical ones; they are:

1. Truth consists in an approporiate correspondence relation holding between language and the world.
2. Truth obtains or fails independently of all epistemic acceptance/ rejection criteria.[18]

Like relativists, most contemporary realists are against a foundationalist epistemology as advocated by (logical) positivists. They also accept that there is no direct access to the knowledge - independent world.[19] The rejection of foundationalism implies that the correspondence theory of truth need no longer be considered as integral to a realist philosophy. The realists are generally sympathetic to the notion of correspondence, but do not want to insist on it.

Contemporary realists accept that there cannot be an ultimate verification or justification of any empirical propostion or scientific theory for the simple reason that we cannot compare our theories and beliefs with the world-as-it-is-in-itself. But they are not only convinced of a realist metaphysics or ontology but also of a realist epistemology and semantics. They admit that though the meaning of truth lies in its correspondence with the reality, it is difficult to be sure of this correspondence. The best we can do is to make two additional assertions of fallibilism and coherentism:

(i) Fallibilism - All our theories and beliefs are approximations to truth, and are open to future revision. Even the best scientific theory or the most fundamental assumptions are open to challenging revisions. The realists, however, feel that the fallibilism of our theories does not undermine ontological realism. It also does not mean that we are incapable of knowing the world. They are firm believers in scientific progress and limited convergence of scientific theories. That is, the realist conceives scientific research as cumulative by successive approximations to the truth.

(ii) Scientific theories can be justified not by comparing with the world that is there, but by a complex method of correlated mutual support which is a form of coherentist method of justification. On the other hand, coherence theory of meaning must be supplemented by the correspondence notion of truth. Here realists are making a distinction between accepting a certain theory as true, and the condition for its truth. That is, a given scientific theory is true in the correspondence sense, but we choose it when it coheres well with other relevant theories.[20]

It seems that the realist is not at present willing to take up the task of developing a suitable epistemology. Her main concern is the assertion of a realist ontology, coupled with the assertion that the world is knowable in everyday perceptual knowledge.

We have given the realist theory of science in such detail above even though it does not seem directly relevant for our ethical problem at first glance. But it is relevant since realist philosophers of science have developed their thesis in response to the postmodernist theses of dualism of scheme and content, and the plurality and incommensurability of these schemes. These theses, as we have found in the 4th Chapter, provide support to ethical relativism.

The realist contends that the world and its furniture are real; that we know the world in our (mostly perceptual) knowledge; that our empirical beliefs and scientific theories are all approximations to truth which are open to further revision; and that we are progressing towards more and more reliable knowledge of the world. Above all, reality is prior to thought.

III. Realism and Ethical Discourse

III.1 But what of minds, society and morality? If scientific realism is naturalist, that is, considers human beings as natural phenomena, then the *sui generis* nature of morality seems to be undermined, as was done by earlier positivists. Hooker has even called his kind of realism as anti-anthropocentricism, by which he means that the humans have no privileged status in the scheme of things; and "what is true is not tied logically or conceptually to human cognition (nor to human culture),..."[21]

Does this anti-anthropomorphism make any difference to ethical discourse? It does; and therefore, our problem is whether we can extend empirical realism to moral field; and if yes, how far? That is to say, is adoption of a realist ontology, as advocated by the above writers, going to help us in asserting some more enduring and conceptual schemes - independent status to the objects or referents of moral discourse?

The naturalist realist declares the world, the objects and their properties as real. What does the moral realist say about the objects of moral discourse? Moral realism makes a few related assertions of its own:

(i) Moral statements (or the propositions they express) are approximately true or false.
(ii) The truth or falsity of moral assertions is largely independent of our moral opinions, theories etc.
(iii) Ordinary canons of moral reasoning, together with scientific or factual reasoning, constitute a reliable method of obtaining moral knowledge. And,
(iv) Moral terms, as 'just', 'good', or 'obligatory' usually correspond to real properties or relations.[22]

Contemporary moral realists, like their scientific counterparts, are anti-foundationalist. More important, they subscribe to causal theory of reference.[23] Many philosophers, including Putnam, have suggested that naturalist theories of reference and definition might be extended to moral discourse. Most realists, such as Richard N. Boyd, affirm the concept of moral properties as actual (natural) properties of actions and persons. In the words of Boyd,

> Our ordinary use of moral terms provides us with epistemic access to moral properties. Moral goodness must, to some extent, regulate the use of the word 'good' in moral reasoning.[24]

According to the realist position, moral goodness is a real property of actions, policies, states of affairs and persons; and our moral judgments are often reflections of truth about them.[25] Boyd contends that goodness is an ordinary natural property, and can be observed as any other natural property. He understands goodness in an utilitarian context, and offers a relatively complex theory of homeostatic consequentialism. All it means is that moral goodness is related to basic human needs. 'Good' is what satisfies these needs, and the latter cluster together.[26]

Boyd and other ethical realists are eager to argue that they are not advocating any purely naturalist or reductionist definition of moral terms. They also insist on the objectivity of moral properties. This is best asserted by the causal connection between the use of a term and its referent.[27]

Boyd further contends that in the last analysis there is a general agreement of major normative theories which should suggest that actual features of goodness regulate the use of the term 'good'. Differences in these theories lie in the different weights that are put on different human goods by different theories.[28]

Jonathan Lear argues that the very possibility of a moral way of life presupposes realism and objectivism. If we thought that moral properties are just mental constructs, we would not be able to sincerely talk of 'right and wrong'. "That vocabulary presents itself", says Lear, "not as one of approval or disapproval of local behaviour, but as a universal standard against which diverse behaviour can be measured." He goes on to say that those who accept this implication of moral discourse cannot go on being relativists for whom all norms and values are equally good.[29]

In a famous essay, Gilbert Harman has argued that moral facts are irrelevant for the making or justification of moral judgments.[30] In response, Nicholas L. Sturgeon argues in detail how all moral judgments presuppose objectivity of moral facts and a causal relation between the two (facts and judgments). He approves of Putnam's suggestion that we "apply a generally causal account of reference.... to moral terms."[31] We have to affirm objective moral facts if we want to be true to the nature of moral discourse. For example, Hitler would not have committed a mass scale genocide had he not been a depraved person. There is no other plausible explantion of his actions. Harman has strongly asserted that the assumption that the children are doing something very wrong (while burning the cat) is "totally irrelevant" to any reasonable explanation of the judgment that it is a wrong act. Sturgeon questions in response whether anyone would have made the same judgment (that this action is wrong) had the children been engaged in an entirely different activity. In order for us to be able to say that children's act is not wrong, the act must lack its main feature of deliberate, pointless cruelty. Same is true of our judgment regarding the depravity of Hitler; we would not have made such a judgment had Hitler been an entirely different person. Our adverse judgments on children's act and Hitler's character seem to be directly determined by the moral quality - positive or negative - of the act, or the person. Sturgeon asserts against Harman that moral facts are relevant for both moral and non-moral assertions, such as our judging the children's act as wrong. They are relevant even in explaining such contingent facts, as revolt by the slaves, and so on.[32]

III.2 David O. Brink argues in detail in defence of moral realism:

> moral realism asks us to take moral claims literally, as claims that purport to describe the moral properties of people, action, and institution - properties that obtain independently of our moral theorizing. Moral realism is roughly the view that there are moral facts and true moral claims whose

> existence and nature are independent of our beliefs about what is right and wrong. A moral realist who is not a skeptic holds related epistemological and semantic claims. The moral realist thinks that our moral claims not only purport to but often do state facts and refer to real properties, and that we can and do have at least some true moral beliefs and moral knowledge.[33]

Brink affirms some form of naturalist realism, which means that moral facts and properties are just like any other natural facts and properties. Alternatively, they are constituted by, or supervene upon, natural and social facts. Moral realism, according to Brink, may be taken as a special case of metaphysical realism. The basic claim of moral realism is that,

> There are facts of certain kind that are metaphysically or conceptually independent of the beliefs or propositions which are our evidence that those facts obtain.[34]

Moral realism, therefore, should be understood as the claim that there are moral facts which are independent of our beliefs. Brink gives two tenets of moral realism:

1. There are moral facts or truths; and,
2. These facts or truths are independent of the evidence for them.[35]

According to Brink, two most important opponents of moral realism - noncognitivism and constructivism (relativism) - deny one each of the above two tenets respectively. Against them Brink reiterates the moral realist's position as one according to which,

> moral claims should be construed literally; there are moral facts and true moral propositions, and moral judgments purport to state these facts and express these propositions. Ethics is objective, then, insofar as it concerns matters of fact and insofar as moral claims can be true or false... Not only does ethics concern matters of fact; it concerns facts that hold independently of any one's beliefs about what is right or wrong.[36]

While the first kind of objectivity distinguishes realism from all kinds of non-cognitivism and cognitive relativism; the second kind of objectivity distinguishes it from all kinds of constructivism, ontological relativism, or even nihilism. Brink convincingly argues that moral realism best explains "the point and nature of moral inquiry." Moral discourse is typically assertive or declarative in form. In moral discourse we are continuously using the vocabulary of perception, and cognition; and affirm that our moral judgments are (objectively) true or false, right or wrong. We engage in argument and deliberation which would be pointless if all moral judgments were valid (for the people who make them), or as good as another. And we believe that people are either right or mistaken in their moral beliefs. All of which proves that moral judgments are capable of being true or false. "Cognitivism", claims Brink, "seems to be presupposed by common normative practices of moral judgment, argument and deliberation." He adds that, moral language

> is putatatively fact-stating (because, it is declarative in form) and certainly seems to ascribe moral properties to persons, actions, policies and so forth.[37]

Brink regards noncognitivism of all hues as anti-realist. First, emotivists were wrong because our moral judgments are not necessarily accompanied by, far less the same as expressions of, our feelings. Secondly, reference to moral facts is integral to moral judgments, but non-cognitivism cannot accept moral facts.Similarly, the relativists reject the objective status of the referents of moral judgments. According to him, this would make the entire spectrum of moral judgments logically impossible; e.g. if no actions are objectively wrong, no one can be blamed for them; and no 'ought' can be attached to them.[38] For Brink and other realists, ethical discourse is essentially cognitive; and that implies realist ontology and epistemology :

> we often *recognize* the existence of moral requirements that constrain our conduct in certain ways. And when we are uncertain about moral issues, we often *deliberate* as if there were a right answer to the issue before us.[39]

Thirdly, Brink contends that since the noncognitivists do not recognize objective moral facts which are recognized in moral judgments, they cannot even accept the possibility of mistakes in moral judgments. Moreover,

> Moral argument and deliberation presuppose not only correct answers to moral questions but also answers whose correctness is independent of our moral beliefs.[40]

Brink is strongly opposed to noncognitivism, as, according to him, it cannot explain those moral judgments which have no emotive or prescriptive force. He feels that most moral judgments are made with no intention of influencing the feelings and attitudes of others. He further feels that noncognitivism cannot even explain the prescriptive force of those judgments because the fact that a person recommends or prescribes an action presupposes that he acknowledges that action as right.[41] That is to say, a cognitive element is always present in all moral judgments, even in those which have a prescriptive form. Thus all ethical realists mentioned above insist that not only ethical discourse is essentially cognitive, it implies a realist ontology and epistemology. Boyd, as we have seen above, argues fervently for 'actual' moral properties as referents of moral judgments. He further recommends that naturalistic theories of reference and of definition might be extended to the analysis of moral language.[42]

The realists' assertion of the objective validity of moral judgments on the basis of moral facts comes very close to Moore's understanding of 'good' as a nonnatural property. I agree with both Moore and the neo-realists when they emphasize the objective reference of our moral judgments and a causal relation between them. We call the act of burning the cut an evil act *because* there is something in the nature of the act itself which makes it morally wrong or evil, and not simply because we feel some emotion, sentiment, or attitude towards that act. While in a large number of moral judgments the emotive or attitudinal element may be absent altogether; in others where it is present it presupposes the *cognition* of the act as right or wrong.

III.3 According to the realists, just as commonsense language assumes the objective reality of the world, commonsense discourse about morality assumes the objectivity of moral characteristics or properties, as well as the truth (or falsity) of moral propositions. Commonsense takes it for granted that we 'know' that stealing or violence is wrong, and that promise keeping is right. Renford Bambrough argues that the emotivist is wrong when he identifies the good with what is approved, just as he would be wrong if he equated true with what is believed. According to him,

> Belief cannot be explained without introducing the notion of truth, and approval cannot be explained without introducing the notion of goodness. To believe is (roughly) to hold to be true, and to approve is (equally roughly) to hold to be good.[43]

Bambrough also argues like Brink that the possibility of error or mistake in moral judgments, and later acknowledgment of that mistake, mean that there is a truth of the matter which is rightly or wrongly comprehended by us.[44] These realists seem to be right when they assert that even our approval and disapproval assume that we *know* the referent of our attitudinal responses to be right or wrong, good or bad.

A skeptic would object here that the justification of our moral judgments does not go very far; and soon we reach a point where no rational justification can be given. Realists generally point out that in empirical reasoning the situation is the same. We justify our empirical knowledge on the basis of sense experience; but we cannot justify that sense experiene in a final manner by referring back to the objective reality.

Brink here contends that all this talk of objectivity of moral judgments, and moral facts does not mean an unconditional universalism or absolutism. Right and wrong are contingent matters and will vary with circumstances. Moral facts vary in accordance with changes in morally relevant circumstances. The moral realist, however, insists that moral facts do not vary with changes in people's beliefs and attitudes.[45]

A moral realist who believes that moral beliefs are objectively true or false, must also believe that in any genuine moral dispute any one party alone can be true. Of course, it does not imply that my own point of view alone is true. To the argument that such a belief would lead to intolerance, Brink answers that noncognitivism and relativism have no special commitment to tolerance either. If all viewpoints are equally good or right, even the question of tolerance does not arise.

On the other hand, realism is saved from intolerance because it believes in fallibilism. A fallibilist believes that no viewpoint can be absolutely right. Every view is open to critical evaluation at some later stage. And if a moral realist asserts that he is right in a moral dispute, fallibilism ensures that he is open to criticisms and corrections from others. Brink thinks that a non-cognitivist cannot be even a fallibilist because, according to him, moral judgments are neither true nor false, and therefore there is no question of some beliefs being mistaken, and in need of later corrections.[46]

The greatest worth of moral realism lies in its closeness to commonsense conception of moral judgments as referring to objective qualities (properties) of facts and persons, and the predominance of cognitive element in them. Even if moral judgments carry a strong or weak feeling tone, their usual form is assertive, e.g. "this act is right or wrong"; "that person is good or bad", etc.

Brink and other realists are right when they point out that a large portion of moral discourse is declarative in nature; and the moral language also suggests that moral properties asserted in moral judgments are real and objective. To that extent moral judgments are true or false. Realists are also right when they assert that moral judgments are influenced, and even determined, by the objective but morally relevant factors of the external situation. That is, we would not make the same judgment if the nature of external action or person were entirely different.

They are also right when they insist that though our moral judgments are determined by contexts and situations which may differ or change, they are independent of our moral beliefs and opinions. In other words, moral properties are objectively real, and independent of our beliefs and judgments. The act of burning the cat would be a morally wrong or evil act even if there was no one there to condemn the act; or even if someone like Harman would raise academic objections to our judgment condemning the act. It is not our opinion, belief, or judgment, that makes the act a morally reprehensible one, but it is the very nature of that act that makes it so.

Thus, the most important contribution of moral realism lies in their emphasis on the objectivity (independence from the subject) and the truth claim of moral judgments. The realists mean by objectivity that our moral judgments are not mere outcomes of our approval or disapproval but are independent of our subjective (or societal) attitudes. They also mean that moral facts have a causal relation with our judgments. Moral assertions do not express our affective attitudes but describe objective moral properties. These realists believe that their assertion of objective moral properties of acts and traits of character is not naturalism; nor does it undermine the normative character of ethics. Our moral judgments still remain normative because they are not talking of natural properties but of moral properties. These moral properties have two characteristics - they are consequential or superimposed upon a cluster of natural properties (such as the details of children burning the cat); and they are causally related to our moral judgments, that is, they *make* us pronounce a certain act as right or wrong.

III.4 At the same time, moral relativism is open to several criticisms. First, J.L.Mackie has given an 'argument from queerness' which challenges the idea of objective being of moral properties. According to it, if there were objective ethical values, then they would be very strange or queer entities. Moreover, it would be very difficult to assess the relation between natural features and objective moral qualities. Mackie further says that such objective moral properties can only be apprehended by intuition, and intuition has been suspect in philosophical circles for a long time.[47] It is clear that moral rightness, goodness, or their opposites cannot be some sort of 'non-natural' properties. If we were to acknowledge them as such we would have to first identify the 'faculty' by which we are able to 'know' or 'perceive' these qualities. Secondly, we would have to explain to the relativists how one and the same objecive quality or property elicits so many different (culturally conditioned) judgmental responses.

Thirdly, if the 'objectivity' and 'reality' of moral properties is emphasized too much, it undermines the *sui generis* nature of morality, its normative character, and the role of will therein. These are the three things emphasized by Kant and prescriptivists like Hare. When the realists try to understand moral properties as real and objective, they often take up a naturalist position which seems to reduce the normative character of ethics to a mere descriptive one.

Fourthly, too much emphasis on the objective properties of the act seems to eliminate the distinction, so rightly emphasized by Charles Stevenson, R.M.Hare and others, between descriptive and evaluative judgments. According to these non-cognitivist scholars, the reasons for, or justification of, our beliefs about objective facts are very different from the reasons for, or justification of, our evaluative judgments. While the former appeal to empirical facts, the latter refer to our attitudes.

Hare has emphatically challenged any attempt at reduction of normative judgments to descriptive ones. "No moral system", Hare argues, "whose principles were regarded as purely factual could fulfil its function of regulating our conduct."[48] In other words, moral judgments and imperatives cannot be *entailed* by factual premisses.[49]

Hare takes strong exception to Brink's views. I give below his main arguments against Brink. First, Brink insists that there is no prescriptive force in moral judgments unless they are first thought to be true. Hare argues that there is a large class of prescriptive judgments which make no claim to be true. According to Hare, Brink is not able to do justice to the prescriptive element in moral discourse.[50]

Second, in response to Brink's realism - externalism, Hare reiterates his internalist view of moral judgment and motivation. He contends that it is right to accept that non-moral facts in some way constitute moral rightness or wrongness, but our moral principles (which are chosen by our rational will) determine which non-moral facts are taken as constituting moral properties. He adds that while a prescriptivist can explain the supervenience of moral facts over non-moral ones, a realist cannot, since "nobody has explained how we observe moral facts."

Third, Hare thinks that Brink's position, like that of Rawls, is an intuitionist-coherentist one, and is open to several criticisms. According to him, intuitions alone cannot provide a basis for the assertion and justification of our moral judgments; and we cannot escape the fact that intuitions conflict. He therefore contends that intuitionist level should find its corrective at the level of 'critical thinking.'[51]

Fourth, Hare's main objection against Brink's realism is that it cannot explain the sense of obligation. The externalism of realists means that we recognize the rightness or wrongness of given acts or traits by their proprties which are independent of the perceiver. Hare argues that moral obligations arise due to our recognition of some moral principles as supreme, true, or universal, and a mere perception of the rightness or wrongness of an action cannot obligate us.[52]

It seems to me that the positive assertions of both Brink and Hare are separately true, but their negative claims, i.e. their mutual criticisms, are only partially true. And possibly the two views can be brought closer.

The objectivity of moral judgments and their claim to truth are better emphasized by the realists, whereas their essential normativity and universality are brought out more clearly by the imperativists. Of course, the realists equally recognize the universality of moral assertions, for every such assertion explicitly or implicitly includes the affirmation that this act and all similar acts are right or wrong. Similarly, the imperativists cannot but recognize the 'objectivity' (independence from the subject) of moral judgments if they want to empasize, which they do, the universality thereof.

Most moral assertions include both a reference to 'moral facts' relating to the objective situation, the subject of a particular judgment, and moral principles which serve as standards of our judgment. These principles constitute the normative or prescriptive part of our moral assertions, and explain the sense of obligation which is integral to any normative assertion. Any understanding of moral discourse which exclusively concentrates on any one of the two constituents of moral assertions would not be able to do justice to them.

If we grant the above, we are faced with two philosophical problems. First is the old one which we encounter whenever we discuss Hare's moral philosophy, that is, the relation between the descriptive and the normative parts of a moral assertion. I feel that if we could modify both Hare's and the realists' positions a little, we would be nearer to the nature and intention of moral discourse; and bridge (even if partially) the gulf between description and prescription in a moral assertion. For this we would have to say that moral judgments do refer to, what the realists insist, the moral characteristics of acts, persons etc., and these characteristics are somehow 'consequential', or 'supervenient' upon the non-moral characteristics of the object of the judgment. But, according to a modified version of Hare's position, these moral characteristics or 'moral facts' come to us as already interpreted or mediated by our moral principles. That is, there is no clift between the physical description of the boys' act of burning the cat and its cruelty which is inherent in the very nature of the act. And yet, our judgment of the act as morally wrong is mediated by our moral principle that all acts of needless violence or cruelty are morally wrong.

The second problem related with the above position is regarding the source or locus of moral principles or standards, whether it is the moral subject (either the agent or the appraiser), or the community (of either the agent or the appraiser), as in relativism; or universal reason shared by all humanity, as in Kant. (Hare's position is not very clear on this point.) For me, it is perhaps the most important issue to be tackled in our controversy between relativist and universatist approaches in ethics.

I believe with Kant, Singer, and Hare that universality (or universalizability) is perhaps the most important characteristic of all moral assertions. But I feel that this universalizability can be achieved only if we accept together the two basic theses of the rival groups in ethics, i.e. the imperativists and realists. This brings us to ethical universalism,

IV. Ethical Universalism

IV.1 The foremost philosopher, almost the prophet, of universal morality is, of course, Kant who advocated a morality which is valid for all rational human beings. He sought to provide an ultimate justification of morality, first, by rejecting the relevance of empirical content for universal moral principles; and second, by affirming universal human reason as the source and authority of all moral principles. Marvin Fox observes :

> Kant formulates the supreme principle of morality, arriving at it in what he takes to be purely *a priori* manner. By a categorical imperative... he means a moral command whose force is absolute, which applies equally to all men and in every actual or possible moral situation.[53]

In Kant's own words:

> we must admit that its [morality's] law must be valid not merely for men, but for all *rational creatures generally*, not, merely under certain contingent conditions or with exceptions, but *with absolute necessity*.[54] (original italics)

Kant takes it as self-evident that moral law applies to all rational beings, and that would not have been possible "if they were merely empirical and did not take their origin wholly *a priori* from pure but practical reason."[55] And,

> it is clear that all moral conceptions have their seat and origin comletely *a priori* in the reason,...... that they cannot be obtained by abstraction from any empirical, and therefore merely contingent, knowledge; that it is just this purity of their origin that makes them worthy to serve as our supreme practical principles.[56]

Kant did not know of the contemporary relativism, but it is as if he antcipated it and answered it once for all. That is, if any laws or norms are culturally conditioned, or derived from experience, or history, or anthropology, they do not deserve to be categorized as moral. A mxim of our actions deserves to be called moral only when it conforms to a universal law, and "it is this confority alone that presents the imperative as necessary."[57] The supreme principle of morality or the categorical imperative tells us to act only on that maxim which one can at the same time will that it should become a universal moral law. [58]

By universal law Kant means a law which is applicable to, or valid for, every rational being, and also a law which can have no exceptions. He denies the possibility of exceptions to moral principles by the well-known argument that if the maxim which seeks to justify a particular exception were universalized, it would result in self-contradiction (as in the example of promise breaking). Kant, thus, seems to equate uiversality with necessity and absoluteness. The latter apparently is based on Kant's *a priori* conceptions of morality as obedience to moral law, and of moral law as an expression of universal human reason.

The conception of a person as both noumenal and phenomenal is basic in his ethics. The person, by virtue of its very rationality, is such that its "*existence* has in *itself* an absolute worth, something which being, an *end-in-itself*, could be a source of definite laws,...[59] (original italics) The universality and necessity of moral law both presupposes and implies the autonomy of will (as determined by pure reason) and the dignity of person. The foundation of the categorical imperative lies in the axiomatic truth that "*rational nature exists as an end in itself*." (original italics) Hence the second formulation of the categorical imperative which commands to treat humanity in every person as an end-in-itself, and never as a means.[60]

The will of every rational being is a "universally legislative will". The authority of the universal moral law derives from the fact that its source is the will itself, and that will, in turn, is determined by universal reason. Autonomy or freedom is the property of all rational beings, and reason and freedom are equated, together characterizing the person or moral agent.[61] Reason is in some sense transcendental and the human will or person shares in that transcendental nature.

It seems that while the universality, necessity or absoluteness of the moral imperative are natural or indubitable within the Kantian (metaphysical) system, once his transcendental or metaphysical presuppositions are questioned, the necessity or absoluteness of the moral imperative can no more be upheld. Kant has been persistently criticized on several counts. We would very briefly take up only two of them here. It is argued first, that Kant's categorical imperative is empty or without content, and therefore fails to provide any supreme norm or standard for morality in general. Secondly, Kant's ethics of the categorical imperative allows of no exceptions, and is therefore said to be an absolutist and rigorous doctrine.

Though Kant's categorical imperative does not seem to have a normative content, it is still the fundamental principle which gives the most essential condition or basis for all other normative principles. If it had a positive content, it would be one of a large number of normative principles or maxims, and not their supreme guiding principle. It lays down that any maxim of our actions cannot claim to be moral unless it is at the same time applicable to, or valid for, all rational beings.

The second criticism of Kant's ethical system concerns his alleged rigorism. When Kant calls his categorical imperative absolute, he seems to reject any possibility of exceptions to moral principles or imperatives. He seems to say that the moral law and the maxims based on it are applicable to, or obligatory upon, every human being under all possible circumstances, and can allow of no exceptions. Especially, in his later writings Kant tended to be more rigid and uncompromising in his understanding of the categorical imperative.[62]

M.G. Singer has argued in detail how Kant has interpreted his categorical imperative in such a rigid manner that leaves no scope for considerations of the special circumstances or demands of particular situations. If we take the hackneyed example of the case where lying can save an innocent person's life, it seems only too obvious that exceptions must be granted even in cases of apparently most universal and uncontroversial moral imperatives, such as the rule against lying. According to Singer, the term 'categorical' may mean either as opposed to hypothetical, and as such not dependent upon our purposes and desires; or as unconditional, absolute and exceptionless. He believes that Kant confuses the two senses of the 'categorical' and thus makes an easy transition from the first innocent meaning of the 'categorcal' to the second meaning which is contestable.[63] Singer concludes that Kant's ethical arguments only prove that lying (or making false promises) is generally wrong, and not that it is unconditionally wrong, i.e. wrong in all circumstances.[64]

Though we cannot say with Singer that Kant misunderstood his own conception of the categorical imperative, we have to make a distinction between an absolutist conception of the moral law, and a universalist one. Kant's own ethics can be interpreted in a way so that the universality, and to same extent necessity, of the moral law are affirmed without rejecting the need for making exceptions.

Also, Kant's second and third formulations of the categorical imperative, regarding each person being an end-in-herself and all together forming a kingdom of ends, together give a substantive principle which is fundamental and normative. The idea of every human being as a person who is an end in herself and who can never be made a means of anyone else, when combined with the conception of kingdom of ends, gives us the principle of justice. Justice, along with universality and rationality, seems to be the fundamental guiding principle of all moral imperatives (maxims of actions). No maxim can claim to be moral unless it is fully rational, universal and just. For Kant justice is included or implied in the doctrine of the innate dignity and inviolability of all persons. In its positive version, it asserts the absolute equality of all humans by virtue of their innate rationality; and in its negative version it prohibits the treatment of any person as a means to any other.

A universalist approach to ethics is far more defensible than either a relativist, or an absolutist one. A universalist approach accepts the plurality of values and norms, passionately asserted by the relativists, as not only existentially true but also possibly valid or justified for their respective societies. It, however, insists that all these plural values, norms and institutions should be subject to rational-ethical scrutiny, the standards, and rules of which can be provided only by a cross-cultural or universal point of view.

IV.2 Hare develops Kantian ethical philosophy and modifies it. He agrees with Kant in : (i) conceiving ethical assertions as imperatives; (ii) asserting the essentially universal character of all moral imperatives; and (iii) affirming freedom or autonomy of will as equally essential for the authenticity of ethical imperatives. But while Kant could construct his elaborate ethical system on the foundations of his implicit metaphysical assumptions of the universal reason shared by all human beings, and the freedom or legislating power of the noumenal self, Hare cannot take recourse to such a metaphysics. His self-assumed task of justifying both universality and freedom becomes therefore more difficult, as well as more relevant and interesting. Hare is right when he rejects Kantian metaphysics, though his values and perspective are all through Kantian. Having shed Kantian transcendentalism, Hare further rightly rejects Kantian absolutism, and accepts various possibilities of exceptions to a given moral law. At the same time, he argues that all these exceptions - provided they are justified on relevant grounds - give rise to new moral principles which, in turn, become universal moral rules in their own right.

Hare develops his universalist prescriptivism in contrast to the naturalist-cognitivist theories. He affirms first, that "No imperative conclusion can be validly drawn from a set of premisses which do not contain at least one imperative."[65] Secondly, he rejects the idea that any descriptive assertions can ever function as regulating principles of our conduct.[66] Therefore,

> What is wrong with naturalist theories is that they leave out the prescriptive or commendatory element in value judgement, by seeking to make them derivable from statements of fact.[67]

Facts are less important for Hare, as for Kant, because he is chiefly concerned with universal moral imperatives. These moral imperatives, though universal, become authoritative for the individual agent only when she chooses one of them by an act of decision. Principles and decisions are integrally related. Not only do we choose our principles through our decisions of will, we modify them, or even create new ones according to the demands of the situation.[68] Moral principles are necessarily universal, and a moral judgment necessarily

> commits the speaker to the further proposition that any thing exactly like the subject of first judgement, or like it

> in the relevant respects, possesses the property attributed to it in the first judgment.[69]

While the normative or prescriptive element is more important in ethical assertions, Hare regards the descriptive element or meaning which is concerned with the sense and reference as responsible for the universalization of the moral imperatives. He gives credit to the naturalists for duly recognizing the descriptive element in moral judgments. He calls these two elements in value judgments as two kinds of meaning: descriptive meaning made up of criteria of application, and evaluative meaning made up of its commendatory or prescriptive use.[70] This distinction between two types of meaning bears a close resemblance to Stevenson's distinction between descriptive and evaluative meanings of moral judgments, and faces the same problems.

First, the main problem with Hare's thesis is to specify the relation between the descriptive and evaluative meanings of a moral proposition. If the descriptive element in moral judgments consists of the criteria of application, and commendatory element or meaning of the judgment is entirely different, then it seems that we are left with moral judgment or evaluation which is without any rational ground. Secondly, if the descriptive meaning alone is responsible for the universalizability of moral judgments, it may suggest that the prescriptive element in them is not universalizable; or that moral judgments are both rational and universal due to the descriptive element in them alone. In order to have meaning and validity as a whole there must be a logical connection between the description and evaluation in them. For Hare, they can be connected only through a major premiss which embodies a moral principle. But then this major premiss needs to be integrally connected with the minor premiss or descriptive criteria in order to lead to a universal moral judgment.

Thirdly, there is the problem of justifying or even explaining the moral principles themselves by ascertaining their source, locus and status. As George C. Kerner points out: "The connexion between evaluation and description depends on standards and principles and those, in turn, on decisions."[71] The emphasis on the element of decision comes from Hare's desire to preserve subject's freedom and autonomy in moral life. The prescriptions are not commands from some external authority but are 'chosen' by the subject herself.[72] Hence the internalism of Hare: the reasons or motives of an action come from within oneself. Though Hare is a stout believer in the rationality of morality, he does not explain how the decisions of principles can be defended rationally. He seems to suggest that morality rests on decisions and commitments which either cannot be justified, or do not need any justification. The emphasis on human freedom gives the suggestion that we can create our own moral principles.[73]

While deciding on (creating?) any moral principle the subject might well insist that her principle is universalizable, that is, everyone else must act on that principle. But what if the subject's principle is against those of others? How can she insist that others must act upon her principle? Otherwise also, the principle of A would be heteronomous or external to B,C,D; and following that principle would mean undermining their freedom and contradicting the internalist conception of ethics, as propounded by Hare. That means each one of us would have to choose, decide (or 'create') her own moral principle(s). But this is pure relativism, and Hare never intended it.

Hare's thesis is really very complex, but his universalizability principle is very important for us. If *ex hypothesi* moral judgments are necessarily those which can be universalized, then universality of morality, at least of fundamental moral principles, would be vindicated. As Hare puts it :

> What the thesis does forbid us to do is to make different moral judgements about actions which we admit to be exactly or relevantly similar.[74]

As Hare presents it, if universalizability is a necessary or logical requirement of all moral judgments, ethical relativism becomes self-contradictory. Universalizability of moral judgments assumes the commitment to deliver the same judgment in all relevantly similar circumstances. It means that of the two acts which are exactly similar in all relevant aspects, one cannot be right and the other wrong.

It is quite possible that the two acts, though they appear similar, are actually quite different due to the different cultural contexts. That is why the phrase 'similar in all relevant aspects' is important.

Let us take up the hackneyed example of particide. It has been argued that the meanings of the act are different in different cultures; and therefore while the act of patricide would be wrong in developed societies, it would be right in societies with different conditions and concepts. But the thesis of universalizability makes this view implausible. The two acts of patricide are similar in all relevant aspects. Though local conditions may be different, they are not relevant in the sense that they cannot justify patricide. It is the nature of the act which is relevant here, and not cultural concepts. The latter are relevant for fixing blame upon or exempting someone from it for the act, but they cannot determine the rightness or wrongness of the act.

Hare contends that universality does not mean generality. A moral principle or moral judgment must be such that it can be applied to different but relevantly similar cases, i.e. it must be universalizable. But it need not be general. The assertion of the universality (universalizability) of moral judgments does not imply absolutism, or a rejection of exceptions of a given moral rule. Hare asserts the need of modification of an already established moral rule when confronted with a case of exception to it. This modification is brought about by incorporating the exception into the moral rule, thus creating a new modified moral rule which equally claims universal applicability.[75] That is, moral principles and rules can be very specific, and yet universalizable. However, for Hare, universalizable moral principles are not objective in the realist sense, but are rather created in an act of rational freedom.[76]

IV.3 Singer's explication of uniersalizability principle is simpler and hence somewhat more convincing. According to him,

> The generalization principle must be understood in the sense that what is right for one person must be right for every *relevantly* similar person in *relevantly* similar circumstances. An important or relevant difference is one that "can be stated as a *reasonable ground* for difference of treatment (Sidgwick)."[77] (original italics)

Singer adds, "the criteria for "all similar cases" are contained in the "general grounds" or reasons on the basis of which an act is, or is said to be, right or wrong."[78] In other words, "What is right for one person cannot be wrong for another, unless there is some relevant difference in their natures or circumstances."[79]

If we apply the above idea to our example, the act of partricide is wrong on two counts the taking of life, and the close relationship between the victim and the agent of the act - (which makes it even more reprehensible). These are the general grounds or reasons on the basis of which the act is wrong. And these general grounds are common in any two acts of patricide which may occur in ancient Rome or in the distant world of Eskimos. An act's rightness or wrongness is decided on 'general grounds', or the reasons in terms of which the act is right or wrong. In our example, if the act is wrong because of taking of life, then the class of persons to which the judgment 'patricide is wrong' is applicable, is exactly the entire class of persons who have ever perpetrated the act, or intend to do it.

Singer quotes Henry Sidgwick frequently in support of his generalization principle. Sidgwick seems to be the first philosopher, other than Kant, who has so clearly visualized the significance of the concept of universality in moral judgments. According to Sidgwick,

> even when a moral judgment relates primarily to some particular action we commonly regard it as applicable to any other action belonging to a certain definable class; so that the moral truth apprehended is implicitly conceived to be intrinsically universal, though particular in our first apprehension of it.[80]

It means that every judgment is intrinsically universal, or involves a generalization. Singer here equates universality with generality.[81] The generality in mral judgments helps in their justification and substantiation by reasoning. He calls it the generalization principle, and,

> The generalization principle is involved in or presupposed by every genuine moral judgment, for it is an essential part

> of the meaning of such distinctively moral terms as "right", "wrong", and "ought", in their distinctively moral senses. It is also an essential feature of moral reasoning, for it is presupposed in every attempt to give a reason for a moral judgment. It thus determines what can count as a moral reason.[82]

Moral reasoning can proceed in different ways; but any moral judgment must include the reasons for it. Singer contends rightly that a reason necessarily makes a claim to objectivity, that is, a reason is independent of the person who so regards it. For us, it would mean that the reasons that are offered for justifying or condmning an act in a particular culture need not force us to a relativistic position that an act is right or wrong if it is so regarded in that culture. The person or culture that makes the judgment is not relevant, because every moral judgment, in order to be one, must be objective and universalizable. Especially, the reasons that are given for justifying the judgment have to be objective and universal. He further contends that a person who asserts that an act is wrong but is unable to give reasons for his judgment is simply expressing his approval or disapproval of the act, and not expressing a moral judgment.[83]

Singer also develops what he calls generalization argument. It says that "If the consequences of everyone's doing X would be undesirable, then no one ought to do X."[84] Generalization argument, like the original principle, is applicable only to similar persons in similar circumstances. Without going into details, let us apply the generalization argument to our example of particide. The moment we ask "Wha if everyone acted in this manner (killing off one's parents)?" we would find it impossible to endorse any single act of particide, whatever the local circumstances or cultural conceptions of the perpetrator of the act.

Hare and Singer seem to have given formal (logical) conditions of making a moral jdgment. Hare frankly says that his universalizability thesis is neutral as to normative theories.[85] Since Singer has brought in consequences, his thesis of generaization no longer remains neutral and fully formal. Yet the generalization principle - not argument- remains a formal condition for him.

Singer distinguishes moral principles from the generalization principle. Like the latter the former are universal, and hold in all circumstances, and generally allow of no exceptions; but they are not formal as they have content. He cites his generalization argument as one of the substantive universal moral principles.

Generalization principle, according to Singer, provides the standard or criterion for all moral principles. For example, it would endorse the principle that says that if everyone does not have the right to act in a certain way, then no one has the right to act in that way without a reason.[86] The phrase 'without a reason' implies that moral principles cannot be unconditional in the Kantian sense. There can always be exceptions to the moral principles or rules. These exceptions can be granted with reference to the circumstances. For example, the rule against lying is universalizable (generalizable) but also admits of exceptions, such as lying may be permissible in order to save the life of someone, or even to avoid unnecessary suffering to others. Alternatively, exception to a moral rule or principle can be admitted only in deference to some higher rule or principle. Exception to a rule against lying is accepted only when speaking the truth violates a 'higher', more basic, or preferred rule regarding the sanctity of life, or rule against causing (unnecessary) pain to others. In our example, there is no such higher rule which can be appealed to for accepting the patricide committed by Eskimos and some other preliterate tribes as an exception to the moral rule regarding the sanctity of human life.

We noted earlier that Hare has contended that the moral principles which are universalizable need not be general, and can be very specific. A moral principle in this case would include all possible exceptions, or rules specifying reasons for those exceptions. Moreover, from time to time we would be modifying the given moral principles in order to accommodate new cases. Singer, on the other hand, regards the moral principles as general, and by this he means that a moral principle is generally applicable in all similar cases, but also admits of exceptions. But those exceptions do not modify the original principle; that is, we are not constantly 'creating' our moral principles. Rather, they are accepted as objectively true, or independent of this or that person's beliefs and attitudes. In admitting an exception, we are not adding a sub-clause for some known rule, or creating a modified rule, but rather simply saying that the particular rule does not apply in the given case, due to special circumstances; or that there is another more basic principle which overrides the earlier one.

Herein lies the difference between absolutism and universalism which was perhaps not so well appreciated by Kant. Morality, not only at the commonsense level but also at the critical level, admits of pluralism of circumstances, and even that of moral principles. It also admits of exceptions to a moral rule. If we do not allow these exceptions, morality would become authoritative, dogmatic and extremely limiting. There would be no scope left for conceiving and practising morality as a practical discipline which is developed in response to practical situations and their demands. Perhaps no moral principle can be applied to any given case without taking into consideration the context of the case. Acknowledging this, however, does not mean rejecting the thesis of universality of basic moral principles.

V. Are Realism and Universalism Complementary?

V.1 Realism asserts that the referents of moral judgments are moral properties of acts and persons, and these properties are objective in the sense that they exist independently of all our opinions and norms. The realist thesis does justice to our understanding of moral judgments as declarative.

This view is however open to two major objections : First, its assumption of moral properties in a typically naturalistic language seems dogmatic and untrue to actual facts. That is, we can never identify 'good' 'bad' 'right' and 'wrong' as properties 'out there', in addition to other natural properties. I think the relation between natural and moral properties is best described as that of supervenience, as suggested by G.E. Moore, W. D. Ross and Hare. When certain natural properties exist together, the act or character to which they belong also possesses a moral property of being good or bad, right or wrong. This moral property is a resultant of, or supervenient upon, the cluster of natural properties. An act of burning the cat is morally wrong *because* its inherent quality is cruelty and getting pleasure out of giving unnecessary pain to others; and both these natural properties result in, or imply, the moral property of the act being an evil one.

Here we need not suppose that the moral property is something in addition to natural properties actually existing out there. The contention that a whole can have more than its parts can be readily understood in everyday life, and has been supported by philosophers. When the realists say that moral properties are objective, they do not mean that they exist as other objects of the world; but only that moral quality of an act or a person inheres in that act or person and is not a creation of the subject of judgment (appraiser). By the objectivity of moral judgments and their referents, moral realists simply mean that our moral beliefs, approval, or disapproval, of various acts and persons do not create those moral properties. As contended by Ross long back, "Rightness is always a resultant attribute, an attribute that an act has because it has another attribute."[87]

Of course, Ross believed that these moral attributes are recognizable by intuitive insight. But even if we have discarded the faculty psychology, there still seems to be no reason why we cannot speak of 'perceiving' or recognizing something directly without the mediation of our conceptual framework or reason. Ross rejected reason as the source of our knowledge of right and good, or their opposites, as he believed that we do not deduct the rightness, or otherwise of an act from some more basic principle, but rather 'perceive' it directly. There is some truth in this. When we see the children burning the cat we are horrified and pronounce the act as evil, which suggests a 'cognition' of the evil character of the action. We hardly refer to some universal principle and then go on developing a syllogistic argument and a conclusion from it. Even the archetypal relativist, Harman recognizes the intuitive character of our moral judgments or cognitions:

> You can observe someone do something, but can you ever perceive the rightness or wrongness of what he does? If you round a corner and see a group of young hoodlums pour gasoline on a cat and ignite it, you do not need to

> *conclude* that what they are doing is wrong; you do not need to figure anything out; you can *see* that it is wrong.[88] (original italics)

He, however, contends that while in scientific experiments one has to make assumptions about certain physical facts, no such assumption about moral facts is needed in order to explain the occurrence of the "so-called moral observations." That is, our observation or contention that the cited act is morally wrong or evil has nothing to do with the actual facts having a moral quality of being wrong or evil. But how to explain his own phrase "you can *see* that it is wrong". The seeing is possible only when there is something to be seen, some objective facts out there. In perceiving an act with moral overtones we 'perceive' the physical details, as well as its moral quality, call it intuition, reason, or whatever. There is no other mysterious faculty but the mind which 'perceives' or 'intuits' rational ideas, moral facts, and the states of other minds.

The contention of Harman and other relativists that observations are theory-laden may be true. Some of us are more sensitive to the suffering of animals and some less so, and possibly our metaphysical or religious beliefs play a role here. But almost all persons - to whatever culture and conceptual framework they might belong - who chance upon the above mentioned scene would be both horrified by it, and declare it as morally wrong. Academicians are further fond of citing the hypothetical example of skinning a child alive. There could hardly be any person on earth who would not declare such an act as absolutely evil.

Our perception of the good or evil character of an act is not a deduction from any primary moral principles; nor is it theory-laden; rather it is a perception of objective 'moral facts' which is comparable to the perception of physical facts. The quality or nature of our cognition or perception of the rightness or wrongness of an act is such that it is best explained by the assumption of 'moral facts'. Even this assumption is not a part of the initial perception/ cognition / intuition of the moral quality of some act, or trait of character. It is needed only for *a posteriori* explanation. Harman further contends that,

> The fact that you made a particular moral observation when you did does not seem to be evidence about moral facts, only evidence about you and your moral sensibility.[89]

This expresses only partial truth; such moral observations do require a minimum of moral sensibility. But had there been no objective moral facts our moral judgments would have been an example of mistaken beliefs or want of proper moral sensibilities. In spite of what Harman says, moral facts do explain or justify moral observations or judgments. If there were no moral facts, we would as well pronounce an act of kindness as wrong or evil, and an act of cruelty as right. Moral facts also make it possible to assert that moral propositions are right or wrong, true or false. Our moral vocabulary does contain these terms, and we routinely talk of our moral judgments ('observations' for Harman) as right or wrong.

Thus, moral realism asserts that the objectivity of moral properties (moral facts) is implied in most moral discourse. The ontological status of these moral properties is problematic. Some moral realists want to give a real and objective status to moral properties; and Mackie's argument against 'queerness' holds against any such proposition. That is to say, we cannot rationally conceive moral properties as existing 'out there', just as the physical properties do. But such an actual existence is not required by moral discourse, because otherwise moral properties would be reduced to physical or natural properties.

Moral properties are comparable to aesthetic qualities. A thing- a flower or a painting - is beautiful not simply because the perceiver calls it so. There is something inherent in the object itself - its colours, its proportion or harmony - which makes it beautiful. A piece of music is melodious, not because the listener regards it so, but because its very constitution, its combination of various *svaras* (notes) is melodious. Now, both beauty and melody are not properties which exist separately from their constituents, and yet at the same time they have a nature and worth of their own. The latter is a resultant quality of the combination of natural factors of colours and sounds.

Similarly, an act is morally right because it is an act of helping out the needy, an act of kindness; and its moral rightness is a resultant quality of the whole nature of that act. Another act is evil, and its moral quality does not exist out there as a separate quality other than the nature of that act, but is supervenient on it. It is the quality that the act as a whole possesses, and so is neither reducible to the natural facts of the case, nor is it something that exists out there over and above the natural facts.

I can see no objection to moral realism as presented here. It makes ethical relativism reasonably impossible. The act of burning the cat is an evil act, and whether the people of any given culture condemn or endorse it does not make a bit of difference to the moral fact that it is an evil act. Same is true of medieval Hindu practice of *sati* (self-immolation of widows). No amount of religious and sociological beliefs, or the so-called conceptual framework can make that practice valid for medieval Hindus and deserving our tolerance; it was an evil practice, and that is all. Here the claim of moral qualities for independent, objective being is even stronger than that of aesthetic qualities. The latter are more intimately related to the tastes and capacities of the subject (viewer/listener); but the moral qualities claim to be totally independent of the experiences, beliefs, and norms of the appraiser. It means that the act of burning the cat, or any similar act is wrong or evil in every culture and under all circumstances. It is so because it is an inherently cruel act, and cruelty is morally wrong. No elaborate cross-cultural criterion is required for declaring cruelty as evil. It is still more wrong when it is perpetrated on hapless beings like young children or animals.

To a certain extent the idea of universalizability is integral to that of objectivity. Realism implicitly asserts that if a certain act is right or wrong because of its inherent properties (i.e. properties which are independent of the beliefs and emotions of any person), then any act which is similar to it in all relevant aspects would be similarly right or wrong. The objectivity of moral properties presents an important counter to ethical relativism.

Moral discourse, both at the commonsense and the critical levels, also assumes the objectivity of moral principles. Realism does not only advocate objectivity of moral principles in the sense of intersubjectivity, but also in the sense of moral principles being right or true whether anyone believes in it or not.

V.2 It is true nevertheless that realism pays much less attention to moral principles than to individual acts. Kant and Hare, on the other hand, emphasize moral principles, and conceive morality in terms of universal imperatives. But other than these, there is a large class of normative judgments (e.g. "Hitler was an evil person"; "the act of burning a cat is wrong or even evil" etc.) which are not apparently prescriptive.

We are not always conscious of any moral prohibitions or prescriptions when we offer a moral judgment. While some moral judgments which relate to acts against which there are well recognized rules may carry an implicit reference to the relevant prescriptions (e.g. "A did wrong in cheating or breaking his promise."), others may not. The judgment condemning practices of slavery or *sati* need not contain a prescription against them. When I assert that *sati* is an evil practice, I am not at the same time prescribing for myself that I must not assist the practice; there is so little chance of my doing so.[90] When I praise Mother Teresa for her philanthropic work, I do not necessarily thereby prescribe that I must also do exactly that. Take another example, Bertrand Russel opposed world wars, especially the policy of conscription, even through being old, he himself was beyond the purview of the law of conscription.

The greatest problem, however, is the authority or source of the moral principles or prescriptions. If it is the individual will, as Hare seems to imply, then other persons have no obligation to act upon those principles, in spite of all claims of universality on the part of the moral agent. Kant was saved from this dilemma by taking recourse to an elaborate metaphysics of kingdom of ends, and so on. But Hare simply says that each act is a matter of decision of principle, through which we also change or modify the earlier maxim. To say that we accept exceptions to a moral principle is one thing, and to say that we modify older principles, or create new principles is quite another. If we were to accept this position, it may open the doors to all kinds of new (amoral) principles which individuals can 'create' out of their decisions.

The metaethical or metaphysical status of moral principles is difficult to determine. It seems that the demands for the objectivity and universality of moral principles precludes the view that they are the creation of individual wills. Of course, Hare does not say this; he simply says that we choose our moral principles in an act of decision.[92] But the universality and objectivity of moral principles seems to be jeopardized by the idea that we (freely) choose our principles. In the final analysis, for Hare, the way of life we want to adopt, and the principles we want to follow are a matter of individual decision.

It seems that the individual decision refers to the 'choice' of the principle to be applied in a certain situation; and that choice is not the source of that principle. While the way of life we choose to adopt may (or may not) be a matter of individual decision, moral principles are not so (excepting in the Kantian metaphysical framework). Whatever principle or whatever modified form of the original principle we decide upon in a given situation, it can still be asked whether the principle we have 'chosen' or decided upon, or the modifications we have included in the original principle, are 'correct' or 'true' from the moral point of view; or are 'appropriate' for that situation.

At the same time, Hare understands prescriptions in terms of 'ought'. But the 'ought' or obligatoriness of a moral prescription or principle implies both universality and objectivity or subject-independence. Again, Kant could reconcile the obligatoriness of the categorical imperative with the autonomy of the will, since its source is universal reason as embodied in the rational person belonging to the kingdom of ends. But if the individual subject is a part of the phenomenal world, a historical being, then the 'ought' of his moral principles cannot have its source in the autonomous will of the moral agent.

On the other hand, realism tries to preserve the objectivity of moral principles which can do better justice to the sense of 'ought'. According to it the moral principles would be true or valid, even if no one affirmed them. It means that if the objectivism of realism is reconciled to the universal prescriptivism of Kant and Hare we can have both universality and objectivity.

CHAPTER 6

The Moral Point of View

I. Overridingness

So far I have mostly concentrated on the issue of relativism versus universalism in morality. Having first given the relativist perspective, as developed in both modern and postmodern Western thought in my 1st and 2nd Chapters, I have sought to critically evaluate them in my 3rd and 4th Chapters. Then in my 5th Chapter I have given a general account of two non-relativistic trends in contemporary Western thought, that is, realism and universalism.

In the present Chapter my aim would be to develop the idea of a universal moral point of view which does not negate or even undermine separate moralities, but which still claims to have an overriding authority over them, that is, which has cross-cultural validity. Having *presumed* this, I shall try to understand and explicate the nature of this moral point of view.

When the relativists contend that a people's morality is relative to their culture and its conceptual framework, the crucial concept of morality is deliberately left undefined by them. The ambiguity in the conception of morality helps them in clubbing together all kinds of beliefs, practices, mores, customs, taboos and norms as morality; and thereby overemphasizing their immense diversity.

What is morality, and what is its extension? The idea that morality covers the whole of life has a natural appeal at first glance. But this broad understanding of morality involves a big confusion between customs, norms and rules of interpersonal behavior in a particular society on one hand and morality proper on the other. If Westerners take off their hats and Indians cover their heads to show respect, this has nothing to do with morality. Not only customs associated with different occasions but also patterns of customary behaviour are different from society to society (e.g. Indian bride is dressed in red, heavily bejewelled and is expected to act subdued and coy, as against her Western counterpart who is dressed in white and is vivacious and bubbling). These patterns of behavior are naturally related to, or conditioned by, the system of moral norms and values of that society. And yet, there is every need to make a distinction between these customary norms and patterns of behaviour which are totally culture-specific, and morality proper. Failure to make this distinction results first, in undermining the normative or regulative character of morality, and second, in encouraging relativistic arguments which cash in on this confusion.[1]

If having described the various practices and ways of a different society, an anthropologist or sociologist goes on to assert that these different 'patterns of life' are deserving equal respect etc., she is guilty of two confusions. First, she is confusing morality proper with the culture-specific norms and patterns of behaviour etc. And second, she is declaring all of them as valid for that particular society and immune from rational criticism.

A large number of social practices, role models, and patterns of interrelationships are totally culture-specific and relative; they are also in most cases beyond rational criticism or an evaluation from a moral point of view, that is, they are morally neutral. At the same time, no social practice, norm, or pattern of behaviour is beyond the purview of critical evaluation from the moral point of view. Neither the practice of untouchability in India, nor that of slavery in the West, was a moral institution. But they could still be evaluated from the moral point of view, and found immoral or wrong.

I am here trying to put two counter-theses to the relativist thesis based primarily on cultural diversity. First, not all social norms and patterns of behaviour are morality proper. And it means that any observation regarding their relative character can have no bearing on the relativity or otherwise of morality. Second, while many of these social practices are morally neutral, many others are not so, and should be judged or evaluated from the moral point of view. Rather, all social practices are potentially objects of moral evaluation. The latter observation strengthens the first, that morality should be necessarily distinguished from social customs and practices as a normative discipline which claims to guide, regulate, and critically evaluate all our activities.

Arguably, the claim to overridingness on the part of the moral point of view requires rational justification. Kurt Baier has tried to present the moral point of view which is at once universal and applicable in the context of a particular society. Baier recognizes that morality can be conceived and practised only in the social context, because society, its institutions and rules are necessary for the realization of all human goals. Each society further develops primary and secondary moral rules to regulate interpersonal behaviour. Above all, these moral rules are applicable to everyone and are for the good of everyone alike. Moral rules have overriding authority over reasons of self-interest because they are expected to produce a state of affairs which serves everyone's interest much better than if everyone pursued her interest exclusively. The moral point of view is that of everyone and anyone, and hence is superior to the point of view of individual interests:

> The very *raison d'etre* of a morality is to yield reasons which overrule the reasons of self-interest in those cases when everyone's following self-interest would be harmful to everyone. Hence moral reasons are superior to all others.[2]

I am afraid that Baier is here not able to give a rational justification for the moral point of view, except the egoistic argument that it is in the interest of everyone alike to follow the moral rules. He is also not able to do justice to the other-oriented nature of morality.

R.B. Perry similarly understands morality in terms of its social function. He defines morality as "man's endeavour to harmonize conflicting interests : to prevent conflict when it threatens, to remove conflict when it occurs." Unlike Baier and Rawls, Perry believes that the interests of totality, being more inclusive, are superior to those of separate individuals.[3] This is a utilitarian position; but Perry is saved from the inconsistencies of the former by understanding the interests of the whole in terms of harmony, rather than as maximization of satisfactions.

For both Baier and Perry, however, self-interest remains the main motive of moral conduct; and moral imperatives, indirectly at least, are reduced to rules of expediency. If morality could be justified only on the ground that following moral rules is in everyone's self-interest through creating societal conditions which are conducive to the harmonious realization of everyone's (separate) goals, then the normative and overriding character of morality would remain unjustified. Moreover, such views still fail to answer the question, "Why should I be moral?" Arguably, a person can realize all her goals through immoral means in a well-ordered society where everyone else follows the moral rules.

Significantly, the idea of overridingness is included in the Indian conception of morality. The term unanimously used for morality in various Indian religio-cultural traditions is *dharma*. *Dharma* is a nebulous concept and means several things, but above all, it means duty and/or virtue. The latter two concepts are mostly used interchangeably, the idea being that duty performed without a virtuous frame of mind cannot have moral worth.

The Vedic-Dharmaśātric tradition expresses a very positive spirit of world-and-life-affirmation, which recognizes *artha* (prosperity) and *kāma* (pleasure) as legitimate goals of human life. At the same time, it affirms *dharma* (morality or righteousness) as the supreme regulating authority, or the supreme normative principle of conduct which must regulate or govern all other pursuits of life. *Dharma*, *artha* and *kāma* were together known as the *trivarga* or the three goals of human life (*puruṣārthas*); and *mokṣa* or liberation was added to them only later on. Significantly, *dharma* or righteousness was given first place in any enumeration of the goals or values of life, thus proclaiming the supremacy or overriding character of *dharma*. In other words, the pursuit of all other goals of life should be governed by the principles of *dharma* or morality.[4] Even the pursuit of the supreme religious goal of life - *mokṣa* or *nirvāṇa* (liberation)- was declared by one school of thought as illegitimate unless that person had discharged all his sociomoral obligations first.[5]

But why should I follow the dictates of *dharma* at all? The answer is, you should do so, because there is a witness to all your acts and motives, call it God, soul, or conscience.[6] The conception of *dharma* is integrally related to that of debt (*ṛṇa*). A person is said to owe his/her life to various sections of the society, eg. to parents and teachers, to fellow human beings, as also to the tradition; and finally to the entire creation. Since the moral subject owes debts to so many persons and nature, he/she is expected to lead his/her life in such a way that all these debts are paid fully in the process.[7]

This conception of morality includes : first, the idea of every person being integrally related to the society and the entire creation; and second, the idea of morality or *dharma* as the supreme regulating principle of human life, both at the personal and interpersonal levels. At the social level *dharma* was the principle of harmony between various sections of society, and was declared as the basis of the social order.[8] Whether at the individual or the social level, the overriding claim of *dharma* as the supreme regulating principle of all aspects and activities of human beings was emphasized at every stage.

The conception of morality, *dharma*, or the moral point of view implies the idea of some supreme regulating principle(s). Various sociological phenomena can be understood from different points of view, as anthropological, sociological, historical, psychological and moral. The moral point of view may be conceived as one of the several points of view; or as one which claims the right to offer the supreme criteria of judgment over and above all other points of view.

The assertion of a distinct (universal) moral point of view means that it has superior authority than the customs, mores and other sociological aspects of human life. It also means that it is some unique or rationally superior point of view which can in no way be equated to the diverse moral codes or moralities. When we talk of 'moralities', which talk is right from an anthropological-sociological point of view, we are taking a naturalistic position. When we talk of the moral point of view, we are not denying the existence, value and even limited validity, of separate moralities which are suited or integral to different societies and their ways of life. We are rather affirming the moral point of view in addition to all these moralities, and contending that the latter are subject to critical evaluation from the moral point of view. We are asserting the supreme authority and the universal or cross-cultural validity of the moral point of view.[9]

The moral point of view is at once different from other points of view which are concerned with other areas of human activity, such as science, sociology, art and religion, as well as from separate moralities. It makes an overriding claim. Art and literature, and even religion to a certain extent, are culture-specific; so are all other human sciences, as sociology, economics and history, as also socio-political ideologies. They are the products of their times, and are relative to their respective cultures, and conceptual frameworks. They cannot, therefore, claim universal validity. Also, these points of view or perspectives conflict with each other even within a given culture.

The same is true of separate moralities. They are culture-specific and have limited validity, as the relativists so candidly admit. The moral code of your society is not applicable to, or valid in, my society. And the code of my society leaves all other human beings, except those belonging to my society, untouched. These moral codes or moralities are further supposed to be extremely diverse, contradictory, or incommensurable.

The moral point of view claims to be overriding; that is, when an action, character trait, practice, or state of affairs is being considered from different points of view, and the evaluations from them come out divergent and heterogeneous, then the evaluation from, and the demands of, the moral point of view have the highest authority which can under certain circumstances override the claims of other points of view, as well as of separate moral codes.[10]

This overriding claim of morality is liable to be challenged by religion (excepting perhaps contemporary Protestant Christianity). Semitic religions which are based on distinct historical 'revelations' claim their respective revelations as the supreme arbiter or determiner of all aspects of human life. If religion is 'the ultimate concern of man' (Paul Tillich), it cannot allow itself to be judged or sanctioned from the moral point of view. It is, of course, being taken for granted here that religion can never sanction immoral activities, and insofar as it does (as in fanatic acts) it is open to criticism from the moral point of view. But when religions claim to determine the entire personal and interpersonal lives of their followers, there is bound to be a conflict between the claims of two points of view -moral and religious. Various practices, enjoined, allowed, or prohibited, by various religious texts, such as untouchability in Hinduism and practices of polygamy and instant divorce in Islam, are open to criticism from the moral point of view, if they contradict our sense of justice, the dignity of the individual, or some other humanitarian considerations. Take another example: the refusal for blood transfusion to save a human life by Seventh Day Adventists is totally unacceptable from a moral point of view. None of these practices can claim immunity to criticism from the moral point of view simply because it is prohibited or permitted in a particular religion.

Of course, the highly secularized Western societies do not need any convincing regarding the superiority of the moral point of view to the religious point of view. But Islam, Hinduism, and to some extent Catholic Christianity, persist in their separate claims to provide norms and rules which have superior or overriding authority in all fields of human life.

The problem of the relative superiority of moral and religious points of view is too profound and complex to take it up here. I would, however, refer the readers to my views, presented elsewhere, regarding the need to distinguish the essential from the peripheral matters of a religion.[11] I believe that while the essence or faith of any religion is above all critical evaluation, including the one from the moral point of view, the peripheral beliefs, laws, taboos, and practices sanctioned by different religions are open to critical-moral evaluation and sanction. All the practices referred to above are peripheral to their respective religions - so I believe- and can therefore be challenged from a rational-moral point of view.

I am assuming here : First, no amount of relativistic reasoning can make such practices which undermine justice and other humanitarian considerations immune to sanction from the moral point of view, even though they have all the support of some religious tradition, or the other. Secondly, any criticism of religious practices is possible only from the 'moral point of view', and not from the points of view of various moralities.

Generally speaking, we can say that the moral point of view's claim to overridingness, or what is the same, the right to judge the beliefs, activities and values of other fields of life is quite sustainable. Morality probably is not the highest activity, or goal of human life, and so possibly cannot judge other human goals or values. But it still remains the supreme judge to decide which beliefs, activities, norms and values are morally and rationally justified; which are not; and which are morally neutral, and can be pursued provided they do not conflict with fundamental moral imperatives.

II. Objectivity and Universality

II.1 The overriding claim of the moral point of view is based on, or follows from, the essentially rational nature thereof. The moral point of view, as I am trying to develop it here, is that of universal morality, as distinct from separate moralities. As such, it has to be rational, objective and universal, that is, it cannot represent or embody any particular culture-specific conceptual framework and must have (or try to achieve) cross-cultural validity. This presupposes its rational, objective and universal nature and approach.

The moral point of view has to be rational in order to be an acceptable judge over separate mores and moralities. While customs and mores, as well as human approbation or disapprobation, are contingent and local, reason alone can claim to have certain universality. R.M. Hare rightly calls morals a rational activity which consists in the search for moral principles, and the testing of them against particular cases.[12]

According to Kurt Baier, the best course of action from the moral point of view would be "the course of action which is supported by the best of reasons." Rationality or a critical approach to the conventional rules of conduct is regarded as the chief criterion of morality by Baier :

> We could not properly speak of *morality*, as opposed to a system of conventions, customs, or laws, unless the question of the correctness or incorrectness, truth or falsity, of the

> rules prevalent in a community is asked, unless, in other words, the prevalent rules are subjected to certain tests.[13]

Baier questions the practice of anthropologists and sociologists of listing various divergent beliefs and practices of different peoples; and contends that such practices can at best establish that these types of conduct are *believed* to be right or wrong in their respective societies. But this cannot even prove that those types of conduct are right or wrong in those particular societies. This can far less prove that they are right or wrong from the moral point of view.[14]

Not only the relativists, even other thinkers like Toulmin have asserted that whatever is prescribed in the moral code of a community *is* right for its members. Baier criticizes this view by saying that such persons ignore the crucial question - "Is what the morality of that group forbids really wrong?" Or, "Are the moral convictions of that group true?"[15] He contends that the mere fact that certain norms or rules of conduct are included in the moral code of a society cannot be taken as a guarantee or proof that those norms or rules are genuinely moral. Any given moral rule or conviction may be either right or wrong, true or false. And their truth or falsity can be decided only on the basis of critical scrutiny[16]

Baier further believes that while the concrete moral rules which constitute a given moral code are developed in the context of concrete or historically developed institutional demands of a particular society, and are therefore naturally culture-specific, the standards or principles with reference to which they are to be critically or rationally evaluated must be universal, or having cross-cultural validity. In other words, morality proper, as against separate moral codes, is a rational discipline. And as such, it is not tied or limited to a particular culture or conceptual framework but claims to have universal authority. That authority comes from its rational character.[17]

By the rationality of the moral point of view we mean : first, that our moral judgments and even imperatives have a strong cognitive element; and second, that we can give reasons for them.

Even our moral approvals and disapprovals have a rational element in that we are willing to give reasons for our emotional attitudes. Suppose we make a moral judgment that a particular act of willful cruelty is wrong or an evil act, and then we appeal to a moral principle "Do not hurt others", in support of our judgment, we are indulging in a rational activity. We can give reasons for our adverse judgment against an act of cruelty, such as that it is morally wrong because it violates the principle of the sanctity of all life; or undermines the bond that unites the agent with all human beings or the entire creation. Or, we can simply say that it hurts the victim as much as it would have hurt the perpetrator of violence; and so on. By rationality of a point of view is simply meant that reasons can be given for all our assertions.[18]

II.2 The claim to rationality presupposes certain objectivity in our moral judgments. We have discussed this issue in the previous Chapter.

Very briefly, rationality and universality of moral judgments imply their being true or false, and that in turn implies their objectivity. By the objectivity of moral judgments we simply mean that our moral beliefs, values and judgments, and above all, our sense of 'ought' are not mere products of our approvals or disapprovals, or attitudes; nor are they fully determined by different cultures' divergent conceptual frameworks. As a contingent fact, this may be so, that is, our moral judgments may seem to accrue from our attitudes, which latter may seem to be derived from our society's traditional norms and conceptual framework. But when the question of truth, validity or correctness of moral judgments, norms, or moral principles arises, or when we undertake to justify our moral assertions, we simply cannot go back to those attitudes and/or conceptual frameworks for their rational justification. As far as moral approval, disapproval, and any other sentiment or attitude are concerned, we can be pretty sure that they are not the source, far less the justification or authority, of moral laws, imperatives or judgments.

There is a cognitive element not only in moral judgments, but also implicitly in moral laws or imperatives. Especially, moral judgments imply an assertion of some positive or negative moral quality in its object (some act or character trait). This is a typically realistic position which may not be acceptable to other ethicists. It seems quite justified to me, provided we do not get entangled in any realist ontology regarding moral qualities. As understood by me, it simply says that some basic moral principles and judgments based on them are not determined by our culture-specific moral code but are objectively right or true. When we pass a moral judgment that the act of burning the cat is a wrong or evil act, we do so because we 'perceive' that act or trait to be so. Whatever our attitude towards animals, and whatever our conceptual framework, the act of burning the cat has a 'causal' relation to our judgments, that is, our moral judgment is 'determined' in some way by the nature of the act.

The idea of objectivity need not mean any ontological status for the objects (goodness or badness of acts or character traits) of our judgments. It simply means that they are not the products of our sentiments, or attitudes, or even our conceptual frameworks; and their normative value, truth, or validity are independent of all these sentiments, attitudes and concepts. It is the subject-independence of the moral judgment or imperative that is mainly implied by the objectivity of moral assertions. Again, it is not to deny that our moral judgments are conditioned by what Hans Georg Gadamer calls 'prejudices', as well as by the conceptual framework and the moral code of the subject's society. But a moral assertion (it may or may not be a part of the moral code of the society), in order to claim its superiority to other points of view, must be supra-personal, or independent of the subject or society who is making that judgment.[19]

Moral assertions assume that the rightness or wrongness of a particular act, or class of acts is not a matter of subject's attitudes, or conceptual framework, but in some way inheres in the act itself.[20] That is, if I pronounce the burning of a cat by children, or skinning a child alive (the examples are taken from the usual works on the subject) as evil acts, it is not because I feel a disapproval towards those acts; nor is it because my moral code prohibits such acts; but *because* I *see* that this act, and all acts of this kind are morally wrong or evil.

Jocl J. Kupperman presents a strong case for his thesis that ethical assertions are largely cognitive. He argues first, that the commonsense language in moral discourse is cognitive, that is, consistently speaks of the moral subject as 'knowing' that a certain act is right or wrong. Secondly, the correctness or truth of moral judgments is independent of its acceptance or rejection by the moral subject, appraiser, or any society. Moral assertions, like any other cognitive assertions, have a truth claim which cannot be sustained if they were conceived in a relativistic manner.[21] The limited validity of moral claims to a particular society asserted by the relativists is not satisfying from the moral point of view.

A moral imperative such as "Do not hurt others" (*ahiszmsa* in Indian religions) claims universal validity. This claim implies objectivity, that is, independence from the moral rules and imperatives of separate subjects and moral codes. Our moral judgments refer to both the qualities or characteristics of their objects (acts or character traits) and the appraiser's choice or decision of some moral principle as applicable (or suited) to a particular situation. This choice or preference of some moral principle would, however, be arbitrary or unjustified if it were not rooted in, or supported by, the demands of the practical situation (e.g. when speaking the truth would endanger the life of an innocent person).

Moral terms are like the A words of P.H. Nowell-Smith which "indicate that an object has certain properties which are apt to arouse a certain emotion or range of emotions."[22] Let us substitute the phrase 'the choice or decision of moral principles' for "certain emotion or range of emotions", and we get what I have been trying to argue. That is, moral terms and judgments refer to some characteristics of their objects which are judged by us as 'good-making' or 'bad-making' characteristics. Our decision as to whether those particular characteristics are 'good-making' or 'bad-making' in turn, is determined by our moral principle(s). According to W.D.Ross, the terms 'good' and 'right' are resultant or consequential properties.[23] That is, an act is right, or wrong; and a character trait is good or bad, because it has certain other natural characteristics.

Baier calls the features of the empirical situation, act, or character trait 'considerations', and our moral principles 'consideration - making beliefs'. He explains the latter in a propositional form, according to which any moral principle, such as 'stealing is wrong', "is a reason (a moral one) against doing it." That is, in any moral reasoning we can cite both facts and moral principles, former as considerations in our judgments and the latter as consideration-making beliefs which give us reasons for our judgments and decisions.[24]

As we shall see in our next section, in order to avoid lapsing into mere tautology, universalizability is always explained by ethicists as applicability of a moral judgment to all relevantly similar cases, or to all relevantly similar persons in relevantly similar circumstances. This reference to relevant similarity suggests both the need to take into consideration the objective circumstances and demands of the situation, and the need to understand the similarity of any two cases with reference to moral principles. Only those objective characteristics are to be accepted as similar which are morally relevant, and this, in turn, requires a careful consideration of the objective situation, and the (subject-independent) nature of the object of moral judgment.

The same idea is expressed by the understanding of moral property of an act or character trait as being consequential or supervenient upon certain objective characteristics of that act or person. An act or character trait is right or good if it responds well to the demands of the objective situation, and conforms to a well-established universal moral principle. The objective validity of our moral judgments means that their object or referent has certain objective (subject - independent) characteristics; and that those characteristics are found by us as 'good-making', or 'bad-making' with reference to some moral principle. The latter is not arbitrarily chosen, but is intimately related to the demands of the objective situation. Furthermore, the moral principle that is appealed to in our moral judgment is a universal one, and its universality can be attested to by rational argument.

II.3 Perhaps the most important characteristic of the moral point of view is that it can only be universal, that is, it necessarily claims universal validity. Kant's moral philosophy is the paradigm of universal ethics. His categorical imperative, "Act only on that maxim which thou canst at the same time will that it should become a universal law" provides perhaps the most important and necessary condition of (universal) morality, or the moral point of view. In other words, only those maxims can be truly moral which can be followed by all humankind in different cultures and times, and even under all possible circumstances. While the relativist says that no moral rule can have any validity beyond the limited confines of one's group, Kant says that no rule or action can be moral unless it is such that it is applicable to the entire humankind, irrespective of their different cultures, moral codes and ways of life. If a person has promised, then it is her duty to keep the promise, period, and the fact that she lives in contemporary Western society or in some preliterate one does not make the slightest difference. Nor is the fact that promise keeping or speaking the truth can only be done under certain circumstances at greatest cost (even that of some one's life) is relevant for Kant. The only thing that counts is that it is the moral law that one should speak the truth, or keep one's promise, and that moral law is binding on all rational human beings.[25]

Arguably, a carefully formulated universalism is a much more defensible philosophic position than Kant's normative absolutism. The idea of the categorical imperative or any universal moral principle becomes more acceptable if the absoluteness of the categorical imperative is substituted by its applicability to the entire humankind under 'relevantly similar' circumstances.

As we have seen, R.M. Hare and M.G. Singer have opted for a universalist approach to morality, as against the absolutist one of Kant. Both acknowledge the need for exceptions to universal moral rules. While Hare contends that we modify an already well-recognized moral rule in order to accommodate a need for exception[26] Singer says that in such situations we prefer some other moral rule to the one that is apparently applicable to the given situation.[27]

Whether it is the same rule that is being modified, or it is another rule that is being substituted for the earlier one in accordance with the needs of the situation, two things are clear : First, some cases must be acknowledged as exceptions to the original moral rule. And second, the modified or the preferred rule must be as universal in its application as the original one. The acknowledgment of the need of exceptions does not undermine the universality of moral principles and judgments. The conception of relevance becomes crucial here. How do we decide which aspects of an act or a person are morally relevant ? Relevance is not an absolute term; it is rather relevance to a particular argument, judgment, decision, or relevance for our purpose, here relevance from the moral point of view. If so, then the aspect of the act or the agent which should be relevant to determine the class of acts or persons to which a given moral principle or a moral judgment applies could only be a moral one. The identification of the members of the appropriate class to which our moral principle applies presupposes a moral standard which helps us in finding the class of acts or character traits to which that principle applies. When we describe an act of killing as 'murder' we say something more than giving a mere physical description of the events resulting in the death of someone.

Hare affirms that, in order for a moral judgment to be universal, direct reference to some universal moral principle or standard which has application to all other similar cases is required. He has somewhat weakened his position by emphasizing the distinction between the descriptive and normative meanings of moral assertions or imperatives.[28] However, reference to some moral principle is inherent in any morally relevant description, or descriptive criteria.

When we talk of universalizability in the moral context we mean something more than the mere universalizability of all rational judgments; and the criteria that is adopted in order to define the class of relevant acts or persons includes both a certain description of the act and a moral standard or principle. In order to argue for the universalizability of moral judgments we must bring forward not some morally neutral description of the act or character trait, but a morally relevant one. That is, a moral judgment is universalizable, as it is applicable to all such cases which are judged as right or wrong by an appeal to some moral standard. As J.M. Brennan says,

> Thus, when we want to judge like cases alike we are not looking for some morally neutral similarity between them, but for a similarity in accordance with certain standards of justification.[29]

This is very clearly stated by Singer. Having explained the generalization principles in terms of relevantly similar persons in relevantly similar circumstances, he explains the concept of 'relevance' by asserting that, "the criteria of all similar cases are contained in the general grounds or reasons on the basis of which an act is, or is said to be, right or wrong."[30]

D.H.Monro gives a sensible piece of argument. According to him, to say that the terms, yellow, good etc., are universalizable is merely to mean that if something is yellow or good, then something else with similar relevant characteristics is also yellow or good. It would be different from saying that if something is yellow or good to you or me, it *is necessarily* yellow or good to everyone else.[31] First assertion refers to moral properties, or rather, to the referents of such terms as right or good; and the universalizability of such judgments which appeal to some descriptive (even implicitly evaluative) criteria is easy to accept. But the second assertion refers to moral principles. It asserts that if a moral principle is applicable to a certain person, it is necessarily applicable to all persons under relevantly similar circumstances. And 'relevantly' similar circumstances are decided on the basis of some universal, rational principle which gives us grounds or reasons for our identification of relevantly similar cases. In other words, moral discourse is above all "about standards which we apply in appraising the object of our commendation, praise or approval."[32] And these standards have to be universal in order to constitute the moral point of view.

Though concrete moral judgments cannot be applied to all human beings without reference to the relevant difference between them; in another sense, all rational beings are potential objects of moral imperatives or judgments. As Kant said, a moral rule is applicable to all rational beings who are capable of acting on them. According to Bernard Gert, "a basic moral rule is one that concerns actions open to all rational persons in all societies at all times.[33] He adds that,

> a moral rule cannot be limited to any group smaller than this class [of all rational persons]. If a rule applies to any group smaller than the class of all rational persons it is not a moral rule."[34]

Theoretically, every moral rule is applicable to every rational human being, that is, every rational being is a potential subject to whom all relevant moral rules are applicable. The class of persons to which a moral rule applies is a sub-class of all rational persons. This class would be defined by the nature of the particular act they are contemplating, or undertaking to do. For example, the rule against injury to living beings is potentially applicable to all human beings; it becomes more stringently applicable if someone undertakes an act prohibited by that rule.

Several other ethical philosophers have emphasized that universalizability is integral to all moral rules and judgments. To quote W.T. Stace,

> What do we *mean* by a universal morality ? We do *not* mean a moral principle which is, as a matter of empirical fact, believed and accepted by all men. We mean a moral principle which is *applicable* to all men in the sense that even if they do not accept it, they ought to do so. What we have to show is that the same moral obligation in reality falls upon all men. We do not have to show that all men know what this obligation is, or there is among them any agreement about the matter. We have to show that what really *is* right is the same for all men. We do not have to show that what men *think* right is everywhere the same.
>
> For even if it were the case that not a single moral opinion could be found upon which all men were in agreement, it might still be true that there *is* some principle which is in reality binding upon all men in the sense that they *ought* to accept it and act upon it.[35] (original italics)

Stace is contending here that the same morality is applicable to all human beings, irrespective of all conventional differences. Applicability suggests an 'ought' on the part of humankind regarding some basic moral principles and obligations. The need here is to make a distinction between what people think as right, and what *is* morally right. Though what people think and practice as right may be quite divergernt, there still remains a strong case for saying that what *really is* right or moral is the same for all.[36]

According to Brennan, moral judgments necessarily make a universal claim. This is a claim on the judgment of others that they should agree with our judgment, provided we are sure that we have reached our conclusions through the application of appropriate moral standards and reasoning. If a person makes a certain moral judgment, but adds that others are free to arrive at their own judgments which may be contrary to the one arrived at by our subject, then it would mean that the person herself is not sure of the validity of her own judgment.[37]

A universalist ethical thinker distinguishes between moral 'truth' or universally valid moral norms or principles and local changing moral norms. Granting that moral rules of conduct are local and variable, a universalist hopes to find norms and principles which are sufficiently permanent and universal, though not absolute or infallible; and which can be taken as standards to judge and evaluate the more variable elements in morality.

The idea of the universalizability of moral judgments is related both to the idea of rationality of moral assertions, and to their claim to objectivity, or some kind of truth.[38] To say that "killing is wrong" is to utter a universal moral principle. Its claim to universality cannot be sustained except by arguing (i) that it is a rational moral principle; and (ii) that it is in some way rooted in the matter of the case. In other words, the above three characteristics of morality, i.e. rationality, objectivity and universality, are integrally related and are mutually supported or justified. And it is because the moral point of view is all three, that is, is rational, objective and universal, that it can claim overriding authority over all other points of view (the latter includes perspectives belonging to different fields of human knowledge and activity, as well as different moral codes). These four characteristics of the moral point of view hang together, or are closely related; though there is no necessity about their interrelationship.

III. Impartiality and Reversibility

III.1 An important characteristic of the moral point of view is impartiality. It is integrally related to the principle of universalizability. Generally, impartiality is conceived as applying the moral rule to all relevant acts or persons without making exceptions in favor of anyone, especially oneself. Impartiality can be conceived on a narrower or wider canvas. It can be explained in terms of the class of persons towards whom the subject is impartial, and the rule or criterion which the subject is trying to apply. On the other hand, impartiality can be conceived on a universal scale. Then the class of persons towards whom one is expected to be impartial consists of all present and future rational beings. The main idea of impartiality is that it should be irrelevant for making a judgment as to who would benefit or lose from the making of our judgment, decision, or act. It also means that no exception can be allowed in favour of some particular person which is not at the same time allowed to all relevantly similar persons. In the words of Baier,

> The supreme principle of the application of moral rules is that in the absence of morally relevant differences between people, moral rules must be applied to everyone alike.[39] And,
>
> since from the point of view of morality, all are to be regarded equally, we would expect that the rules should *affect everyone alike*.[40] (original italics.)

Impartiality means nondiscrimination, that is,

> the principle that all rules *qua* moral apply to everyone alike. That is to say, a moral rule must not discriminate between people, i.e. differentiate between them on morally irrelevant grounds.... The system of these grounds of differentiation rests on the principle of equality, that to begin with all other things being equal, i.e. unless there are some specific grounds

for differentiation, all moral rules must, therefore, be equally applied to all.[41]

This idea is developed in an elaborate hypothesis by Rawls. He imagines an original state in which there is no laws or authority. The individuals in the original state are rational persons who want to legislate laws to create a just social order. But in order that they do not create laws which are beneficial to this or that person, or group, Rawls hypothesizes that they are under the veil of ignorance which hides from them all contingent circumstances regarding their relative places in the society, their capacities and needs. He believes that in such a position no one will be able to "tailor principles for his advantage", for the simple reason that no one knows what his empirical circumstances will be.[42] Actually what Rawls has done is to strip his rational persons of all individuality. Such disembodied persons, having no interests of their own, are expected to be capable of reaching an agreement as to the socio-moral laws which should govern a harmonious and stable society.

Rawls has been criticized for supposedly conceiving his rational human beings as self-centred or selfish beings competing for limited natural resources. That is more or less how Hobbes conceived the original human condition. Hence the need of the veil of ignorance which hides the empirical circumstances from the rational persons while contemplating ideal moral laws.

Whether the critics' interpretation of Rawls' views is correct or not, it seems obvious that true (moral) impartiality cannot be achieved if the moral agent or rational person has no knowledge of her own interests. Impartiality need not be, cannot be, ensured by a forced veil of ignorance. Both moral knowledge and praxis demand real moral agents with real desires, goals, capacities and weaknesses, deciding and acting in the context of real life situations. The veil of ignorance makes impartiality almost mechanical. Real impartiality which would be a moral virtue, as well as a necessary condition of moral judgments, is more profound and difficult to achieve. From the moral point of view, impartiality is the attitude of a person who knows who would benefit and who would not from her decision, or act, and yet sets aside all these considerations while applying a moral principle or norm to a given case.

The first two formulations of Kant's categorical imperative express the virtue of impartiality. A moral maxim cannot be applied universally unless the empirical circumstances of all individuals are first set aside as irrelevant, and that is what impartiality means. Impartiality also means that all rational persons are regarded as equal in the sense that no person can be treated as a means of the realization of the goals or interests of another person,

The concept of impartiality is integral to the very ideas of moral judgment, evaluation, law, norm and imperative. A moral judgment must apply the relevant moral principle to all relevantly similar persons and acts absolutely impartially. A moral imperative must be applicable to all (potential) moral agents impartially. Impartiality means the rejection of any exceptions, unless strictly based on rational considerations of relevance; as also universality (universal applicability) of basic moral principles; above all, impartiality means an assertion of fundamental equality of all human beings.

The value of impartiality has been well recognized in Indian thought, especially in the context of jurisprudence.[43] But generally its context and conception are quite different from those of Western moral discourse, and it is often conceived not in the moral context *per se* but in that of religio-spiritual quest.[44] Such conceptions do not easily fit in a discourse, such as ours, which is largely carried out in the Western conceptual framework.

III.2 Reversibility is another very important constitutive characteristic of the moral point of view. Reversibility, according to Baier, means that "the behavior in question must be acceptable to a person whether he is at the "giving" or "receiving" end of it." While other tests, such as universalizability, rationality, assessment of consequences and conformity to moral code, may be somewhat doubtful, reversibility is the surest test of rightness or wrongness of a certain mode of conduct. Nonreversible behaviour is "wrong-in-itself" irrespective of individual or social recognition, irrespective of the consequences it has.[45]

Hare first suggested the idea of reversibility as a test of universalizable behaviour. In order to assess the universalizability and moral correctness of a principle, we have only to imagine a hypothetical case which is precisely similar to the case being considered in all relevant aspects, except for the fact that the roles of the people involved are reversed. Here Hare gives the long argument about the person who wants to put his debtor in prison. Such a person should be asked whether she would still endorse the policy of putting all debtors into prison if she herself was the debtor who could be put into prison. It is expected that when confronted with this reverse possibility, a normal person would back out of her unjust position, though a fanatic may still persist in her original assertion.[46]

It is perhaps to avoid any such complications that Rawls has put the hypothesis of the veil of ignorance. Rawl's rational persons do not know whether they would be in a position of the debtor or the financier. But somehow the veil of ignorance makes the rational persons so impersonal or almost disembodied that the actual idea of reversibility loses its experiential basis, and hence its strong appeal. Let us suppose that a person who is willfully torturing another is confronted with the possibility that some day he/she may be in the position of the person being tortured. The immediate confrontation of the possibility of being tortured some day not only horrifies any normal person, but it also brings the realization of the intensely unjust and cruel character of the act of torturing or inflicting any injury on another person, or any living being. This ensures the subject's adopting a just, moral, or even a compassionate point of view.

P.F. Strawson's version of the condition of reversibility is quite convincing. He calls the rules of morality, or the moral code of a society as some form of "socially sanctioned demands on its members." But such social demands on the members get their legitimacy only when they are such that the demands on each person or group are balanced by the demands on others on the former's behalf. He locates the essence of morality or a moral point of view in the reciprocal acknowledgment of rights and duties." He contends that "a demand made on an individual is to be regarded as a moral demand only if it belongs to a system of demands which includes demands made on others in his interest."[47] Strawson has sometimes been labelled as a relativist. In fact, he emphatically affirms that there is,

> something genuinely universal in morality: the necessary acceptance of reciprocity of claim. And one way in which a demand made on one individual in the interest of others can be balanced by a demand made on others in his interest is through the operation of a general rule or principle having application to all alike.[48]

He accepts that it does not follow that all moral claims have universal applicability, or that the system of moral demands is identical in different societies. And yet, there is a core of universal moral principles in every system of moral demands or moral code:

> What is universally demanded of the members of a moral community is something like the abstract virtue of justice: a man should not insist on a particular claim while refusing to acknowledge any reciprocal claim.[49]

The idea of reversibility is perhaps absent in ancient Greek thought; but it is quite clearly affirmed in Indian thought, though therein it is presented in a form which is different from the clearly articulated idea of reversibility. The Golden rule, recognized in all religions and cultures as the most fundamental guiding principle of all morality, expresses this very idea of reversibility when it says : "Treat others as you would like them to treat you." Or, "Do not do unto others what you would not like to be done to you."

Golden rule is the idea of reversibility stated in the form of a direct and noncontroversial proposition which tells us that all moral behaviour is implicitly reversible. It tells us to imaginatively exchange the place with the other, that is, to recognize that there is no one more privileged than others in the field of morality, and the roles can be reversed any time. Therefore it asks us to treat others as we would like to be treated ourselves by them.

It has been often argued that the Golden rule appeals to the lowest motive of morality, that is, self-interest. Or, that it presumes that self-love is our only motive, or we love ourselves the most, so that we could be moral only when we treat others as we would like to be treated. It is also said that the morality of the Golden rule being based on self-love belongs to a lower level of morality, and is superseded by other-based or socio-centric morality.

This is an entirely mistaken conception of the Golden rule. It definitely does not treat self-love as the only motive of morality. "Treat others as you would like to be treated yourself," is not an appeal to self-love but a suggestion to understand morality in an existential or experiential context. Hare's position is nearer that of the Golden rule rather than Rawl's. Hare asks the subject to imaginatively conceive herself in the position of the 'other', or the object (victim) of her (mal)treatment. How would she feel if she were in the position of the object of (unjust) treatment? He expects that confronted by this imaginary possibility, the agent of unjust, harsh, or cruel treatment would refrain from it. It is not so because the agent loves herself most (which may well be the case), but because existential or experiential confrontation with the position of the object (or victim) of the unpleasant treatment meted out by the subject makes her realize the true meaning or nature of her act. A person who is torturing another or contemplating murder would realize the immorality or unjustfiability of her behaviour, when told by the Golden rule that one must not treat another in a way in which one would not like to be treated oneself.

While reversibility, as conceived by Hare and Rawls, is mostly a negative conception, the Golden rule is stated both in negative and positive forms. The maxim "Do not treat others in a way you would not like to be treated yourself" resembles Hare's position, and only asks us to refrain from morally wrong or unjust actions; while its correlate "Treat others as you would like to be treated yourself" presents the same idea of reversibility in a positive form. In this it goes beyond both Hare and Rawls and implicitly enjoins upon us the duties of kindness, compassion and helping others. When it reminds us that when in need we would like others to help us, and adds that we should treat others similarly, i.e. help them etc., it is not appealing to our self-love, but is rather helping us to found our morality on an experiential basis. The idea, "I would like to be treated (or not treated) in this way," is not an expression of self-love or egoism, but is just a sensible appeal to human nature and its needs. It also implies that any moral principle cannot be developed and sustained by purely formal reasoning but needs a basis in human nature. It rightly presumes that human beings can feel pleasure or pain and other desires and needs only in themselves and not in others. It also recognizes that abstract recognition of one's duties towards others cannot motivate a person in the way in which a sensitive personal realization of their suffering or needs can motivate her. And since we cannot experience pleasures or pains of others, the best that we can do is to imaginatively identify ourselves with them, and realize that they feel pleasure, pain and other needs as we do, and that they want to be treated justly and kindly as we naturally do.

To understand others on the analogy of oneself is not an expression of self-love or ego-centricity. Rather, it means transcending the empirical distinctions between oneself and others and affirming the fundamental affinity, if not unity, of all selves or persons. Regarding and treating others as oneself means expanding the limits of one's self (ego) to embrace the entire humanity, and in the Indian context, entire living beings. It makes no distinction between our own interests and those of others, our own self and others. Where is the place for any self-love here ?

Perhaps the above interpretation of the Golden rule is an idealized one. Yet perhaps it was conceived and interpreted through the centuries in two different ways - one that simply relied on human beings' self-love, and the other that asked them to transcend the limits of 'I' and 'thou' and treat all human beings absolutely equally. The latter version is idealistic as it takes morality to a higher level; and also as it implies an idealistic or spiritualistic version of the basic affinity, or even unity of all selves.

My understanding of the idea of reversibility and interpretation of the Golden rule are largely influenced by Indian thought. Reversibility is understood in ancient Indian texts, not as a tentative hypothetical exercise but, as something more fundamental, and as integrally related to the idea of ontological unity or affinity of all living beings.

Christ's injunction to "love thy neighbour as thyself" presumes the basic affinity of all human beings (though not all living creatures) as children of one Father; and so, loving one's neighbour, the 'other', as oneself means transcending the demands of self-love, and not being motivated by it.[50]

IV. Equality and Justice

IV.1 The idea of reversibility brings in the idea of basic or inherent equality of all human beings. While universalizability emphasizes the similarity of and affinity between human beings, so that a moral law can be applicable to all rational human beings; the idea of reversibility translates that similarity or affinity into complete equality.

The idea of equality of all human beings *qua* humans was not favoured by most ancient Greek thinkers, except Stoics, and medieval feudal European societies which clearly opted for a hierarchical social order. Not only Plato starts with the natural differences and inequality of different groups of humans, his famous discussion of justice justifies a hierarchical social order. Certain aspects of Christian creed (e.g. the doctrine of predetermination) go against any possible assertion of the inherent equality of all human beings, which would have been natural if it had sufficiently emphasized Christ's assertion regarding all humans being the children of one Divine Father, and so on.

In India, while certain relatively esoteric groups emphatically asserted the Divine Being's immanence in all creation, or one Self being the self of all, the predominant Dharmaśāstric tradition strongly supported the hierarchy of classes (*varṇas*) and castes, and even conceived justice as apportioning of punishment relative to the castes of the perpetrator and the victim. Perhaps the factual inequality of different human beings, and their hierarchy according to their abilities, social status etc. were accepted as natural, and hence justified by the ancient and medieval societies.

The Renaissance first brought in the idea of humanism which found a stronger support in the Enlightenment thought. J. Rousseau and John Locke separately advocated the basic equality of all human beings. For both, as well as for Thomas Paine and other protagonists of French and American revolutions, the idea of basic equality of all human beings was integrally related to the idea of natural law, and the rights of humans as per that natural law. Locke asserted:

> And reason, which is that law, teaches all mankind who will but consult it that, being all equal and independent, no one ought to harm another in his life, health, liberty,

> or possessions.... And being furnished with like faculties sharing all in one community of nature there cannot be supposed only such subordination among us that may authorize us to destroy one another, as if we were made for one another's uses, as the inferior ranks of creatures are for ours.[51]

Locke sensibly qualifies his statement as referring, not to unconditional equality, since men differ as to "age or virtue", but, to "the equal right that every man hath to his natural freedom." The natural equality of men should be the basis of their equal socio-political rights. For the first time in the history of Western thought, Locke, Paine and Bayle advocated the right of freedom of conscience and the idea of religious toleration. It was the assertion of the individual's right to think and act for herself. For Locke, the equality of all persons is based on their supposedly essential or inherent nature which they share between them. He asserted the equality of all human beings not only regarding their basic rights (to life, liberty and property) but also regarding their capacities and general nature. The declaration of human rights by the pioneers of American and French revolutions assumes that the equality and dignity of human beings is not merely an ideal or a normative principle but is a factual assertion. That is, not only all humans ought to be treated equally, they are equal according to the law of nature. When Rousseau declares, "Men are born free but everywhere they are in chains", he assumes the *natural* equality of all humans; and contends that the existing inequalities are due to the society's unjust institutions which need to be changed.

However, a glance at the natural differences between the capacities, inclinations and achievements of different persons makes it clear that equality of all human beings can only be a normative principle and not an empirical or factual statement; whereas for some ancient Indian and Enlightenment thinkers it seems to have been both. For the moral point of view, the assertion of the equality of human beings *qua* humans is a normative assertion, and the affirmation or denial of their natural equality does not make much difference to the normative rule that they *ought* to be, or are entitled to be, treated equally in spite of all contingent differences.

From the moral point of view, all human beings possess a dignity and inviolability in view of their essentially rational nature. I am here referring to Kant's second formulation of the categorical imperative - "So act as to treat humanity whether in thine own person, or in that of any other, in every case as an end withal, never as a means only." This imperative is derived from what for Kant is an exiomatic truth, that "rational nature exists as an end in itself."[52] Add to it, Kant's assertion of the autonomy of will; and his third formulation of the categorical imperative regarding all rational beings together forming a kingdom of ends; and there emerges a categorical assertion of the equality, dignity, autonomy and inviolability of all persons *qua* rational beings. His universalism-absolutism is derived from this intuitive and axiomatically conceived truth regarding the essential rational nature of all persons.[53] His categorical imperative prohibits that any person can ever be made a means for the realization of the ends of any other person. This rejects in one sweep all attempts at coercion and exploitation.

Kant's conception of the person is somewhat metaphysical; the rational nature of the moral agent, the autonomy of self-legislating will, the supreme value of the absolute good will, are not argued by Kant but are accepted as axiomatic truths. None of these assertions is acceptable to those contemporary philosophers who are not directly influenced by Kant. However, the equality, dignity and inviolability of human person can be asserted at the normative level without presupposing Kantian metaphysics. As contended by Thomas K. Abbott, the second formulation of the categorical imperative is a purely normative principle which affirms "the duty to recognize the dignity of every man, to pay homage before the absolute and ultimate worth of every human personality."[54] And this as such can be affirmed without any metaphysical commitments.

Recognition and respect for the dignity of every person can be asserted on the basis of *a priori* acknowledgement of the rational nature of man, or the autonomy of the will but it can also be asserted as a normative principle which is essential or basic for all morality. Being *ex hypothesi* fundamental or basic to all morality, such a normative principle does not need any rational justification.

The same idea is expressed in the utilitarian principle - "Everyone is to count for one, and no one is to count for more than one." It is the basic liberal principle according to which, each individual person has a natural worth, dignity, or inviolability simply by virtue of her being a human person. Those contemporary thinkers for whom the terms 'essence', or 'basic', or even 'natural' are an anathema still need not reject the normative principle of the dignity and inviolability of all human persons. (Of course, while it is natural from a liberal point of view, it becomes problematic from a communitarian point of view. We shall briefly discuss the issue in the next Chapter.) From the moral point of view, as I am trying to develop it here, the idea of 'person' necessarily includes equality, dignity, and inviolability. Each person is an end-in-herself; and no one can claim greater worth for herself, or exempt herself from the applicability of universal moral law.

Absolute equality of all human persons, *qua* human beings, is the central theme of Rawls also:

> Each member of society is thought to have an inviolability founded on justice, or as some say, on natural right, which even the welfare of everyone else cannot override.[55]

The conceptions of impartiality and reversibility are integrally related in Indian (both orthodox and heterodox) thought with the belief in the unconditional equality of all living beings. (Indian thought does not make any distinction between humans and other living beings.) Apparently, equality of all living beings is not a normative assertion for Indians, but is understood as a factual one, or a truth which transcends all empirical inequalities. Equality, in turn, is derived from the religio-philosophical faith in the immanence of one Divine being or Self (*Atman*) in all. There has been no attempt to develop these ideas separately at the moral level. Even though these ideas are developed in a different conceptual framework in Indian thought, they deserve greater attention, as the conceptualization of these ideas therein is very positive, highly moral and idealized (spiritual). (We would have occasion to discuss Indian conception briefly in our next Chapter.)

IV.2 Justice is another substantive principle of our proposed universal morality, or the moral point of view. Justice presupposes the normative equality of all human beings as regards their basic rights, personal dignity and inviolability. It also aims at achieving maximum possible equality among the members of any society. This aim is achieved by a just distribution of the benefits and obligations among all persons, and taking measures to ensure maximum possible equality of rights and opportunity for all. Justice further consists in taking socio-legal steps so as to correct the imbalances in the working of social institutions, resulting in unequal or unjust distribution of goods and opportunities among the members of a society. Justice is required to correct the inequalities inherent in any social order and its institutions. The inequalities of race, religion, economic class, power group, social status, education and sex etc. are natural, and perhaps social life cannot function without some or most of these inequalities. They become undesirable when they are extreme, or when they result in degrading certain groups of persons to a position of poverty and deprivation.

Justice is also required to correct the imbalance created by an indiscriminate application of the principle of equality to everyday functioning of the society. Thus, the equality of opportunity when it is offered to persons belonging to very unequal economic and social (including educational) backgrounds results in an enhancing of existing inequalities. Equality of political rights results in the tyranny of majority over the minorities, whether racial, ethnic, or religious, The allocation of rewards or wealth according to merit, though apparently a just idea, similarly leads to socio-economic inequalities.

Justice is further required to correct the imbalance created by some one or some group's activities which might have resulted in disadvantage or loss to another person or group. Administration of justice then means taking from the party responsible for the loss and compensating the party who has suffered the loss. This is, according to H.L.A. Hart, "providing for the restoration, after disturbance, of the moral *status quo* in which victim and wrongdoer are on a footing of equality and so alike."[56] Justice, therefore, is "traditionally thought of as maintaining and restoring a *balance* or *proportion*, and its leading precept is often formulated as 'treat like cases alike.' "[57] (original italics)

The conception of justice has a strong element or idea of distribution of benefits and responsibilities, or what is called distributive justice. Justice has long been conceived as "giving each person his due" (Ulupi). It is a conception of some kind of distributive justice, and includes the idea of retributive justice.

In whatever way we conceive justice, it includes the idea of equal or fair distribution of goods. Distributive justice is usually based on the idea of basic equality of all human beings, so that the benefits and responsibilities are distributed among them as equally as possible. But distributive justice, unlike the normative principle of basic equality of all human beings, is mainly concerned with treating like cases alike. The class of persons to whom a legal or moral law is applicable, or who deserve punishment, moral sanction, or special benefits, is clearly defined in cases of legal-moral offences as murder or cheating. But most of the time the class of persons who are to be treated equally is already determined by social institutions and prejudices, which undermines the very idea of justice.[58]

For example, the class of persons who were to be treated equally in ancient India was determined by their hereditary *varṇas* (larger caste groups), and śūdras were totally excluded from any claim to equality. Similarly, in ancient Greece and Rome equality existed only among citizens; and slaves were totally excluded from any claim to equality. And till sixties of the last century, blacks were treated as a separate class altogether in the U.S., so that there was no question of the whites and blacks being equal on the socio-moral plain, even if they were given equal political and legal rights.

Whether we conceive justice as "maintaining or restoring balance or proportion" (Hart); or "giving each man his due"; it leaves the most crucial question, "What is everybody's due?" unanswered. This latter question may, in turn, be translated as : "Which cases are alike so that they ought to be treated equally?" The question "What is everyone's due?" however, seems to better focus the issue involved.

Socio-political thinkers have rightly pointed out that the problem of determining everyone's due, or fixing the class of persons who should be treated equally or differently, is already decided by the socio-institutional structure, the established customs, or even legislation,. Thus, if justice was giving everyone his/her due, and if every person's due was already decided (as in ancient India, Greece, Rome and medieval Europe) by the existing social order, then the dues of aristocracy in Greece and Rome, of brāhmṇas and kṣatriyas in ancient India, and of feudal lords in medieval times, would far exceed those of the slaves or śūdras. A system of justice which sought to distribute benefits and disadvantages according to the hierarchy of social classes, and understood it as "giving everyone his due" would be a travesty of justice.

It is sometimes suggested that justice simply means "treating equals equally." But this conception of justice is as much unable to answer the crucial question as to who are equal, who are not, as any other conception. In fact, the determination of equals and unequals has already been carried out by the social institutions, which themselves may be very unjust. The two formulations of justice - "giving each one his due", and "treating equals equally" - take for granted the initial inequalities of the socio-political order; and then understand justice as the regulating principle of that social order. They do not face the possibility that the social institutions and the rules that decide the worth and dues of different groups may themselves be unjust. If so, the function of justice is to challenge those institutions, and not to take them for granted.

Justice is to treat all beings in a way so as to maximize equality among them. Justice does not start with, but seeks to achieve, equality among persons. It rather starts with a state of inequality, and its task is to correct the imbalances in society due to some act of aggression by some individual(s), or due to the working of some social institution(s). Hart's definition of justice as maintaing and restoring " balance or proportion" brings out this aspect of justice very well.

A related task of justice is to determine the bases or grounds of inequality or differential treatment by the law or society, so that those who are responsible for rendering justice may be guided by right moral rules in their allocation of unequal shares of gains or losses to different people. That is, justice seeks to develop the criteria for classifying people as equal or unequal in order to guide their different or differential treatment. The aim of differential treatment is to bring about greater measure of equality in the society, or in a particular institution. The number one question remains as to which of existing differences, e.g. those of race, ethnicity, economic or social status, sex, and expertise or merit, are relevant for the allocation of different benefits or losses.[59] Most of the above criteria are morally and legally irrelevant for differential treatment. An important aspect of justice is to decide which differences among people are relevant for meting out different treatment to them. Justice is expected to declare most empirical differences as irrelevant and reject them as bases for difference in treatment. In fact, that is the main function of justice in a societal context, i.e. to challenge unnecessary or unjustified inequalities in the social order and declare them as irrelevant in the administration of justice. However, merit, efficiency, sincerity of effort, and hard work are worthy of reward, even though this would naturally result in increased inequality in riches, power, and social status. The task of justice, therefore, is not to erase all inequalities but to minimize them as far as possible, especially those which are not related to individual talents or efforts, but are a product of the functioning of the socio-political order.

Rawls has added to the above another task of justice, that is, positive discrimination towards the most disadvantaged sections of the society, so as to minimize the ill effects of socio-economic and other inequalities. Rawls starts with offering two principles of social justice :

> the first requires equality in the assignment of basic rights and duties, while the second holds that social and economic inequalities, for example inequalities of wealth and authority, are just only if they result in compensating benefits for everyone, and in particular for the least advantaged members of society.[60]

While Rawls feels that the corrective measures (i.e. positive discrimination) are the responsibility of the society, or the state, Rawlsian conception of justice can as well be accepted as one of the two or three most fundamental principles of morality, as universally applicable to individual moral agents. "Justice as fairness" transcends the demands of equality as generally understood in socio-political discourse (e.g. "equal treatment of equals", or "giving each person her due"). When confronted by the inherent inequalities of the social order, justice seeks to right or correct the imbalances and inequalities, so that optimum conditions of equality can be realized. In trying to rectify the social inequalities the principle of justice may demand preferential treatment towards the least advantaged sections of society; or the arrangement of social and economic inequalities in such a way that "they are to the greatest benefit of the least advantaged."[61] It would also include any other corrective measures required to restore "balance or proportion" in the functioning of the social order.

Even though "justice as fairness" is conceived in the socio-political context, it can equally be a worthy and fundamental regulating principle of individual conduct. It means the duty of "giving each person her due" when that due is conceived not in terms of the rules of existing socio-political order but in those of what would be morally right, just, equitable, or fair settlement of the other's dues. Thus, it not only forbids us to make others a means of our personal goals (Kant), but also forbids us to take advantage of others' socio-economic, educational, or political disadvantageous position. "Justice as fairness" means to work, as far as it lies with us, to achieve 'fair equality' in our interpersonal relations.

As understood here, justice is integrally related to the principles of impartiality, recirprocity and equality. The four concepts together mean that from the moral point of view all persons are equal (normatively, if not empirically); and that justice and morality demand from us that we should treat all human beings equally, or impartially. The concept of reciprocity adds something more to that of impartiality by recognizing the mutual obligations of all individuals in a society. Justice consists in the practice of impartiality and reciprocity; and all three presuppose and imply absolute (normative) equality of all human beings (or as Indians say, of all living beings). Justice is thus the recognition of equality and inviolability of all persons at both the socio-political and personal levels, and is the source of the obligation to impartiality and reciprocity on the part of the moral agent.

Reciprocity of demands can be ensured by the restructuring of the social order, or by enjoining upon the individual the duty to acknowledge and act upon reciprocal demands. Reciprocity becomes justice when an individual fulfills her obligations to others in response to the debts incurred, or acknowledges the moral right of others to make demands on the moral agent. It means at the individual level that we cannot make others a means of the fulfillment of our goals; and they have legitimate moral demands upon us which we cannot ignore. A reciprocal acknowledgement of rights and duties, as pointed out by Strawson, leads to the establishment of a just social order.[62] Significantly, if justice is giving each one her due, not only it is I who have to give to others their respective dues, others - each single recipient of my giving - have as much obligation to give me my dues. The imbalance created by social inequalities is righted by the acknowledgement of the reciprocity of demands.

Thus, justice is a principle which presumes the basic equality of all human beings, and seeks to restore the balance in social relationships and institutions when it is disturbed by the activities of some individuals, groups, or institutions. Justice is also giving each person her due. But justice is not ready to leave the decision of what is every person's due to the blind functioning of social forces. Instead, it seeks to determine that due itself by taking into consideration various factors that result in inequalities and imbalances in social relationships. Justice keeps the principle of equality as its guiding principle or aim, when trying to determine the dues of various individuals and groups and correcting the effects of various contingent inequalities. It is also, perhaps above all, reciprocity of demands and duties, so that it would not allow any person or group to be reduced to a mere instrument of others' interests. It insists that any demands on one person or group can be legitimate only when they are matched with equal demands on behalf of that person or the group on all others. And when we say that justice seeks to correct the imbalance created by social inequalities, we mean, with Rawls, that justice particularly takes care of the interests of the most disadvantaged sections of society, often by offering them preferential treatment so that they are brought to the level of minimum equality with others.

I feel that there is something still lacking in the above discussion of justice. Plato was right when he considered justice both as a regulating principle of the society, and as a personal virtue. However, almost all Western writers on justice, including Rawls, conceive justice as a social institution, or at best a normative principle for the regulation of social institutions. The state is mostly regarded as the agency for rendering justice, or the just distribution of benefits or disadvantages. But as far as I have been able to understand the issues involved in the foregoing discussions, it is the moral agent and not the society, far less the state, who is the basic unit or main referent of all moral principles and judgments. That is why, I feel that understanding the principle of justice as a regulative principle of society or state does not do full justice to it. What, then, is justice at the level of the individual moral agent? Who is the just individual?

Among modern Western thinkers only Kant has given some consideration to the personal aspect of justice. Kant understands justice in terms of the moral agent's indebtedness to others. Justice is giving others their due when that due is understood as the debt one owes to others either because the moral agent has benefited from them, or because she has deliberately or otherwise acted in ways which has resulted in some loss to them.[63] The regulative principle of justice becomes the virtue of justice at the personal level. It then means integrity, rectitude or truth, and a commitment to pay off all one's debts and fulfill all one's obligations. It again implicitly means giving each person her due; only now the 'due' is being interpreted in terms of fairness.

This conception of justice as a personal virtue was developed and emphasized in Indian thought a good deal (as we have briefly seen in section I *supra*). According to it, everyone is born with certain debts (*ṛṇas*) to parents, teachers and humanity (society), as well as to entire creation (nature). A person is what he (she) is because of his (her) parents, hereditary culture and knowledge of earlier generations, the contribution of other human beings to his (her) welfare, as well as due to the bounty of nature. He (she) that seeks his (her) own interests without paying off all his (her) debts to others - from parents to all living beings - lives in sin. Justice which is mostly expressed by the comprehensive and nebulous term *dharma* means paying off one's debts, or giving positive contribution to the welfare of society, nature and even gods.[64] Of course, this exalted conception is nowhere developed fully, and is often vitiated by a certain confusion between universal and particular or caste-based duties.

But the idea is there that justice means paying off one's debts, when those debts are generously conceived as consisting in doing one's utmost for the welfare of others, and understanding this contribution as merely paying back what one has received from them. This is a wider concept than Ross' duties of gratitude, because we are talking here of the requiredness to pay off all the debts of the moral agent not to this or that person (excepting parents) but to the entire humanity by helping the traveller or guest (stranger), contributing towards the maintainence of teachers' hermitages, and so on.

IV.3 To recapitulate, I have sought to argue in this Chapter that there is a core universal morality which consists of a minimum number of basic or fundamental moral principles. At first it seemed to me that perhaps this core universal morality cannot have a full-fledged content in view of the fact that, as relativists insist, different moralities have drastically different contents. Therefore I tried to search for some formal characteristics of universal morality which would provide a common framework within which moral discourse can be carried out cross-culturally. I preferred to call it 'the moral point of view' in order first, to distinguish it from what is generally understood by the term 'morality'; and second, to emphasize that it provides standards to judge not only different acts and character traits but also different moral codes and socio-moral institutions. This is what is meant by the 'overridingness' of the moral point of view. Apart from overridingness, I found rationality, objectivity and universality as the formal or definitive characteristics of the moral point of view. The idea was that these characteristics would help us identify the moral point of view as against the separate moral rules, or even separate moral codes. Any principle or assertion, which (i) makes an overriding claim; (ii) is rational or rationally justifiable; (iii) is objective or subject-independent; and (iv) is universal (universalizable), belongs to the moral point of view, as against that of individual moralities. On the other hand, the principles of impartiality, reversibility, equality and justice are constitutive of the moral point of view. When we assert that moral judgments have overriding claim, and are necessarily those which can be universalized, we are not giving any normative principles. But when we say that the moral point of view consists of the principles of impartiality, reversibility, equality and justice, we are prescribing normative principles which constitute universal morality, a morality which is different from, and overrides, the claims of all separate moralities.

However during the course of my discussion I realized that even universalizability is not a mere formal condition. It presupposes some generally agreed principle or standard for identifying the class of relevant cases to which a moral judgment can be (universally) applied. And such a principle will have to have some moral content. Same is true of objectivity because it not only implies subject-independence but also reference to the demands of the objective situation, and so cannot but have some content. Even rationality would be value-neutral and vacuous unless conceived in the context of day-to-day life.

Anyway, the understanding of the moral point of view or universal morality by citing these four semi-formal characteristics is very incomplete. Gradually I could think of so many other characteristics of the universal moral point of view, 1. impartiality, 2. reversibility, 3. equality and 4. justice. Impartiality is closely allied to universalizability, and the two together form one of the few most fundamental principles of morality that moral principles and judgments are potentially applicable to all human beings, or are meant for everyone alike.

This brings in the very substantial principle of equality of all human beings. As a normative principle, the equality of all human beings *per se* can claim to be the universal (cross-cultural) and overriding criterion to evaluate all other moral norms and institutions. Universality and equality are again integrally related to the idea of reversibility on the one hand and justice on the other. As Baier has pointed out, while we can have exceptions to other moral rules, non-reversible behaviour *per se* is immoral. So, reversibility becomes one of the most important substantive principles which constitute universal morality. In a way, reversibility, like impartiality, is very akin to the ideas of universality of moral judgments and principles and equality of all human beings.

The principle of justice is equally fundamental, and is also closely related to the idea of (normative) equality of all human beings. I have tried to understand justice as the principle that aims at achieving maximum possible equality in the society through corrective measures that seek to rectify the imbalances and inequalities which already exist in the social order. As such, it is related to, but different from, the normative principle of equality.

Some of the characteristics discussed above can be combined together in order to reduce their number and achieve a somewhat greater focus in our discussion. Thus objectivity can be included in rationality; impartiality is easily combined with the need of universality; and reversibility could be included in a more comprehensive concept of equality. Generally speaking, we can accept four basic characteristics of the moral point of view or universal morality: rationality, universality, equality and justice. They are not mere formal characteristics but provide substantial criteria for moral decisions and moral judgments. Any act, character trait, or societal institution, is moral, right or good if (i) Reasons can be given for that act, decision, judgment, social institution, or practice. (ii) Our moral principle and/or judgment is universalizable, that is, applicable to all persons under relevantly similar circumstances where the relevant similarity is decided according to some moral principle. (iii) The given act, decision, or policy is guided by the normative principle of equality of all persons. (iv) And the ideal of equality is sought to be achieved through the functioning of the principle of (corrective) justice.

To a certain extent, the principles of equality and justice can alone form the core of universal morality. However, this still seems to be an incomplete picture of the proposed universal morality. It leaves the personal element out of morality, and still sounds somewhat formal. The above also leaves out all considerations of human welfare which makes such a conception of universal morality incomplete or unsatisfactory.

V. Towards Universal Morality

V.1 When I or any other philosopher argues for a minimum universal morality, we are neither trying to reject cultural diversity, nor even cultural relativism, but are rather trying to search for our common humanity. To quote Bimal K. Matilal,

> The claim of the non-relativist is minimum: certain basic moral principles are neither agent relative nor contingent upon any specific type of social order. These principles are sometimes claimed to flow from the "nature" of human needs. One may understand this as an attampt to uncover a core of shared rationality that is reached by gradually peeling off or stripping down the overlay of distinctive cultural mores, local customs and individual idiosyncrasies.[65]

The moral principles I am here trying to advocate as substantive principles of universal morality would be both universal and foundational in the sense that they would have cross-cultural validity, and also would be expected to form the basis or core of all particular moralities. They would further provide the criteria for the critical evaluation of separate moralities and a corrective to them where needed. As such, without negating the separate moralities, our moral principles would have overriding authority on us inasmuch as they are conceived in a universal, rational and objective perspective. Let me quote Baier in same detail :

> I shall, then, distinguish between true moralities and absolute morality. True moralities are actually embodied moralities, those forming part of a given way of life of a society or an individual which would pass a certain test, if they were subjected to it. Absolute morality, on the other hand,

> is that set of moral convictions, whether held by anyone or not, which is true quite irrespective of any particular social conditions in which they might be embodied. Every true morality must contain as its core the convictions belonging to absolute morality, but it may contain a lot more that could not be contained in every other true morality.[66]

It seems to me that the several characteristics of the moral point of view that I have been trying to develop directly or indirectly presuppose the axiomatic assertion of the fundamental equality of all human beings. Universality of moral principles means their universal applicability, which, in turn, implies the basic or 'natural' equality or affinity of the entire humankind. If it were not so, there would be no point in asserting that our moral principles and judgments should be universally applicable (to all relevantly similar cases), and that we should be impartial towards all humans while trying to reach a moral decision or pass a moral judgment. Reversibility is another important characteristic of the moral point of view, that is, a genuinely moral act should be one which would be acceptable to the moral agent even if the roles of the agent and the object are reversed. This again presupposes natural equality and affinity of all human beings, because if they were not so, there would be no possibility of even hypothetical reversal of roles. (Even in theory the roles of the citizens and slaves in Greece and brāhmaṇas and śūdras in India could not be reversed due to the deep-rooted hierarchical social order.)

The principle of universalizability also assumes the 'natural' equality of all human beings. Similarly, the principles of impartiality and reversibility presuppose equality of all persons. A conduct which assumes the fundamental distinction and conflict between the interests of the self and others, and is guided by self-interest, is immoral, or at best amoral. It is so, not because morality is chiefly concerned with our duties towards others but, because the moral point of view asserts the equality of all living beings as an axiomatic truth, thus leaving no scope for making an exception in favour of oneself, or someone else. We can, therefore, accept equality as one of the most fundamental principles of morality which can rightfully claim universal validity. I also think that the principles of universalizability, impartiality and reversibility, if not reducible to equality, are quite akin to it and presuppose it, so that for the sake of simplicity, instead of three or four substantive principles of morality we can have one only, that is, equality.

V.2 Justice is the second most fundamental or substantive principle of morality or the moral point of view. Justice starts with the normative principle of equality and ends with restoring the equality in the social order through compensation to the victim, punishment to the aggressor, and other relevant ways. The further task of justice is to help the most disadvantaged sections of society so that they can come up to a position of minimum equality with others. As such, the principles of justice should claim universality as a normative principle which provides both the standard for assessing morality and institutions of any society, and certain guiding norms (vide Rawls) to correct the initial inequalities and injustices.

As we have seen, a very similar conception of justice in terms of agent's indebtedness (*ṛṇa*) to others was developed and advocated in ancient India's socio-moral thought. Thus, the two principles of equality and justice seem to have emerged from our discussion as the most basic, comprehensive and substantive principles of any universal morality, or what I have called the moral point of view. (We would have occasion to discuss the views of Kant and Indian thinkers in our next Chapter, Sections III and IV.)

V.3 I would like to add to them 'truth' or truthfulness as a third substantive ethical principle. All my life I was puzzled by the fact that a large portion of Western moral discourse seems to be centred round the obligation of promise-keeping, until I realized that the obligation of promise-keeping accrues from the larger principle of truth, or the obligation of being truthful. Kant first affirmed promise-keeping as a universal or categorical imperative of morality, which means that no exceptions can be made to this principle, and it must be obeyed even at the greatest cost. Ever since, both Kantians and their critics have been discussing the obligation of promise-keeping as the paradigm of universal categorical imperative.

Sometimes we get the impression that promise-keeping exhausts the entire moral discourse. It seems (as in the article of Sealre) that if anything is argued (and proved) about promise-keeping, it automatically holds good for the rest of morality, or our sense of 'ought'. The duty of promise-keeping is arguably one of the most important and fundamental universal duties; and is given great importance in Indian moral thought also. But it definitely is not the whole of morality; and Ross was right when he included it as (only) one of the six fundamental duties.[67] Possibly, what Western ethical thinkers are trying to affirm through their discussion of promise-keeping is the virtue of (or obligation to) truth or truthfulness. The latter includes the imperative against lying, and is a much more comprehensive concept. As such, it deserves to be included in our enumeration of fundamental moral principles, not as promise-keeping but as truth.

The three principles of universal morality, namely equality, justice and truthfulness, cover a substantial part of morality and can be unhesitatingly declared as universal moral principles with overriding authority vis-a-vis all other moral codes. All the same, the three principles do not seem to be sufficient, that is, cannot constitute the whole of universal morality. I would like to add here a fourth substantive principle of morality which is as foundational and universal as the first three, that is, the principle or imperative against hurting others or non-violence (*ahiṃsā*).

While *ahiṃsā* (nonviolence) is the pivotal principle of Buddhist religio-moral thought, it has gradually become equally prominent in the Hindu conception of morality (*dharma*), so much so that it is often declared as the supreme duty.[68] On the other hand, the duty not to hurt others and the virtue of compassion or benevolence are given relatively less priority in Western thought, with the possible exception of Christian texts and writings. Of course, Hume, Butler and other proponents of the moral sentiment theory recognized a universal sentiment of sympathy and benevolence; but even they (perhaps with the exception of Hume) did not give any central importance to the sentiment of benevolence in their moral theory. The place of sympathy or benevolence became even more secondary in the Western ethical thought with the decline in the respectability of the moral sentiment theories.

Kant discussed the duties of benevolence perhaps in greater detail than any subsequent moral philosopher. But his attitudes towards such duties is rather equivocal. While he often downgrades duties done out of benevolence, as they are motivated by our emotions and are not done out of pure respect for the moral law, he also gives a beautiful justification for the duties of benevolence in terms of the moral agent's indebtedness towards others.[69]

Ross has given a list of six fundamental prima facie duties, and includes duty not to hurt others in his list. But somehow the duty of non-violence-being squeezed between various duties and unrelated with them - does not come out as an important constitutive principle of universal morality even in Ross.

However, a morality which mainly consists of equality, justice and promise-keeping (or truthfulness) would be a very incomplete and unsatisfactory one. A person who does all her moral duties but not only does not feel pity for the suffering of others but also does not bother if her actions hurt others, even though they may be according to the moral law, lacks something very vital in her personality. Therefore the principle of non-violence (*ahiṃsā*) should be emphatically recognized as the fourth universal and overriding moral principle. While the duty of not hurting others would be a duty of perfect obligation (to borrow Kantian terminology), perhaps benevolence or compassion cannot be enjoined upon us in the same fashion. That is, non-violence, in order to be included as a substantive and constitutive principle of universal morality, is best understood with a slight negative connotation.

Thus, the above discussion gives us four substantive principles of any system of universal morality, i.e. equality, justice, truth and non-violence.

My intention in proposing these four principles of universal morality as fundamental and overriding is not to suggest any comprehensiveness or finality for my understanding of universal morality. The principles of equality, justice, truth and non-violence are not exactly *a priori*. Moral experience or our everyday moral responses, decisions and judgments provide an occasion for 'cognizing' these principles as objectively (subject-independently) true or valid. But in another sense, they are *a priori* or axiomatic, that is, they do not need any rational justification. They are also 'fundamental' or 'foundational' in the sense that they provide a basis for the justification of all other moral principles and imperatives. They have overriding authority over all other moralities because of their foundational and axiomatic character. That is how, they can provide the much talked of cross-cultural framework and/ or criteria with reference to which all other moralities and ways of life can be critically evaluated.

I am fully aware that not only my position is anti-relativist, but also all its contentions, e.g. the cognitive character of morality, foundationalism in justification, and the possibility of cross-cultural rational-moral criteria of judgment, have been relentlessly rejected by the postmodern thinkers. On the other hand, I can say in defense that the postmodernist relativism is equally vulnerable to several criticisms (see Chapter 4, Sections III and IV *supra*). Also, our position does greater justice to both commensense and morality as it has been understood through the centuries both in the West and the East.

CHAPTER 7

Self and Others

I. Early Views

I.1 I have so far talked about the relativist and universalist approaches to morality, the latter including the realistic interpretation of moral discourse. Even though I have tried to argue for a universalist approach to morality, I may not have proved my point. A universalist ethics, as is well known, can be defended in two versions - absolutist or unconditional universalism such as the Kantian, and cautious or conditional universalism, such as that of Hare and Singer. I have tried to argue for the latter point of view. It does not only not deny the existence of a large number of moralities, it also accepts that to a certain extent they are authentic or valid for their respective societies. It differs from relativism in that it does not accept the relativist claim that the separate moral codes are the only, and in some sense, absolute authority for the members of their respective societies.

In other words, the universalist point of view that I am advocating accepts pluralism of moralities and even their authority for their respective societies, but rejects - first, the conception of those moralities as closed systems of thought and praxis resembling the windowless monads of Leibnitz; second, the thesis of mutual incommensurability of these moralities and their conceptual frameworks; and third, the relativist claim on the part of these plural moralities that they provide the only or final source of the moral principles and standards of a people. A cautious universalist does not question the usefulness and even correctness of different moralities because she recognizes that only particular moralities are capable of responding to the needs of that particular social order and its institutional structure. But she claims for the universal morality the right to critically and even comparatively evaluating these moralities on the basis of the criteria provided by the former, such as justice of their respective institutional structures; and the reasonableness of the hierarchy of their moral principles. Universal morality claims to override the particular moralities where they are found unjust, or violating human dignity, or being governed by a hierarchy of moral principles which does not seem reasonable or correct from the (universal) moral point of view.

Now, the relativists would question the right of any universal moral point of view to question the justifiability or moral worth of particular moralities; they would even question the very possibility of such a universal moral point of view. While the first objection is based on the preconception of the morality of a group being a closed system having no communication with other groups; the second objection implies the thesis of the impossibility of any cross-cultural understanding. I do not find any rational justification for both assertions, as also for the thesis of incommensurability.

Communication and dialogue at the rational level are not only possible, they may lead to the emergence of a universal moral point of view. But before I come to rational dialogue as our main hope for arriving at, and justifying, a system of universal morality, or a universalist moral point of view, I would like to discuss one moral issue - that of the relative importance of the individual moral agent and the community or society in moral discourse. As I understand the issue, our answer to the problem of self and others (or community) would have a decisive impact on our central problem of relativism versus universalism.

If an ethical thinker or a society understands morality as sociocentric and institution-based, then she/it also has to assert its relative nature. If some other person or society understands morality as agent-centred; or at least regards the human person, her character and motives as of equal importance as the norms and interests of the society, then the moral agent or person would be naturally considered in her capacity as a rational person; and such rational persons would spontaneously provide cross-cultural bridges, thus making the assertion of universal morality possible.

A basic question of morality or the moral point of view is, therefore, whether morality is mainly interested in regulating interpersonal behaviour in the society by defining and emphasizing our duties towards others; or whether we also have duty towards our own selves. A second related question would be whether the person of the moral agent is totally constituted by the society, its institutions, norms and conceptual framework, or whether the moral agent is a person in her own right; that is, a person is at least partially what she is because she is a rational being, or because she is a human being who shares with other human beings not only certain bio-psychological needs, but also ways of thinking, and (as Hume believed) certain sentiments (e.g. that against cruelty).

I.2 I will first take up the second question, i.e. whether the person or the moral agent is what she is because of some inherent characteristics, e.g. reason or moral sentiment; or whether her person is totally determined by the norms and values of her society. Answer to the first question - whether morality consists of our duties towards others alone, or whether one has a duty towards oneself also - would depend upon our answer to the second question regarding what constitutes the moral person.

Plato's conception of man was that of a social animal whose personality was determined by the role he was to play in the society, which role, in turn, was conceived according to a strict hierarchical social order.

Similarly, in Indian socio-political thought, a person's identity was generally recognized not as an individual in his (her) own right, but as a member of larger family (*kula*) and professional or caste group. While saluting others a person was expected to introduce himself (herself), by naming one's family, caste etc. And a person's duties (*dharma*) were determined by his (her) various roles as a son or daughter-in-law, master or servant, and member of some professional group etc.

Medieval society everywhere was structured on a hierarchy of social classes - feudal lords, peasants and slaves in Europe; brāhmaṇas, kṣatriyas (upper castes), middle castes and śūdras in India. Duties were strictly defined in terms of this hierarchical social structure in which the uppermost class hardly had any duties. Above all, the common bond of humanity among persons of different classes or communities was explicitly or implicitly rejected.

Both the humanism of Renaissance (which did not even try to question social inequalities), and the emphasis on the rights of the individual as against the Church in Reformation (which soon got undermined by the dogmatism of the reformers) made a substantial beginning towards the assertion of the identity of the individual as a person.

It was during the period of Enlightenment that the twin ideas of the individual as a person, and the natural affinity and equality of all human beings based on their shared rational nature found definite expression. John Locke is the foremost among early Enlightenment thinkers who asserted the 'natural' right to life, liberty and equality, as well as to property.[1] Locke's emphasis on equality and liberty for all became the hallmark of later liberalism.

The two revolutions - American and French - were inspired by the ideas of 'natural' equality of all human beings, and the declarations of human rights by them assume that the equality and dignity of all human beings is not merely a normative principle but is a factual assertion. That is, human beings not only *ought* to be treated equally, they *are* equal according to the law of nature. "Man is born free but everywhere is in chains"- this dictum of Rousseau assumes the natural equality of all humans, and contends that the existing inequalities are due to the society's unjust institutions which need to be changed.

In Kant, the ideas of dignity, inviolability and absolute equality of all persons are asserted both as a normative principle, as also expressive of the 'natural' sharing of universal reason by all human beings. (We would come back to Kant in a later section.)

First half of nineteenth century saw the development of idealist philosophy in Germany (e.g. J.G.Fichte and G.W. Hegel). These philosophers were not content to develop philosophical systems, but applied their philosophical principles to socio-political fields; and influenced and strengthended the nationalist sentiment and some kind of totalitarianism in politics. The State is placed very high in Hegelian hierarchy and is perceived as a living expression of universal Reason, Mind, Objective Spirit, or Divine Idea (*Geist*). It is only as a citizen of a State that the individual becomes wholly free and possesses rationally defensible rights. State is conceived as an organic unit in Hegel whose citizens have no separate or independent identity other than that of being the citizens of a particular state. The role of the State in Hegel's thought is quite extensive.[2] Inasmuch as the State is the source of both laws and moral standards or norms, the morality of any particular society as determined by the State would be naturally different from that of other societies. Hegel's moral philosophy sometimes comes very close to the later communitarian point of view.

Though the emphasis on the State as the integrated whole, having greater worth than its parts or individuals, was more prominent in German philosophy than in the English speaking world, F.H. Bradley's conception of the whole as being richer and larger than its parts, comes very near the German idea of the State. The state-society is an example of the 'concrete universal' which is a community of its members. A society brings into unity the diversity of its members or sub-sections, but it is more than them; it is an individual. The interests of the whole are always larger, have greater worth and are more important than those of the parts, and the society is a higher level of being than the individuals.

Nineteenth century liberalism was the true heir to the spirit of the Enlightenment, and carried forward its ideas. There was a continued emphasis on equality, liberty and individual dignity of all human beings *qua* their humanity. The individual's right to think, choose, and act for herself without any interference from others is the pivotal idea of nineteenth century liberalism. It is expressed beautifully in J.S. MILL's much quoted passage:

> If all mankind minus one were of one opinion, and only one person were of the contrary opinion, mankind would be no more justified in silencing that one person, than he, if he had the power, would be justified in silencing mankind....
>
> We can never be sure that the opinion we are endeavouring to stifle is a false opinion; and if we were sure, stifling it would be an evil still.[3]

The ideas of equality and liberty go back to the social-contract theory of Hobbes and Locke which conceives the society as a product of social contract or agreement among free individuals. The social order created by the social contract has nothing sacrosanct about it and is merely meant to facilitate the realization of the goals of free individuals. It was also assumed that the dignity and inviolability of the human person, and her rights to freedom and equality are 'natural' or 'innate' to the human person, and are prior to the formation of the society. Even the contribution of society in the formulation of human personality, beliefs and values was undermined in early liberalism. Its assertion of the rights of the individuals vis-a-vis the society expressed an extreme kind of individualism. At the same time, liberalism also emphatically affirmed the values of pluralism and tolerance which have been generally associated with relativism in contemporary thought.

II. Existentialist View

Existentialists deserve a special mention in the context of our problem of the relationship between self and others from the moral point of view, as they have discussed this problem in great detail, though in an existential context. Though existentialists' main concern is the individual subject of experience, they have emphatically recognized that individual's personhood is constituted by her relationships with others. For example, Martin Heidegger develops his philosophy in conscious contradistinction to the Cartesiarn idea of the subject's certainty of herself ("I think, therefore I am") as the only truth in one's experience. He opposes the concept of the subject as some-one standing over against, or confronting, an alien and unknowable objective world, including other selves.

In contrast, he develops the concept of *Dasein* or being-in-the-world. Knowing and acting no longer have to be conceived in terms of the subject - object relationship, but are modes of *Dasein* or being-in-the world. That is, human person is an existence-in-the-world, and is conditioned in every mode of her thought and action both by the external world or her material situation, and by other people in the world. Being related to other people is an essential aspect, or even constitutive, of the being and existence of each person.[4] The being of a person is 'being with' others. An individual could not have been what she is without her relationship with others. Her knowledge, perspectives and private concerns exist only against the background of the ways of thinking and responding shared by members of a social group. Part of our self-awareness is derived from our awareness of the world. Our relationship with others, which the existentialists call our 'being for others', is a part of our being ourselves. The entire idea of *Dasein* or our being-in-the-world, or our being-with-others, should suggest an integral relationship between different selves. But it is not the case.

Though the various existentialist writers differ widely among themselves, they all emphasize the essential solitude of the human person as she faces anxiety, guilt and above all death alone. Even Heidegger who emphasizes the self's relationship with others more than other existentialists comes close to Nietzsche in his arrogant affirmation of the solitary existence of the human person.

J.P. Sartre emphasizes this solitariness of human person even more in his concept of the authentic existence which consists in "treating ourselves as isolated, unique and free." Authentic life is one in which we are prepared to take full responsibility for our lives.[5] Our reason for doing an act must not be that society demands it, or that others expect us to do certain things, or play a certain role in society, but that we have chosen to do that act, or live in a particular way through an authentic act of decision.

Sartre talks of 'Bad Faith' which is understanding ourselves as others understand us, and living in a way which is expected of us from others. Authentic existence consists in total rejection of bad faith, that is, refusal to be what others want us to be. Authentic existence is being and living on the basis of our free decisions.[6] Sartre even says that each person must devise her own system of values or morality, and make her own absolutely unaided choices. Choosing something for oneself is to set a value to something. The individual thus becomes the source of all values.

While both Heidegger and Sartre acknowledge the importance or influence of others in shaping up of our personality and life, their conceptions of human solitariness and authentic life undermine the importance of others. Sartre goes beyond this and declares that the self is irremediably opposed to the 'other', and there is no area in which the self can address the 'other' as a 'thou'. For him the very being of the 'other' challenges or even poses a threat to my existence. As against Heidegger, Sartre is closer to the Cartesian position. My self is the only sure thing, others' being is either a matter of doubt, or a threat. Freedom is the watchword, a freedom which mainly consists in putting aside societal bonds, and asserting that 'I' am the source of whatever happens to me.[7]

Strangely enough, Heidegger as he grew older became very close to Nazi ideology; and Sartre became a communist in his later years. While in the case of Heidegger, Nazism was an extension (though a distorted one) of his conception of being-in-the-world or *Dasein*, especially as he started identifying *Dasein* with the nation;[8] in the case of Sartre, communism, being a strictly communitarian ideology, just does not fit in his conceptions of human solitariness and authentic existence.

Existentialism is an interesting study in our context, as it brings into focus -- first, that the self's existence or individual's personality presupposes the existence of and interaction with other selves; and second, that at the existential level, the self's interests or goals and above all authenticity imply a natural conflict with those of others. I do not agree with the second proposition at all, and find that the two assertions are at variance. The emphasis on authenticity which can be achieved only by rejecting the place of others and their demands in our lives is at variance with both their first assertion of the existence of the subject as 'being-in-the-world', and the moral point of view. If authentic existence can be achieved only by the subject or person living and facing guilt, anxiety and death alone, or by acknowledging and emphasizing the solitarianess and total freedom of the subject, then it seems to mean that morality's main referent is the subject alone. How can this emphasis on human solitariness be reconciled with the conception of 'being-in-the-world', or 'being-with-others'?

What their discussion brings out is that morality cannot be conceived or practised without the presence of others, that is, without the context of human interrelationships. Whether we consider other selves as integrally related to the moral agent, or as hostile beings, a major part of morality would still consist in specifying our duties towards others; or in defining rules and norms to regulate interpersonal behaviour in the society.

Another important contribution of existentialism is highlighting that the human person owes duty to herself. It may mean living an authentic existence (existentialists); living according to the moral law, or living as a rational person (Kant); or simply realizing one's potentialities, or living in a way which would bring fulfillment to one's self.

III. Liberals and Communitarians

III.1 (i) This brings us to contemporary liberalism, because for liberals, as for existentialists, the individual person, her goals, desires, and rights are of central importance. We have briefly discussed liberalism in our first section; the need to discuss it again arises from the fact that Rawls has not only renewed liberal ideology in the West, contemporary communitaririan writers whose thought has relativistic overtones have also concentrated on his thought and developed their theses in conscious contradistinction to his views. Typically, Rawls puts great emphasis on the right to liberty of the individual subject or agent.[9] The central ideal in Rawls is that of a positive conception of liberty for achieving one's goals; but inasmuch as this liberty is to be extended to all persons, the assertion of equality of all human beings becomes crucial. But liberty and equality are not always compatible, as given the inborn inequalities of human beings, the exercise of liberty by individuals with different capabilities and goals always tends to increase and strengthen economic and other inequalities in the society. Rawls therefore takes extra care to insure minimum equality among different groups. This can be realized when the principle of liberty is complemented by the principles of equality and justice. And justice demands that each member of society has "an inviolability founded on justice or, as some say, on natural right, which even the welfare of everyone else cannot override.[10]

This, of course, is again a liberal ideal, very different from the usual utilitarian point of view proclaiming the greatest happiness principle. Rawls takes further care to ensure that the exercise of the right to liberty does not result in an excessive increase in social inequalities, or disadvantage to the lesser privileged sections of the society. Hence he puts forward his famous principle of justice as fairness:

> Social and economic inequalities are to be arranged so that they are both (a) to the greatest benefit of the least advantaged and (b) attached to offices and positions open to all under conditions of fair equality of opportunity.[11]

(ii) Rawls' conception of the person has been severely criticized by the communitarians. First, they contend that when Rawls emphasizes the separateness of persons, he fails to understand either the intimate relationship between the individuals and society, or the fact that it is the society in which people live that shape or determine what they are and the values that they have.[12] They repeatedly assert that the selfhood or moral identity of the individual, consisting of her beliefs, norms, values and standards, is determined, or even constituted, by the traditional beliefs, norms etc. of her community. They particularly criticize the conception of rational persons implied in Rawls' hypothesization of the original position in which all rational persons come together to plan and formulate principles of a future just society.[13] This implies, they argue, as if the individuals are prior to, and independent of, the society, whereas the society or community is in fact the source of whatever we are.

Secondly, it is argued, that the entire liberal, particularly Rawlsian, conception of the relationship between the individual and the society is faulty. According to the communitarians, the liberals conceive society as if it were a mere cooperative venture for the pursuit of individuals' advantage; or a private association formed by the individuals whose essential interests are independent of, and in a sense prior to, the existence and institutions of the community of which they are members.[14]

Thirdly, communitarians point out that liberals, particularly Rawls, are suggesting that there is some universal essence of human beings - for Rawls it is the rational nature which is common to and overrides the particularities of various cultures. Liberals, it is argued, "characterize people in a way that detaches them from what it is that makes actual people different from each other..." Rawls' theory of justice and its implicit claim to universality are said to neglect the factors that make actual people different from each other, that is, the variety or diversity of various cultures and their ways of life. Communitarians further talk of "the moral importance of different cultures in which people live and in whose terms they conceive themselves and the meaning of their lives."[15]

Fourthly, communitarians argue that Rawls is always taking for granted a liberal conception of the person, and a democratic conception of the state. Does Rawls intend, they ask, that his conceptions and the institutions they envisage are right or true for every social set-up; or are they true only for modern Western societies ? They support the latter alternative, whereas Rawls implies that the ideas of human beings as free and rational persons with natural claims to liberty and equality; of justice as fairness; and of democracy as a political system which best ensures these values, have universal validity.

III.2 The two criticisms against Rawlsian liberalism regarding the supposed priority of the individuals to the society; and the conception of society as if it were a voluntary association, are interrelated and can be taken up together. I agree with both these criticisms that the conception of individuals as separate and semi-independent subjects and agents; and the conception of society as a product of some hypothetical social contract between persons who are chiefly interested in securing their personal interests, are not justified by sociological facts. It is true that the individual person, her perfection and welfare are of supreme importance in Rawls' thought. There is also a suggestion that (political) society has been developed so as to create conditions in which individuals' goals can be realized best. Any such view would be a faulty understanding of social reality, or even life. Individuals do not exist as independent, separate units of society. They are mutually interdependent for their various needs and even for their inner health and happiness. The welfare of an individual is integrally related to that of others; and it is so obvious that I need not labour the point.

At the same time, Rawls is not as much individualistic in *A Theory of Justice* as some of his critics suggest. Though his rational persons are individuals - may be separate individuals - they are interested in forming a social order based on the principle of justice as fairness. And most of the work is devoted to the problem of how to achieve such a social order. Moreover, in his later work, *Political Liberalism,* Rawls further acknowledges the important role of the society as a political community in shaping up the entire personality of the individual. Even in his earlier work he has clearly acknowledged the role of "a social setting as well as a system of belief and thought that is the outcome of the collective efforts of a long tradition."[16] Elsewhere also he acknowledges the role of the community:

> In the well-ordered society of justice as fairness citizens....share a common aim, and one that has a high priority, namely the aim of political justice, that is the aim of insuring that political and social institutions are just and of giving justice to persons generally, as what citizens need for themselves and want for one another. It is not true, then, that on a liberal view citizens have no fundamental common aims.[17]

That is, justice itself becomes the common aim which is given priority over the interests of individuals. The vision of the society that emerges is "a society in which each citizen acknowledges the freedom and equality of all other citizens and is committed to maintaining the institutions and practices that preserve it...."[18] Of course, a just social order is expected to be inducive to the individuls' welfare. However, justice is not conceived as an instrument of ensuring the individuals' welfare but as a moral or normative principle which is good-in-itself. The point of view of justice is that of impartiality.[19] As conceived by Rawls, justice or impartiality has a special connotation. It is not merely and passively treating all human beings as equal, it is arranging or modifying social institutions so that the least advantaged sections are taken care of, and a fair amount of equality of opportunity, liberty etc. is actually realized by all in real life. Justice conceived as such is definitely a social ideal to which individual interests are to be subordinated.

The third criticism of Rawlsian liberalism by communitarians concerns the supposed negation by the liberals of bases of differences between human beings which consist of different ways of life of separate communities. To a certain extent I agree with this view. It is true that our values and norms of both thought and praxis, as well as our patterns of behaviour, are different in various cultures. It is also true that generally we respond to apparently similar cases differently according to our inherent biases and moral conceptions, all of which might have been learnt from our society but have now become an integral part of our mental make-up.

On the other hand, those relativists or communitarians, who exclusively emphasize and base their entire understanding of human person, society and even morality on empirical differences between various cultures, fail to do justice to either human nature or morality. Can we go beyond that, and say that when two persons, belonging to very distant cultures, meet for the first time they would fail to recognize each other as human persons; or they would not have any natural affinity which can pave the way for mutual communication or dialogue ? Differences are not only there as an empirical fact, they may also constitute a major part of our personality. But let these cultural differences not make us blind to, first, differences of capacities, inclinations and even values among individuals belonging to the same culture; and second, very significant differences between various ethnic, linguistic and religious groups within the larger culture.[20] However, the acknowledgment of various-level differences need not lead us to the negation of the basic affinity between, or common traits and needs shared by, all or most human beings. (Let us forget the secluded far-off preliterate cultures for the time being, for in all probability, the anthropologists might really not have understood them due to the difficulties in intercultural understanding which they are so fond of emphasizing!)

I do not see how the emphasis on the rationality of human persons, affirmed by both Kant and Rawls, needs to negate the differences between various cultures. While emphasizing rationality, or just humanity, of all human beings these thinkers are not necessarily rejecting their differences. Differences and common points are complementary aspects of humanity, and the recognition of these differences need not imply the rejection of either the rationality of human beings, or the fact that they share common ways of thinking and responding to life's situations. In other words, there is a common bond of humanity which does not contradict the various-level differences between human beings.

Here communitarians have not been able to take due cognizance of internal differences within each society which are almost as important as those between any two societies. On the other hand, liberals are truer to reality in that they firmly assert the value of pluralism, both between and within different societies.[21]

This brings us to the fourth criticism of Rawls by the communitarians, that his philosophy is simply a product of his culture and times; and therefore he cannot claim universal validity for the same. It seems to me that liberalism, with its emphasis on the values of liberty of the individual moral agent, equality and impartiality, and its conception of justice as fairness, may well be a product of some definite culture, but it can justifiably claim certain universal validity and applicability. True, liberal emphasis on the individual moral agent cannot fit into the cultural ethos of a communitarian morality with its emphasis on the common good. But it is not that the liberals reject the idea of the common good; they conceive it instead, as we have seen, as the shared good of all members of a society, and not as a good which transcends all individual goods.

III.3 Having criticized the assumed liberal conception of society, communitarians present their own version as an alternative and preferable understanding thereof. Generally, "they regard the good life for human beings as that devoted to participation in political life, so that the content of individual well-being is inherently communal - and communal at the level of political society..."[22] Our good as individuals is to be found primarily in our interpersonal relationships in the society, or in our various social roles. It is realized through voluntary associations or institutions, and above all, through our political community or society. Moreover, the individuals' good consists in shared goods that can exist and be realized only through the community or society.[23] According to MacIntyre:

> For I am never able to seek for the good or exercise the virtues only *qua* individual....But it is not just that different individuals live in different social circumstances; it is also that we all approach our own circumstances as bearers of a particular social identity..... Hence what is good for me has to be the good for one who inhabits these roles.... This is in part what gives my life its own moral particularity.[24]

The self of the moral agent, including her values, standards and norms, as well as the ways she responds to particular situations, is constituted by the fact of her being a member of this or that society. All thought and praxis are possible only in the context of specific socio-cultural traditions, or what the postmodernists prefer to call conceptual frameworks of particular societies.[25]

The communitarians often use the terms, political community, society, or community, as interchangeable concepts, whereas they definitely are not. But communitarian writers, such as Michael Walzer, Michael Sandel and Alsdair MacIntyre, have often talked as if they are near synonyms.

There is a general lack of a clear conception of the nature and extension of the term 'community'. Leaving aside very small nation-states, every modern society consists of several ethnic, regional, linguistic and religious groups. These intracultural differences are as prominent and determinative of the individual's identity as intercultural ones. For example, Indian society has a mixed and heterogeneous population belonging to different religions, speaking different languages, and consisting of groups with their own distinct cultures. Apart from language and region, religion is a very important factor in avowedly providing separate identities to its members in Indian society. (Religious factor becomes more prominent in the case of multi-religious societies such as India's than in unireligious ones where it can not offer any basis for the breakup of those societies into separate communities.)

We cannot neglect here the all important economic factor. People belonging to the same economic strata feel an affinity to each other and socialize among themselves, and are mostly cut off at the social level from those belonging to markedly different economic levels.

For example, slum dwellers in any third world country have a bond of sharing together the same hardships and other vicissitudes of life, which is what community feeling is all about. Neighborhood provides another important basis for community feeling. Then there are distinctions in educational levels, and distinctions between people with rural or urban backgrounds. These distinctions are much more marked in the third world countries than in the developed societies. In societies such as India's, where these differences markedly exist, they provide bases for communal fellow-feeling.

It would be naive to think that any individual can ever belong to one community alone, as certain religious groups in India seem to think. Each of us belongs to so many communities at once, and our various identities-regional, linguistic, religious, economic and socio-political - necessarily overlap. If so, which of these innumerable communities can justifiably claim to be the determiner of the individual's identity and her moral values and standards ? That is, which of the various communities to which an individual belongs is primary or primordial, so that it would command overriding loyalty from its members?

Perhaps it follows that none of these smaller communities or groups forming the nation-society is primary or most basic in providing us our complete moral identity. And definitely they cannot claim to provide conditions for the realization of such common goals as justice.

It is perhaps for this reason that communitarians have chosen the political community as the primary community. They mostly choose to understand the political community as a homogeneous whole which is a historical society with a common language, culture, common meanings, and shared sensibilities. I wonder which political community these writers have in mind. I also feel that in the name of giving cognizance to the uniqueness and plurality of different communities, the understanding of the political community as some sort of monolithic whole in communitarian writings negates the natural plurality and diversity of attitudes and ways of life of different groups or communities within a nation-state. It also negates the natural affinity of humankind, and the common shared elements of human nature.

Of course, communitarians do not totally reject the possibility of certain universal basic moral principles, but nevertheless assert that all substantive moral rules and standards of judgment come from our political community. According to MacIntyre, even such apparently universal virtues as truthfulness, justice and courage cannot be realized or practised without the context of social relationships. Even if we acknowledge a few basic moral principles or virtues, this would not be incompatible with "the acknowledgment that different societies have and have had different codes of truthfulness, justice, and courage. [26] In short, morality can be understood only in the context of social institutions or traditions, and these differ from society to society.

Thus, morality is for the communitarians first and last a matter of social practice; my moral identity being totally determined by my society's norms and standards, as also by my role in the society. Our community determines what *is* right or wrong, what *is* worthwhile to pursue, and so on. Moral understanding and motivation can be sustained only in the context of one's community, here political community, which provides all our standards of judgment. Hence preserving one's way of life and one's identity through loyalty to one's (political) community and its norms is the moral way of life. MacIntyre acknowledges both the plurality of goods and the continuously changing nature of traditions. But the emphasis throughout is on socially determined identities, roles and their accompanying obligations.

III.4 The role of social customs, practices, and traditions cannot be belittled. Perhaps the liberals, being preoccupied with the individual and her dignity and liberty, have not properly recognized the contribution of cultural traditions in making us what we are. On the other hand, communitarians not only overemphasize tradition as constitutive of our moral identity, they also speak of it in singular. In real life we never come across members of a society who are all determined by one tradition. Such a uniformity of beliefs, attitudes and moral standards is both inconceivable in real life and undersirable, as well as against the idea of plurality which the communitarians are supposed to advocate above all.

Another important objection to the communitarian point of view is their practice of identifying three terms - community, society and political community. Leaving aside the term community which is used too loosely, the identification of society and political community is unjustified. There is no denying that these two concepts overlap and in many cases have the same referent. Nor is there any denying the fact that the individual's day-to-day life and the realization of her goals are possible only because of the rule of law by the state; and therefore the individual has certain very definite duties towards the state. But when the two concepts of society and state are identified, the idea of power or superior authority enters the concept of community or society. And this idea of the power and authority of the community has played a very important role in communitarian thought.

Communitarians have frankly acknowledged that the state is the primary or most important community, demanding unconditional loyalty. The latter, in turn, may mean that the nation-state is accepted as beyond all rational scrutiny, and its interests, or the so-called common good is to be pursued by its citizens even when they are against the best interests of humanity. M. Walzer even asserts that acts of aggression against, or oppression of, other societies by some one society is just so long as such acts are instrumental to its common good.

If the above interpretation of the communitarian point of view, as the theory of political community being the source of all our norms etc., as well as of our very moral identity, and therefore deserving citizens' unconditional loyalty, and being itself beyond all moral criticism, is right, then it is just not acceptable to us, or for that matter to any one who enters the discourse from a moral point of view.

First, the idea of the nation-state as beyond all moral criticism and the idea of the common good of the state entitling it to override the rights and interests of the entire humanity takes us to the rule of the jungle which could never be accepted from the moral point of view.

Second, the idea that all our moral norms and standards and even our moral identity are determined by the state, and hence it deserves unconditional loyalty of its citizens, is equally unacceptable from the moral point of view. Suppose a person belongs by birth to a totalitarian state, such as Nazi Germany, Stalin's Russia, F . Castro's Cuba, or modern communist China. Does it mean that the citizen of Nazi Germany should have endorsed the genocide of the Jewish community; or a citizen of China should have condoned and perhaps helped in the brutal suppression and massacre of students in the Tiananman Square ? No moral thinker can endorse the view that citizens of every state should committedly support and even contribute towards the realization of all the aims pursued by the state (including acts of agression). Decisions for such acts are made by power hungry politicians, and the hunger for power on the part of the rulers has been the cause of innumerable wars and untold misery to the humankind throughout its history.

Third, the conception that an individual's moral identity is constituted by the norms and standards of her political community is wrong from another point of view also. Does it mean that if an individual refuses to accept the norms and standards of her political community, she would lose "all genuine standards of moral judgment"(as MacIntyre suggests); or even her identity as a moral agent ? Does it mean that the only moral way of life is one that consists of blind and exclusive loyalty to one's community ? When MacIntyre and others are criticizing the liberal emphasis on individual liberty, do they mean to suggest that their ideal state would be one in which individuals are less free, and generally enjoy less rights than in a liberal state? That is, do they approve of a state of affairs in which individual moral agents would not be able to take their own moral decisions on the basis of their reason and valuational preferences but would act as directed (or coerced) by the authority of the state?

If communitarians mean what I have understood them to mean, then they are definitely not talking of morality. An act would definitely not be moral unless it has been freely chosen, or unless the moral principle under which it comes is agent's own. The authority and overriding nature of the moral law comes from the fact of its being autonomously chosen and not being forced upon the subject by an external authority. Freedom to choose what act one wants to do, what goals or values one wants to pursue, and how one wants to live is an integral aspect of one's identity as a moral agent. A person who is fully conditioned or determined by the norms and standards of her society, and constrained by the duty of loyalty to her state as the supreme duty, cannot act freely, and hence cannot be a genuine moral agent. That is to say, the communitarian conception of both the moral code and the moral identity of citizens misses a very fundamental truth about morality, that it cannot be forced upon someone from outside but must be chosen freely.

Fourth, the communitarian conception of political community as the supreme object of one's loyalty cannot claim to be a normative or moral contention because it arbitrarily chooses one aspect of human life, i.e. political as of supreme importance. If asked for a justification for their standpoint, communitarians contend that the political community is the source or determining factor in the development of our moral ideas and identity. But this is a totally indefensible moral position. MacIntyre and others are right when they emphasize the role of traditions in constituting our views, attitudes and standards of judgment. But these traditions - plural - have very different sources - history, customs, religion(s), literature, moral code(s) and political order. The political institutions are not the determining factor but are themselves influenced by the ethos or predominant values of that particular culture. State laws have only limited applicability, and have nothing to do with the morals proper.

Of course, there is no end to debate between liberals and communitarians, and I am not qualified to make a worthwhile contribution to it. It seems to me, however, that they can be quite complementary if their respective emphases on the individual and community are moderated a little. Liberals are right when they assert the importance of the moral agent to whom the moral imperatives apply. Communitarians are right when they point out the essentially social or other-regarding nature of all morality. The two points of view do not seem contradictory to me. If the two groups could mutually recognize the strong points of the other, the conception of morality that would emerge would be more balanced, comprehensive and definitely universal.

III.5 The above discussion has made one more point clear, that the two questions posed by me in the beginning of the Chapter, i.e. first, as to which of the two, 'self' and 'others' (community), is the focal concern of morality; and second, what constitutes the selfhood of the moral agent, cannot be treated separately. In a way, the quarrel between liberals and communitarians is primarily over the question as to what constitutes the person. For communitarians, it is the community, society or state that forms and determines the human person. For liberals, it is the innate nature or reason which constitutes the self; hence their emphasis on liberty of the individual.

Any answer to the second question would naturally result in an answer to the first. That is how, communitarians, believing that it is the society that constitutes the self, also assert that the individual's primary duty is to the society, and a moral way of life is one of sharing of common interests and working for common goals along with other members of the nation-society. Liberals, regarding the moral agent as the primary referent of moral discourse, emphasize the rights of the individual vis-a-vis the society. But if the individual is the primary unit of morality, not only her rights but her duties towards herself and others must be specified. I do not think that liberals have tried to answer this question.

Whether morality is conceived as a system of regulative principles of interpersonal behaviour in order to achieve a state of lawfulness and harmony; or as justice which is concerned with the interests of the least advantaged; or as the fulfilling of our social obligations *qua* our various roles assigned to us by the society or state - our obligations to others are prominent in all conceptions of morality. As one of the participants in the dialogue regarding "Self and Others" (W.D. Falk) says:

> Only insofar as you ought to do things..... for the sake of others, is the reason a moral reason, and the ought a moral ought. Reasons of self-regard are not moral reasons at all, and you can forget about them in the reckoning of your moral obligations.[27]

It is true that a greater part of our morality is concerned with our obligations and conduct towards others; and duties towards oneself are not given equal prominence in morality, as the natural prudential egoism of human beings generally takes care of one's interests. Interests of the subject are further taken care of by commonplace morality that seeks to bring out a state of social equilibrium or a well-ordered society in which the interests of all members are most likely to be achieved through sensible (and not ideal) moral rules. Such a morality has per force to be relative to the society's institutional structure and traditions.

Any universal morality, however, would have to be distinct from everyday moralities consisting of traditional rules of conduct and patterns of behaviour. Now, would this morality be interested only in our duties towards others, or also in our duties towards our own selves? Falk argues that a person has a moral duty to herself also, and all one's interests need not be sacrificed for the sake of others. For example, a daughter need not sacrifice all her interests to the demands of her parents.[28] That is, the moral agent's duties towards others are to be balanced by the recognition of her duties towards herself. And this, in turn, implies a recognition of the moral agent as a person in her own right. Perhaps both our questions are best answered in Kantian thought.

IV. Kantian Perspective

IV.1 Kant's answers to my two questions discussed above are crystal clear. To the question, whether morality is concerned exclusively and primarily with others, or whether the moral agent has any duties towards herself, Kant emphatically answers that the person or moral agent owes very definite duties to herself. To the question as to what constitutes the personhood of the individual, his answer is again very clear and I may say categorical. Though the moral agent is also an empirical self with various inclinations (and we may add culture-specific beliefs and prejudices), the essence or personhood of the moral agent is constituted by universally shared reason, or rational will. Here Kant adds a significant dimension to the moral discourse by asserting that the motives of the moral agent are of primary importance in morality.

While for Kant the good will that acts out of pure respect for law is of ultimate worth; and Hare hardly tries to tackle the question directly; most ethical philosophers have emphasized the social context of morality almost exclusively. This conception of morality not only underlines the other-oriented nature of morality, it also implicitly suggests first, that external acts done in obedience to the moral laws of the society constitute morality, perhaps irrespective of the motives or internal state of the moral agent; and second, that in some way the moral agent is a means to the interests of the society.

Falk's contention that a moral agent need not sacrifice all her interests or goals seems reasonable in terms of Kantian philosophy, as according to the second formulation of the categorical imperative, a person is an end-in-herself and must never be treated as a means to the ends of others. The moral agent, being a rational person, need not let herself be used by others as a means.

It should however be noted that the interests and goals of the subject that she should be morally free to pursue even in disregard to the demands of others on her could not be ordinary interests. Suppose a son or daughter neglects to look after his/her parents when they are old and destitute, simply because he/she wants to have a good life, we would not be able to endorse his/her conduct. According to Kant, not only the moral agent is allowing herself to be used as a means when she is succumbing to the demands of the parents or any other person (or section of society); she is also using herself as a means of her own self-indulgence if she does not devote herself self-consciously to her own perfection.[29]

In the very beginning of his *Fundamental Principles of the Metaphysics of Morals*, Kant declares the absolute worth of two things - the moral law or the categorical imperative and the good will. While the goodwill is understood as one which is exclusively determined by the moral law, the law, in turn, is explained as one which is given by the rational-autonomous (self-legislating) will to itself. Moreover, inasmuch as the determination of the will by the moral law is a self-determination, the dignity and worth of the rational-autonomous will or person are preserved. According to W. Windelband:

> *reverence for the worth of man* is for Kant the material principle of moral science. Man should do his duty not for the sake of advantage, but *out of reverence for himself*, and in his intercourse with his fellow-men he should..... honour in him the *worth of personality*.[30] (original italics.)

The concept of the person is pivotal to Kant's moral philosophy. The worth of the person is due to both, the moral law by which the rational will is determined, and the universal practical reason which every person embodies in herself. Kant insists on the supreme worth of rational will or person as an end-in-itself, and as a source of all moral laws. And the absolute worth of the person is based on the axiomatic principle that "rational nature exists as an end-in-itself." Kant regards non-rational beings as things, and adds that "rational beings on the contrary, are called *persons*, because their very nature points them out as ends in themselves."[31] This universal practical reason not only possesses absolute worth but is also *a priori*, that is, presupposed in all moral judgments and decisions. It is in a certain sense transcendental, though Kant does not always say so explicitly. The idea that the personhood or rational nature of human beings should be respected in all our thought and praxis is central to Kantian ethics, and provides us with the basis for, or source of, all our duties, both towards others and towards the self. This axiomatic assertion is also perhaps the greatest contribution of Kantian ethics to human thought.

The dignity and inviolability of persons arises out of two metaphysical propositions in Kant : first, the supremacy of reason, and reason forming the core or essence of a person; and second, the freedom or autonomy of the person, so that the laws which a moral agent obeys are those which she has given to herself.[32] These two are complex propositions and imply a distinction between two aspects of our personhood. I refer here to the only too familiar distinction between our noumenal and phenomenal natures which are postulated as locuses of the rationality and freedom or autonomy of the person on one hand, and the general heteronomy of the human will, the emotions and inclinations of the moral agent which are necessarily in conflict with the moral law, on the other hand. The necessity of acting in obedience to the moral law further presupposes a distinction between, or our person as consisting of, two aspects - the phenomenal and the noumenal. To quote Kant,

> Now man really finds in himself a faculty by which he distinguishes himself from everything else, even from himself as affected by objects and that is *reason*. This being pure spontaneity is even elevated above the *understanding*....
>
> For this reason a rational being must regard himself *qua* intelligence.... As belonging not to the world of sense, but to that of understanding; hence he has two points of view from which he can regard himself..... *first*, so far as he belongs to the world of sense he finds himself subject to the laws of nature (heteronomy); *secondly*, as belonging to the intelligible world, under laws which being independent of nature have their foundation not in experience but in reason alone.[33]

The entire Kantian metaphysics of morals, especially his three formulations of the categorical imperative are best understood and justified in the Kantian conceptual framework. It has no parallel in the Western thought, excepting Bradley's distinction between appearance and reality. But in Indian philosophy, especially in the Vedãntic tradition, the distinction between the transcendent self (*pārmãrthika satya*) and the empirical self (*jiva or vyãvahãrika satya*) is foundational to their religion and ethics.

Kant further distinguishes between duties towards others and those towards ourselves. It is taken for granted that a person's perfection which consists in the fullest realization of her potentialities can be realized only through her own efforts. It follows that we can only bring about the happiness (welfare) of others, that is, our duties towards others are limited to promoting their welfare or happiness. In addition, we have a definite duty towards our own selves, and it consists in working for the fullest realization of our potentialities or self-perfection. What is more,

> Far from ranking lowest in the scale of precedence, our duties towards ourselves are of primary importance and should have pride of place; for..... it is obvious that nothing can be expected from a man who dishonours his own person.... Thus a man who fails in his duty to himself loses worth absolutely; while a man who fails in his duty to others loses worth only relatively. It follows that the prior condition of our duty to others is our duty to ourselves; we can fulfil the former only in so far as we first fulfil the latter.[34]

This seems to be a radical statement indeed. While most Western ethicists give an almost exclusive importance to our duties to others, Kant not only gives primary importance to our duty towards our own selves, he even declares that neglect of our duties towards others is of lesser moral importance than the neglect of our duties to ourselves.

IV.2 Kant makes another distinction between the duties of perfect obligation and those of imperfect obligation. The former, i.e. duties of perfect obligation are duties of indebtedness or justice, that is, the duties to pay back to others what is due to them. Keeping one's promise is the paradigm of duties of perfect obligation which can have no exception:

> Here there is no question of inclination, only of the rights of others.... It is not a question whether my neighbour is needy, wrechedly poor, or the reverse; if his right is concerned, it must be satisfied.[35]

For him, each human being is a rational person and as such claims dignity and inviolability as an end-in-herself. These claims are the rights of a human person which become the duties of perfect obligation for all other persons. Since the claims to personal dignity etc. on the part of human beings necessarily follow from the fact of their essential and universally shared rational nature, these claims are a part of our personhood, and are inviolable; and their corresponding duties are unconditional or duties of perfect obligation.

In addition to the duties of perfect obligation are those of imperfect obligation which include duties of benevolence. Kant here goes beyond the limits of his own philosophy. While he has mostly downgraded duties done out of benevolence, in this context he acknowledges the moral worth of such actions. He argues that the bounty of nature is a common property of all human beings and must be shared by us all. Benevolence or charity simply means giving to others what as a matter of fact belongs to all of us. Through acts of benevolence we restore "what we have unrighteously (though unknowingly) procured." Although we may be acting according to the rules of the land,

> we may nevertheless be participating in general injustice and in giving to an unfortunate man we do not give him a gratuity but only help to return to him that of which the general injustice of our system has deprived him.... Even charity therefore is an act of duty imposed upon us by the rights of others and the debt we owe to them.[36]

Thus, not only the duties of perfect obligation, such as promise keeping, are resultant of, or consequential upon, our previous indebtedness to others, even duties of imperfect obligation, such as acts of charity, indirectly involve the idea of our indebtedness to fellow human beings.

While the duties of perfect obligation are universal (universally applicable) and unconditional or absolute, the duties of imperfect obligation, though universal, are optional. Performing them may mean additional merit for the moral agent, but their non-performance brings no demerit. Kant goes on to tell us that if a person obeys the moral law under all circumstances, and performs all the duties of perfect obligation, but has never performed an act of charity or benevolence, she would still remain a morally worthy agent.[37]

However, our duties of perfect obligation cannot exhaust all our duties. It is true that while some of our duties are both universal and necessary (though they may still have exceptions), as the duty to keep one's promise, others, such as helping the needy, sick, or old, would be optional; but they would nevertheless be our duties.

Mostly duties which are universal and necessary are those which have a negative connotation, e.g. duties implied in the Ten Commandments. Duties which have positive connotation and which involve our going beyond our duties of perfect obligation, arising out of our explicit indebtedness to others, have to be voluntary. While we cannot ask everyone to act like Mother Teresa, we can ask everyone not to hurt others.

The above discussion may suggest first, that the duties of perfect obligation have an overriding force or are universally obligatory, and therefore, our proposed universal morality would largely consist of duties of perfect obligation. Secondly, it may suggest that duties of perfect obligation or universally obligatory duties are largely negative in character. Abstaining from wrongful acts is more crucial for social relationships than doing good works; that is why, the moral principles prohibiting us from undertaking immoral acts are perceived as more compelling and even universally applicable than positive moral imperatives. It may be the case that most positive acts and duties are done in response to the demands of institutional roles and related values and patterns of behaviour. Particular duties, such as those of the son in the Indian joint family, cannot possibly be declared as universally obligatory; while the duties not to hurt others, or to abstain from falsehood can clearly be declared as universally obligatory.

I feel however that Kant did not intend his duties of perfect obligation as having only negative connotation. For example, his paradigmatic duty of promise-keeping is a positive one in character. Also, we cannot speak of 'universal morality' from the Kantian point of view, as morality *per se* is universal. So either the duties of imperfect obligation are universal, or they are not moral at all. That means any proposed system of morality need not consist only of duties of perfect obligation, or those having negative connotations only; but would include duties of imperfect obligations as well.

Thus, Kant makes a fourfold division of duties : First come the duties towards ourselves, and they involve duties of self-preservation and avoidance of acts and ways which would be harmful to our higher or rational self, e.g. indulgence in carnal pleasures. These are the duties of perfect obligation to ourselves. In addition, we have duties of imperfect obligation to ourselves, and they consist in developing our higher (rational) faculties. The second group of duties consist of those towards others. Kant lists several duties in this context: there are some which arise out of our duty to respect the personhood in others;[38] and there are others which are duties of beneficence, gratitude, love and sympathy. Here also the emphasis is more on avoidance of the vices directed towards others, such as hatred, mockery, avarice, etc. and less on the performance of acts of benevolence; though he recommends such acts, as also the duty of friendship as morally worthwhile.

Significantly also, all these duties of perfect and imperfect obligations, duties towards oneself and those towards others, are included under the head of duties of virtue. Duties of virtue, in turn, presuppose inner freedom, and it is these duties alone which have ethical worth for Kant. On the positive side, "virtue signifies a moral strength of will", or self-mastery.[39] In his *The Doctrine of Virtue*, Kant seems to contend that duties of perfect obligation alone are duties proper, while duties of imperfect obligation are virtues. But Kant's own conceptions of duty and virtue are so integrally related that it is difficult to distinguish the two.

IV.3 The two contentions of Kant, regarding morality as mainly consisting of our duties of perfect obligation; and the latter having mostly negative connotation, do not follow from Kant's own moral philosophy. According to his own conception of justice and duty as mainly consisting in the payment of our debts to others, we just cannot claim that all our morality is exhausted by our performance of certain duties of perfect obligation, mostly having negative connotation. If the other members of society have rights and we owe debts to them, either because of some previous transaction on our part with them, or because of our having participated in social processes which have resulted in their loss or disadvantage, then our duties extend much beyond those of perfect obligation. If all persons *qua* their personhood have right to dignity and inviolability, then the society and the individuals in it have a duty towards all persons, especially those who are in a disadvantageous position because of the unjust social processes.

Kant's main concern, however, is the purity of motive or attitude in the performance of one's duties. To repeat a well-known aspect of his philosophy, morality consists, for him, only of those acts that are done out of pure respect for the moral law. He understands the categorical imperative as giving the form or the principle of all moral actions. And "what is essentially good in it consists in mental disposition, let the consequence be what it may. This imperative may be called that of morality."[40] If so, then the distinction between duties and virtues crumbles down. Virtues are those which are concerned with purity of motive, inner freedom and restraint; and duties are those which are performed with the sole motive of conforming to the moral law through self-restraint. Moreover, Kant himself persistently suggests that all our duties are finally reducible to the need for restraint over our lower passions, self-mastery and purity of motive. This idea of doing one's duties without regard to the consequences does not hold much appeal to the modern mind. I have a few comments in favour of Kantian moral philosophy.

First, I feel that the idea of a desireless performance of one's duties paves the way for a universal morality. It is so because deciding one's duties on the Kantian principle means deciding under the Rawlsian veil of ignorance without the artificiality of the latter. It cuts out all considerations of personal interests, thus indirectly rejecting any sharp distinction between our duties towards the self and towards others.

Secondly, of course, Kant's conception of the categorical imperative as universal and absolute, i.e. without the possibility of exceptions, is the most clear cut assertion ever made regarding the necessity of universal morality. The universality and necessity of the categorical imperative mean that neither the differences in the empirical circumstances, nor those due to the fact of any two moral agents belonging to different cultures, are relevant for the moral point of view. For Kant, it is as simple as this that morality consists in acting from pure respect for the moral law; and the moral law, being the law given by the universal reason, is a categorical imperative, applicable to all rational beings.

Thirdly, the three formulations of the categorical imperative are not merely formal, as being synthetic they must have content. The first formulation regarding the universality and absoluteness of the moral law implies the equality of all persons, and even justice. Second and third formulations are even more substantial, as they emphasize the dignity and inviolability of the person, and the need for reverence for the personhood in every one of us. This principle alone can provide the most universal regulative principle of morality.

Another comment in passing. Some aspects of the Kantian moral philosophy are so akin to the ancient Indian conception of morality (*dharma* or a righteous way of life) that this affinity itself should prove that human reason and intuitions are basically universal.[41]

V. Indian Perspective

V.1 Hinduism is not a religion of the Book, nor is it based on one single 'revelation' and creed; it is rather a conglomeration of various religio-moral traditions. Each tradition has its own set of metaphysical beliefs, and a system of morality. I would concentrate here on two such, probably most fundamental, traditions : the liberation (*moksa*) - centric tradition of Vedānta and the socio-centric tradition of Dharmaśāstras and Epics etc.[42] Thus it came about that the problem of self and others in morality has been discussed and understood in two very different metaphysical-valuational contexts in Hinduism.

According to the liberation-centric tradition, the universal transcendental self (*Atman*) resides, or is immanent, in all selves, inspiring and energizing all their experiences. The human goal is perceived in this tradition as the realization of the subject's total identity with the universal or Divine Self (*Atman*) through the transcendence of our empirical self and all the dualities and conflicts associated with our empirical (*vyāvahārika*) life. These ideas were developed in the Upaniṣads, which are popularly known as Vedānta, and then in a more moderate form in the *Bhagavadgitā*. There are various versions of Vedānta, some are more esoteric and extreme, as that of śaṁkara; others are milder and more accommodative of the requirements of the social order and its related duties, as those of Rāmānuja, the *Gitā* and a few Purāṇas.

While the first or Vedāntic tradition concentrates on spirituo-moral questions and is world-and-life-negating to some extent, the more predominant Hindu tradition as expounded in the Dharmaśāstras, Epics and popular literature, is extremely world-and-life-affirming and socio-centric. Moreover, it perceives the individual, not as a transcendent self but, as a unit of society whose goals and duties are both directed towards and determined by the social order, its norms and role models.

This tradition of Indian thought emphasizes the duties towards others. A person's duties towards herself or her rights vis-a-vis others are not discussed much. Whenever rights of certain persons need to be discussed, they are presented as the duties of some other persons in certain roles towards those persons with different institutional roles. It must be admitted that the ancient Indian conception of the moral agent's duties towards others was mostly determined by their acceptance of a caste-based social order. Duties were largely determined by a person's caste, and there were apparently unjust caste-based norms which regulated the interpersonal relationships in the society.

On the other hand, the socio-centric tradition in particular, and the entire Hindu moral thought in general, uphold a unique understanding of duty based on the concept of debt (*ṛṇa*). A person is what he/she is because of the contribution of so many persons, humanity in general, and of nature. His/her duties towards others arise out of his/her indebtedness to them. Fulfilling one's obligations to various persons and to the whole of humanity consists in acts aimed at paying off one's debts to all those persons, humanity and nature.[43] Now, different societies would have different coneptions and norms of interpersonal obligations according to their institutional structures and traditional role models. But the idea of duty as paying off of one's debts to others is universal and independent of any historico-cultural context.

V.2 That is why, Indians made a clear distinction between particular duties (*viśeṣa or varnāśrama dharma*) which arise out of social institutions and their norms, and universal duties (*sādhāraṇa dharma*). While the particular duties are different for different individuals according to their status and role in society, the universal duties are meant for, or applicable to, everyone, irrespective of all societal and other empirical differences. They are the duties that are obligatory for all human beings *qua* their humanity. As such, the inner attitude is more important in them; and they are best described as virtues.

There is not much systematic thinking in Indian ethical thought, and ethics is not generally recognized as a separate discipline. This may be confusing for a person who is unfamilier with the Indian ethos, but it has some advantages also. The same term *dharma* is used for both particular or institutional duties and universal duties; it is also indiscriminately used for duties and virtues. As such it comes closest to the Western conception of morality, though in some ways it is a more comprehensive and profound concept than that of morality. The sense of 'ought' is central to it, but this 'ought' belongs to both duties and virtues. And no distinction is made between our duties towards others and those towards our own selves. Universal duties, that is, duties or obligations that belong to us *qua* human beings, are conceived and understood as virtues, as the emphasis in them is on inner motives and states of mind. While the aim of the other - regarding virtues is the good of others, those concerning the self aim at achieving moral discipline or purity of self. In fact, all universal duties cum-virtues (*dharma*) are conceived as qualities or attitudes of the moral agent; as a result even the virtues regarding others are difficult to distinguish from self-regarding virtues.

I quote here a few such lists of universal virtues at random. Manu, the most famous and authoritative law-giver (where law is understood as *dharma* or the righteous way of life), enumerates 10 universal virtues which are - forbearance, forgiveness, self-discipline, nonappropriation of others' wealth, cleanliness, control of senses, intelligence, knowledge, truth and nonanger. Later on he adds nonviolence to the list.[44] Gautama, an earlier law-giver, lists eight virtues of the self (*ãtma guna*) : kindness towards all, forbearance, nonhostility, cleanliness, quietude, doing good acts, and freedom from avarice and cevetousness.[45] Yãjnavalkya, another respected law-giver, gives two lists of virtues : First list includes non-injury, purity, control of senses, charity, mercy, self-restraint and forbearance. The second list consists of the virtues of patience, absence of pride, intelligence, absence of anger, spiritual knowledge, modesty, non-appropriation of others' property and restraint of senses.[46]

Mention should be made here of the five *yamas* or fundamental moral laws which have their origin in the Yoga system of philosophy, but which are equally recognized and valued in all Indian traditions. They are : truth (or truthfulness - *satya*), nonviolence (*ahimsã*), non-stealing (*asteya*), non-hoarding (or limiting one's possessions to basic requirements - *aparigraha*), and restraint of sexual desires (sometimes interpreted as celibacy - *brahmacarya*).[47] *Yamas* are basic moral laws or normative principles which apparently have negative connotation, and aim at self-purification. On the other hand, they are open to positive interpretation, and are mostly understood as virtues which signify a purified mental state. For example, *satya* is abstaining from lies, as also truthfulness, or abiding by truth whatever the consequences. *Ahiṃsā* is not only non-violence, but is also friendliness or compassion towards all. Similarly, *aparigraha* is not merely nonhoarding, it is an attitude of mind, a virtue, which requires very little for oneself, and is always ready to share one's wealth with others.

Let me repeat : there is no distinction between duties and virtues in the Indian mind, and possibly no difference between duties to oneself and to others. In fulfilling our duties to others we fulfil ourselves. Let us take a glance at some of these virtues:

Self-regarding Virtues	**Other-regarding Virtues**
1. forbearance (*dhṛti*)	1. forgiveness (*kṣama*)
2. self-discipline (*dama*)	2. non-violence (*ahiṃsā*)
3. non-appropriation of other's property (*asteya*)	3. kindness (*dayā*)
4. clealiness (*śauca*)	4. nonhostility (*anasūyā*)
5. control of senses (*indriyanigraha*)	5. charity (*dāna*)
6. intelligence (*dhī*)	
7. spiritual knowledge (*vidyā*)	

8. truth (*satya*)
9. nonanger (*akrodha*)
10. freedom from covetousness (*aspṛhā*)
11. non-hoarding (*aparigraha*)

It is interesting to note that while self-regarding virtues given in the above list are 11, other-regarding ones are only 5. It definitely does not mean that ancient Indians (Hindus in popular parlance) conceived morality mainly as self-regarding. However, it is true that Indians gave great importance to the purity of self, that is, the inner attitude of the moral agent, so that often the practice of other-regarding virtues was perceived as a means of self-purification. On the other hand, a large number of those virtues which we have included in the column of self - regarding virtues can be practised only in the social context, that is, are directed towards others. Take for example, the virtue of forbearance which is given a prominent place in all discussions of universal virtues (or duties). It is understood as a part of self-discipline or self-purification, but in practice it is directed both towards the vicissitudes of one's life, and towards others' treatment of one's self. As such, it is almost indistinguishable from forgiveness which is an other-regarding virtue, but which is also cultivated as a means of self-purification or self-discipline. Nonappropriation of others' property is obviously other-regarding, though it is again cultivated as part of self-discipline. Truth or truthfulness is a personal virtue in Indian thought, but it would lose its meaning unless practised in a social context. Similarly, freedom from anger and avarice are meant as part of self-discipline, but can be practised only in the social context. Thus, as far as I can understand, self-control, including discipline of senses and mind, as well as freedom from evil passions, to some extent truth (truthfulness), and spiritual knowledge, are the only virtues which are exclusively self-regarding; other virtues have a definite and even basic reference to our relations with others.

On the other hand, what we have listed as other-regarding virtues, such as nonviolence, forgiveness, kindness, charity and nonhostility, are closely related to one's efforts to purify one's self of all negative feelings, such as violence, anger and avarice. Of course, nonviolence, kindness and charity are definitely other-regarding and should be valued as such.

The problem of classification of virtues recognized in ancient Indian thought is both interesting and a profound one; there is no clear-cut division between other-regarding and self-regarding virtues, because there is no marked distinction between myself and other selves. And it is by directing our thoughts and efforts towards the welfare of others that we do the maximum good to ourselves, which consists in total purity of the self and its freedom from negative emotions (mostly towards others). So by being forbearing and forgiving to others; by avoiding injury to others; by restraining from the emotions of avarice, anger, hatred etc. towards others; by cultivating kindness to others; and by giving or sharing what one has with others, the moral agent's inner self is purified, and she reaches a higher, spiritual level of being.

An interesting and enlightening example of the above observation is the group of four very positive virtues: friendship towards all (*maitrī*), mercy towards the suffering of others (*karuṇā*), gladness at the good of others (*muditā*), and indifference towards evil persons, or their treatment of us (*upekṣā*). There cannot be any more positive and more clearly other-regarding virtues. And yet, they are advised in the *Yoga Sūtras* as antidotes to our negative feelings, and as aids for self-discipline.[48]

It means that though a major portion of morality is concerned with our duties and obligations towards others, it is also or equally concerned with the subject or moral agent. The concern of morality for the subject does not imply concern for her everyday interests, or for her happiness; rather it is for the purity and perfection of her inner self. While our duties towards others are an outcome of our being indebted to them, our duty towards our own self arises out of the moral law to respect a person; or in the Indian context out of our realization that our self is a spiritual entity (*ātman*).

The Indian conception of the ideal moral life as being devoted to the performance of our duties in an equanimous frame of mind is best expressed in the *Bhagavadgitā*.[49] The moral philosophy of the *Gītā* resembles that of Kant in a marked way, or rather, the other way round, i.e. the Kantian conception of duty and morality comes very near that of the *Gītā*. For both, the *Gita* and Kant, duty has moral worth only if it is undertaken out of a pure regard to duty without any reference to its consequences. For both, a major or perhaps the supreme aim of the performance of duties is self-mastery or self-purification.

V.3 Our discussion in Chapter 6 has brought out four substantive principles of universal morality : equality (which includes the ideas of universalizability, impartiality and reciprocity), justice, truth and non-violence.

Generally speaking, the ideas of innate equality of all human beings, impartiality towards all persons, and reversibility, as another way of emphasizing the unconditional equality of all persons (and all living beings), are emphatically asserted in Indian moral thought. The absolute equality of all persons, rather of all living beings, is forcefully recognized by various religious traditions, and is asserted in remarkably different religio-metaphysical conceptual frameworks. The concept of equality of all human beings (i.e. their right to life and even their personal dignity) is integrally related to the virtue of impartiality and the idea of reversibility of all behaviour as the root or ultimate test of morality. As usual, Indians do not distinguish and define their concepts, so that the above three concepts of equality, impartiality and reversibility are all mixed up, or stated as different expressions of the self-same principle.

Impartiality (*samabhāva*) towards all living beings characterizes a morally and spiritually perfect person, and results from the vision of the essential sameness of all living beings. The virtue of impartiality has been highly valued in the Indian religio-moral traditions. Impartiality means nondiscrimination between various persons including oneself which leaves no scope for making an exception of oneself to any moral rule. To quote the *Bhagavadgitā*:

> He who is equal-minded among friends or companions, foes and those who are neutral; among those who are hateful and those who are related (to oneself); among saints and sinners, he excels,[50]

Indian religio-moral thinkers recognize that it is egoism or concern for one's own welfare that makes a person deviate from the path of duty. So the best way to achieve religio-moral perfection is to get rid of one's desires, attachments and egotism. The attitude that rejects one's egoistic desires etc. as irrelevant when deciding on a course of duty is called detachment (*udāsinatā*).[51] There is no need here of the veil of ignorance because the personal desires, attachments and egotism are already recognized as hindrances in the path of duty (*dharma*). So they are simply to be disregarded when deciding upon a course of duty. The very meaning of impartiality in Indian thought means a total disregard for contingent differences among living beings, and an equal disregard for, or equanimity towards, one's own interests or considerations of what would benefit or what would harm the moral subject.[52]

The virtue of impartiality includes or implies two other values or characteristics of the moral point of view : first, universalizability of moral principles and moral judgments; and second, equality of all persons. It is because of their basic affinity to each other that moral principles should apply to them equally, irrespective of differences in their contingent circumstances. And it is because they are absolutely equal, or have some basic ontological affinity, that the moral agent is expected to be impartial towards them, including herself. She must be impartial because *there is no fundamental difference* between them all.

The idea of reversiblity of human behaviour as a test of its moral worth is included in the idea of impartiality. The Upanisads and the *Bhagavadgītā* assert one transcendent Self (*Ātman*) in all living beings. The *Gītā* adds to this esoteric spiritual vision an apparently moral principle :

> He, O Arjuna, who sees with equality everything in the image of his own self, whether in pleasure or in pain, he is considered a perfect yogin.[53]

The phrase "he sees everything in the image of his own self" may be integrally related with the Vedāntic metaphysics, but it also expresses the quintessence of all morality, at least as Indians understood it. The *Gitā* is telling us here that there is no fundamental (metaphysical) difference between I and other selves. Just as Kant's persons are worthy of equal respect by virtue of their rational nature, so all human (in fact all living) beings are worthy of equal treatment by virtue of the transcendent Self which is immanent in all.[54]

If the above sounds too esoteric, the *Mahābhārata* simply asserts the sameness of all living beings on the basis of the commonsense experience of similarity and affinity between myself and all others. The Epic derives the Golden rule from this perception of essential affinity:

> Don't treat others in a way in which you would not like to be treated by others.....
>
> A man who is guilty himself has no right to point to the guilt of others....
>
> How can a man who wants to live himself kill another? Therefore, you should wish for others whatever you want for yourselves....
>
> We should treat others in a way which is desirable for ourselves. And we should not act towards others in a way which is undesirable or unpleasant for us.[55]

The Epic does believe in the individual soul and in the immanence of the Divine Being in all hearts; but its stress is mainly on the normative values of equality and impartiality. It generally does not bother about philosophical consistency, and the words life (*prāṇa*) and self (*ātman*) are used indiscriminately as the common element in all human (living) beings. Life or self is shared by all living beings, and that makes them all essentially equal. This equality does not follow from, that is, is not additional to, their essential affinity, rather, the two conceptions are two sides of the same medal.

The distinction between self and others which is so prominent in Western thought is almost absent from Indian philosophy (with a few exceptions). Equality is integral to the very conception of the individual self (*jīva*), all of whom contain the same Divine spark, or in all of whom the same Divine Being is immanent. And if we choose to steer clear of all religious terminology, equality of all living beings has still to be asserted, as there is no essential distinction between all these selves. The *Tirukkuṛāl*, a lesser known Tamil text, expresses this idea :

> If a person does not protect other beings from injury, realizing that their pain is his own pain, then what use is his knowledge?[56]

One of the basic tenets of Buddhism is its denial of self (*anattā*). The idea of absolute equality of all living beings is asserted therein, not on the basis of one self in all, but, on that of no-self. It is a difficult metaphysical doctrine and need not be discussed here in detail. What concerns us here is that Mahāyāna Buddhist texts constantly extol the virtue of compassion (*karunā*) on the basis of their belief that all living beings are basically the same. There being no immortal soul or a permanent substantial individual principle which could provide the basis for individual's separate identity or agoism, it follows that all living beings are absolutely equal, or even the same. It is egoism or excessive attachment to one's self which is the cause of all moral vices (such as selfishness, avarice, anger and animosity towards others). Once this attachment is given up because there is no separate self to be excessively concerned about, a morality of total impartiality and universal compassion comes naturally.[57]

Such a morality consists in realizing the equality of oneself and others (*para-ātma-samatā*), and practising the substitution of others for oneself (*para-ātma-parivartana*). It is significant that the idea of substitution of others for oneself is nothing but the idea of reversiblity, as so laboriously developed by Hare and others; and here we have this idea clearly stated in texts which belong almost to two millenniums ago.[58]

Indian moral thought typically goes beyond even the idea of reversiblity. When a Buddhist spiritual aspirant (*bodhisattva*) realizes the equality of oneself and others, he gets rid of the ideas of I and you, mine and yours. He learns to feel the joys and sorrows of others like his own, and does not prefer his own happiness to that of others. When a moral agent or spiritual aspirant thinks of others in the same way as he thinks of himself, the words self-interest (*svārtha*) and altruism or concern for others (*parārtha*) lose their distinction.[59] It is repeatedly affirmed that the aspirant (*bodhisattva*) must not bother about the pain and suffering of his body and ego more than those of others, because there is nothing (no soul) which distinguishes oneself from others.

Of course, a total rejection of distinction between self and others would be unacceptable to the modern mind. Morality, as it is conceived in the West (and that conception is probably right), presupposes a moral agent who is not only distinct from others but whose interests and desires may also be in conflict with those of others. At the subjective level, morality is acting according to the moral law in conscious contradistinction to the agent's interests and inclinations (Kant).

On the other hand, it would be wrong even to suggest that Indian thinkers undermined plurality and diversity in favour of some idealized conception of the metaphysical unity of all living beings. In everyday life they perhaps overemphasized differences and structured their society in a hierarchical manner. Not only the society was based on a strict hierarchy of social groups (*varṇas*), interpersonal morality was conceived and practised in accordance with such an unequal social order. Even in jurisprudence, justice was to be accorded in strict accordance with this hierarchy.[60]

Indians seem to have advocated two quite divergent moralities-first, that of *varṇāśrama dharma* (duties according to the caste and stage of life) which was discriminatory and inequitable, but which emphasized interpersonal duties, and second that of *sādhāraṇa dharma* (universal duties or virtues expected from all human beings *qua* their humanity). The latter were idealistically conceived, and emphasized the metaphysical equality of all living beings and the virtue of impartiality; but to some extent they undermined a person's institutional or social duties. There seems to be a vast gulf between the two conceptions of morality, and we have to accept them as they are.

V.4 However, truth (*satya*) and nonviolance (*ahiṃsā*) are two principles of morality which seem to be almost unanimouly accepted by ancient Indians. The concept of truth, like so many other concepts, has metaphysical connotation in Indian thought. But when stripped off of all its metaphysical associations, and understood as a purely spirituo-moral virtue or value, truth or truthfulness emerges as a strong universal moral principle in Indian ethical thought. Truth takes the first place in any enumeration of universal moral obligations or virtues (such as the *yamas* mentioned earlier). *Satya* is conceived in India on a wider canvas so that truthfulness is speaking the truth and keeping one's promises; but more than this, it is being true to one's own self. And a person who is true to herself cannot indulge in immoral acts. Any person, while doing things which ought not to be done, need not think that no one is perceiving her doing it, because the Divine being immanent in every heart or the inner Witness sees and hears everything. This understanding of truthfulness is not necessarily religious, because we can substitute 'Divine Being' by conscience, and still the meaning would remain the same.[61]

Thus, not promise-keeping but truth or truthfulness, as conceived in Indian ethical thought, should be included in universal moral principles. An action is not moral if it is not performed in a truthful frame of mind, or if the agent cannot truthfully claim that it is a moral course of action. Being true to oneself here also means being absolutely just. Of course, a person's conscience may be distorted, and her understanding of what is moral or immoral may be vitiated by prejudices or self-interests. Or a society's moral code may itself condone acts of untruthfulness because that society encourages other things such as success and power. But these would be failures in practice, and unlike Hare, I do not think that failure in practice diminishes the worth of a moral principle.

Ahiṃsā is the second most important cardinal virtue in Indian ethics, and is the fourth substantive principle of universal morality, as I am trying to develop here. *Ahiṃsā* means nonviolence, and it is the second virtue in the five universal moral rules of conduct, i.e. *Yamas*. It is also often hailed as the supreme duty of human beings.[62] (The ideal of *ahiṃsā*, was more or less heterogeneous to the Vedic-Dharmaśāstric tradition, and was imported therein from the heterodox or śramaṇic tradition, i.e. Buddhism and Jainism; but once it was accepted by the mainstream tradition, it became integral to it. *Ahiṃsā* is not merely abstaining from hurting others or causing physical pain to others, it also means desisting from causing any mental pain, worry, or fear in another being. *Ahiṃsā* or nonviolence means giving the gift of fearlessness to all living beings.[63] It is an all-encompassing ideal, both in its conception and scope.

True worth of *ahiṃsā* lies in its exceptionally broad application. All living beings from gods to the smallest creatures are *jīvas*. The word *jīva* means both the individual soul, as also simply whatever has life. *Jīva* is one who has life, and the element of life (*prāṇa*) is common in all living beings. Life is dear to all living beings as it is to us; and all beings feel pain and suffering as we do. Therefore, it is incumbent upon us not to cause injury or hurt to any living being. The moral obligation of *ahiṃsā* goes beyond our obligations to other human persons and extends to all living beings. In this it is unique or different from the Semitic and Western conceptions of morality which exclude animal kingdom from the realm of moral action. Moral obligations, even for Kant, are directed towards persons, and animals are not persons.

Thus *ahiṃsā* or non-violence is the fourth constitutive principle of universal morality. It has broader application than even the first three principles, i.e.equality, justice and truth. No morality can be complete without the principle of nonviolence, or our universal duty not to hurt others, or cause pain to them. We may or may not conceive it as including compassion (*karuṇā*), and as demanding from us active contribution towards their general welfare. Possibly, *ahiṃsā* is best understood as a slightly negative principle prohibiting violence to others. But its comprehensive and overriding nature cannot be neglected.

To conclude, I started with the question whether morality is chiefly or exclusively concerned with our duties towards others, or it is also concerned with the motives, intentions, will and personal goals of the moral agent. The above discussion seems to have proved that morality is concerned both with the self and others. Perhaps it is more concerned with others because we naturally tend to take care of our interests, and neglect those of others; and morality seeks to ensure that the rights of others are respected by us, and our debts to them are paid. The principles of equality and justice enjoin certain universally obligatory duties of the moral agent towards others. Nonviolence adds another dimension to the moral point of view. We have not only the duty not to hurt others or cause pain to them, this duty is also in a way independent of all considerations of justice and debts. Since *ahiṃsā* in the Indian context presumes the basic affinity of all living beings, it is integrally related to the assumption of both innate and normative equality of all. The three principles of equality, justice and nonviolence are thus harmoniously related.

However, the moral point of view is equally concerned with the motives and character of the moral agent. In Kant and Indian philosophy, this aspect of morality is emphasized much more than even the duties towards others. The moral principle of truthfulness (*satya*) refers mainly to the subjective aspect of morality. As we have seen, truthfulness not only includes abstaining from lies and promise - keeping, but also several other virtues, such as good will or respect for the moral law, rejection of the relevance of considerations of self-interest and freedom from moral vices. A person who is truthful to herself cannot demean herself by succumbing to moral vices, has self-restraint, and moral integrity, which latter includes acknowledgment of our obligations to others.

Any effort to divide universal moral principles into self-regarding and other-regarding cannot do justice to the comprehensive and 'foundational' nature of universal morality. While the regulative principles of interpersonal behaviour are generally culture-specific and hence relative, the universal element of morality directly or indirectly refers to the inner states of the moral subject. As Kant so rightly asserts, the moral worth of an action lies in the good will, or the will that acts out of pure respect for the moral law. In Indian ethical parlance, the same idea is expressed in terms of purity of self. That action is morally worthy which is done with an equanimous frame of mind and with an exclusive regard to one's duty without any reference to the consequences.[64] Once this is acknowledged, the self-regarding and other-regarding duties seem to merge together.

Let us take a few principles of universal morality, as equality, impartiality, reversibility, and justice. All of these are other -regarding principles, that is, refer to our attitudes towards, or our relations with, others. They, at the same time characterize the self. To affirm the (normative) equality of all persons and the 'ought' of impartiality, reversibility and justice is to say that the moral subject ought to be equitable, impartial, and just. A person who acts in this way would act morally, whatever the socio-cultural circumstances.

I have tried in the last two Chapters to explore and identify some principles of morality which seem reasonably free from culture-specific conditions and can therefore claim universal validity. I have also realized that these principles, such as universality, rationality, justice etc., are not merely formal principles of morality but are constitutive of universal morality, or the moral point of view. I would have preferred to call them the core or the foundational principles of morality. But we can easily avoid the foundationalist terminology and say that these are the ethical or normative principles which are both directly (intutively) realized as true or right, and rationally justified as universally (cross-culturally) valid.

I have also tried to argue that the individual moral subject or agent is probably the primary referent of all ethical discourse. Even if it is not so, the individual's motive and her frame of mind are very important and relevant factors in determining the moral worth of an act, practice, or even way of life. Moreover, the individual agent owes duties to herself as much as she does towards others. If so, the community alone cannot be the source of all the beliefs, moral norms and standards, of a person, or group; and there can be ethical principles and standards which can be recognized universally or cross-culturally. The principles of the moral point of view that I have tired to develop here may well be some such universal normative principles.

CHAPTER 8

A Rational Approach to Universal Morality

I. Objectivity and Validity

I.1 As we have seen in Chapter 6, the moral point of view is characterized by rationality, universality, ojectivity and overridingness. That is, if an assertion is not uiversalizable, cannot claim certain objectivity for itself, cannot be either questioned at the rational level or be capable of rational justification, and does not claim for itself some form of overriding authority, then that assertion, and the point of view from which it is made, are not ethical.

The claim to objectivity and interpersonal validity is inherent in an ethical assertion. If I assert, first, that Hitler's act of genocide was an evil act or that he was evil, and second, that all meaningless cruelty is evil, I intend my assertions to be taken literally as cognitive assertions. I expect at the same time that others would agree with me, since what I am asserting is objective, true, or interpersonally valid. If my ethical principles and judgments were a creation of my subjective idiosyncrasies or my society's norms and prejudices, they could make no claim to interpersonal validity.

The term 'objectivity' in rational judgments has two quite independent meanings. According to the first, objectivity in moral discourse means independence of the subject of judgment from the approval or disapproval and other emotional responses, as well as from cultural prejudices and narrow culture-specific beliefs and values of the individual or society. That a moral judgment is objective simply means that it is independent of the subjective beliefs and prejudices which are almost always relative to the subject's culture and its specific conceptual framework. Barring some hard core relativists, most other ethical thinkers accept this objectivity as an essential condition of the moral point of view and subsequent moral discourse.

Objectivity also means that the object or referent of a moral judgment exists in some way independently of the subject of judgment. The objectivity of moral properties is strongly advocated by the realists[1], and even more strongly opposed by the relativists who reject the independence of all objects of our experience. I am sympathetic to the realist view, and believe that there is something in the object (act, situation, or character of the moral agent) which in some way governs or determines my moral judgment. It is not only that we judge the act of burning a cat as morally wrong, the act *is* wrong and would have been wrong had there been no judgment to that effect.

Most ethicists do not want to go this far, yet insist on the objectivity of moral judgments, that is, their independence from the subject pronouncing that judgment. W.T. Stace, M.G. Singer and others have emphatically expressed the view (quoted earlier) that what really *is* right is independent of what people *think* right. If some act or character trait is good, or some moral principle is right or true, it is so irrespective of whether anybody believes in it or not.[2]

Kurt Baier has insisted that the moral point of view is both universal and objective; and by objectivity he means total independence of the moral principles and norms from social opinions and conditions.[3] Moral convictions, such as "killing is wrong", "lying is wrong", etc.

> are true quite irrespective of the particular setup of given societies. If there are true moral convictions at all, then they must be absolutely true, for they are based solely on human nature.[4]

Baier goes beyond this and claims that these objective, universal moral principles constitute absolute morality. "Absolute morality", according to him, "is that set of moral convictions, whether held by anyone or not, which is true quite irrespective of any particular social conditions in which they might be embodied."[5] Specific moralities are the outcome of the application of these absolute moral principles to specific social conditions. Baier does not mean by the term 'absolute' unconditional, final, or without exception, as the term is understood in Kantian philosophy. Perhaps the choice of the term is wrong because all he means is that there are certain fundamental, universal ethical principles, which are often at the core of specific moralities but which are independent of any socio-cultural context. This implies that if the norms and rules of separate moralities go against these fundamental moral principles, the former should be overridden by the latter.

Joel J. Kupperman similarly asserts that the moral judgments are cognitive, and they can rightly claim objective validity. If someone insists on some moral principle, and also accepts that the principles being asserted would be right or true even if neither he nor anyone else affirmed it, then that would be a case of ethical knowledge.[6]

When we say that Jones' ethical judgment is correct, we mean that this is the case independently of what he or anyone else (including us) thinks. We would be prepared to say that his judgment would be correct even if he were somehow convinced no longer to make it, and we and everyone else were convinced somehow no longer to agree to it. If it is correct, then it is correct independently of all these circumstances.[7]

It means that even though our ethical assertions are often influenced by sociological factors, in order to be right or correct, they must be understood and justified without reference to them. He further distinguishes between correctness in a qualified sense and that in an unqualified sense. The qualified correctness is where validity of an assertion is made logically dependent on the opinion of some individual or the group. On the other hand,

> The correctness of judgments which are correct in an unqualified sense is independent of (not simply a function of) the attitude or the opinion of the person making them, the agreement of the person responding to them, or the opinion of the society.[8]

He adds that, "to claim that there is ethical knowledge implies the claim th-t ethical judgments may be correct in an unqualified sense."[9] The word 'know' is appropriate in these circumstances, e.g. when we say that someone 'knows' that killing a human being or stealing an art object is wrong. "What we normally speak of 'knowing' in an ethical sense," says he, "has a close similarity to knowledge that something is the case."[10]

That is to say, when we assert something regarding moral matters, we are not merely expressing an opinion or attitude, but are telling what we 'know'. And 'knowing' mainly means here that our assertions are not based on subjective or sociological factors, but claim objective, interpersonal, and even cross-cultural validity.

At the same time, Kupperman seeks to qualify his own view that ethical assertions are cognitive. He says that 'ethical knowledge' need not be knowledge in the usual sense but has a definite family resemblance to other kinds of knowledge; or simply that it has a close affinity with knowledge that something is the case.[11]

Kupperman need not have qualified his contention regarding the cognitive character of ethical assertions. Whatever else we may or may not agree upon, we have to admit the necessary (integral to it) universality and objectivity of ethical judgments. This, in turn, means a claim to truth or correctness on their part. It is difficult to acknowledge one, i.e. objectivity and reject the other, i.e. the claim to cognitivity and correctness. Though our emotions and some sociological factors influence our ethical assertions, the latter are neither mere emotive utterances, nor mere socially-determined opinions. Ethical assertions, at least at the 'higher' or critical level, are universal,, objective, rational and overriding.

When Kupperman and others recognize the cognitivity and objectivity of ethical assertions, but hesitate to call them knowledge, they seem to be influenced by the common notion of knowledge as empirical, that is knowledge of facts which can somehow or other be verified or falsified. Instead, we have knowledge in several fields of human culture and experience which is neither empirical, nor verifiable in the positivists' sense of the term, but which is still knowledge as it can be rationally proved. In this category not only should we include aesthetic and religious assertions but also sociological and scientific theories and hypotheses.

Kupperman further contends that substantial ethical claims or fundamental ethical principles are presupposed in all rational moral discourse, and hence do not need any further rational justification.[12] If we demand or try to justify these moral principles, we would be led to infinite regress. Since we cannot carry the process of rational justification indefinitely, we have to stop at some place, and certain fundamental moral principles, such as were suggested at the end of our Chapter 6, are the best point to stop further rational justification.

But how do we arrive at our moral principles ? We cannot derive them from experience. Experience or what 'is' cannot provide a basis of the 'ought' of morals. And I reject any claim that our most fundamental moral principles are simply a part of specific moral codes. This leaves us the option that in some sense our moral assertions are a case of knowledge, that is, we 'know' that "the act of burning a cat is a cruel and wrong act;" that "giving pain to others is wrong;" or, "we should keep our promise;" and so on. How do we know this ? What is the form of our 'knowledge' in ethical matters? And how can such supposedly cognitive assertions be justified?

I have a natural sympathy with intuitionism as advocated by Moore and Sidgwick. Intuitionism is supposedly closely related with the presumptive thesis of there being nonnatural properties of the objects of our judgment which are intuitively recognized. Intuitionists are also supposed to equate normative judgments with descriptive ones. I think that Sidgwick and Moore did not mean all that they are accused of; or even if they meant all this, the conception of intuition can not only be freed of all the semi-metaphysical beliefs of its advocates, but it can also be demystified. That is, intuition is not some 'higher' or unique (mystical) faculty but just another name for an immediate rational awareness of our duties, some basic values and some basic moral principles. This intuition or cognition is not unique to morality but is a very important mode of knowing in almost all fields of knowledge, from mathematics and logic to science.

W.D. Ross has compared the comprehension or cognition of ethical principles to the direct perception of the truth of mathematical principles. We are directly aware of universal moral principles, such as "promises must be kept," which are self-evident and need no further proof. Our particular moral judgments are discursive and derived from, or based upon, those self-evident or intuitively apprehended fundamental moral principles.

However whether we say that we directly apprehend (intuit) the moral quality of the object of our ethical judgment; or that we cognize certain ethical principles directly or intuitively, there are problems in any such position. First, we have to explain the nature of this direct apprehension; and second, we have to defend its truth claim. Obviously, the truth or falsity of ethical assertions cannot be understood naively in terms of actual (empirical) verification, or correspondence theory of truth. Though ethical discourse implies the cognitive nature of our moral assertions, the terms 'knowledge', 'cognitivity' and 'truth' are not free from problems in the ethical context.

'Intuition' alone cannot explain the cognitivity, objectivity and truth claim of our ethical assertions. If we were all intuitively certain of the truth of our moral principles and judgments, moral disagreements could not be explained. Intuition, being direct and non-mediate, would not accept either its fallibility, or exceptions to its principles. Such a dogmatic position is unacceptable to the contemporary mind.

At the same time, the claim to objectivity seems to be integral to an ethical assertion, and this claim is closely linked to the claim to cognitivity. Perhaps the most important relation in a cognitive assertion, whether empirical or ethical, is not between different concepts and words of the language (as the postmodernists contend); nor is it between the speakers and language (as the positivists claim) ; but rather it is between the language and the object or referent thereof. Both knowledge and its truth claim imply objective reference. Every cognitive assertion has a clearly identifiable referent (in spite of the postmodernist contention to the contrary) which can be perceived and described by different persons according to their different perspectives. But these different versions of objective 'facts' would not only be comparable but also in most cases mutually compatible, due to the fact of their having the same referent. Ethical assertions, though not descriptive in their meaning, have a descriptive content whose object can be identified and described explicitly or implicitly in all value judgments.

The element of description in all evaluations guarantees their objective reference or indicative character. That is why, value judgments are very different from emotive utterances. Unlike the latter, value assertions, including the prescriptive ones, seek to tell us something about their object, i.e. an action, a character trait, or a situation. Above all, value judgments are ones about which we can give reasons, reasons which claim to have objective or interpersonal validity, that is, reasons which can be understood, agreed to, or controverted by, other people in a moral discourse.

I.2 The claim to cognitivity and hence to some kind of truth is inherent in ethical assertions. This claim, however, cannot be a claim for necessary truth or infallibility, which claim on the part of any human knowledge or judgment can never be sustained. Therefore, scholars have translated this claim to truth into a claim to reasonableness, or claim to rational justifiability.

This means, above all, that the correctness or incorrectness, or truth or falsity, of a given assertion is independent of the subject who asserts it. The assertion may owe its origins to sociological factors, but its truth or falsity, or justifiability from a rational moral point of view is independent of those sociological factors. For example, most of the rules and norms of customary morality owe their origins and even authority to sociological factcrs, but they cannot be morally and rationally justified just by reference to the prevailing moral code, as the ethical relativists do.

When we say that a certain ethical assertion A is right, correct, or true, we mean first, that the assertion is independent of who (or how many) make it; and second, that there are good reasons to make or support it. It also means, though there is no general agreement among ethicists over the issue, that in case two persons or societies make very different or contradictory judgments over some issue, it cannot be that both of them are right. Baier insists:

> When two people have contradictory beliefs, then the question which is true necessarily arises. Similarly when two

> peoples or two societies regard one and the same fact.....the one as a prima facie presumptive reason *for*, the other as a prima facie presumptive reason ag*ainst* doing it, then the question who is right necessarily arises. We cannot just leave the matter at that and be satisfied with their just being different, as we can with regard to the brute facts.[13]

What these scholars want to assert is that to say that "we know that....." implies a claim to the truth or correctness of our assertion. If we go on to say that those who contend that they 'know' something entirely different from us about the same subject matter, are equally justified in their claim; or that their claim, even though contrary to ours, is equally true, then we are being inconsistent. We cannot simultaneously claim truth or knowledge (here they are being treated as equivalent) for two contradictory contentions.

But any assertion to the effect that out of the two contradictory opinions, beliefs, or principles, only one can be correct or true implies an absolutist or unipolar conception of truth. Only when we conceive the truth or falsity of any assertion as unconditional or absolute do we claim that only one of the two opposing judgments can be true. Of course, there is nothing logically wrong in saying that out of the two contradictory views on *one* subject both cannot equally be right.

The argument by Philippa Foot and others, to the effect that two mutually contradictory judgments can both be right since the same subject is being judged with reference to two different standards, is not convincing.[14] It would be the case only if the two different assertions belonged to two different points of view, e.g. when an act or a person is being assessed in physical, historico-sociological and moral contexts. Thus, we can describe the physical characteristics of Hitler, and even the physical movements and other details involved while ordering the extermination of Jews; we can also discuss in a detached scientific manner the historical consequences of his policy; and finally we can judge his acts and character from a moral point of view. These three different assertions regarding Hitler do not contradict each other because they are made from different points of view.

But the different moral judgments of one and the same act cannot be all true simply because they are being offered by persons belonging to different cultures supposedly having different standards. If they are moral judgments they must share some characteristics of the moral point of view, or at least there should be a family resemblance between them all in order for them to claim being moral. If they make this claim, they cannot at the same time claim to be made from entirely different perspectives, the judgments from which can be incommensurable and yet right, and so on. If I declare Hitler's act of genocide a morally evil act, and another person commends it as a morally justified act, it does not make a whit of difference that I and the other person belong to two different cultures and are supposedly making our *moral* judgments with reference to two culture-specific standards. What counts is that we are both claiming that our different judgments regarding one and the same act are moral judgments; and as such they cannot be contradictory and yet simultaneously true.

Different moral judgments are somewhat justified in the case of the conduct which is necessarily determined by society's institutions and their norms; while differences in judgments become progressively unjustifiable as we move from concrete cases to more abstract moral principles. We would not therefore pronounce Eskimos' practice of letting the old people die as morally right for them even though most of us would not blame those who practise it for various considerations. It is because in this case a fundamental moral principle is involved, regarding the sanctity of human life, and we cannot say that this principle is different for different cultures.

In other words, if two judgments are supposedly made from the moral point of view, they cannot at the same time contradict each other. At the practical level, such contradictions are found, and are to be accepted as such both from the relativist and the liberal points of view. But where fundamental moral principles are involved, e.g. the sanctity of life, the duty of truthfulness or promise-keeping, then we cannot take the pretext of two moral judgments being made from two different cultural points of view to claim that both are true, even if they contradict each other. Implied here is the claim that only one of the two assertions can be true.

However, to say that out of two or more contradictory judgments only one can be true is one thing; and to try to decide which one of them is the 'true' one is quite another. Any such position invariably leads to ethnocentricism and fanaticism which, of course, are highly undesirable. Similarly, to say that out of two or more contradictory judgments, standards, or principles on *one and the same* subject, all cannot be equally true is one thing, and to claim finality or infallibility for any particular ethical assertions is quite another. No human knowledge, particularly no linguistic proposition can ever be so. It means that all moral judgments are subject to critical evaluation and modification; and therefore no moral assertion can claim finality in the sense that it can declare all other judgments wrong.[15]

I.3 Thomas D. Perry contends that the claim to interpersonal validity, correctness, or truth for any moral judgment made by some person means the claim that anyone who would consider the matter in a reasonable manner is likely to arrive at the same decision as she has done. What is being asserted here is that different persons arguing in a clear and reasonable manner are likely to appeal to the same moral principles and give the same weightage to the facts of the case; and therefore in reasonableness lies the hope for consensus. Perry goes on to assert that the truth or validity of a moral assertion is to be found in consensus of opinion among people who are capable of arguing in a rational manner. According to him, a moral statement is true if and only if practically everyone who might consider it in the proper manner would concur in it.[16]

Like Perry, Kupperman believes in the consensus of competent judges over some subject as a proof of the validity of a particular opinion. To quote him:

> There is a genuine relation between the amount of consensus which surrounds a view and one's right to claim knowledge that the view is correct. It is this: where intelligent men differ it is, or ought to be, harder to feel sure or confident of the correct answer.[17]

It is significant that both Kupperman and Perry are not talking of general agreement among the majority of people over some ethical issue, but of consensus among competent judges who are expected to judge the issues involved in a reasonable manner, and arrive at an agreed conclusion through reasoning and dialogue. At the same time, both scholars go on to acknowledge that such a consensus is mostly possible among people belonging to the same culture or form of life. If consensus among qualified people or experts (which claim is seriously challenged by the postmodernists) guaranteed the truth of an assertion, and if such a consensus can be achieved only among people belonging to the same culture or form of life, then we come back to ethical relativism.

On the other hand, I have tried to argue in this work, and cited other ethicists in support, that the claim to correctness or truth of an ethical judgment is a claim to universality and objectivity which, in turn, implies the independence of that judgment from the person or society that holds it. It is further the claim that agreement or disagreement among different people on the issues involved would not make a difference to its truth or falsity, correctness or incorrectness. As Carl Wellman says not only do we judge some ethical assertions as correct, right, or true, but also,

> the notion of correctness brings with it the assumption that correctness or incorrectness of a proposed answer is fixed independently of any one's acceptance or rejection. In some sense the answer is there to be discovered, thinking cannot make it so.[18]

So the fact that a majority of those who can argue reasonably arrive at a consensus on some ethical issue need not guarantee its truth. Actually what we can reasonably (to borrow Perry's phrase) claim here is that the consensus of belief and judgment among those who consider it reasonably and in all its dimensions is neither a source, nor a proof, of the rightness of that view, but it can be an *indication* of the greater possibility of its rightness.

Of course, agreement in moral issues is always welcome. Arriving at some form of agreement is the goal of most ethical discourse. Hume genuinely believed that human beings share the same emotional responses to morally good or bad acts or traits. Hare at one place grounds the possibility of agreement in human emotions and needs, and asserts that, "People's inclinations about most of the important matters tend to be the same."[19] He even contends that in most cases the agreement already exists and "all that is needed is to think clearly and to make it evident."[20]

There is another dimension to the worth or otherwise of agreement or consensus over an ethical issue. If the truth of moral assertions is irrespective of who or how many assert it, then agreement or consensus about some moral issue cannot claim any privileged position. and there is no point even in moral discourse or dialogue. It seems that we have to acknowledge agreement among rational persons arguing in a reasonable manner as an important element in rational discourse, even though we cannot accept it as the final arbiter or criterion of the 'truth'. of ethical assertions.

On the other hand, while acknowledging the value of consensus, moral philosophers, including Hare and Thomas D. Perry, have insisted on the freedom or right of the moral agent to decide for herself the guiding principles of her actions, or the way of life she wants to live. Even if my moral assertions make a claim to correctness or truth, or there is a general consensus about some particular moral issue, we have no right to declare any other person's moral judgment as false. According to Perry, it is especially so if the other person is arguing reasonably and still arriving at a different judgment. To quote Perry in some detail:

> A person is always entitled to judge reasonably for himself whether a certain moral principle or criterion is valid, and whether it should be allowed to determine a particular moral question in a particular way. Even if there would be a consensus of fully informed or reasonable moral judges about the question before him....he is not bound by that consensus and meaning. A moral critic is still entitled by the 'rules' of moral thought and discourse to reject that principle in that application if he finds it objectionable when considering the subject of evaluation in the morally reasonable way.[21]

I have reservations about this liberal thesis that every moral agent is the best judge of the rightness or wrongness of a proposed act, or the appropriateness or otherwise of a moral principle to that situation. When Kant talked of the autonomy or freedom of will, the will to which he was referring was in some way a noumenon. Being transcendental and universal, its laws are naturally authoritative or applicable to all persons who in some way share the noumenal will. When we talk of the freedom of will of the moral agent, we are talking of the empirical self or the phenomenon in Kantian terminology. In what sense is the moral agent free ? She is definitely free to choose or decide to act or not act on a moral principle. She is also free, as Hare says, to choose whether or not she wants to act morally, that is, she is free to choose the way of life she wants to live by.

But it is a different thing to say that a moral agent is free to decide what is right or wrong in a given case, or to decide which moral principle should be correctly applicable to a given case, or which of the several moral views is the right, correct, or true. That is, a moral agent may have her value preferences, but she is not the source or authority of the moral law. She cannot be the final arbiter of what is right or wrong; nor can she freely legislate ultimate moral principles.

Hare has argued that in every moral situation we have to decide not only which universal moral law would be applicable but also whether that particular law needs modification; and the modified moral law would, in turn, be a universal principle.[22] This in some way makes the moral agent the final authority regarding moral law, as well as its final critic (when she decides to modify it). I would like to contend here that the moral laws 'preexit' the choice of the moral agent, if not in any ontological sense, then in a logical or epistemological sense. Or, we can say that the moral laws are existentially prior to the agent's choice. The moral agent does not legislate the laws (as in Kant), but discovers them, and in some cases chooses them. The simple fact that a moral agent has arrived at that particular decision by exercising her freedom or, as some others insist, through rational thinking, does not make her judgment or decision necessarily correct or true, even as the simple fact that a society believes certain acts to be right does not make those acts right.

II. A Rational Approach

II.1 It has been my contention in this work, supported by a large number of ethical thinkers, that a morality would not be worth being called one unless it is willing to be put to rational tests and to provide a rational justification for its principles and standards when called to do so.[23]

Kant, of course, is the foremost philosopher who asserted that our moral principles have their source in reason which is both universal and transcendental. The rational categorical imperative, in turn, is the source of, and provides the formal criterion for, the maxims of our actions. The conceptions of the moral imperative as categorical and of reason as universal and transcendental provide the surest foundation to any proposed universal morality. Kant's founding of morality on universal reason or reason which is shared by all persons could provide the greatest ground support for any assertion of universal morality. As Thomas K. Abbott comments:

> In appealing to the reason which Kant thought to be universally the same in all men, we transcend the limitations of particular societies and cultures, and we free ourselves from any considerations of individual differences among men....For to consider differences among men and cultures would mean to restrict morality to a relativistic or even an individually subjectivistic foundation. The good would then differ from person to person, and society to society. If on the other hand, we are able to ground the morality in reason alone, then we have achieved the foundations of a universal morality, whose basic principles, like the rules of logic and mathematics, are the same for all men, in all places and for all times.[24]

While the maxims of our actions can be justified on the basis of the categorical imperative, the latter, being a rational principle, does not need another principle to justify it. A rational principle is self-validating and thus helps us to avoid infinite regress in moral reasoning.[25]

To quote Abbott again:

> A rational principle carries its own obligatory force for all rational creatures. When for example, a man recognizes the validity of a conclusion, he is no longer able to deny its logical claims. It forces itself upon him, and he cannot escape it...In precisely similar fashion the rational moral principle is self-validating, and carries its own binding force. To a rational creature its obligatory character becomes immediately evident,...[26]

The obligatory force of the moral law is further justified by the fact that it is a law which is given by the rational will to itself. The rational will is an end-in-itself; and it is also autonomous or self-legislating.[27] However, Kant's moral philosophy is so integrally related to his philosophical system that it cannot be easily offered as a foundational support for the assertion of universal morality outside his metaphysical framework.

Hare argues, as is well known, first, that moral assertions are normative and prescriptive in character, and second, that they cannot be derived purely from factual premisses.[28] The latter contention means that evaluation (prescription) and description are basically different activities with very different functions, in both ordinary language and moral discourse.[29] He makes a further distinction between descriptive criteria and evaluative conclusion in moral argument. But he has never properly explained the exact relationship between the descriptive criteria and final evaluation. Hare himself recognizes that there has to be some logical connection between description and evaluation or prescription : "To know the descriptive meaning is to know by what standards the speaker is judging."[30] There is need to relate the two, descriptive criteria and evaluation, by presuming a causal relationship of some kind. Then we can say that a car is good *because* it runs smoothly; and an act is wrong *because* it is an act of cruelty.

It was perhaps the need to underline the objectivity of value judgments that Hare brought in descriptive criteria as an important ingredient of moral judgments. The element of description in all evaluations guarantees their indicative character or objective reference. All value assertions, including the prescriptive ones, have an objective reference, that is, seek to say something about an object (act or situation).

Hare seems to acknowledge some such relationship in his *Freedom and Reason* where he contends that our moral judgments are made *because* of the possession by the object of certain non-moral properties, and are based on, or made for, reasons.[31] These reasons are provided by a combination of moral principles which are axiomatically accepted and certain descriptive criteria which elaborate these principles and apply them to concrete life situations.

Above all, value judgments are ones for which we can give reasons-reasons which claim to have objective or interpersonal validity, which emotive or culture-specific assertions cannot have. Moral reasons are ones which can be understood and agreed to, or controverted in, a moral discourse.

What exactly is an ethical reason, and what do we mean by validating an ethical assertion by giving reasons for it ? Hare has started wrongly by conceiving moral argument as a piece of syllogistic reasoning in *The Language of Morals*. As a result, he has to conceive reasoning in a linear fashion in which each principle is justified by reference to a higher, more fundamental or second order principle which, in turn, needs justification in terms of even more basic principles which may be called third order principles, and so on. In order to avoid infinite regress one has to stop at some place which Hare calls a way of life, and which is a matter of personal choice.[32]

One thing however is clear even from this syllogistic form of reasoning that the two most fundamental elements of moral reasoning are our fundamental or axiomatic ethical principles and assessment of facts which, according to him, constitute the major and minor premisses of any moral argument. I also believe that we have to presume or presuppose - and not assume - certain fundamental moral principles which cannot be challenged by any rational person. These principles plus the assessment of the nature and demands of the given situation give us our basic material for moral arguments.

At the same time, there is much to be said for the view that we do not 'presume' these principles but rather arrive at them through a complex process of reasoning. Ethical reasoning tries to understand and elaborate these principles, and apply them to concrete cases. In short, ethical reasoning is exploratory, as Hare acknowledges in his later work:

> There is no reasoning which proceeds from the data of observation to the *truth* of a hypothesis. Scientific enquiry is a kind of *exploration*......
>
> moral reasoning..... too is a kind of exploration, and not a kind of linear inference, and.... the only inferences which take place in it are deductive. What we are doing in oral reasoning is to look for moral judgments and moral principles which, when we have considered their logical consequences and the facts of the case, we can still accept.[33]

And,

> morals, as a serious endeavour, consists in the search for principles and testing of them against particular cases. Any rational activity has its discipline, and this is the discipline of moral thought : to test the moral principles that suggest themselves to us by following out their consequences and seeing whether we can accept them.[34]

Like all other reasoning, ethical reasoning is a form of exploration which may take different exploratory directions, and appeal to different factors, such as moral principles, a description and interpretation of the facts, a consideration of alternative courses of action and their possible consequences. There may also be a reference to, or expression of, our intuitive and emotional responses to the object of judgment, as also the use of descriptive criteria. Thus, moral reasoning is both exploratory and multidimensional. It has its own rules of relevance and standards to evaluate its correctness, validity, or otherwise. Stephen Toulmin is right when he describes moral reasoning as:

> an ethical argument, consisting partly of logical (demonstrative) inferences, partly of scientific (inductive) inferences, and partly of that form of inference peculiar to ethical arguments by which we pass from factual reasons to an ethical conclusion. What we may naturally call 'evaluative' inference.[35]

Though Toulmin has given the moral code of the society a prominent place in his account of ethical reasoning - with which view I do not fully agree - he also rightly distinguishes this common morality from the critical morality. The latter is one which has a predominance of rational element and which, like scientific assertions, aims at "universality and impartiality." Critical morality is not derived from either our experience, or our society's moral code. Instead, just as science's concern is to understand the real colour of the sun as against what appears, similarly critical morality's concern is understanding "what is really good and right", as against what is believed to be good or right in a given moral code.[36] Toulmin further contends that ethics has an important rational element which is analogous to the role of reason in science; "and it is only the judgments in which the rational element predominates which can be called 'fully developed'."[37] However, he does not fully develop these ideas in his work.

Kurt Baier, Joel A. Kupperman, Thomas D. Perry, Carl Wellman and others have strongly argued for a rational approach to morality.

As we know, like Toulmin, Baier distinguishes between everyday morality and critical level of morality. But unlike Toulmin, he makes everyday morality or the moral code of the society fully subject to critical evaluation by the rational moral point of view The moral point of view is that of universal morality which, without rejecting the differences and uniquenesses of different moralities, reserves for itself the right to critically examine, evaluate and override them.[38] The principles of universal or critical morality are neither culturally inherited, nor arbitrarily chosen, but are arrived at after a long process of reasoning. Those moral convictions are true which are required by, or acceptable from, the universal moral point of view. And this moral point of view is that of "acting on principle."[39]

He also argues for the relevance of facts in moral judgments. Both the assessment of facts and of alternative courses of action require an additional factor, what Baier calls "consideration-making beliefs" or "rules of reason". These beliefs and rules often form the major premisses of our ethical arguments. These consideration-making beliefs are per definition universal, or as he calls them "person-neutral". That is, "They are simply true or false, not true for me and false for you and vice versa." On the other hand, considerations or reasons are particular facts to which, in particular contexts, universally true (or false) consideration-making beliefs apply."[40]

These consideration-making beliefs are actually moral principles; and considerations are assessments of facts. So in the end, we are left with two basic ingredients of moral reasoning, i.e. universal moral principles and assessment of facts or considerations of relevance of facts. These two principles are the same ones that we arrived at in our discussion of Hare's ethics, as the most fundamental or constitutive principles in all moral judgments and discourse. While at the first level of everyday morality these consideration-making beliefs are generally those of the moral code of the agents's society, at the critical or 'higher' level, they are universal moral principles.

He sums up the rational approach to morality in a clearly articulated assertion that the best course of action is the course of action which is supported by the "best moral reasons."[41] Equally important, our moral convictions or moral principles act as moral rules of reason which ensure the correctness of our moral conclusions. Our moral reasoning helps us in arriving at a reasonably true or correct moral conclusion that a proposed course of action, or an act which is already done, is morally right or wrong.

The principles of critical morality, according to him, are neither inherited from one's culture or moral code, nor are they freely chosen. They are rather arrived at the end of a long process of reasoning; and hence can be true or false like any other conclusion of reasoning. The question regarding the truth or falsity of any moral assertion is, according to him, "an eminently sensible question."[42]

He further argues that "our moral convictions are true if they can be seen to be required or acceptable *from the moral point of view*"; and the moral point of view is one according to which the right or the good is whatever accords with the moral principles. Above all, the moral point of view is necessarily universal, that is, it is meant for everybody, without exceptions (except on morally relevant grounds).[43] He, however, adds that "our moral convictions hold only presumptively,"[44] that is, there can be situations which demand exceptions to our moral principles; or in which some other principle is found as having an overriding claim.

How do we arrive at these principles? Baier thinks that we can abstract from all concrete moralities, "true moral convictions whose content is completely independent of the particular conditions of this or that way of life."[45] Above all, the moral point of view is a rational point of view in which rules of reasoning and of relevance which are peculiar to moral situations guide our discourse. The rational nature of morality is also a guarantee of its universality, objectivity and overriding character.

M.G. Singer declares reason a basis for any claim to objectivity or truth :

> In giving a reason, my reason, for believing something, I am attempting to give you a reason for believing likewise. A reason necessarily makes a claim to objectivity. My reason makes a claim for being a reason, that is, independently of the person who so regards it......To regard something as a reason for arriving at a certain conclusion is to assume that everyone who knows the fact or whatever it is that is regarded as reason ought to arrive at the same conclusion, and will so far as he is rational.[46]

Similarly, Carl Wellman contends,

> Whether or not ethical sentences can make good their claim to objective validity depends upon whether or not there are good reasons for and against them. If there are considerations which rationally determine the correctness of an agent's choice, ethical judgments are objectively valid.[47]

Like mathematics or empirical sciences, ethical sentences make a claim to objective validity. And, "This claim rests upon the possibility of supporting these sentences with reasons."[48] "In making any assertion", he says, "one tacitly claims that he is in a position to give reasons for it." A rational, reasonable, or responsible assertion is one, according to him, in which we are prepared to respond to, and defend our judgment against, criticism.[49] The claim to objectivity and truth on the part of any ethical assertion, according to Wellman, as well as Kupperman and others, "is the claim that there are good reasons or determining grounds for the acceptance of our judgment among conceivable alternatives."[50]

Thomas D. Perry emphasizes that the guarantee for the correctness of a moral judgment lies in the rationality or reasonableness of the way that judgment is arrived at and later on justified. To offer any rational argument is to use an objective standard, that is, a standard which is independent of the beliefs and biases of the person using that standard. It is also a claim to know what we are asserting, and the claim to know, in turn, is a claim that anyone else who knew the facts of the case and considered them in a reasonable way would arrive at the same conclusion. A rational or reasonable way of arriving at morally correct judgments not only involves using of objective standards but also arguing according to 'the relevant rule of reasoning' which tells us how to identify certain factors of practical situation which can provide a basis for our moral judgment.[51] A valid moral reasoning which can justify the claim to know further implies that,

> in order for some concrete action to 'satisfy the criteria of wrongness', it must not only be the case that it has one or more 'wrong-making' characteristics, but that its having them should 'control' or be the dominant consideration in its moral evaluation.[52]

This is exactly what I have been trying to argue in this work; that is, in order to make a truth claim, any moral assertion must have two constituents : First, it must apply objective moral standards which are independent of the subjective biases and sentiments, because only then they can have interpersonal validity. And second, it must not only have a clearly identifiable objective referent, the object of judgment and its qualities (which need not be assumed as nonnatural properties having ontological status) must in some way determine our judgment. For example, our judgment that the boys burning a cat are indulging in an evil act is determined by the nature of the act. Obviously, had the boys been doing something else, we would not have made that judgment. This is a typically realist position. I feel that its main contribution regarding the intimate relation between the facts or nature of the objective act or character trait and our moral judgment thereof must be taken more seriously than it is generally done.

This, however, does not mean subscribing to the correspondence theory of truth, or verification theory of meaning. All I want to contend here is that our moral judgments in order to justify their claim to correctness must be somehow based upon, and if not determined at least directly influenced by, the nature of the 'object' of judgment.

On the other hand, if it were so, that is, if our moral judgments were in some way determined by the objective situation, then there cannot be any justified moral disagreement, which is definitely not the case. Moral disagreement, in turn, would depend upon what characteristics of the case are considered relevant by different participants in the dialogue. While some moral disagreements may be on moral principles; some others on the preference of moral principles; a majority of them are due to different perceptions of relevance. And these considerations of relevance are mostly influenced by socio-cultural factors. That is why, not only the relativists, but also the rationalists, such as Kupperman and Perry, have ended up saying that agreement in moral matters (on relevance of factual considerations) is easier to arrive at among those who share a common form of life. However, I do not agree with this delimitation of the truth claim of moral judgments.

On the other hand, we may presuppose or presumptively accept a certain hierarchy of moral principles; or this hierarchy may result from prolonged rational dialogue between people holding different points of view in morality. The very purpose of declaring reason as a ground for the correctness or validity of a moral assertion is this only that we can enter into discourse with others who are different from us about moral matters, and try to arrive at some agreement about them which may not be a guarantee of the truth of our assertions but which still would be an indication thereof.

Reasoning in moral discourse that claims its own validity, or the correctness or truth of the moral judgment arrived through it, has to be a very complex and open-ended process. It includes:

(a) A recognition of the important role of fundamental moral principles. (b) A recognition that they are not entirely a matter of personal choice or decision (which may play a role only in one's personal conduct) but are to be recognized as given *a priori* to the human mind. (c) Either experience or cultural influence can be an occasion to make us conscious of those principles, and strengthen their appeal to us ; but none can guarantee the truth or correctness of those principles. Nor can the sense of moral obligation be derived from experience. (d) The sense of moral obligation is often said to be derived from the authority of the existing moral code. But such an authority destroys the freedom of the moral agent without which no act can be moral. (e) Above all, the norms and standards of any given morality must be open to critical scrutiny, since the mere fact that they belong to the moral code or a way of life of a particular people is no guarantee of their truth or correctness.

(f) Right moral reasoning further has to recognize the importance of facts of the case in arriving at either a decision about what ought to be done; or a moral judgment about the act which has already been done. (g) But this brings in the all important issue of the relevance of facts which are being taken as considerations for our moral judgment. The parties disagreeing on an ethical issue may not disagree about the facts of the case, their disagreement arising out of their different judgments regarding which facts are to be regarded as relevant and which not, or which facts are to be given greater weightage than others in our moral judgments. The problem of the relevance of facts cannot be expected to be solved by the 'rules of relevance' to which some philosophers as Perry have appealed, mostly because these rules of relevance have never been clearly spelt out. (h) Instead, the relevance of considerations should be an outcome of the application of what Baier has called "consideration- making beliefs", or moral principles. As I have argued, the facts of the case and our *a priori* moral principles are to be considered together, and our moral judgment is an outcome of the interplay between the two. We choose facts of the case which are found to be relevant in the light of our *a priori* principles. At the same time, not only our choice of principles which would be relevant in a given case is influenced or even determined by the facts of the case, we are often forced to acknowledge some exceptions to our chosen principles if the latter do not fit in, or appear appropriate to, the facts.

This means that moral reasoning is exploratory, multi-dimensional, takes into consideration several factors, and open-ended, that is, it is an ongoing process, and at no stage can its conclusions claim finality and infallibility.

The contention that our principles and norms must be critically or rationally questioned, evaluated, and rationally justified, along with the acknowledgment of disagreement about moral issues among peoples of different times and cultures, may imply the faith that these disagreements can be more or less resolved through rational moral discourse.

III. Reason and Dialogue

III.1 My particular problems in this work arise out of my desire to have the cake and eat it too! I want to preserve the objectivity of moral judgments in a somewhat stronger sense than simple intersubjective validity. I want to assert that unless there is a definite referent in two contradictory moral judgments, there is no sense in talking of either moral agreement or disagreement. At the same time, I do not wish to populate the world with nonnatural qualities or "queer objects" (Mackie's phrase).

Similarly, I do contend that a moral judgment is correct (true) or incorrect (false) regardless of who or how many assert it, or dissent with it. But I can neither suggest a fool-proof criterion to judge the truth or falsity of moral judgments; nor can I squarely face the important problem of moral disagreements. If moral judgments can be true or false, then perhaps out of several mutually dissenting moral judgments only one can be true. This leads us to absolutism, and above all, to the problem as to which of the several judgments is to be declared true.

Both objectivism and relativism have their own theoretical problems to which I have been referring from time to time. Does truth of the matter lie somewhere between the two positions? Can we even talk of the 'truth of the matter?' Is there any philosophic position which goes "Beyond Objectivism and Relativism", as Richard J. Bernstein claims?

Perhaps reason can help us? Let us take another look at reason as a means of arriving at and justifying ethical assertions. *A posteriori* reason alone cannot lead us to the truth or validity of moral assertions. I feel that some form of intuition is an important element in our moral judgments and discourse. But then intuitions are conditioned by our socio-cultural background, and people's intuitive judgments do disagree. Without giving up my 'intuitive' preference for 'moral intuitions', I would here concentrate on reason alone.

I have questioned both consensus and personal decisions of principles as the final authority for validating any moral assertion. Earlier I have rejected societal code and experience as the source and ground of justification of any moral principles and judgments. I especially reject societal norms, commands and standards as the final authority for a higher or critical level of morality. My objection to consensus of opinion about some moral issue is mainly that this is likely to take us back to cultural-ethical relativism. That is, if we accept consensus of opinion as the final authority in controversial ethical matters, and also admit that such a consensus is easier to achieve within some particular culture, then it simply means that societal consensus, as expressed in the society's norms and standards, is the final authority. Of course, this implies ethical relativism. On the other hand, if we leave the matter to the individual, that is, give her the right to deliberate and decide on fundamental ethical matters (no one is questioning her right or freedom in taking day-to-day decisions), then also we are making basic moral issues relative to the subjective idiosyncrasies and prejudices, and hence making them contingent, relative and variable.

I have argued that there are moral principles which are fundamental in the sense of being *a priori*, that is, they are presupposed or axiomatically accepted in all moral discourse, and need no rational justification. Since we cannot take the process of justification indefinitely backwards we have to stop at some place, and that place is what I have called fundamental, universal ethical principles.

But how do we arrive at these fundamental principles, if we have already rejected consensus, experience, societal moral code and individual decision as the possible sources and grounds of justification of our moral principles? Significantly, the philosophers referred to above who have advocated either consensus or personal decision, such as Kupperman, Perry and Hare, have also argued for a rational approach to ethics. It is not consensus as such but the consensus reached through rational argumentation among competent, reasonable persons that they are advocating. The same is true of personal decision; it is not decision as such that they are advocating (though in the practical context Hare does), but decision arrived at the end of a long process of rational deliberation.

It seems to me that it would be easier and less controversial if we accepted reason, neither consensus nor personal decision, as the final source or ground of justification of all moral assertions.

III.2 Alan Montefiore has discussed the issue in a very clear and reasonable manner. He starts by reminding us that all propositions are either analytic or synthetic; and that analytic propositions are necessary and *a priori*, while synthetic ones are contingent and *a posteriori*. Having followed Kant so far, he then takes up a position markedly different from him. He contends that all synthetic propositions are *a posteriori*, and such that further observations can challenge or falsify them, whereas the conception of necessary truth entails that it cannot be contradicted by any amount of empirical observation. Therefore synthetic propositions cannot make a claim to necessary truth.[53]

The truth or falsity of two kinds of propositions is to be decided in two different ways. While analytic propositions are to be validated with reference to the rules of language or the symbols involved; "The truth or falsity of a synthetic proposition depends upon the state of facts."[54]

According to Montefiore, moral judgments are neither analytic which, of course, is obvious; nor are they synthetic, since synthetic assertions are per definition those which can be proved or falsified by any present or future observations. Moreover, moral judgments are not statements or propositions. He further contends that the notions of 'true' and 'false' are bound up with the notion of 'statement' (or proposition).[55] It seems to follow that since ethical assertions are not propositions, they cannot be true or false. He, however, believes that ethical judgments can still be true or false. But "the truth of a value judgment remains entirely independent of any factual observations." That is to say, "value judgments are not open to falsification by experience in the same straightforward manner as ordinary factual statements." He clarifies that he is not trying to suggest that, "value judgments are totally independent of facts, but that they are not totally dependent on them either."[56]

Here Montefiore is making three related contentions : First, ethical assertions are not about facts, and therefore, cannot be either validated or falsified by reference to facts. Second, only statements can be true or false, as they alone can be validated or falsified by further observations. And third, ethical assertions can still be true or false. In order to reconcile all three contentions, he brings in the well-recognized distinction between evaluation and description, or between the meaning of the term and the criteria of its application; and understands the distinction largely in Hare's terminology.[57] In order to explain his distinction he refers to the term 'good' as a quintessential value term and argues that,

> someone who has said that something is good, should provide his reasons for having said so; that is that he should say clearly what were the factual characteristics which served him in this context as criteria for his evaluation.[58]

This position, is in no way better than that of Hare. Not only does he distinguish like Hare between the criteria of evaluation and evaluation proper, he also emphasizes, even more than Hare, that value judgments are independent of facts. How then can he claim that the reasons for value judgment are the factual characteristics of the case? The need here is to underline a more intimate relationship between the relevant facts of the case, our basic moral principles and our moral judgments.

He however goes on to argue that it is reasons alone which provide a basis for any claim to objectivity or truth.[59] In fact, all genuine moral judgments are about their objects. A moral assertion is "*an assertion about something* that might be true or false", and is not about our *"feelings towards something,"* which cannot be true or false,[60] (original italics.)

To clarify, a moral judgment, even if it is not a statement which alone is usually true or false, can still be true or false, since it is "an assertion about something." We can surely ask whether what is being asserted about some objective act, character trait, or cultural institution is true or false.

Now, what do we mean by 'true' or 'false'? Montefiore here claims that the term 'true' is an evaluatory term like 'good' and not a descriptive term. He interprets 'true' as affirmable, meaning thereby something that one is justified in affirming.[61] And, "we are only justified in affirming which we have every reason to *believe* to be true."[62]

Montefiore makes another valuable suggestion that apart from analytic and synthetic assertions, there is a third class of assertions, i.e. ethical judgments which class is entirely different from the first two classes. The meaning of truth as what is affirmable or confirmable applies to all the three kinds of assertions - analytic, synthetic and ethical; though the criteria by which we are able to determine the truth or falsity of any given assertion would be different in these three different kinds of assertions.

These three classes of assertions are validated or falsified in very different manners. We know that analytic and synthetic propositions are validated in different ways. Similarly, moral assertions are validated or falsified in a third manner, i.e. by giving reasons in favour or against particular judgments. He rightly describes moral reasoning as a complex and multi-directional process. It may involve reference to more and more general principles. It would also involve reference to other related moral principles, and arguing that they support each other.[63]

The difference between three kinds of assertions is mainly based on ways in which they can be confirmed. He believes that "to say that something is true is always, in part at least, to confirm or affirm what is being asserted in a way that involves very special commitments or guarantees on the part of the speaker." He adds that, "to say that a value judgment is true would be to commit oneself to belief in and defence of that value judgment."[64]

It reminds us of Hare's distinction between the 'phrastic' and 'neustic' elements in both empirical and normative assertions. He explains the term phrastic as meaning to point out or indicate (the objective reference in value judgments), and 'neustic' as meaning 'to nod assent' (the confirmatory element that comes from the subject). The neustic phrase (assenting to an assertion) is common, Hare believes in both indicative and evaluative assertions. It is something that is done by anyone who uses a sentence in earnest, and does not merely mention it or quote it in inverted commas; and is something essential to saying and meaning anything.[65]

Further, "If we assent to a statement we are said to be sincere in our assent if and only if we believe that it is true....." Hare adds that, while assenting to a statement is believing it, assenting to a command or moral imperative means acting on it. Assenting to, or 'affirming', any assertion implies confirmation of what is being said, and this is what the term 'true' and 'false' mean (though he has not used exactly this language).[66]

But somehow these suggestions regarding the truth or falsity, or correctness or otherwise, of moral assertions as consisting in, 'consenting to', asserting with confidence, and 'committing to', some moral assertion do not seem very satisfactory. If I say that cruelty to other living beings is morally wrong; or that a particular moral act of cruelty is wrong or evil, I am *not* saying that I am asserting this with confidence, or that I am committing myself to this judgment. Psychologically it may be what my moral judgment involves; but what I *intend* by my moral judgment is that what is being asserted therein would be true, even if no one else, including myself, ever asserted, or committed oneself to, it. My 'assenting to' a particular judgment implies my prior recognition that it is true. I have consistently argued for the objective validity of moral assertions, which assertion cannot be sustained if it is reduced to mere 'assenting to' a particular judgment.

I also do not agree that the conception of 'truth' is a valuational concept comparable to that of 'good'; nor do I think that the truth claim of any assertion simply amounts to our assernting to it. However, I find one suggestion of Montefiore very significant, that is, regarding ethical assertions being an entirely new class of assertions, different from both analytic and synthetic ones. Its corollary is that the three classes of assertion - analytic, synthetic and ethical - require three different methods of rational justification. As against the first two, value judgments (ethical assertions) are justified by offering reasons in their support. Of course, this argument would be rejected by W.V.O Quine and others who reject the distinction between analytic and synthetic judgments. But since I do not agree with Quine's view, I can very well accept Montefiore's threefold distinction of various kinds of linguistic assertion.

However, if moral assertions are fully separated from synthetic assertions, and the latter are considered as ones which are validated or falsified by reference to facts, then moral assertions would be fully cut off from facts, or real life situations. Montefiore is right when he says that no amount of factual assertions can prove or disprove an ethical principle, such as "aimless cruelty is wrong". But surely actual facts of life, some of which may be even called 'moral facts', are not only relevant but are also the cause or basis of our moral judgments, such as that the boys' burning a cat is an evil act. Montefiore does not seem to have properly distinguished moral principles from moral judgments While the former do not require validation through an appeal to empirical facts, the latter do. Even if all moral assertions are best justified through reasoning, in the case of moral judgments, important reasons in their favour would be the citing of the facts of the case, and the relevance of those facts to our judgments. The problem of Montefiore is the same as that of Hare. They first make a sharp distinction between the evaluative and the descriptive aspects of moral judgment; and then fail to connect the two in a convincing manner.

Nevertheless, Montefiore's contention, that ethical assertions should be considered a class apart from the analytical and synthetic assertions, and therefore need a very different kind of justification, deserves serious consideration. This may not only help us to finally reject the positivist undermining of ethical discourse, but may also provide a basis for the justification of a rational approach to moral issues; or rational moral discourse.

III.3 Admittedly, reasoning directly or indirectly aims at reaching consensus. We argue in order to prove our point to others with the specific purpose of convincing others. And if we are arguing rationally, we are equally ready to be convinced ourselves by others' reasons. Obviously the aim of various participants in a moral discourse is to reach some kind of consensus over the issues being discussed.

I am somewhat sceptical about the consensual approach to ethics. Truth or falsity of a moral assertion, I believe, depends fully on, first, the nature of the case; and, second, the fundamental and overriding principles involved. It does not depend upon who or how many assert it, so that whether there is a general agreement about the issue involved, or a marked disagreement, the truth of the matter would be found independent of the number of persons assenting or dissenting with a particular view. And yet, consensus is implicitly the goal of moral discourse. Denying any value to consensus may mean undermining the worth of the very moral discourse which is what we are engaged in at present.

In this context Jürgen Habermas' views are valuable. Among postmodernist writers he is almost the lone, or at least the most prominent, thinker who has tried to put reason back on its throne where the Enlightenment has put it, and from where most postmodernist writers have dethroned it. Habermas' philosophy is developed in the context of postmodern Continental thought, and addresses itself to those problems which are currently occupying the minds of Continental thinkers. Only the general thrust of his arguments is relevant to us for our problem. I will briefly discuss here a few points of his philosophy which help in strengthening my somewhat nebulous position.

(i) Both Hans George Gadamer and Habermas believe in dialogue and consensus. While Gadamer makes this consensus, especially in the form of language, primordial, Habermas considers it as the end point of rational discourse.

Habermas starts by pointing out that the common semantic conception of truth considers the objective world as correlative of all true assertorial sentences. If we accept this conception and then try to argue for the 'truth' of normative assertions, 'worlds' analogous to the world of facts would have to be postulated, which, of course, is not a philosophically defensible position. He adds,

> By contrast as soon as we conceive of knowledge as communicatively mediated rationality is assessed in terms of the capacity of responsible participants in interaction to orient themselves in relation to validity claims geared to intersubjective recognition.[67]

Habermas thus presents his consensual conception of truth in counterdistinction to the semantic conception of truth as correspondence. According to him, constant interaction with others - at both levels of theory and praxis - results in the emergence of consensus about different issues. And it is this consensus alone that provides us with some guarantee of truth.

(ii) Communication at both levels makes social life possible. The latter implies that direct participants "can act communicatively only under the presupposition of intersubjectively identical ascriptions of meaning."[68] Even our personhood is developed through "intersubjective relationship between individuals who are socialized through communication and reciprocally recognize one another."[69] This implies that consensus is more easily reached in "particular totalities."[70]

However, unlike other postmodernist scholars, Habermas does not regard the consensus within "culturally embodied self-understanding", or lifeworlds as the final criterion for the truth of a given assertion. In fact, "Everyday communicative practice, in which agents have to reach an understanding about something in the world, stands under the need to prove its worth."[71] That is, the consensus achieved within a lifeworld cannot claim to be beyond critical scrutiny. He clearly recognizes the need for, and possibility of a distinction between true and false consensuses. At the same time, if the truth is reached through consensus, then we are apparently left with no criterion to distinguish between true and false ones.

(iii) Habermas' main contribution lies here in trying to provide a profounder conception of truth as consensual. The consensus reached within a culture or lifeworld is not final, as it is mostly not carried out in ideal conditions and is, therefore, likely to be mistaken. His conception of truth presupposes "the ideal speech situation" which is characterized by the exclusion of extraneous pressures. Ideal speech conditions mean rationality, freedom from prejudice, the will to understand the other's points of view, and freedom from any kind of coercion. The main emphasis, however, is on freedom from extraneous pressures, whether they be authority, or the determining influence of societal norms and beliefs.[72] He expects that if rational persons enter into dialogue or communicative discourse with each other under ideal speech conditions, then they are more likely to reach agreement on the issues being discussed.

This communication or dialogue is an ongoing process, so that we cannot stop at some point and say that the conclusions of these people, or this period, are the final truth about the fundamental moral principles, or criteria of what is morally right or wrong. Rather, the hope lies in what Habermas calls "communicative rationality" as an ongoing process :

> This communicative rationality recalls older ideas of logos, inasmuch as it brings along with it the connotations of a noncoercively unifying, consensus-building force of a discourse in which the participants overcome their at first subjectively biased views in favour of a rationally motivated agreement. Communicative reason is expressed in a decentred understanding of the world.[73]

The last phrase "decentred understanding of the world" implies Habermas' rejection of the conception of subject-centred reason and autonomy of the will of the moral agent. But it is the individual who is the locus of reason, and who enters into dialogue with 'others' and it is the individual who tries to, and often achieves, agreement with those others.

Habermas' intention seems to underline the need for the participants to "overcome their at first subjectively biased views in favour of a rationally motivated agreement." If so, I am fully in agreement with him. A person is supposedly made up of her 'prejudices' inherited from the society, as Gadamer and other postmodernist thinkers never tire of asserting. She cannot communicate with the 'other' in the proper sense of mutual understanding and dialogue. Dialogue or communication does not merely mean that we express our views, and try to convert others to them; nor even that we try to understand them in our own culturally conditioned terms and mind set, but it means that we try to understand the 'other' as the 'other' understands herself. The first step to communication or dialogue is, therefore, shedding off of our prejudices in order to understand the 'other' better, and the second is trying to build bridges between the self and the 'other' by searching for and underlining the common points between the two. It would be absurd to say, in spite of the incommensurability thesis, that there are no such common points which two individuals or two groups can find and share during the process of dialogue. These shared principles and sentiments provide the basis for further understanding of each other's uniquenesses; an attempt at appreciating and incorporating some of the views and values of the 'other' in our moral code and conceptual system, and expecting that the 'other' would also do so. To quote Habermas:

> Agreement arrived at through communication, which is measured by the intersubjective recognition of validity claims, makes possible a networking of social interactions and lifeworld contexts. Of course, these validity claims have a janus face; as claims they transcend any local context; at the same time, they have to be raised here and now and be de facto recognized.......The transcendent moment of *universal* validity bursts every provinciality asunder; the obligatory moment of accepted validity claims renders them carriers of a *context bound* everyday practice.[74]

That means Habermas is not talking of consensus as such, but of consensus which is arrived at through rational discourse under ideal conditions. This has been well recognized by other scholars who have affirmed reasoning as the most important means of arriving at correct or true moral judgments.

(iv) Even more important for us is Habermas' assertion that there is more than family resemblance between various cultures or lifeworlds. Admittedly, reason as expressed in communicative action in everyday context of particular totalities is culturally embodied. But,

> These particular forms of life, which only emerge in the plural, are certainly not connected with each other only through a web of family resemblances; they exhibit structures common to lifeworlds in general.[75]

And,

> Moreover the different lifeworlds that collide with one another do not stand next to each other without any mutual understanding. As totalities, they follow the pull of their claims to universality and work out their differences until their horizons of understanding "fuse" with one another, as Gadamer puts it.[76] (original italics.)

This possibility of fusion of the mental horizons of different lifeworlds goes against various postmodernist theses regarding the closed character of different cultures and their conceptual frameworks or lifeworlds, the incommensurability of these conceptual frameworks, and the mutual untranslatability of different languages. The entire idea of rational discourse with ever widening horizons implies the possibility of communication, mutual translation, and even commensurability. The possibility of communication implies that the lifeworlds are not closed systems and various rational persons coming from different lifeworlds can easily enter into rational dialogue with each other.

The next step is to develop universal principles and criteria through mutual dialogue which, in turn, are expected to regulate further discourse, leading to wider and wider consensuses. He proposes what he calls a thought experiment, that of "the abstraction of *universal* lifeworld structure from the particular configurations of totalities of forms of life that arise only as plural." For example, at the cultural level, the mythical and other culture-specific contents are separated from abstract concepts of the objective, social and subjective worlds, presuppositions of communication, procedures of argumentation, abstract basic values etc. The three, culture, society and individual, are transformed, become more generalized and abstract through the process of rational discourse.[77]

When persons who are relatively free from the determining influence of their traditions and are rational enter into communication with others, certain consensuses are reached. These consensuses, in turn, are not final, and need further discourse. There are two conditions for such a rational discourse to be meaningful: First, it should be carried out in "ideal speech situations", that is, should be free from any coercion of authority, or cultural bias. Second, this rational discourse should not be limited to some particular culture but should include in it wider and wider segments of humanity.

IV. Concluding Note

I do not claim to have fully succeeded in proving my thesis of a minimum basic universal morality, for the simple reason that there cannot be any end point to a philosophical controversy. That does not mean, however, that all points of view are equally right or correct; otherwise taking up a position in a philosophical - ethical, discourse would be meaningless. To argue for a particular approach to, or a distinct understanding of, an issue implies a claim to be right, correct, or even true; but it does not mean a claim to infallibility, as every assertion or perspective is fallible and every discourse open-ended.

I have argued for a universalist approach to ethics in this work which includes the following contentions :

(i) A universalist approach to ethics does not mean either a rejection of cultural plurality, or that of cultural ralativity. Not only does it not undermine cultural diversity, it also accepts the values of pluralism and tolerance. At the same time, it does not accept cultural determinism, though it does not deny the role of socio-cultural factors in the formation of beliefs, values and praxis. It, however, questions the conception of culture as a self-enclosed monolithic whole, and suggests that we must take into account both intracultural diversity and intercultural communications and mutual give and take.

(ii) Neither the contingent fact of cultural diversity, nor the value of pluralism, nor the theory of cultural relativism, even if all of them were fully true, can prove ethical relativism. What is approved of, prescribed, or practised, in a given culture or society need not be what *is* right or good, or what *ought to be* so approved of, prescribed and practised. Hare is right when he contends that normative conclusions cannot be drawn from empirical premisses. Ethical relativism, or the doctrine that what is believed in and practised *is* right and valid for the people who believe in and practise it, is an indefensible thesis.

(iii) A sincere recognition of cultural diversity and cultural relativity, and an equally sincere assertion of a minimum universal morality seem contradictory. But they can be reconciled if we are able to appreciate a distinction between particular moralities, or moral codes, and the point of view of universal morality which is cross-culturally valid, and which overrides all the claims of other points of view, including particular moralities. Like Baier, I have called this universal morality 'the moral point of view'. The moral point of view necessarily implies both universality and overridingness; and it claims to provide criteria or standards for critically evaluating all other points of view and moralities.

(iv) Both ordinary language and ethical discourse imply universal applicability of moral assertions. That is, whatever moral judgment I (or any other moral subject) deem right, correct, or true, in a particular case, I at the same time presume that the same is applicable to all relevantly similar cases. And whatever moral principles I (or any other moral subject) regard as right or true, I believe that they are so for every other rational being. In this aspect, my position is similar to that of Hare (though I do not concur with his radical distinction between descriptive criteria and evaluative judgments).

The idea of universality is so integral to the idea of morality or ethics that any assertion to the effect that a particular judgment is right or true in a particular case but wrong in another (relevantly) similar case, or vice versa, because of cultural differences, is immediately seen as unreasonable or unjustified from the moral point of view.

(v) When we assert that a given moral judgment is universally applicable to all relevantly similar cases, we mean that the factors that are relevant for moral discourse are not those which are related to cultural or sociological differences, but would be those which are judged relevant on the basis of *a priori* universal ethical principles. The considerations of relevance are determined by what Baier calls 'consideration-making beliefs', or fundamental ethical principles.

This, in turn, implies the assumption of certain ethical principles as 'given' or fundamental, in the sense of providing the basis for justification of all other moral principles and standards, while themselves needing no justification.

Put in this way my position sounds like foundationalism; and foundationalism in knowledge and justification has been found problematic. On the other hand, we have only two alternatives, either to accept the extreme ethical relativism of the postmodernists (e.g. Harman), or to acknowledge that there are certain fundamental ethical principles which have universal or cross-cultural validity and which provide the basis for the justification or validation of other moral principles, norms and practices. This is not to declare some particular moral principles as fundamental or foundational; nor does it mean to say that any principles that we arrive at today are, to use a famous phrase of Quine, 'immune to revision'. These principles are also not 'given' or foundational in the sense the positivists regarded empirical data to be so. The difference between the relativist position and mine is not that I regard some ethical principles as foundational in the 'modern' sense of the term, which is unacceptable to the relativists. Rather, my position differs from the latter in that I am claiming universal or cross-cultural validity for some, yet unspecified, 'basic' ethical principles, which, of course, is also unacceptable to the relativists in general and postmodernists in particular. But this is far from foundationalism.

(vi) The universalist approach to ethics further implies the objectivity of moral principles and judgments. 'Objectivity' of any assertion is generally taken as meaning its independence from the subject of that judgment or assertion, whether it is the individual or society. It also means that in some way the object of moral judgment 'determines' the judgment. This, however, does not mean a naive realist position which assumes objective moral properties having ontological status. In fact, contemporary ethical realists make no such claim. All that we - the realists and I - are trying to say is that the 'moral properties' attributed in a moral judgment to its object (an act, character trait, or practice) are not a product or construct of that judgment, but rather the judgment itself is determined by the character or nature of the object. The act of burning a cat is not evil because my society's moral code says so, but *because* the act itself is so.

Moreover, not only our moral judgments are thus objective, our basic ethical principles are also objectively valid or true and *a priori*; that is, they are there to be acknowledged and articulated, and are not a product of the conceptual framework of any society or culture.

(vii) Objectivity of moral assertions implies their cognitivity. I support a commonsense conception of knowledge which is nearer the realist position. According to this view, not only do we 'know' the external world and other selves; we also have knowledge in such fields of life, as sociology and ethics, though presumably it would be different in nature from empirical knowledge.

Ethical discourse is cognitive in nature. We declare that an act is right or wrong; and a universal moral principle is true, not because we approve them, or they are determined by our lifeworld or conceptual framework but, because we 'know' that it is so. In some cases our knowledge would be unjustified and wrong, but the admission of fallibility does not detract from the cognitivity of our ethical assertions.

(viii) The assertion of the cognitivity and objectivity of knowledge challenges the postmodernist thesis of a radical distinction between the scheme and content of knowledge, along with its corollaries, i.e. the immense plurality of these schemes, and the impossibility of knowing the world-as-it-is-independent-of-our-knowledge. Davidson is probably right when he says that relativism is a product of scheme-content dualism, and once that dualism is rejected, relativism automatically becomes questionable. Thus, while the postmodernist approach makes the very concept of knowledge problematic, a moderately realist position, such as I have tried to develop in this work, aims at reestablishing knowledge and epistemology where they belong.

The relativist hypothesis stands rejected by the very possibility and familiarity of intersubjective communication and dealings in a common world in day-to-day life. In ethical discourse we may not agree with each other, but we do understand what the 'other' is saying. Even moral disagreement implies knowledge of the 'other'.

(ix) The twin theses of incommensurability of different lifeworlds and mutual untranslatability of different languages, as we have seen, contradict each other. In order to challenge them nothing else is required except pointing out that if we cannot translate the other's language into ours, and cannot understand (at least fully) what the 'other' is asserting and practising, we cannot say that the two lifeworlds are incommensurable.

The limited overlapping of our world and knowledge, admitted by moderate postmodernist relativists like Richard Bernstein, is not sufficient. I, along with the realists, would like to make a stronger submission that not only do we share a common world, but we also share common ways of perceiving, thinking and responding to that world. In spite of all our disagreements, most of the time we can understand and empathize with what the 'other' believes in and values.

(x) It is because the postmodernists make the community as the basic unit of ethical discourse and conceive the community as a self-sufficient monolithic whole, that they are able to argue for ethical relativism. Instead, if we were to make the individual moral subject and agent as the basic unit of ethical discourse, the plural identities of the individual and her basic affinity with other human beings would help us in building cross-cultural bridges. Communitarianism is right when it emphasizes the social character of all morality; but it is wrong when it neglects the primary importance of the purity of motive and the moral agent's recognition of the obligatoriness of certain acts as her duties, as has been emphasized in Kantian and classical Indian thought.

(xi) We need not assume a neutral conceptual framework in order to admit the possibility of mutual understanding. The possibility of mutual understanding between peoples belonging to different cultures or lifeworlds suggests the possibility of rational dialogue with the 'other'.

It is argued by the relativists that all rationality is culture-specific, and therefore there cannot be any meaningful rational dialogue between persons belonging to different lifeworlds. I do not believe in the total culture-specificity of rationality, such as argued by Peter Winch and others, and I do not accept Azande black magic as a unique form of rationality. On the whole, the Enlightenment conception of rationality, as that form of communication for which reasons can be given which can claim cross-cultural validity, has its merits, and I subscribe to this view.

If reason is conceived as exploratory, multi-dimensional, open-ended and corrigible, it can provide a means of mutual understanding, dialogue and agreement about a minimum universal morality. Dialogue and agreement do not prove the validity or truth of fundamental ethical principles; their aim is to search for them. Once they are arrived at through reason and dialogue, they are in some sense 'intuitively' apprehended as right, valid, or true. At the same time, the ever-continuing process of reasoning and dialogue ensures that no ethical principle or standard becomes so sacrosanct that it cannot be critically examined and modified, if required. And thus the process of rational moral discourse goes on.

Notes

Chapter 1. Cultural and Ethical Relativism

1. In this work, I have deliberately used the two terms, morals or morality and ethics, interchangeably, mostly to avoid any confusion. Personally, I have a preference for the term morality as having wider connotation.
2. *Manu Smṛti* II. 1. 18; II. 6. 12,; *Gautam Dharma Sutra* I. 1-2.
3. *Baudhāyana Dharma Sūtra* I. 1. 19-26.
4. *Manu Smṛti* I. 85-86. See writer's *Aspects of Hindu Morality*, 1989, pp.73 ff., 76 ff., and article "An Inquiry into Ethical Relativism of Hindu Thought", in *Indian Philosophical Quarterly*, July-Oct. 1996, pp. 263 ff. Also see P.V. Kane, *A History of Dharmaśāstra,* 1974, Vol. III, Ch. 34; Vol. V, Part II, Ch. 29 for a discussion of relativism in Hindu thought.
5. *Mahābhārata, Śānti Parva*, 252 : 6-19.
6. Even if we do not go to the preliterate cultures, we would still find marked differences in the moralities of different modern socieities, e.g. the moral codes concerning extra-marital relations and values relating to family structure in the Western and Indian societies; the differences become more marked if we include Islamic fundamentalist societies. Changes in norms and values are equally marked with the passage of time; e.g. slavery was naturally accepted in the West till well after Reformation, and is now considered reprehensible. In India, several practices, such as *sati* and untouchability which were respected in medieval times are now condemned.
7. See W.T. Stace, *The Concept of Morals*, 1962, pp. 14 ff.
8. In the above discussion I am generally indebted to Milton Singer, "Culture", in *International Encyclopaedia of the Social Sciences*, ed. David L. Sills, Vol. 3, pp. 527 ff., especially p. 530.

9. "Introduction", in John Ladd, ed., *Ethical Relativism*, 1973, p. 2.
10. *Ibid.*, pp. 2-3.
11. *Ibid.*, p. 3.
12. *Op. Cit.*, "Preface", p. ix.
13. *Ibid.*, p. 1.
14. "The principle of cultural relativism briefly stated is as follows: *Judgments are based on experience and experience is interpreted by each individual in terms of his own enculturation.*" M.J. Herskovits, "Cultural Relativism and Cultural Values", in *Ethical Relativism*, p.61. Herskovits quotes a psychologist, M. Sherif: "The psychological basis of the established social norms.... is the formation of common frames of reference as a product of the contact of individuals." *Ibid.*, p. 63.
15. "Of Virtue and Vice in General", in W.T. Jones, Frederick Sontag, Morton O. Beckner, Robert J. Fogelin, eds., *Approaches to Ethics*, 1962, p.260.
16. *Ibid.*, p. 263.
17. *Principia Ethica*, 1956, p. 39.
18. "Introduction (to Ethical Relativism)" , in Paul W. Taylor, ed., *Problems of Moral Philosophy*, 1967, p. 43.
19. "The Sociology of Knowledge", in James E. Curtis and John W. Petras, eds. *The Sociology of Knowledge : A Reader*, 1970, pp. 111 ff.
20. *Ibid.*, p.113.
21. *Ibid.*, p.115.
22. *Ibid.*, p.116.
23. "it is not at all true that concepts, even when constructed according to the rules of science, get their authority uniquely from their ojective value. It is not enough that they be true to be believed. If they are not in harmony with other beliefs and opinions, or, in a word, with the mass of other collective representations, they will be denied;" *Op.Cit.*, p. 152.
24. *Ibid.*, p. 152.
25. " the sociological character of all knowledge, of all the forms of thinking, perception, cognition, is indubitable : not, of course, the content of all knowledge, and still less its objective

validity, but the selection of its objects according to the ruling social-interest perspective...." Max Scheler, "The Sociology of Knowledge : Formal Problems", in *The Sociology of Knowledge: A Reader*, p. 175.

26. Quoted in R.B. Brandt, *Ethical Theory*, 1959, p. 166.
27. *Ibid*., p. 167.
28. See "Elementary Forms of Religious Life", in *The Sociology of Knowledge: A Reader*, pp. 150 ff.
29. *Op. Cit*., pp. 44-45.
30. "With the possible exception of technological aspects of life, however, the proposition that one way of thought or action is better than another is exceedingly difficult to establish on the grounds of any universally acceptable criteria." Herskovits, *Op. Cit*., p. 67.
31. *Op. Cit*., p.8.
32. "For cultural relativism is a philosophy that recognizes the values set up by every society to guide its own life and that understands their worth to those who live by them, though they may differ from one's own. Instead of underscoring differences from absolute norms that, however objecively arrived at, are nonetheless the product of a given time and place, the relativistic point of view brings into relief the validity of every set of norms for the people who have them, and the values these represent." Herscovits, *Op. Cit*., p. 74.
33. Quoted in "Introduction", John Ladd, *Op. Cit*., p. 9.
34. *Op. Cit*., p. 76.
35. W.G. Sumner, "Folkways", in *Ethical Relativism*, p. 32.
36. *Ibid*., p. 35.
37. *Ibid*., pp. 35 ff.
38. *Ibid*., p. 34.
39. *Ibid*., p. 39, also pp. 35 ff.
40. See "Moral Relativism", in Michael Krausz and Jack W. Meiland, eds., *Relativism :Cognitive and Moral*, 1982, pp. 152 ff.
41. *Ibid*., p. 161.
42. *Ibid*., pp 162 ff.
43. "Local truth is the only substantive truth that we have, and

it is this truth that we tacitly claim for our opinions when we expres them...... Why is it not enough that we should claim relative truth for our moral judgments., taking it as truth relative to either local standards, or to individual standards, according to our theory of moral judgment?" *Ibid.*, p. 161. Also see Foot, "Moral Arguments", in Kenneth Pahel and Marvin Schiller, *Readings in Contemporary Ethical Theory*, 1970, pp. 145 ff.

44. *The Structure of Moral Code...*, 1957, pp. 46-47.
45. See Karl Dunker, "Ethical Relativity ? (An Enquiry into the Psychology of Ethics)", in *Ethical Relativism*, pp.43 ff.
46. *Ibid.*, p. 48.
47. "Social Psychology", in R.B. Brandt, ed., *Value and Obligation: Systematic Readings in Ethics*, 1961, p.481.
48. *Ibid.*, p. 483
49. *An Examination of the Place of Reason in Ethics*, 1970, pp. 132 ff.
50. "The only fact at issue is whether the action in question belongs to a class of actions generally approved in the speaker's community." *Ibid.*, pp. 144-45.
51. *Ibid.*, pp. 148-49.
52. *Ibid.*, pp. 149, 152-53.
53. *Ibid.*, pp. 149 ff.
54 "You cannot evaluate or appraise any given practice or institution or behavior pattern, in any given community, out of relation to the multitude of other practices, institutions and behaviour patterns which are common to that community. This means that if you wish to praise or censure, as morally desirable or undesirable, a particular practice or institution, you have got to take into account the whole way of life of the community concerned." "The Moral and the Non-Moral", in *Problems of Moral Philosophy*, p. 25.
55. *Ibid.*, pp. 36-37.
56. "Social Morality and Individual Ideal", in *Readings in Contemporary Ethical Theory*, 1970, p. 347.
57. *Ibid.*, p. 349.
58. *Ibid.*, p. 353.
59. *Ibid.*, p. 347. However, Strawson's distinction between ethics and morality is untenable.

60. *Ibid.*, p. 166.
61. "Two Concepts of Rules", in *Ibid*, pp. 225 ff.
62. *A Theory of the Good and the Right*, 1979, p. 180.
63. We will have occasion to discuss existentialism in some detail in our Ch.7, Sec. II infra.
64. Lucius Outlaw, "Lifeworlds, Modernity and Philosophical Praxis : Race, Ethnicity and Critical Social Theory", in Eliot Deutsch, ed., *Culture and Modernity*, 1994, p. 35.
65. *Ibid.*, pp. 34 ff.
66. See Ch. 2, Sec. III.2, infra for a detailed discussion of the thesis of incommensurability.
67. "Is There a Single True Morality ?" in Michael Krausz, ed., *Relativism: Interpretation and Confrontation*, 1989, p. 147.
68. "Post-Nietzschian Anthropology : The Idea of Multiple Objective Worlds", in *Ibid.*, p. 99.
69. "There Kinds of Incommensurability", in *Ibid.*, p. 147.

Chapter 2. Positivism, Postmodernism and Ethical Relativism

1. See R.M. Hare, *Freedom and Reason*, pp.88ff.; W.K. Frankena, *Ethics*, 1993, pp. 95 ff.
2. *Language, Truth, and Logic*, quoted in J.O. Urmson, *The Emotive Theory of Ethics*, 1968, p.25.
3. *Ibid.*, in W.T. Jones, Freederick Sontag, Morton O. Beckner, Robert J. Fogelin, eds., *Approaches to Ethics*, 1962, p. 545.
4. "In short, we find that argument is possible on moral questions only if some system of values is presupposed.... Given that a man has certain moral principles, we argue that he must, in order to be consistent, react morally to certain things in a certain way. What we do not and cannot argue about is the validity of these moral principles. We merely praise or condemn them in the light of our own feelings." *Ibid.*, p. 547.
5. *Ibid.*, p. 547.
6. See *Facts and Values*, 1963, pp.18 ff.
7. *Ethics and Language*, in *Approaches to Ethics*, p. 549.
8. In the following account of the 'postmodern' I am generally

indebted to Hans Bertens, *The Idea of the Postmodern*, 1995, "Introduction".

9. "Introduction" to Jürgen Habermas, *The Philosophical Discourse of Modernity*,1995, pp. viii-ix.
10. *Philosophy and the Mirror of Nature*, 1979, p. 178.
11. *Farewell to Reason*, 1987, pp. 52 - 53.
12. *Ibid.*, pp. 104 ff.
13. *Mind and the World Order*, 1956, p. 38.
14. "Just the Facts, Ma'am!" in Michael Krausz, ed., *Relativism : Interpretation and Confrontation*, 1989, pp. 80-81.
15. *Ibid.*, p. 81.
16. *Ibid.*, p. 83, also see p. 84.
17. "Post-Nietzschian Anthropology : The Idea of Multiple Objective Worlds", in *Relativism : Interpretation and Confrontation*, p. 132.
18. "The Fabrication of Facts", in Michael Krausz and Jack W. Meiland, eds., *Relativism : Cognitive and Moral*, 1982, p. 19. Cf. Rorty, *Op. Cit.*, pp. 268 ff.
19. *Ibid.*, pp. 195 ff., 268 ff.
20. *Ibid.*, p. 275.
21. ".......to think of knowledge which presents a "problem," and about which we ought to have a "theory", is a product of viewing knowledge as an assemblage of representations - a view of knowledge which.... was a product of the seventeenth century." Rorty, *Op. Cit.*, pp. 136, also 180 ff.
22. See Rorty, *Op. Cit.*, pp. 149 ff., 168 ff., 268 ff; Cf. "After all, each of the world's languages is "specialized" in saying particularly well those things necessary to address the unique features of its own natural and social conditions, and hence, the greater the degree of difference among cultures, the greater the degree of difference in translating among the languages that express them." Roger T. Ames, "Meaning as Imaging : Prolegomena to a Confucian Epistemology," in Eliot, Deutsch, ed, *Culture and Modernity*, 1994 p. 227.
23. See Richard Bernstein, "Incommensurability and Otherness Revisited"; Alsair MacIntyre, "Incommensurability, Truth and Conversation Between Confucians and Aristotelians about the

Virtues"; A. C. Graham, "Conceptual Schemes and Linguistic Relativism in Relation to Chinese"; and Ames, *Op Cit.*, in *Ibid.*, pp. 85 ff.; 104 ff.; 193 ff.; 227 ff.; also see Rorty, *Op. Cit.*, pp. 274 ff.

24. "Conceptual Schemes and Linguistic Relativism in Relation to Chinese", in *Ibid.*, pp. 193 ff., Especially pp. 198-99, 207.
25. "Incommensurability, Truth, and the..... Virtues", in *Ibid*, p.109.
26. *Ibid.*, p. 109.
27. *Op.Cit.*, p. 269, also see pp. 268 ff., 275 ff.
28. See *Ibid.*, pp.174 ff.; 223 ff.; Bernstein, *Beyond Objectivism and Relativism: Science, Hermeneutics and Praxis*, 1983, pp. 8, 16 ff. etc.
29. Quoted in *Beyond Objectivism and Relativism*, pp. 81-82.
30. In the above account I am generally indebted to *Ibid.*, Chapter one, "....An Overview."
31. *Ibid.*, p. 8.
32. *Ibid.*, pp. 11-12.
33. "I think, the concerete existential concerns and actions of specific groupings of people to realize their particular(istic) interests, when pulled into the bounds of the theoretical and practical legacies of the project of modernity, have generally been poorly accommodated, if not eclipsed or eliminated, by the twin pressures of reductionist moves to individualism, and flights into abstract universalism, derivative of subject-centred reason. The historical, cultural, social lifeworld is the foundation and context of our lived experience, of our very being." Lucius Outlaw, "Lifeworlds, Modernity, and Philosophical Praxis", in *Culture and Modernity*, 1994, p. 35.
34. *Op. Cit.*, p. 50.
35. *Ibid.*, p. 261.
36. *Ibid.*, p. 249.
37. *Op. Cit.*, pp. 327 ff., especially 329.
38. *Ibid.*, p. 331.
39. See Outlaw, *Op. Cit.*, Jiang Tianji, "The Problem of Relativism", in *Culture and Modernity*, pp. 35 ff.; 164 ff.
40. Quoted in Jiang Tianji, *Op.Cit.*, p. 164.
41. See Barry Barnes and David Bloor, "Relativism, Rationalism, and the Sociology of Knowledge", in Martin Hollis and Steven

Lukes, eds., *Rationality and Relativism*, 1994, pp. 22 ff.

42. See *Beyond Objectivism and Relativism*, pp. 8 ff.; "Incommensurability and Otherness Revisited", in *Culture and Modernity*, pp. 89 ff.
43. See Charles Taylor, "Rationality", in *Rationality and Relativism*, pp. 88-89.
44. Quoted in Bernstein, *Philosophical Profiles: Essays in Pragmatic Mode*, 1986, p. 83. Cf. ".....reason itself is never "pure", never without specific historical and cultural clothing appropriate to the particular projects of particular persons of particular groups situated in particular ways in a particular social order." Outlaw, *Op. Cit.*, p. 35.
45. "For every statement (theory, point of view) that is believed to be true with good reasons there may exist arguments showing that either its opposite, or a weaker alternative is true." *Op. Cit.*, p. 74.
46. "The Myth of Subjective", in *Relativism: Interpretation and Confrontation*, pp. 159 ff.; "On the Very Idea of a Conceptual Scheme", in *Relativism: Cognitive and Moral*, pp. 66 ff.
47. See "True For", in *Relativism Cognitive and Moral*, pp. 84 ff., especially pp. 103-5.
48. See Joseph Margolis, "The Truth About Relativism", in *Relativism: Interpretation and Confrontation*, pp. 232 ff.
49. "Kuhn's Epistemological Relativism: An Interpretation and Defense", in *Relativism : Cognitive and Moral*, pp. 113 ff.
50. *Op. Cit*, pp. 127 131-33.
51. "Incommensurability and Otherness Revisited", *Op. Cit.*, p. 92.
52. *Ibid.*, p. 93.
53. See ref. nos. 31, 32 supra.
54. "Solidarity or Objectivity ?" in *Relativism: Interpretation and Confrontation*, p. 37.
55. *Ibid.*, pp. 42 ff.
56. "Relativism, Power, and Philosophy", in *Ibid.*, p. 193 ff.
57. *Ibid.*, p. 199.
58. *Truth and Method*, tr. by Joel Weinsheimer and Donald G. Marshall, 1995, pp. 270 ff., 277 ff.

59. "Moral Relativism", in *Relativism: Cognitive and Moral*, pp. 152 ff.; especially 155, 161; also see, Barnard Williams, "The Truth in Relativism", in *Ibid.*, pp. 175 ff.
60. See *After Virtue*, 1984, pp. 194 ff., 220.
61. *Ibid.*, p. 246.
62. "Relativism, Power, and Philosophy", in *Op. Cit.*, p. 188.
63. *Ibid.*, p. 189.
64. *Ibid.*, pp. 190-91.
65. In *Relativism : Cognitive and Moral*, p. 189.
66. *Ibid.*, pp. 189 ff. especially 202-3.

Chapter 3. Cultural-Ethical Relativism: A Critique

1. *Aspects of Hindu Morality*, 1999, pp. ix - x, 1.
2. *Secularism in India*, 1995, p. 109.
3. See Ch. 1. Sec. I; Ch. 2, Sec. III supra.
4. *Aspects of Hindu Morality*, pp, x, 3 ff.
5. Sec Ch. 1, Sec. I, ref. nos. 23-26.
6. See D.H. Monro, *Empiricism in Ethics*, 1967, Ch.s 4 to 9, for a general review of the naturalist-empiricist position.
7. See Ch. 1, Sec. II, ref. nos. 23-26; and Mannheim, "The Sociology of Knowledge", in J.E. Curtis and J.W. Petras, eds., The *Sociology of knowledge : A Reader*, 1970, pp. 113 ff.
8. *Ibid.*, p. 124.
9. *Ibid.*, p. 125.
10. "The Sociology of Knowledge : Formal Problems", in *Ibid.*, p. 175.
11. *Ibid.*, pp. 178-79.
12. Hans Speier, "The Social Determination of Ideas", in *Ibid.*, p. 275.
13. See Toulmin, *An Examination of the Place of Reason in Ethics*, 1970, pp. 149-50.
14. See "Two Concepts of Rules", in Kenneth Pahel and Marvin Schiller, eds., *Readings in Contemporary Ethical Theory*, 1970, pp. 225 ff.
15. "Moral Relativism", in Michael Krausz and Jack W. Meiland, eds., *Relativism : Cognitive and Moral*, 1982, pp. 155-57.

16. See Ch. 1, Section II. 2, ref. nos 33-34 supra.
17. *Op. Cit.*, p. 263.
18. *Principia Ethica*, 1956, pp. 39, also 40, 41, 58.
19. *Ibid.*, p. 132.
20. *Ibid.*, p. 132.
21. *Ibid.*, p. 134.
22. *Ibid.*, p. 135.
23. "The Naturalistic Fallacy", in *Readings in Contemporary Ethical Theory*, pp. 32 ff.
24. *The Language of Morals*, 1956, p. 82.
25. *Ibid.*, p. 91.
26. *Ibid.*, p. 28.
27. "How to Derive "Ought" from "Is"," in *Readings in Contemporary Ethical Theory*, pp. 156 ff.
28. "The Promising Game", in *Ibid.*, pp. 168 ff., especially pp. 178-79.
29. "Moral Arguments", in *Ibid.*, pp. 145 ff., especially p. 151.
30. See Ch, 1, ref. no. 33 supra.
31. "Folkways are the right ways to satisfy all interests, because they are traditional and exist in fact.... The tradition is its own warrant. The notion of rightis in the Folkways .... In the Folkways whatever is, is right.," "Folkways", in John Ladd, ed., *Ethical Relativism*, 1973, p. 31.
32. *Ibid.*, pp. 34-35.
33. "The fact that a man believes that the action is required does not actually make it required. If the whole society believes that the action is required, then the whole society is mistaken. We might, in some circumstances, excuse people because they could not know better, but we can still say that the action is wrong." *Moral Philosophy*, 1967, pp. 172 and ff.
34. *Ibid.*, p. 172-73.
35. *Ibid.*, pp. 173.
36. *Ibid.*, p. 173.
37. *Ibid.*, p. 175.
38. "Social Science and Ethical Relativism", in Paul W. Taylor, ed., *Problems of Moral Philosophy*, 1967, p. 67.

39. *Ibid.*, pp. 67-68.
40. *Generalization in Ethics*, 1961, pp. 332-33.
41. *Ibid.*, p. 333.
42. See "Introduction [to Ethical Relativism]", in *Problems of Moral Philosophy*, 1967, p. 46.
43. *Ethical Theory*, 1959, p. 84.
44. *Ibid.*, p. 84.
45. "*Ethical Relativity* ? (An Enquiry into the Psychology of Ethics)", in *Ethical Relativism*, 1973, p. 47.
46. *Ibid.*, p. 48.
47. *Ibid.*, p. 47.
48. *Social Psychology*, in Richard B. Brandt, ed., *Value and Obligation: Systematic Readings in Ethics*, 11961, p. 483.
49. "General Theory of Value", in W.T. Jones, Frederick Sontag, Morton O, Beckner, Robert J. Fogelin, eds., *Approaches to Ethics*, p. 498.
50. "Social Morality and Individual Ideal", in *Readings in Contemporary Ethical Theory*, pp. 347 and ff., especially, 349.
51. *The Moral Point of View : A Rational Basis of Ethics*, 1967, pp. 112 ff.
52. *A Theory of the Good and the Right*, 1979, pp. 176 ff.
53. See Toulmin, *Op. Cit.*, pp. 284 and ff.
54. *Freedom and Reason*, 1963 pp. 87 ff.
55. *Op. Cit.*, pp. 84 and ff.
56. "The Point of View of Morality", in *Readings in Contemporary Ethical Theory*, pp. 334 and ff.
57. *The Moral Point of View*, p. 89.
58. "The Point of View of Morality", *Op.Cit.*, p. 343.
59. *The Concept of Morals*, 1962, pp. 51-52.
60. *Ethical Theory*, pp. 288 ff.
61. "Relativism and Tolerance", in *Relativism : Cognitive and Moral*, pp. 238 ff.
62. "Moral Relativism Defended", in *Ibid.*, pp. 189 ff.
63. It does not mean either that any one has a right to think and act as the moral police of entire humanity. This attitude that we know what is right or wrong for everybody and we have

been chosen (by God?) to force everyone to comply with our value perceptions and norms was prominent among the Europeans in eighteenth and nineteenth centuries, and was nicknamed as 'whiteman's burden' The same approach is being adopted by the United States in contemporary world, and is regrettable.

64. "The Sociology of Knowledge and Epistemology", in *The Sociology of Knowledge : A Reader*, pp. 238-39.
65. "The Social Determination of Ideas", in *Ibid.*, p. 276.
66. *Ibid.*, p. 277. Cf. "a great number of philosophical problems are given by human existence as such, independent of any historical constellation of needs." *Ibid.*, p. 276.
67. "Introduction", in Ladd, *Op. Cit.*, pp. 8-9.
68. *Ibid.*, p. 10.
69. *Op. Cit.*, p. 45.

Chapter 4. Relativism: Positivist and Postmodern: A Critique

1. Rorty, *Philosophy and the Mirror of Nature*, 1979, pp. 176 ff., 180 ff.
2. *Ibid.*, pp. 136 ff.
3. See *Ibid.*, pp. 274 ff.; Bernstein, *Beyond Objectivism and Relativism*, 1983, pp. 8-9; articles by Bernstein, "Incommensurability and Otherness Revisited"; Jiang Tianji, "The Problem of Relativism", in Eliot Deutsch, ed., *Culture and Modernity*, 1994, pp. 85 ff., 161 ff.
4. Bernstein, *Op. Cit.*, p. 84; also see pp. 11-12, 84 ff.
5. See Ch. 2, Sec. III, ref. nos. 18-26, 31-33 supra.
6. *Realism and Reason : Philosophical Papers*, Vol.3, 1983, p. 168.
7. "Relativism, Rationalism and the Sociology of Knowledge,"in Martin Hollis and Steven Lukes, eds., *Rationality and Relativism*, 1994, pp. 22 ff.
8. See Rorty, *Op. Cit.*, pp. 328 ff.; and Ch. 2, Sec. III, ref. nos. 36-39 supra.
9. *Op. Cit.*, pp. 236 -38.
10. *Ibid.*, pp. 238 ff.
11. See Ch. 2, Sec. III, ref. nos. 22-25 supra.

12. See Rorty, *Op. Cit.*, pp. 194 ff.; also see articles by Barnstein, *Op. Cit.*; A.C. Graham, "Conceptual Schemes and Linguistic Relativism in Relation to Chinese"; and Roger T Ames, "Meaning and Imaging: Prolegomena to a Confucian Epistemology," in *Culture and Modernity*, pp., 85 ff.; 193 ff.; and 227 ff.
13. Putnam, *Op. Cit.*, pp. 192 ff., especially 194.
14. "True For", in Michael Krausz and Jack W. Meiland, eds., *Relativism : Cognitive and Moral*, 1982, pp. 92 ff.
15. "Relativism and the Possibility of Interpreation", in *Rationality and Relativism*, pp. 106 ff.
16. *Ibid.*, pp. 113-14.
17. See articles by Graham and Ames, *Op.Cit.*, pp. 193 ff.; 223 ff.;
18. *Op.Cit.*, pp. 275-76; also 266 ff.
19. Quoted in the Bernstein, *Op. Cit.*, p. 82.
20. *Ibid.*, p. 8.
21. *Ibid.*, pp. 11-12, also 8 ff.
22. See *Ibid.*, pp. 8 ff; Rorty, *Op.Cit.*, pp. 178 ff.
23. "Just the Facts Ma'am!" in Michael Krausz, ed., *Relativism : Interpretation and Confrontation*, 1984, pp. 80 ff.
24. *Op.Cit.*, p. 193; Cf. Ernst Gellner, "Relativism and Universals", in *Rationality and Relativism,* pp. 185-86.
25. Quoted in Bernstein, *Op. Cit.*, pp. 53-55.
26. Quoted in *Ibid.*, pp. 84-85,
27. *Ibid.*, p. 85.
28. *Ibid.*, pp. 84-85.
29. *Ibid.*, p. 86.
30. See *Ibid.*, pp. 25 ff.
31. See Ch. 3, Sec. I.3 supra.
32. Let us take a few examples from Indian history. Kabir, the 15th cent. saint of Bhakti (devotional faith) tradition vociferously condemned all distinctions of creed (religion) and caste between men and men, as well as all externalistic rituals, and he did that at a time when all these factors were determinative of Indian social life. In 19th cent. Rammohan Roy successfully fought a sustained battle against the practice of *sati*. There

followed several thinker-reformers who aggressively attacked several undesirable religio-social practices in Indian-Hindu society, and thereby ushered in a new more liberated and enlightened era in Indian history. None of these thinker-reformers were prisoners of their society's normative and conceptual frameworks, because if they were, they could not have transformed their society almost beyond recognition.

33. Putnam, *Op.Cit.*, pp. 178-79.
34. *Op.Cit.*, pp. 80-81.
35. *Ibid.*, p. 83.
36. "The Myth of the Subjective", in *Relativism : Interpretation and Confrontation*, pp. 165-66.
37. *Ibid.*, p. 166.
38. *Ibid.*, p. 171.
39. "On the Very Idea of a Conceptual Scheme", in *Relativism : Cognitive and Moral*, p. 79.
40. *Op. Cit.*, pp. 238-39.
41. *Ibid.*, p. 193.
42. See David B. Wong, "Three Kinds of Incommensurability", in *Relativism : Interpretation and Confrontation*, pp. 142 ff.; Bernstein, *Beyond Objectivism and Relativism*, pp. 27 ff.
43. *Op.Cit.*, pp. 176, 195-96.
44. *Ibid.*, p. 195.
45. *Ibid.*, p. 196.
46. Bernstein, *Op. Cit.*, pp. 68 ff.
47. *Gandhi Reader for 1988*, p. 35.
48. *Ibid.*, p. 31.
49. *Ibid.*, pp. 22-23.
50. *Ibid.*, p. 34.

Chapter 5. Anti-Relativist Trends: Realism and Universalism

1. For a detailed critique of various postmodern theses see Ch. 4, Secs. III and IV.
2. See Hilary Putnam, *Realism and Reason :Philosophical Papers, Vol 3*, 1983, pp. 162 ff.,176-79.
3. See "The Fabrication of Facts", in Michael Krausz and Jack W.

Meiland, eds.., *Relativism : Cognitive and Moral*, 1982, pp. 18 ff.

4. See Michael Devitt, *Realism and Truth*, 1984, pp. 12 ff., 35 ff., 64 ff., 140 ff.; C.A. Hooker, *A Realistic Theory of Science*, 1987, pp. 42 ff. 48 ff. 58, 256 ff.
5. *Op.Cit.*, p. 13.
6. *Ibid.*, p. 140.
7. *Ibid.*, pp. 112, 142 etc.
8. *Ibid.*, pp. 29; 110 ff; 140 ff; 149 ff.
9. *Op.Cit.*, p. 256.
10. *Ibid.*, p. 98.
11. *Ibid.*, p. 256.
12. *Ibid.*, pp. 48 ff.
13. Devitt, *Op.Cit.*, pp. 152 ff.
14. *Ibid.*, pp. 87; 105 ff; Putnam, *Op.Cit.*, pp. 192 ff.
15. Hooker, *Op.Cit.*, pp. 28, 279 ff.
16. Devitt, *Op.Cit.*, pp. 113 ff.; Hooker, *Op.Cit.*, pp. 45 ff., especially 58.
17. *Op.Cit.*, pp. 33 ff.
18. *Ibid.*, p. 256
19. *Ibid.*, pp. 21 ff.
20. *Ibid.*, pp. 34.
21. *Ibid.*, pp. 260 ff., 264 ff., especially p. 265.
22. Richard N. Boyd, "How to Be a Moral Realist", in Geoffrey Sayre-McCord, ed., *Essays on Moral Realism*, 1988, p. 182.
23. *Ibid.*, p. 195
24. *Ibid.*, p. 201.; also pp. 182, 195, 199.
25. "It follows form moral realism that such moral terms as 'good', 'fair', 'just', 'obligatory' usually correspond to real properties or relations and that our ordinary standards for moral reasoning and moral disputation - together with reliable standards of scientific and everyday reasoning - constitute a fairly reliable way of finding out which events, persons, policies, social arrangements etc. have these properties and enter into these relations." *Ibid.*, p. 182; also see pp. 200-1.
26. *Ibid.*, pp. 196 ff. 208 ff.
27. *Ibid.*, p. 211.

28. *Ibid*., p. 214.
29. "Ethics, Mathematics and Relativism", in *Essays on Moral Realism*, p. 93.
30. "Ethics and Observation", in *Ibid*., pp. 119 ff.
31. Quoted in Sturgeon, "Moral Explanations", in *Ibid*., p. 235.
32. *Ibid*., pp. 243 ff.
33. *Moral Realism and the Foundations of Ethics*, 1989, p. 7.
34. *Ibid*., p. 15.
35. *Ibid*., p. 17.
36. *Ibid*., p. 20.
37. *Ibid*., pp. 24-25.
38. *Ibid*., pp. 26 ff.
39. *Ibid*., p. 29.
40 *Ibid*., p. 31.
41. *Ibid*., pp. 78-79.
42. *Op.Cit*., pp. 182,199,200.
43. "A Proof of Objectivity of Morals", in Robert L. Cunningham, ed., *Situationism and the New Morality*, 1970, p. 113.
44. *Ibid*., pp. 107 ff.,112 ff., especially p. 113.
45. *Op.Cit*., pp. 7, 91, 197 ff.
46. *Ibid*., pp. 92 ff.
47. "The Subjectivity of Values", in *Essays on Moral Realism*, pp. 111 ff.
48. *The Language of Morals*, 1952, p. 44.
49. *Ibid*., pp. 28, 91 etc.
50. See "Internalism and Externalism in Ethics", *The British Tradition in 20th Century Philosophy, Sonderdruck*, Vol. 22. Reprint, pp.258 ff.
51. "The intuitionist level of moral thinking.......cannot be the whole of moral thinking. If it were, there would be no way of resolving the conflicts that frequently arise between our moral intuitions. This demands a higher level of moral thinking, which I have called 'critical thinking'." *Ibid*., p. 265.
52. *Ibid*., pp. 262 ff.
53. *Fundamental Principles of the Metaphysics of Morals*, tr. Thomas K. Abbott, 1949 "Introduction", pp. xiii-xiv.
54. *Ibid*., p. 26.

55. *Ibid.*, p.26.
56. *Ibid.*, p.29.
57. *Ibid.*, p.38.
58. *Ibid.*, p.38.
59. *Ibid.*, p.45.
60. *Ibid.*, p.46.
61. *Ibid.*, pp. 48,52,54,64-65.
62. "Truth in utterances that cannot be avoided is the formal duty of man to everyone, however great the disadvantage that may arise to him or any other...." "On a Supposed Right to Tell Lies from Benevolent Motives", quoted in Marcus G. Singer, *Generalization in Ethics*, 1961 p. 228.
63. *Ibid.*, pp. 223-24,
64. *Ibid.*, pp. 229 ff., 231.
65. *The Language of Morals*, p.28.
66. *Ibid.*, p. 44; ref. no. 48 supra.
67. *Ibid.*, p.82, also pp. 44, 91.
68. *Ibid.*, pp. 60 ff.
69. *Freedom and Reason*, 1963, p. 12.
70. *The Language of Morals*, pp. 111 ff.
71. *The Revolution in Ethical Theory*, 1966, p. 169.
72. See *The Language of Morals*, pp. 60 ff.; 64 ff.
73. "if pressed to justify a decision completely, we have to give a complete specification of the way of life of which it is a part.... If the inquirer still goes on asking, 'But why *should* I live like that?' then there is no further answer to give him.... We can only ask him to make up his own mind which way he ought to live; for in the end everything rests upon such a decision of principle." *Ibid.*, p. 69.
74. *Freedom and Reason*, p. 33.
75. *Ibid.*, pp. 38 ff.
76. *Ibid.*, pp. 93 ff.
77. *Generalization in Ethics*, pp. 19-20.
78. *Ibid.*, pp. 21; also see pp. 21 ff., 32.
79. *Ibid.*, p. 31.
80. Quoted in *Ibid.*, p. 36.

81. *Ibid.*, pp.36-37.
82. *Ibid.*, p. 34.
83. *Ibid.*, pp. 53 ff.
84. *Ibid.*, pp. 66 and ff.
85. *Freedom and Reason*, p. 88.
86. *Op.Cit.*, pp.123 ff.
87. "The Knowledge of What is Right", from *The Foundations of Ethics*, in R.B.Brandt, ed, *Value and Obligation*, 1961, p. 343; Cf. Hare, *Freedom and Reason*, pp 19 ff.
88. "Ethics and Observation", *Op. Cit.*, p. 120.
89. *Ibid.*, p. 122.
90. Using Barnard Williams' terminology I may say here that a moral judgment may carry a moral prescription, if there is actual, and not merely notional, confrontation, i.e. if there is some actual possibility of our facing that situation in which we would be called upon to act according to the prescription. But a large number of our judgments are not made prescriptively.

Chapter 6. The Moral Point of View

1. "On the specious pretext that morality should "cover the whole of life", it is first conceived in such wise that it includes the manner in which people get married, the customs they adopt at burials, their habits in regard to social gathering, eating, drinking..... Since in most of these matters there are no definite rules of right and wrong, save such as are determined by tradition, custom or personal preference, morality so defined is seen to be purely relative. From this wide and loose sense of the word "morals" we then slip over, unconsciously perhaps, to real morality, that is, morality in a narrower, stricter, sense." W.T. Stace, *The Concept of Morals*, 1962, p. 74.
2. *The Moral Point of View*, 1967, p. 150; also see. pp. 148 ff.
3. "The Meaning of Morality", from *Realms of Value : A Critique of Human Civilization*, 1954, in W.T. Jones, F. Sontag, M.O. Beckner, R.J. Fogelin, eds., *Approaches to Ethics*, 1962, p. 498.
4. "Let him avoid wealth and desire if they are opposed to sacred

law (*dharma*) and even lawful acts which may cause pain in the future, or are offensive to men." *Manu Smṛti* IV. 176; also see IV. 155, 161.

5. *Ibid.* VI. 35-36; *Mahābhārata, Śānti Parva* 109 : 3ff.; also see writer, *Aspects of Hindu Morality*, 1989, 101 ff., 173 ff.
6. "If thou thinkest, ... with reference to thyself, "I am alone," (know that) the sage who witnesses all virtuous acts and all crimes, ever resides in thy heart." *Manu Smṛti* VII. 91.
7. *Taittirīya Saṁhitā* VI. 3.10.5.
8. *Mahābhārata, Śānti Parva* 91:5; 101:11.
9. "What do we mean by a universal morality ? We do *not* mean a moral principle which is, as a matter of empirical fact, believed and accepted by all men. We mean a moral principle which is *applicable* to all men in the sense that, even if they do not accept it, they ought to do so. What we have to show is that the same moral obligation in reality falls upon all men." Stace, *Op.Cit.*, pp. 102-103. (original italics).

   The moral point of view is "a standpoint from which rules are considered as being acted on by everyone. Moral rules are not merely rules to which a person must not make exceptions in his favor but they are principles *meant for everybody*."(original italics.) Kurt Baier, *Op.Cit.*, pp. 100-101. Cf. Baier "The Point of View of Morality", in Kenneth Pahel and Marvin Schiller, eds., *Readings in Contemporary Ethical Theory*, 1970. pp. 322 ff.
10. "Moral rules are universal rules designed to override those of self-interest when following the latter is harmful to others." *Op. Cit.*, p.149.
11. *Secularism in India*, 1995, pp. 77 ff, 108 ff.
12. *Freedom and Reason*, p. 92.
13. *Op.Cit.*, p. 84.
14. *Ibid.*, p. 85.
15. "a person likewise does not know what he is talking about if he believes that finding out whether some course of action is contrary to the morality of a certain group settles the question whether this course of action is morally wrong. For he ignores the crucial question, "Is what the morality of that group forbids really wrong?" or put differently, "Are the moral convictions

of that group true?" *Ibid.*, pp. 85-86.

16. *Ibid.*, p.89.
17. "The Point of View of Morality", *Op.Cit.*, p. 343.
18. "The best course of action..... is the course of action which is supported by the best reason." *The Moral Point of View*, p. 28 also see pp. 28 ff., 84 ff., 90 ff.
    J.M.Brennan makes a strong case for his thesis that moral judgments are based on rationally justifiable standards which, in turn, claim universal, or objective (interpersonal) validity. *The Open Texture of Moral Concepts* 1967, pp. 67 ff., 89 ff.
19. "The notion of correctness brings with it the assumption that correctness or incorrectness of a proposed answer is fixed independently of anyone's acceptance or rejection." Carl Wellman, quoted in Joel J. Kupperman, *Ethical Knowledge*, 1970, p. 46. "Moral argument and deliberation presuppose not only correct answers to moral questions but also answers whose correctness is independent of our moral beliefs." David O. Brink, *Moral Realism and the Foundations of Ethics*, 1989, p. 31; also quoted in Ch. 5, ref. no. 40 supra.
20. "Our ordinary use of moral terms provides us with epistemic access to moral properties. Moral goodness must, to some extent, regulate the use of the word 'good' in moral reasoning." Richard Boyd, "How to Be a Moral Realist", in Geoffrey Sayre-McCord, ed., *Essays on Moral Realism*, 1988, p. 201; also quoted in Ch. 5, ref. no. 24 supra.
21. *Op.Cit.*, pp. 46 ff., 68 ff., 76 ; also see discussion of moral realism in Ch. 5, Sec. III, ref. nos. 22-45 supra.
22. *Ethics*, 1954, p. 72.
23. "it is in virtue of my thinking the act to have some other character that I think I ought to do it. Rightness is always a resultant attribute, an attribute that an act has because it has another attribute." "The Knowledge of What is Right", from *The Foundation of Ethics*, 1939, in Richard B. Brandt, ed., *Value and Obligation*, 1961, p. 343.
24. *Op.Cit.*, pp. 82-83 and ff.
25. See Ch. 5, Sec.IV, ref. nos. 53-64 supra.

26. See *Ibid.*, ref. nos. 65-76.
27. See *Ibid.*, ref. nos. 77-86.
28. *Freedom and Reason*, pp. 30 ff.
29. *Op.Cit.*, p. 57.
30. *Generalization in Ethics*, 1961, p. 21, quoted in Ch. 5, ref. no. 78 supra.
31. *Empiricism and Ethics*, 1967, pp. 164-65.
32. *Ibid.*, p. 166.
33. *Morality : A New Justification of the Moral Rules*, 1988, p. 68.
34. *Ibid.*, p. 69.
35. *Op.Cit.*, pp. 102-103.
36. *Ibid.*, pp. 102 ff. ; also see Ch. 3, Sec. III, ref. nos 33-43 supra.
37. *The Open Texture of Moral Concepts*, 1977, pp. 74ff.
38. "It is most fundamentally because moral judgments are universalizable that we can speak of moral thought as rational (to universalize is to give the reason);" Hare, *Op.Cit.*, p. 5.
39. "The Point of View of Morality", *Op.Cit.*, p. 331.
40. *Ibid.*, p. 337.
41. *Ibid.*, p. 342.
42. *A Theory of Justice*, 1973, pp. 11 ff., 136ff., 139.
43. See *Manu Smṛti* VIII. 335-336.
44. "He who is equal-minded among friends, companions and foes, among those who are neutral and impartial, among those who are hateful and related, among saints and sinners, he excels." *Bhagavadgītā* VI.9
45. See Baier, *Op.Cit.*, p. 108.
46. Hare, *Op.Cit.*, pp. 90 ff.
47. "Social Morality and Individual Ideal", in *Readings in Contemporary Ethical Theory*, p.352.
48. *Ibid.*, p. 353.
49. *Ibid.*, pp. 353-54.
50. *Matthew* 22 : 39-40; 25 : 34-45.
51. Quoted in Maduabuchi Dukor, "The Concept of Justice in Liberalism", in J.I.C.P.R. (Journal of Indian Council of Philosophical Research), Vol XIV, no. 3, May-Aug. 1997, p. 21.
52. *Fundamental Principles of the Metaphysics of Morals*, tr., Thomas K. Abbott, 1949, p. 46.

53. "rational beings, on the contrary, are called *persons*, because their very nature points them out as ends in themselves...." *Ibid.*, p. 45.
54. "Introduction", *Ibid.*, p. xv.
55. *Op.Cit.*, p. 28.
56. *The Concept of Law*, 1978, p. 161.
57. *Ibid.*, p. 155.
58. "It is easy to show that this (to give to each his own) is an empty formula, because the decisive question, what is that which is everybody's own, is not answered, and hence the formula is applicable only under the condition that this question is already decided by a social order - legal or moral - established by custom or legislation, that is to say, by positive morality or positive law.." Hans Kelson, "What is Justice?" in *What is justice? Justice, Law and Politics in the Mirror of Science* 1957, p. 13.
59. "This idea of justice starts from the presupposition that men are by their very nature equal, and results in the postulate that all men shall be treated in an equal way. Since, however, the presup-position is evidently wrong, men being in fact very differrent, no two men being really equal, the only possible meaning of the postulate is that a social order, in conferring rights and imposingduties on men, should ignore certain diffferences, only certain, not all differences... But which are the differences that should, and those that should not be taken into consideration? this is the decisive question; and to this question the principle of equality is no answer."*Ibid.*, p. 14.
60. *Op.Cit.*, pp. 14-15. Rawls later modifies and elaborates his Two Principles of justice as:

    "First : each person is to have an equal right to the most extensive basic liberty compatible with a similar liberty for others.

    "Second, social and economic inequalities are to be arranged so that they are both (a) reasonably expected to be to everyone's advantage, and (b) attached to positions and offices open to all." *Ibid.*, p. 60
61. *Ibid.*, p. 83.

62. See ref. no. 47-49 supra.
63. *See Kant, Lectures on Ethics*, in *Op. Cit.*, pp. 294-95; *The Moral Law: The Metaphysics of Morals*, Mary J. Gregor, 1964, pp. 115 ff.
64. See writer, *Op. Cit.*, pp. 101 ff.
65. "Ethical Relativism and Confrontation of Cultures", in *Relativism: Interpretation and Confrontation*, 1989, p. 358.
66. *The Moral Point of View*, 1967, p. 115.
67. "Prima Facie Duties", from *The Right and the Good*, in Paul W. Taylor, ed., *Problems of Moral Philosophy*, 1967, pp. 266 ff. 269-70.
68. *Mahābhārata, Anuśāsana Parva* : 98:13, 37-38.
69. *The Doctrine of Virtue*, *Op. Cit.*, pp. 118 ff.

Chapter 7. Self and Others

1. "reason, which is that law, teaches all mankind who will but consult it that, being all equal and independent, no one ought to harm another in his life, health, liberty and possessions.... And being furnished with like faculties, sharing all in one community of nature, there cannot be supposed any such subordination among us that may authorize us to destroy one another...." Quoted in Maduabuchi Dukor, "The Concept of Justice in Liberalism", in J.I.C.P.R. Vol. XIV, No. 3, May-August, 1997, p. 21.
2. "Hegel understood by *Objective Spirit* the active and influential body of individuals, which is not created by these, but rather forms the source from which they proceed... The subjection of subjective dispositions of the individual to the commands of the common consciousness the philosopher calls "*morality*", while he retains the name of "Sittlichkeit" (social morality or the moral order) for the realisation of the common consciousness in the *State*." W. Windelband, *History of Philosophy*, 1957, p. 613.
3. *On Liberty and Other Writings*, ed., Stefan Collini, 1989, p. 21.
4. "In clarifying being-in-the-world we have shown that a bare subject without a world never..is..given. And so.... an isolated "I" without others just as far from being proximally given."

Heidegger, quoted in Jürgen Habermas, "The Undermining of Western Rationalism through the Critique of Metaphysics: Martin Heidegger", in *The Philosophical Discourses of Modernity: Twelve Lectures,* tr., Frederick G. Lawrance, 1995, p. 149.

5. "Man is nothing else but what he makes of himself..... "existentialism's first move is to make every man aware of what he is and to make the full responsibility of his existence rest on him."
...“man is condemned to be free.....once thrown into the world, he is responsible for everything he does." Sartre, "Existentialism is a Humanism", in W.T. Jones, Frederick Sontag, Morton O. Beckner, Robert J. Fogelin, eds., *Approaches to Ethics*, 1962, pp. 521-23
6. "Bad Faith and Falsehood", from *Being and Nothingness*, in *Ibid.*, pp. 526 ff.
7. "man being condemned to be free carries the weight of the whole world on his shoulders; he is responsible for the world and for himself as a way of being.....Then whatever may be the situation in which he finds himself, the for-itself must wholly assume....the situation with the proud consciousness of being the author of it." "Freedom and Responsibility", in *Op.Cit.*, p. 534.
8. See Habermas, Op.Cit., pp. 155 ff.
9. "Each person is to have an equal right in the most extensive total system of equal, basic liberties compatible with a similar system of liberty for all." *A Theory of Justice*, 1973, p. 302, also pp. 14-15.
10. *Ibid.*, p. 28.
11. *Ibid.*, pp. 83,302.
12. See Stephen Mulhall and Adam Swift, *Liberals & Communitarians,* 1996, p. 13.
13. See *Ibid.*, p. 15; Cf. Alsdair MacIntyre, *After Virtue*, 1984, p. 250.
14. *Ibid.*, pp. 10 ff.
15. *Ibid.*, p. 19.
16. *Op.Cit.*, p. 522.
17. *Political Liberalism*, p. 146, footnote 13; also see pp. 202-3.

18. *Liberals and Communitarians*, p. 203.
19. "The impartial standpoint commits the liberal agent to treat all persons as equally real, as equally bearers of rights to their own (compossible) values and pursuits, by virtue of their common humanity." Neera K. Badhwar, "Moral Agency, Commitment, and Impartiality", in *Social Philosophy and Policy*, Vol. 13, No. 1, Winter, 1996, p. 3.
20. See Ch. 3, Sec. III.5 supra.
21. "Justice as fairness does indeed abandon the ideal of political community if by that ideal is meant a political society united on one (partially or fully) comprehensive religious, philosophical or moral doctrine. That conception of social unity is excluded by the fact of reasonable pluralism." Rawls, *Political Liberalism*, p. 201
22. *Liberals and Communitarians*, p. 16.
23. ".... my good as a man is one and the same as the good of those others with whom I am bound up in human community." MacIntyre, *Op.Cit.*, p. 229.
24. *Ibid.*, p 220.
25. "What I am, therefore, is in key part what I inherit, a specific past that is present to some degree in my present. I find myself part of a history and that is generally to say whether I like it or not.... one of the bearers of a tradition." *Ibid.*, p. 221; Cf. "All reasoning takes place within the context of some traditional mode of thought." *Ibid.*, p. 222.
26. *Op.Cit.*, p. 192.
27. W.D. Falk, "Morality, Self and Others", in Kenneth Pahel and Marvin Schiller, eds. *Readings in Contemporary Ethical Theory*, 1970, p. 361.
28. *Ibid.*, pp. 377, and ff.
29. *Fundamental Principles of the Metaphysics of Morals*, tr., Thomas K. Abbott, 1984, pp. 45-46; *The Moral Law: The Doctrine of Virtue*, part II of *The Metaphysics of Morals*, tr., Mary J. Gregor, 1964, pp. 84 ff.
30. *A History of Philosophy*, tr. James H. Tufts, 1959, p. 553.
31. *Fundamental Principles*, p. 45.

32. "It is clear that all moral conceptions have their seat and origin completely *a priori* in the reason." *Ibid.*, p. 29; and "supposing however that there were something *whose existence has in-itself* an absolute worth, something which being an end-in-itself, could be a source of definite laws, then in this and this alone would lie the source of a possible categorical imperative, that is, practical law." *Ibid.*, p. 45.
33. *Ibid.* p. 69. Cf. *The Doctrine of Virtue*, pp. 45, 51, 81 ff.
34. "Duties to Oneself", from his *Lectures on Ethics*, in *Approaches to Ethics*, 1962 p. 291. Also see *The Doctrine of Virtue*, 84 ff., 100 ff.
35. "Duties towards Others", from *Lecturers on Ethics*, *Op.Cit.*, p. 294; Cf. *The Doctrine of Virtue*, pp. 131 ff.
36. *Ibid.*, p. 295.
37. *Ibid.*, p. 295.
38. "Every man has a rightful claim to *respect* from his fellowmen and is raciprocally obligated to show respect for every other man. "Humanity itself has a dignity; for man cannot be used as a means by any man (either others, or even by himself) but must always be treated at the same time as an end." *The Doctrine of Virtue*, p. 132.
39. *Ibid.*, pp. 36 ff., especially p. 66.
40. *Fundamental Principles* p. 33; also see, pp. 18, 21, 26 etc.
41. I have equated the Western conception of morality to the Indian conception of *dharma*, both in my earlier work and here. This is generally endorsed by other Indian thinkers. The term *dharma* is at once all-comprehensive, profound and nebulous. It has various religious and ritualistic connotations. But above all it denotes a righteous way of life, which understanding is shared by all Indian traditions. See writer's *Aspects of Hindu Morality*, 1989, pp. 37 ff., 101 ff., 169 ff.
42. For a more detailed description of the socio-centric and liberation-centric traditions and their respective moralities, see *Ibid.*, Chs. III and IV.
43. *Taittirīya Saṁhitā* VI, 3. 10. 5; *Manu Smṛti* VI, 35-37; *Mahābhārata, Śānti Parva* 25:6; 28:54 etc.

44. *Manu Smṛti* VI.92; X. 63.
45. *Gautama Dharma Sūtra* VIII. 22-24.
46. *Yājñavalkya Smṛti* I. 122; III. 65-66.
47. *Yoga Sútra* II. 30
48. *Ibid.*, I. 33.
49. *Gītā* II. 47, 71; III. 18-19; VI. 9 etc.
50. VI. 9.
51. "He who abandons all desires and acts free from longing without any sense of mineness or egotism, he attains to peace." *Ibid.* II. 71, also VI. 6.
52. "He who is satisfied with whatever comes by chance, who has passed beyond the dualities (of pleasure and pain), who is free from jealousy, who remains the same in success and failure, even when he acts, he is not bound." *Ibid.* IV. 22; also II, 47-50; IV. 20-21.
53. VI. 32.
54. "He whose self is harmonized by yoga sees the Self abiding in all beings and all beings in the Self; everywhere he sees the same." *Ibid.* VI. 30.
55. *Mahābhārata, Śānti Parva* 117:18 ff; 251: 19-21 etc.
56. XXXII. 351.
57. For a detailed view of the no-soul (*nairātmya or anattā*) doctrine, see Har Dayal, *The Bodhisattva Doctrine in Buddhist Sanskrit Literature*, 1978, pp. 72 ff.
58. "It (compassion) consist in realizing the equality of oneself with others (*para-ātma-samatā*) and also practising the substitution of others for oneself (*para-ātma-parivartana*). When a *bodhisattva* (seeker of liberation) cultivates the habit of regarding others as equal to himself, he gets rid of the ideas of "I and Thou" and "Mine and Thine". He learns to feel the joys and sorrows of others like his own, and does not prefer his own happiness to that of others.....he gives himself for the sake of others. He returns good for evil, and helps even those who have injured him...." *Ibid.*, p. 179 and ff.
59. "When the *bodhisattva* thinks of others in the same way as he thinks of himself, the words *svārtha* and *parārtha* become synonyms, and there is no distinction between them. In the

highest synthesis, Egoism and Altruism are merged in perfect love." *Ibid.*, p. 181.

60. It is the writer's opinion that justice was conceived and practised in socio-political life in a way which was a total travesty of justice. See *Op.Cit.*, pp. 82 ff. 87 ff.
61. "If you thinkest, O friend of virtue, with respect to thyself "I am alone", (know that) the sage who witnesses all virtuous acts and all crimes, ever resides in thine heart." *Manu Smṛti* VIII. 91; Cf. "When the performance of an act gladdens his heart, let him perform it with diligence, but let him avoid the opposite." *Ibid.* VI. 161.
62. *Mahābhārata, Anuśāsana Parva* 118 : 13, 37-38.
63. *Mahābhārata, Śānti Parva* 154:26-28; 243:5-7; 254: 25 ff, 262:36 ff., *Bhagavadgītā* XII. 13-14; *Manu Smṛti* VI.8 *Bhāgavata Purāṇa*, Book III., Ch. 8.
64. "He who is equipped with Yoga, whose mind is quite pure, by whom the self has been conquered, whose senses have been subdued, whose self has become the self of all beings, though doing he is not tainted." *Bhagavadgītā* V. 7, also See *Ibid.*, II. 55-57; IV. 19-21; XIV. 25 etc.

Chapter 8. A Rational Approach to Universal Morality

1. See Ch. 5, Sec. III.3.
2. See Ch. 3, Sec. III.4.
3. "There may therefore be true moral convictions which, though possibly no one actually holds them, are true in and for all social conditions. But there could be such true moral convictions only if their content had nothing to do with social conditions." *The Moral Point of View*, 1967, p.114.
4. *Ibid.*, p. 114.
5. *Ibid.*, p. 115.
6. *Ethical Knowledge*, 1971, pp. 21 and ff.
7. *Ibid.*, p. 133.
8. *Ibid.*, pp. 24-25. Cf. "ordinary English does not allow us to speak of the goodness of a thing as simply a function of opinions or attitudes. The ordinary translation of 'X is good'

is not anything like 'I (or my society) approve of X'. The ordinary meaning would be more like 'Even if my society and I did not approve of X, X still would be good." *Ibid.*, p. 69.

9. *Ibid.*, p. 25.
10. *Ibid.*, p. 142; Cf. *Ibid.*, pp. 134 ff.
11. *Ibid.*, pp. 142 ff.
12. "substantial ethical claims (e.g. 'it is better that people live than die', or 'pain is bad' - both things that a person who has lived and felt pain is in a position to know) must lie at the foundation of ethical reasoning, and that rational justification has to end somewhere short of the foundation." *Ibid.*, p. 128.
13. "Good Reasons", in Kenneth Pahel & Marvin Schiller, eds., *Contemporary Ethical Theories*, 1970, p. 104.
14. See Foot, "Moral Relativism", in Michael Krausz and Jack W. Meiland, eds., *Relativism : Cognitive and Moral*, 1982, pp. 152 ff., especially p. 157; also see editors' "Introduction to Moral Relativism", p. 150.
15. "It seems to me, however, that my knowledge is never so complete that my ethical principles are not subject to revision in the light of further evidence." Carl Wellman, *The Language of Ethics*, 1961, p. 73.
16. *Moral Reasoning and Truth*, 1976, p.126.
17. *Op. Cit.*, p. 151.
18. Quoted in Kupperman, *Op. Cit.*, p. 46.
19. *Freedom and Reason*, 1963, p. 97.
20. *Ibid.*, p. 98.
21. *Op. Cit.* p. 161.
22. *Language of Morals*, 1952, pp. 62 ff.
23. See Ch. 6, Section II.1.
24. Kant, *Fundamental Principles of the Metaphysics of Morals*, 1984, tr., Thomas K. Abbott, "Introduction", pp. ix-x.
25. "Act upon a maxim which at the same time involves its own universal validity for every rational being." *Fundamental Principles.*, p. 54.
26. *Op. Cit.*, x-xi.
27. *Op. Cit.*, pp. 45 ff.

28. *The Language of Morals*, pp. 28-29, 44-45.
29. "No moral system whose principles were regarded as purely factual could fulfil its function of regulating our conduct." *Ibid*, p. 44. "Value terms have a special function in language, that of commending, and so they plainly cannot be defined in terms of other words which themselves do not perform this function, for if this is done we are deprived of the means of performing that function." *Ibid.*, p. 91;
30. *Ibid.*, pp. 111, 146.
31. "When we make a moral judgment about something, we make it because of the possession by it of certain non-moral properties....moral judgments about particular things are made for reasons,..." *Freedom and Reason*, p. 21.
32. *The Language of Morals*, pp. 68-69.
33. *Freedom and Reason*, p. 88.
34. *Ibid.*, p. 92.
35. Quoted in *The Language of Morals*, p. 45.
36. *An Examination of the Place of Reason in Ethics*, 1970, p. 125.
37. *Ibid.*, p. 129.
38. "We could not properly speak of a morality, as opposed to a system of conventions, customs, or laws, unless the question of the correctness or incorrectness, truth or falsity, of the rules prevalent in a community is asked, unless, in other words, the prevalent rules are subjected to certain tests."

And,

"a person likewise does not know what he is talking about if he believes that finding out whether some course of action is contrary to the morality of a certain group settles the question whether the course of action is morally wrong. For he ignores the crucial question 'Is what the morality of that group forbids really wrong?' or, put differently, 'Are the moral convictions of that group true?' " *The Moral Point of View*, pp.84, 85-86; also see 91 ff.

39. *Ibid.*, p. 34.
40. *Ibid.*, pp. 28 ff., 34.
41. *Ibid.*, pp. 82 and ff. also 28.
42. *Ibid.*, p. 87, also pp. 84 ff.

43. *Ibid.*, pp. 91, 96:ff., 100 ff.
44. *Ibid.*, p. 99.
45. *Ibid.*, pp. 114-15.
46. *Generalization in Ethics*, pp. 56-57.
47. *Op. Cit.*, pp. 62-63.
48. *Ibid.*, p. 63; Cf. "The Crux of the matter is whether or not it is possible to give genuine reasons for or against judgments of value and obligation." *Ibid.*, p. 299.
49. *Ibid.*, p. 258.
50. *Ibid.*, p. 260.
51. *Op. Cit.*, pp. 106 ff.
52. *Ibid.*, p. 140.
53. *A Modern Introduction to Moral Philosophy*, 1958, pp. 26 ff.; 38 ff.
54. *Ibid.*, pp. 38-39, 50-51
55. *Ibid.*, p. 38.
56. *Ibid.*, pp. 52-53.
57. *Ibid.*, pp. 56-57, 60 ff.
58. *Ibid.*, p. 64.
59. "If I say that Brown is a good man and am prepared to support this with reasons, then I claim something that will hold good not only for Brown himself but for all others like him in the relevant ways, ways that are referred to in the reasons that I give." *Ibid.*, p. 66.
60. *Ibid.*, pp. 67, 165.
61. *Ibid.*, pp. 72 ff., 86 ff., 91.
62. *Ibid.*, p. 74.
63. *Ibid.*, p. 82 ff.
64. *Ibid.*, pp. 82 ff., 85-86, 91, 203 ff.
65. *The Language of Morals*, pp. 17-18.
66. *Ibid.*, pp. 19 and ff.
67. "By contrast as soon as we conceive of knowledge as communicatively mediated, rationality is asserted in terms of the capacity of responsible participants in interaction to orient themselves in relation to validity claims geared to inter-subjective recognition,....." *The Philosophical Discourse of Modernity: Twelve Lectures*, tr., Frederick G. Lawrence, 1995, p. 314.

68. *Ibid*., p. 198.
69. *Ibid*., p. 310.
70. *Ibid*., pp. 298 ff., 326.
71. *Ibid*., p. 199.
72. "This conception of truth as consensual in turn pre-supposes - or rather anticipates - the ideal speech situation' which is characterized by the exclusion of extraneous pressures, i.e. it is discussion free from domination." Joseph Bleicher, *Contemporary Hermeneutics: Hermeneutics as Method, Philosophy and Critique,* 1980, p. 163, also pp. 204 ff.
73. *Op. Cit*., p. 315.
74. *Ibid*., p. 322.
75. *Ibid*., 326.
76. *Ibid*., 359.
77. *Ibid*., pp. 344-45.

Bibliography

Ames, Roger T., "Meaning as Imaging : Prolegomena to a Confucian Epistemology," in Deutsh Eliot, ed., *Culture and Modernity: East West Philosophical Perspectives*, Delhi: Motilal Banarsidass, 1994.

Ash, Solomon E., *Social Psychology*, New Jersey: Prentice-Hall Inc., 1952.

Atfield, Robin, "How not to be a Moral Relativist," in *Monist*, Vol. 62, 1979.

Ayer, A.J., *Language, Truth and Logic*, New York: Dover Publications, 1936, reprint 1989.

________ *Logical Positivism*, London: George Allen & Unwin Ltd., 1959.

Badhwar, Neera K., "Moral Agency, Commitment and Impartiality," in *Social Philosophy and Policy*, Vol. 13, No. 1, Winter, 1996.

Baier, Kurt, *The Moral Point of View: A Rational Basis of Ethics*, New York: Random House, 1967.

________ "The Point of View of Morality," in Pahel, Kenneth and Marvin Schiller, eds., *Readings in Contemporary Ethical Theory*, New Jersey: Prentice-Hall, 1970.

Bambrough, Renford, "A Proof of Objectivity of Morals," in Cunningham, Robert L., ed., *Situationism and The New Morality*, New York: Appleton-Century-Crofts, 1970.

Barnes, Barry and David Bloor, "Relativism, Rationalism and the Sociology of Knowledge," in Hollis, Martin and Steven Lukes, eds., *Rationality and Relativism*, Massachusetts: The M.I.T. Press, 1994.

Barnsley, John H., *The Social reality of ethics: The comparative analysis of moral codes*, London: Rotledge & Kegan Paul, 1972.

Baron, Marcia W., Philip Pettit, Michael Slott, *Three Methods of Ethics: A Debate*, Massachusetts: Blackwell Publishers, 1997.

Beardsmore, R.W., *Moral Reasoning*, London: Routledge & Kegan Paul, 1969.

Becker, Lawrence C., *On Justifying Moral Judgments*, London: Routledge & Kegan Paul, 1973.

Benedict, Ruth, "Anthrolpology and the Abnormal," in Brandt, Richard B., *Value and Obligation: Systematic Readings in Ethics*, New York: Harcourt, Brace & World, Inc., 1961.

Bernstein, Richard J., *Beyond Objectivism and Relativism: Science, Hermeneutics and Praxis*, Philadelphia: University of Pennsylvania Press, 1983.

________ "Incommensurability and Otherness Revisited," in Deutsch Eliot, ed., *Culture and Modernity, Op. Cit.*, 1994.

________ *Philosophical Profiles: Essays in a Pragmatic Mode*, Cambridge: Polity Press, 1994.

Bertens, Hans, *The Idea of the Postmodern: A history*, London: Routledge, 1995.

Bhagavadgita, tr., S. Radhakrishnan, Bombay: Blackie & Sons Ltd., 1977.

Bharadwaja, V.K., *Naturalistic Ethical Thoery*, Delhi University Press, 1978.

Bidney, David, "Cultural Relaticism," in Sills, David L., ed., *International Encyclopedia of Social Sciences*, The Macmillan Co., Vol. 3.

Bleicher, Jospeh, *Contemporary Hermeneutics: hermeneutics as method, philospohy and critique*, London: Routeldge & Kegan Paul, 1980.

Boyd, Richard N., "How to be a Moral Realist," in Sayre-McCord, Geoffrey, ed., *Essays on Moral Realism*, London: Cornell University Press, 1988.

Brandt, Richard B., *Ethical Theory: The Problems of Normative and Critical Ethics*, New Jersey: Prentice-Hall, Inc., 1959.

________ ed., *Value and Obligation: Systematic Readings in Ethics*, New York: Harcourt, Brace & World, Inc., 1961.

________ *A Theory of the Good and the Right*, Oxford: Clarendon Press, 1979.

Brennan, J.M., *The Open Texture of Moral Concepts*, London: Macmillan, 1977.

Brink, David O., *Moral Realism and the Foundations of Ethics*, Cambridge: Cambridge University Press, 1989.

Buhler, Georg, tr., *The Sacred Laws of the Aryas, Part I, Āpastamba and Gautama*, Delhi: Motilal Banarsidass, 1975.

_______ tr., *The Sacred Books of the East: The Laws of Manu*, Delhi: Motilal Banarsidass, 1982.

Coburn, Robert, "Relativism and the Basis of Morality," in the *Philosophical Review*, LXXXV, 1, January, 1976.

Crawford, Cromwell, ed., *World Religions and Global Ethics*, New York: Paragon House, 1989.

_______ *Dilemmas of Life and Death: Hindu Ethics in a North American Context*, New York: State University of New York Press, 1995.

Cunningham, Robert L., *Situationism and the New Morality*, New York: Appleton-Century-Crof, 1970.

Curtis, James E. and John W. Petras, eds., *The Sociology of Knowledge: A Reader*, London: Gerald Duckworth & Co., 1970.

Davidson, Donald, "On the Very Idea of a Conceptual Scheme," in Krausz, Michael and Jack W. Meiland, eds., *Relativism: Cognitive and Moral*, Notre Dame: University of Notre Dame Press, 1982.

Desai, M.V., ed., *Gandhi Reader for 1988*, New Delhi: Namedia Foundation, 1988.

Deutsch, Eliot, eds., *Culture and Modernity: East West Philosophical Perspectives*, Delhi: Motilal Banarsidass, 1994.

Devarja, N.K., *The Limits of Disagreement: An Essay in Reasoning in Humanistic Discourse*, Simla: Indian Institute of Advanced Studies, 1993.

Devitt, Michael, *Realism and Truth*, Oxford: Basil Blackwell, 1984.

Dewy, John, *Reconstruction in Philosphy*, Enlarged edition, Boston: Beacon Press, 1959.

Doppelt, Gerald, "Kuhn's Epistemological Relativism: An Interpretation and Defense, in Krausz, Michael and Jack W. Meiland, eds., *Relativism: Cognitive and Moral*, *Op Cit.*, 1982.

Dunker, Karl, "Ethical Relativity (An Enquiry into the Psychology of Ethics)," in Ladd, John, ed., *Ethical Relativism*, California: Wordsworth Co., 1973.

Emmet, Dorothy, *Rules, Roles and Relations*, London: Macmillan, 1966.

Feyerabend, Paul, *Farewell to Reason*, London: Verso, 1987.

Findley, J.N., *Axiological Ethics*, London: Macmillan, 1970.

Foot, Philippa, ed., *Theories of Ethics*, London: Oxford University Press, 1967.

________ "Moral Beliefs," in *Theories of Ethics, Op. Cit.*, 1967.

________ "Moral Arguments," in Pahel, Kenneth and Marvin Schiller, eds., *Readings in Contemporary Ethical Theory*, New Jersey: Prentice Hall, Inc., 1970.

________ "Moral Relativism," in Krausz, Michael and Jack W. Meiland, eds., *Relativism: Cognitive and Moral, Op. Cit.*, 1989.

Frankena, William, "The Naturalistic Fallacy," in *Readings in Contemporary Ethical Theory, Op. Cit.*, 1970.

________ *Ethics*, New Delhi: Prentice-Hall of India, 1993.

Gadamer, Hans-Georg, *Truth and Method*, trs., Joel Weinsheimer and Donald G. Marshall, New York: Continuum Publishing Company, 1995.

Ganguli, B.N., *Concept of Equality: The Nineteenth Century Indian Debate*, Simla: Indian Institute of Advanced Study, 1975.

Garner, Richard T. and Bernard Rosen, *Moral Philosophy: A Systematic Introduction to Normative Ethics and Meta-ethics*, New York: The Macmillan Company, 1967.

Geertz, Clifford, *The Interpretation of Cultures: Selected Essays*, New York: Basic Books, Inc. Publishers, 1973.

________ "Anti Anti-Relativism," in *American Anthropologist*, Vol. 86, 1984.

Gellner, Ernst, "Relativism and Universalism," in Martin, Hollis and Steven Lukes, eds., *Rationality and Relativism*, Massachusetts: M.I.T. Press, 1982.

Gert, Bernard, *Morality: A New Justification of the Moral Rules*, New York: Oxford University Press, 1988.

Ginsberg, Morris, *On the Diversity of Morals*, London: Mercury Books, 1962.

Goodman, Nelson, "The Fabrication of Facts," in Krausz, Michael and Jack W. Meiland, eds., *Relativism : Cognitive and Moral, Op. Cit.*, 1982.

________ "Just the Facts, Ma'am!" in Krausz, Michael, ed., *Relativism: Interpretation and Confrontation*, Notre Dame: University of Notre Dame Press, 1989.

________ "The Myth of the Subjective," in *Relativism: Interpretation and Confrontation*, *Op. Cit.*, 1989.

Graham, A.C., "Conceptual Schemes and Linguistic Relativism in Relation to Chinese," in Deutsch, Eliot, ed., *Culture and Modernity: East West Philosophical Perspectives*, *Op. Cit.*, 1994.

Grice, Geoffrey Russel, *The Grounds of Moral Judgment*, Cambridge: Cambridge University Press, 1967.

Habermas, Jurgen, *The Philosophical Discourse of Modernity: Twelve Lectures*, tr., Fredrick G. Lawrence, Massachusetts: The M.I.T. Press, 1976.

________ *Moral Consciousness and Communicative Action*, trs., Christian Lenhardt and Shierry Weber Nicholsen, Massachusetts: The M.I.T. Press, 1995.

Halbfass, Wilhelm, *India and Europe: An Essay in Philosophical Understanding*, Delhi: Motilal Banarsidass, 1990.

Har Dayal, *The Bodhisattva Doctrine in Buddhist Sanskrit Literature*, Delhi: Motilal Banarsidass, 1978.

Hare, R.M., *The Language of Morals*, London: Oxford University Press, 1952.

________ *Freedom and Reason*, London: Oxford University Press, 1963.

________ "The Promising Game," Pahel, Kenneth and Marvin Schiller, eds. *Readings in Contemporary Ethical Theories*, *Op. Cit.*, 1970.

________ *Essays on the Moral Concepts*, London: Macmillan, 1972.

________ "Internalism and Externalism in Ethics," in *The British Tradition in the 20th Century Philosophy*, Proceedings of the 17th International Wittgenstein Symposium, August, 1994, Sonderdruck, Offprint.

Harman, Gilbert, "Moral Relativism Defended," in Krausz, Michael and Jack W. Meiland, eds., *Relativism: Cognitive and Moral*, *Op. Cit.*, 1982.

________ "Metaphysical Realism and Moral Relativism: Reflections on Hilary Putnam's Reason, Truth and History," in the *Journal of Philosophy*, Vol. 79, 1982.

________ "Ethics and Observation," in Sayre-McCord, Geoffrey, ed., *Essays on Moral Realism*, London: Cornell University, 1988.

________ "Is There a Single True Morality?" in Krausz, Michael, ed., *Relativism: Interpretation and Confrontation*, *Op. Cit.*, 1989.

Harrison, Geoffrey, "Relativism and Tolerance," in Krausz, Michael and Jack W. Meiland, eds., *Relativism : Cognitive and Moral*, *Op. Cit.*, 1982.

Hart, H.L.A., *The Concept of Law*, Oxford University Press, 1978.

Hartland-Swann, John, "The Moral and the Non-Moral," in Taylor, Paul, ed., *Problems of Moral Philosophy: An Introduction to Ethics*, Belmont, California, Dickenson Publishing Co., Inc., 1967.

Hartmann, Nicolai, *Ethics*, Vol. One, *Moral Phenomena*, tr., Stanton Coit, London: George Allen and Unwin Ltd., 1950.

Herskovits, Marville J., "Cultural Relativism and Cultural Values," from *Cultural Anthropology*, 1955, given in Ladd, John, ed., *Ethical Relativism*, California: Wordsworth Co., 1973.

Hollis, Martin and Steven Lukes, eds., *Rationality and Relativism*, Massachusetts: The M.I.T. Press, 1994.

Hooker, C.A., *A Realistic Theory of Science*, New York: State University of New York Press, 1987.

Hourani, George F., *Ethical Value*, London: George Allen and Unwin, 1959.

Hudson, W.D., *Ethical Intuitionism*, London: Macmillan, 1967.

________ General ed., *New Studies in Ethics*, Volume Two, *Modern Theories*, New York: St. Martin Press, 1974.

Hume, David O., "Of Virtue and Vice in General," from *Treatise of Human Nature*, London, 1939.

Jensen, Henning, "Gilbert Harman's Defense of Moral Relativism," in *Philospohical Studies*, Vol. 30, 1976.

Jhingran, Saral, *The Roots of World Religions*, New Delhi: Books and Books, 1982.

________ *Aspects of Hindu Morality*, Delhi: Motilal Banarsidass, 1989, reprint 1999.

________ *Secularism in India: A Reappraisal*, New Delhi: Har-Anand Publications, 1995.

_______ "An Inquiry into Ethical Relativism of Hindu Thought," in *Indian Philosophical Quarterly*, July-Oct. 1996.

Jones, W.T., Frederick Sontag, Morton O. Beckner, Robert J. Fogelin, eds., *Approaches to Ethics: Representative Selections from Classical Times to the Present*, New York: McGraw Hill Book Company, 1962.

Kane, Pandurang Vaman, *History of Dharmaśāstra (Ancient and Medieval Religious and Civil Law)*, Vols III and V, Part II, Poona: Bhandarkar Oriental Research Institute, 1973-1975.

Kant, Immanuel, *Lectures on Ethics*, tr., Louis Infield, London: Methuen & Co., Ltd., 1930.

_______ *Fundamental Principles of the Metaphysics of Morals*, tr., Thomas K. Abbott, Indianapolis: Bobbs-Merrill Educational Publishing, 1949.

_______ *The Moral Law: The Doctrine of Virtue, Part II of the Metaphysics of Morals*, tr., Mary J. Gregor, New York: Harper & Row Publishers, 1964.

Kent, Edward Allen, ed., *Law and Philosophy: Readings in Legal Philosophy*, New York: Appleton-Century-Crofts, 1970.

Kelsen, Hans, *What is Justice: Justice, Law and Politics in the Mirror of Science: Collected Essays*, Berkeley: University of California Press, 1957.

Kerner, George C., *The Revolution in Ethical Theory*, Oxford: Clarendon Press, 1966.

Kluckohn, Clyde, "Ethical Relativity: Sic et Non," in Ladd, John, ed., *Ethical Relativism*, California: Wordsworth Co., 1973.

Krausz, Michael and Jack W. Meiland, eds., *Relativism: Cognitive and Moral*, Notre Dame: University of Notre Dame Press, 1982.

Krausz, Michael, ed., *Relativism:Interpretation and Confrontation*, Notre Dame: University of Notre Dame Press, 1989.

Kuhn, Thomas, *The Structure of Scientific Revolutions*, Chicago, University of Chicago Press, 1970.

Kupperman, Joel J., *Ethical Knowledge*, London: George Allen & Unwin, 1972.

Ladd, John, *The Structure of a Moral Code: A Philosophical Analysis of Ethical Discourse Applied to the Ethics of Navaho Indians*, Cambridge: Harvard University Press, 1957.

_______ ed., *Ethical Relativism*, California: Wordsworth Co., 1973.

_______ "Introduction", Ladd, John ed., *Ethical Relativism*, *Op. Cit.*, 1973.

_______ "The Issue of Relativism," in Ladd, John, *Ethical Relativism*, *Op. Cit.*, 1973.

Lear, Jonathan, "Ethics, Mathematics and Relativism," in Sayre-MaCord, Geoffrey, ed., *Essays on Moral Realism*, *Op. Cit.*, 1988.

Lewis, C.I., *Mind and the World Order*, New York, 1956.

Linton, Ralph, "Universal Values and Social Functions," in Brandt, R.B., ed., *Value and Obligation: Systematic Readings in Ethics*, *Op. Cit.*, 1961.

Mackie, J.L., "The Subjectivity of Values," in Sayre-MaCord, Geoffrey, ed., *Essays on Moral Realism*, *Op. Cit.*, 1988.

MacIntyre, Alsdair, *After Virtue*, Notre Dame: University of Notre Dame Press, 1984.

_______ "Relativism, Power and Philosophy," in Krausz, Michael, ed., *Relativism: Interpretation and Confrontation*, *Op. Cit.*, 1989.

_______ "Incommensurability, Truth and Conversation Bewteen Confucians and Aristotelians about Virtues," in Deutsch, Eliot, ed., *Culture and Modernity: East West Philosophical Perspectives*, *Op. Cit.*, 1994.

Mahābhārata (15 Vols.), Hindi tr., general ed., Damodar Satvalekar, Paradi, Svadhyaya Mandal, 1980.

Mahābhārata, Anuśāsana Parva, Vol. 13, *Op. Cit.*, 1980.

Mahābhārata, Śānti Parva, Vols. 11-12, *Op. Cit.*, 1980.

Mannheim, Karl, "The Sociology of Knowledge," in Kurtis, James E., and John W. Petras eds., *The Sociology of Knowledge: A Reader*, London: Gerald Duckworth & Co. Ltd., 1970.

Manu Smṛti (The Laws of Manu), tr., Buhler, George, *Op. Cit.*, 1982; Hindi tr., Varanasi: Chawkhamba Sanskrit Series.

Margolis, Joseph, "The Truth About Relativism," in Krausz, Michael, ed., *Relativism: Interpretation and Confrontation*, *Op. Cit.*, 1989.

Matilal, Bimal K., "Ethical Relativism and Confrontation of Cultures," in Krausz, Michael, ed., *Relativism: Interpretation and Confrontation*, *Op. Cit.*, 1989.

________ "Pluralism, Relativism and Interaction between Cultures," in Deutsch, Eliot, ed., *Culture and Modernity: East West Philosophical Perspectives, Op. Cit.*, 1994.

McTaggart, J. Ellis, "Personality," in Hastings, James ed., *Encyclopaedia of Religion and Ethics*, Vol. IX, Edinburgh: T&T Clark.

Mill, J.S., *On Liberty and Other Writings*, ed., Stefan Collini, New York: Cambridge University Press, 1989.

Mitchell, Basil, *Morality: Religious and Secular: The Dilemmas of the Traditional Conscience*, Oxford: Clarendon Press, 1980.

Mitchell, Sollace and Michael Rosen, eds., *The Need for Interpretation: Contemporary Conceptions of the Philosopher's Task*, London: The Athlon Press, 1983.

Monro, D.H., *Empiricism and Ethics*, Cambridge University Press, 1967.

Montefiore, Alan, *A Modern Introduction to Moral Philosophy*, London: Routledge & Kegan Paul, 1958.

Moore, George Edward, *Principia Ethica*, Cambridge University Press, 1956.

________ *Ethics*, London: Oxford University Press, 1966.

Mulhall, Stephen and Adam Swift, *Liberals and Communitarians*, Oxford, Blackwell Publishers, 1996.

Nagel, Thomas, *The View from Nowhere*, Oxford: Oxford University Press, 1986.

Newton-Smith, W., "Relativism and the Possibility of Interpretation," in Lukes, Stephen and Martin Hollis, eds., in *Rationality and Relativism, Op. Cit.*, 1982.

Niebuhr, Rienhold, *Moral Man and Immoral Society: A Study in Ethics and Politics*, New York: Charles Scribner's Sons, 1960.

Nikhilananda, Swami, tr., *The Upanishads*, London: George Allen & Unwin Ltd., 1963.

Nowell-Smith, P.H., *Ethics*, Oxford: Basil Blackwell, 1957.

Oppenheim, Felix E., "The Concept of Equality," in Sills, David L., ed., *International Encyclopedia of Social Sciences*, Vol. 5, The Macmillan Company.

Outlaw, Lucius, "Lifeworlds, Modernity, and Philosophical Praxis: Race, Ethnicity and Critical Social Theory," in Deusch, Eliot, ed., *Culture and Modernity: East West Philosophical Perspectives, Op. Cit.*, 1994.

Overring, Joana, ed., *Reason and Morality*, London: Travistock Publications, 1985.

Pahel, Kenneth and Marvin Schiller, eds., *Readings in Contemporary Ethical Theory*, New Jersey: Prentice-Hall, 1970.

Pande, G.C., *Mūlya Mīmāṁsā*, Jaipur: Rajasthan Hindi Granth Academy, 1973.

Passmore, John, *A Hundred Years of Philosophy*, Penguin Books, 1968.

________ Recent Philosophers: A Supplement to a Hundred Years of Philosophy, London: Gerald Duckworth & Co. Ltd., 1985.

Perry, Thomas D., *Moral Reasoning and Truth: An Essay in Philosophy and Jurisprudence*, Oxford: Clarendon Press, 1976.

Polsby, Nelson W., "Community," in Sills, David L., ed., International Encyclopedia of Social Sciences, Vol. 3, Macmillan Company.

Postow, B.C., "Moral Relativism Avoided," in *The Personalist*, Vol. 60, 1979.

Putnam, Hilary, *Realism and Reason: Philosophical Papers*, Vol. 3, Cambridge: Cambridge University Press, 1983.

Pritchard, H.A., "Does Moral Philosophy Rest on a Mistake?" in Pahel Kenneth and Marvin Schiller, eds., *Readings in Contemporary Ethical Theory, Op. Cit.*, 1970.

Quine, W.V.O., "Two Dogmas of Empiricism," from *From a Logical Point of View*, Massachusetts: Harvard University Press, 1953.

Rawls, John, *A Theory of Justice*, Oxford: Oxford University Press, 1972.

________ *Political Liberalism*, New York: Columbia University Press, 1993.

________ "Two Concepts of Rules," in Pahel Kenneth and Marvin Schiller, eds., *Readings in Contemporary Ethical Theory, Op. Cit.*, 1970.

Redfield, Robert, "The Universally Human and the Culturally Variable," in Ladd, John, ed., *Ethical Relativism*, 1973.

Rorty, Richard, *Philosophy and the Mirror of Nature*, New Jersey: Princeton University Press, 1980.

________ "Solidarity or Objectivity?" in Krausz, Michael, ed., *Relativism: Interpretation and Confrontation*, Op. Cit., 1989.

Ross, William David, *The Right and the Good*, Oxford: Clarendon Press, 1930.

_______ *Foundations of Ethics*, Oxford: Clarendon Press, 1939.

Sapontzis, S.F., "Moral Relativism: A Causal Interpretation and Defense," in *American Philosophical Quarterly*, Vol. 24, No. 4, Oct. 1987.

Sartre, Jean Paul, *Being and Nothingness*, tr., Hazel Barnes, New York: Philosophical Library, 1956.

Sayre-McCord, Geoffrey, ed., *Essays on Moral Realism*, London: Carnell University, 1988.

Scheler, Max, "The Scoliology of Knowledge: Formal Problems," in Curtis, James E. and John W. Petras, eds., *The Sociology of Knowledge: A Reader*, *Op. Cit.*, 1970.

Schweder, Richard A., "Post-Nietzchian Anthropology: The Idea of Multiple Objective Worlds," in Krausz, Michael, ed., *Relativism: Interpretation and Confrontation*, *Op. Cit.*, 1989.

Searle, John, "How to Derive 'Ought' from 'Is'," in Pahel, Kenneth and Marvin Schiller, eds., *Readings in Contemporary Ethical Theory*, *Op. Cit.*, 1970.

Shirk, Evelyn, *The Ethical Dimension: An Approach to the Philosophy of Values and Valuing*, New York: Appleton-Century-Crofts, 1965.

Singer, Marcus George, *Generalization in Ethics, With the Rudiments of a System of Moral Philosophy*, New York: Alfred A. Knopf, 1961.

Singer, Milton, "The Concept of Culture," in Sills, David L., ed., *International Encyclopedia of Social Sciences*, Vol. 3, *Op. Cit.*

Smart, Ninian and B. Srinivas Murthy, eds., *East-West Encounters in Philosophy and Religion*, Mumbai: Popular Prakashan, 1996.

Smith, David G., "Liberalism," in Sills, David L., ed., *International Encyclopedia of Social Sciences*, Vol. 9, *Op. Cit.*

Speier, Hans, "The Social Determination of Ideas," in Curtis, James E. and John W. Petras, eds., *The Sociology of Knowledge: A Reader*, *Op. Cit.*, 1970.

Stace, W.T., *The Concept of Morals*, New York: The Macmillan Company, 1962.

Stevenson, Charles L., *Ethics and Language*, New Haven: Yale University Press, 1944.

________ *Facts and Values: Studies in Ethical Analysis*, London: Yale University Press, 1963.

Stewart, Robert M. and Lynn L. Thomas, "Recent Work in Ethical Relativism," in *American Philosophical Quarterly*, Vol. 28, No. 2, April 1991.

Strawson, P.F., "Social Morality and Individual Ideal," in Pahel, Kenneth and Marvin Schiller, eds., *Readings in Contemporary Ethical Theory, Op. Cit.*, 1970.

Sturgeon, Nicholas L., "Moral Explanations," in Sayre-McCord, Geoffrey, ed., *Essays on Moral Realism, Op. Cit.*, 1988.

Sumner, W.G., "Folkways," in Ladd, John, ed., *Ethical Relativism, Op. Cit.*, 1973.

Swoyer, Chris, "True For," in Krausz, Michael and Jack W. Meiland, eds., *Relativism: Cognitive and Moral, Op. Cit.*, 1982.

Taylor, Charles, "Rationality," in Hollis, Martin and Steven Lukes, eds., *Rationality and Relativism, Op. Cit.*, 1994.

Taylor, Paul W., *Normative Discourse*, New Jersey: Prentice-Hall, Inc., 1961.

________ ed., *Problems of Moral Philosophy: An Introduction to Ethics*, Belmont, California: Dickenson Publishing Company, Inc., 1967.

________ "Social Science and Ethical Relativism," in Pahel, Kenneth and Marvin Schiller, eds., *Readings in Contemporary Ethical Theory, Op. Cit.*, 1970.

Thomson, Judith J., Gerald Dworkin, eds., *Ethics*, New York: Harper & Row, 1968.

Tianji, Jiang, "The Problem of Relativism," in Deutsch, Eliot, ed., *Culture and Modernity: East West Philosophical Perspectives, Op. Cit.*, 1994.

Toulmin, Stephen E., *An Examination of: The Place of Reason in Ethics*, Cambridge: Cambridge University Press, 1970.

Toynbee, Arnold, *An Historian's Approach to Religion*, New York: Oxford University Press, 1979.

Urmson, J.O., *The Emotive Theory of Ethics*, London: Hutchinson University Library, 1968.

Vattimo, Gianni, *The End of Modernity: Nihilism and Hermeneutics in Post-modern Culture*, tr., John R. Snyder, Cambridge: Polity Press, 1988.

Wellman, Carl, *The Language of Ethics*, London: Oxford University Press, 1961.

________ "The Ethical Implications of Cultural Relativity," in Pahel, Kenneth and Marvin Schiller, eds., *Readings in Contemporary Ethical Theory, Op. Cit.*, 1970.

Williams, Bernard, *Ethics and the Limits of Philosophy*, London: Fontana Press, 1985.

________ "Ethical Consistency," in Sayre-McCord, Geoffrey, ed., *Essays on Moral Realism, Op. Cit.*, 1988.

Wilson, Bryan R., *Religion in Secular Society*, Penguin Books, 1969.

Wilson, John, *Reason and Morals*, Cambridge: University Press, 1961.

Windelband, W., *A History of Philosophy*, tr., James H. Tufts, New York: The Macmillan Company, 1893, reprint 1957.

Wong, David B., "Three Kinds of Incommensurability," in Krausz, Michael, ed., *Relativism: Interpretation and Confrontation, Op. Cit.*, 1989.

Yājñavalkya Smṛti, Hindi tr., Umesh Chandra Pandeya, Varanasi: Chaukhamba Sanskrit Series, 1994.

Index